MW00613570

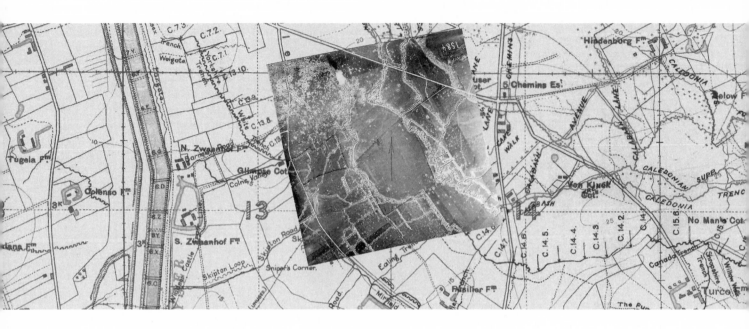

Historical Archaeology of Military Sites

Method and Topic

EDITED BY CLARENCE R. GEIER, LAWRENCE E. BABITS, DOUGLAS D. SCOTT, AND DAVID G. ORR

Texas A&M University Press
COLLEGE STATION

COPYRIGHT © 2011 edited by Clarence R. Geier,
    Lawrence E. Babits, Douglas D. Scott, David G. Orr

Manufactured in the United States of America

All rights reserved

First edition

This paper meets the requirements of ANSI/NISO, Z39.48–1992
(Permanence of Paper).

Binding materials have been chosen for durability.

LIBRARY OF CONGRESS CATALOGING-IN-PUBLICATION DATA

Historical archaeology of military sites : method and topic /
    Texas A&M University Press.—1st ed.
        p. cm.
    Includes bibliographical references and index.
    ISBN 978–1-60344–207–7 (hardcover : alk. paper)
1. Archaeology and history—Case studies.   2. Military
archaeology—Case studies.   3. Archaeology—Methodology—
Case studies.   4. Excavations (Archaeology)—Case studies.
5. Military history—Case studies. I. Geier, Clarence R.
    CC77.H5H576   2010
    930.1—dc22
    2010026335

CONTENTS

"'The time has come' the Walrus said, 'To talk of many things . . .'"

An Introduction

CLARENCE R. GEIER, LAWRENCE E. BABITS, DOUGLAS D. SCOTT, AND DAVID G. ORR

The title of this text relates to issues concerning the methods and topics pursued by historical archaeologists as they address the study of military history and the evaluation of military sites. We do not suggest that this inquiry is new, nor do we suggest that the contents of this book are all-inclusive or an end unto themselves. As the walrus said, however, we believe that practitioners of historical archaeology of military sites have achieved the methodological and topical maturity that requires the significance of historical archaeology to the study of military history be considered. Further, we see the anthropological and historical interests of these researchers contributing to an important and appropriate redirection of the questions pursued in this historical perspective.

In this compilation we seek to provide a setting for field methods that have proven successful in the study of military sites to be introduced to students, professionals dealing with military sites, and the interested public in the context of examples that illustrate their application. Through these examples, we also propose to illustrate a selection of the wide range of topical issues that define the modern study of military history and which serve to validate it as an increasingly significant part of public interpretation, preservation, and historic awareness at a global level.

Our purpose is not to romanticize war or its conduct. Instead, war and aggressive behavior are seen as unfortunate but real expressions of human culture and history that need to be understood and placed in their proper context. Whether studying intertribal warfare in Europe, Afghanistan, or North America, or the aggressive competition of emerging civilizations, tribute states, empires, or colonial states into the twentieth century, war and hostility are established solutions to political, economic, and social problems. Right and wrong, moral or immoral, justified or not, are assessments usually left to the winners and to the cleansing perspective of time. The fact is, however, that as traumatic as war or hostile action is, such conflicts are symptomatic of underlying societal stresses and their conclusions typically mark the beginning of significant processes of change and not necessarily their resolutions.

A number of issues—practical, scholarly, and methodological—prompted this book. While the priority of military sites can be debated, the greatest urgency is created by the rapid rate of residential and industrial development occurring in North America and in many other areas of the world that directly threatens these sites and the unwritten human history that they hold. Today, projects perceived as necessary for industrial, residential, and transport development are being debated relative to the value of history and preservation at local, regional, national, and international levels. Unfortunately, this debate is often uninformed and emotional. In many instances, it is ultimately influenced by entities and individuals who have no vested interest in the history that is being negotiated and often lost. Our principle motives then for publishing this work are described in the following paragraphs.

1. Good scholarship does not simply answer the questions under investigation. Good scholarship provides a better understanding of the complexity of the topic and allows researchers to identify a new set of often more correct questions to ask. The recent

work of anthropologists, historians, and archaeologists has changed the very essence of military history. Certainly, the field retains a continued interest in military engagements and the personalities, tactics, and significance that established their place in the historic record. Yet just as the larger fields of anthropology and history have come to understand the importance of the "common man" for interpreting historic events, so too, military history has begun to see armies and the troops from a different vantage point. Until recently, little effort was made to understand armies as human communities or address the lives of those who comprised them. Armies, or military units within them, were typically attributed to particular military leaders, e.g. the Middle Division, commanded by General Philip Sheridan, the Stonewall Brigade, or Emory's XIX Corps from the American Civil War. In tying a group of men to the successes and failures of particular leaders, there is a dramatic failure to see those groups as distinct social units and, in some instances, self-supporting societies structured around a defined social hierarchy, regulated by law, needing to be supplied and nurtured, and often at odds with the human community of the occupied lands, be they friend or foe. In addition, soldiers of all ranks often died in far greater numbers during long periods of encampment (six of seven men who died during the American Civil War did so off the field of battle) rather than under fire. Efforts to document, understand, and interpret the lives of common soldiers and their sacrifices remain neglected and often unprotected. Increasingly, scholars in military-sites archaeology have come to see encampments, supply depots, supply trains and networks, field and institutional hospitals, training camps, remount stations, etc. and the military structures that integrate them as both worthy of study, as well as the keys to understanding the nature of military life and service and the sacrifices made by soldiers.

2. "You can't save it all." This statement is commonly heard in conversations between politicians and others seeking to develop lands and those seeking to preserve historical heritage. The issue, however, is not really involved with "saving it all" but rather fully and properly understanding the scope of what is being lost or threatened by anticipated development. For those sites that truly contain singular and significant historic insight and potential, efforts should be made to harvest that knowledge before the site is lost, or, as appropriate, efforts should be made to protect and preserve them in "the public interest." In North America, this logic is fundamental to environmental impact and preservation legislation. However, in practice these principles are best accomplished in situations where there is an historic awareness within the public, government, or political leadership, and where development planning includes historical evaluations at the earliest stages of planning, when the results of the studies can be easily (and cheaply) accommodated in subsequent planning and engineering processes. Much of this can be ensured by proactive involvement of state historic preservation offices and local regulatory governmental bodies.

The decisions that are made are only as good as the data available upon which they are based. Unfortunately, for many the learning curve relative to understanding and measuring the historic significance of military sites remains steep. There is a very real need to make the public and those with decision-making responsibilities aware of the historical importance of encampments, hospital sites, training centers, wharves and harbors, transportation routes, military supply depots, remount stations, and numerous other non-battle related military sites. However, sites are now being lost at an alarming rate. There is a need to address the skills and knowledge of historians and historical archeologists involved with locating and assessing military sites and making informed recommendations concerning their historic significance.

A major problem contributing to the study, understanding, preservation, and/or mitigation of many military sites is the scope and complexity that define them. Military encampments for troops can number in the tens and hundreds of thousands. Fortification systems can enclose whole towns and cities, and military actions taking place over days, weeks, and even months, can encompass miles and tens of miles of physical space. Such sites may be the only remaining historical record of the daily lives of soldiers or other aspects of military history. Nonetheless, through ignorance and/or convenience, such sites are often treated by those responsible for enacting preservation law as

common, redundant, and most unfortunately, historically insignificant.

3. Despite the circumstances noted above, by choice
or necessity increasing numbers of historical archaeologists are becoming involved in the study of diverse
military sites. As a result of the creative leadership
of groups such as the National Park Service in many
battlefield parks (e.g., the Little Big Horn, Antietam,
Manassas, and elsewhere), the increasing number of
academic and CRM (Cultural Resource Management)
archaeologists dealing with military sites and features,
and the imaginative research done by private and federal agencies on underwater sites, the study of military
sites has undergone a dramatic revolution in field techniques, methods, and artifact curation.

As will be noted, strategies of site identification
and evaluation that are well established in survey
guidelines provided by many state historic preservation offices are not adequate to reliably locate or
assess many military site types such as battlefields or
encampments. In response, new and creative uses of
a wide range of geophysical evaluation techniques
have revolutionized identification and interpretation
of military sites and site features including those of
considerable scale and complexity. These include
the use of metal detectors and ground-penetrating

radar in conjunction with GIS and GPS mapping
programs, plus more traditional archaeological field
methods.

This text is divided into two sections. Section 1 is
designed to introduce the reader to some of the traditional and innovative methods used by historical
archaeologists in addressing questions presented by the
study of military sites. Two chapters address the issue
of the forensic analysis of human remains in historic
and modern contexts. One chapter discusses methods
of underwater archaeology. Case studies are introduced
that illustrate the utility of the methods along with
some of the problems involved with their application.

Section 2 highlights the breadth of topics included
within the modern study of military sites. Topics
include innovative studies of battlefields and military
fortifications in European and North American contexts. Other chapters address the issues dealing with
the study of military encampment, collateral damage,
the topic of military commemoration, and research
involving Euro-American armies engaged with indigenous Native Americans. Each chapter addresses the
theoretical and historical issues that validate the topic
as an area of study and does so within the context of
an illustrative case study.

Historical-Archaeological Methods and the Documentation, Analysis, and Interpretation of Military Sites

CLARENCE R. GEIER, LAWRENCE E. BABITS, DOUGLAS D. SCOTT, AND DAVID G. ORR

The selection of methods applied to conducting research is logically and inextricably tied to the question(s) that are being addressed. The seven chapters that follow focus on particular categories of method and technique, and their applicability in addressing a range of questions within the modern context of the historical archaeology of military sites. While varying somewhat in style and approach, each chapter is intended to introduce a set of strategies, methods, and/or techniques, issues concerning their selection and use, and illustrations of their application to certain questions. Given their nature and approach, some of the chapters also deal with topics inherent in the modern discourse on military culture and history.

In chapter 1, Whitehorne draws attention to the necessary and dynamic interplay between the historian and archaeologist as colleagues who join their skills, understanding, and methods in the art of historical archaeology. In this dialogue, the historian brings specialized knowledge of the military action to the project in a way that addresses its historical context and which also anticipates what

the archaeologist should look for or might be expected to find. Such information should include: extensive knowledge of the military event and its historical place, the military groups involved, established policies and guidelines that might direct their actions. In addition, the historian has knowledge of, and access to, a whole range of supporting documentation and sources concerning personnel, supply, material culture, and other military issues of a particular time. Beyond the background context, however, the research skills of the field historian will commonly be challenged by the need to provide interpretive insight into the meaning of biological and material finds made by the archaeologist and which may be totally unanticipated from studying available historical records. These points are illustrated with reference to Whitehorne's experience as site historian for burial excavations associated with the War of 1812 Cemetery at Snake Hill, Fort Erie, Ontario, Canada.

The modern field of geophysics is playing an increasingly important role in locating, evaluating, and interpreting military sites. In chapter 2, Hanna introduces readers to

the wide range of new technologies available, discusses their uses and limitations, and considers factors that hinder their utility. In this discussion, he covers use of geophysical technologies at shallow terrestrial sites, particularly soldier gravesites, at battlefields such as Manassas, Antietam, and Mt. Zion Church at Aldie, Virginia.

In chapter 3, Scott addresses several topical areas in the application of forensic archaeological studies to the study of human remains at military sites. The chapter also illustrates how these topics can be addressed through the interplay of forensic analysis of human remains and a scholarly understanding of existing historic records. Topics addressed include the evolution of military medicine over time and the value of the studies of demographic issues of age, ethnicity, and health as they relate to individual soldiers and their military units. While referencing sites such as the 1776 Continental Army hospital at Mt. Independence, New York, and the medical facilities at the latenineteenth century Fort Larned, Kansas, his primary focus is on using existing personnel records and correct enlistment policies and the documentation available on individual recruits in considering the demographic features of members of Custer's 7th Cavalry at the Little Big Horn.

While traditional military studies commonly deal with historical events separated from the present by time and often generations, a growing number of scholars are beginning to study more recent historical conflicts (see de Meyer and Freeman in Section 2) including World War II and even the Vietnam War. At the same time, forensic archaeologists have become increasingly involved with issues of the modern, or more immediate, era and have been confronted by the challenges posed when working on more recent fields of conflict. In chapter 4, Connor confronts the reader with the issues of modern war and genocide in which the role of the archaeologist is to serve as a key part of forensic, often criminal, investigations into military or hostile events. She provides a short history of the field of forensic archaeology and then addresses the differences between the traditional studies (see Scott, chap. 3, Whitehorne, chap. 1) and those conducted as part of legal proceedings such as those carried between 2004 and 2006 on behalf of the Iraqi Special Tribunal investigating the war crimes of Saddam Hussein's administration. She makes strong distinctions between the two areas of application while covering the composition of the field team, the nature of the investigation and its parameters, the physical nature of the artifacts including physical biological remains and associated

material culture, the idea of artifacts as evidence, legal obligations with respect to chain of custody, and the obligation of the archaeologist in providing expert witness. To illustrate the process, she focuses on research done in conjunction with 2004 Tutsi massacres in Rwanda.

Chapter 5 addresses issues of underwater archaeology as they relate to the study of battlefields. Conlin and Russell point out that underwater archaeologists have typically focused on the analysis of single ships and that only recently have the relatively new areas of underwater and battlefield archaeology joined in recognizing the nature and patterning of groups of sunken ships as delineating naval battles and battlefields and providing insights into the study of human conflict (see also Broadwater in section 2). Such studies allow researchers to consider issues involving the larger scale of a naval engagement, patterns of attack, and specific tactics involved as well as the outcome of the action and the historical context in which it occurred. Conlin and Russell discuss the unique potential of naval battlefields and highlight what maritime archaeology offers to battlefield archaeology. Referencing an extended case study focused on the engagement of the *H.L. Hunley* and the USS *Housatonic* off Charleston, South Carolina, during the American Civil War, they discuss a methodological framework for studying naval battlefields and the challenges posed by such research.

The importance of studying military encampments, the daily life of soldiers, and the evolution of

military support systems for troops is of growing interest and importance to students of military history (Geier et al. 2006). In chapter 6, Balicki introduces the reader to the importance of military encampment archaeology. He then provides a substantive discussion of the diverse types of military encampments, the archaeological footprints and feature types that can identify them, and the methods, and procedures that have proven successful in their investigation, interpretation, and recording. The discussion of the use of metal detecting and trained metal detectorists is extremely useful and important (see also Hanna, chap. 2, and Reeves, chap. 8).

The construction of military earthworks (see also Babits, chap. 11) for purposes of short- and long-term defense, is a historically significant feature of many military landscapes. The use of natural and man-made defensive networks is fundamental to security at any level of activity, from temporary encampments and fortified pickets to massive defensive earthworks and walls that can enclose threatened cities or permanent fortifications. In the last chapter of Section 1 (chap. 7), Orr and Steele address the fact that over time, many earthworks are removed to restore the land for more productive purposes after war has ended. Their chapter deals with the particular case of sections of deeply buried earthworks at the Petersburg Battlefield. They illustrate a methodology in which programs of remote sensing (see Hanna, chap. 2), in combination with selective excavation, can be used in some instances to reveal the footprint of reduced earthworks.

CHAPTER ONE

Following the Paper Trail

A Historian's Role at the Snake Hill Excavations, Ontario, Canada

JOSEPH W. A. WHITEHORNE

INTRODUCTION

Archaeologists frequently encounter military sites containing physical evidence that lends itself to a variety of interpretations. The historical paper trail can set this material in a context that narrows possible explanations and interpretations. Historians and archaeologists working together often have a multiplier effect on each other, greatly enhancing and clarifying their respective insights and conclusions. In this dialogue the military historian brings knowledge of the doctrines and practices of a military organization and the numerous ways they can be documented to the equation. In using the paper trail, he can answer the questions that scientists have about military findings, ultimately contributing to a better understanding of the site and the objects found on it.

The growing incidence of historical archaeology at military sites mandates the inclusion of historians on the staff of most excavations. Often, archaeological remains can suggest several tantalizing possibilities that can be resolved only by extensive archival research. The historian can place the evidence from the site in contexts ranging from the very large overview of a campaign down to specifics about events and people related to a particular place. These contexts can then be used to propose the best possible explanation of the physical remains. To illustrate these points, this text describes the experience, and approach used by the author as historian to a major site on the War of 1812 Niagara frontier. Examples of the value of historical contributions to an archaeological end-product are illustrated to provide insights into the sort of historical thinking necessary to be fully effective in that context.

Each site excavation raises unique questions. Initially, the historian should immerse himself into the particular historic era and situation to get a sense of what might be relevant to the archaeologist preparing the excavation strategy. Rarely will one have the good fortune to come across a documented, contemporary explanation for the events that created the site under study. Instead, the historian must use informed imagination and general knowledge of the period to find original sources needed to help build evidence that explains what may be and is found at the site.

A pitfall often encountered by the historian is that persons not familiar with the practices and procedures of another era often assume that they were performed as they are now. For example, archaeologists working on the Fort Erie Site erroneously presumed that personnel records were on file for troops on both the English and American sides of the action. As this practice was not common until the twentieth century, historians had to use their knowledge of earlier nineteenth century military administration to create the needed personnel data, a process that required considerable sifting through primary archival material.

The project historian must also be alert to commentary, innuendo, and allusion in memoirs and other, later, unofficial publications that hint at practices meriting expansion of research and which might prove critical to the final data analysis. For many projects, the historian's imagination, energy, and knowledge can be the only limit on the research and analysis that might be pursued.

The Fort Erie Project involved military units and archives of two governments, British and American. While potentially a source of research difficulty, in this instance it posed no research problem because the armies and their functions were essentially the same. In addition, in this case the current offices of both sides cooperated fully in the research and each office was sensitive to the concerns and idiosyncrasies of the other.

SNAKE HILL PROJECT

In the spring of 1987 developers working along the banks of the Niagara River near Fort Erie, Ontario, began to uncover human remains at a site known locally as Snake Hill (Pfeiffer and Williamson 1991). The area at the confluence of the river with Lake Erie is rich in prehistoric sites and the first assumption was that another native burial ground had been uncovered. This assumption was quickly dispelled when a preliminary archaeological assessment discovered military artifacts indicating that what had been found was probably a graveyard from the War of 1812.

Fort Erie is located across the Niagara River from Buffalo, New York (fig. 1.1). A military site since the Seven Years War, the fort was the scene of major actions in the summer of 1814. U.S. forces captured the fort on 3 July of that year. Subsequently, they fought two severe engagements further north before being pressed back to the fort at the end of the month (Whitehorne 1992). American engineers substantially added to the existing, modest British works by building a berm (parapet or rampart) linking the northeast bastion of the fort to the lakeshore (fig. 1.2). In addition, they built an earthen wall running from the southwestern corner of the original fort nearly one-half mile to the lakeshore at Snake Hill. The hill itself was converted into a fortified artillery bastion supported by infantry. Contemporary maps made by engineers from both sides, revealed details of these efforts (fig. 1.2). These maps were found in official reports on file at the National Archives and in private collections, as well as in published post-war journals.

Following military engagements to the north, the British pursued U.S. forces back to the fort, softened it with artillery fire, and launched a nearly successful attack on 15 August. British infantry simultaneously assaulted both Snake Hill and the northeast bastion of the fort but suffered heavy losses. Repulsed, they

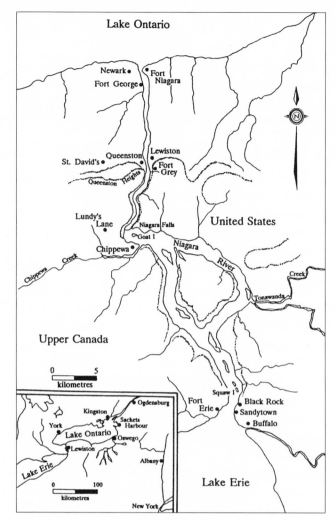

FIGURE 1.1. Map of the Niagara Frontier. Courtesy The Nautical & Aviation Publishing Company, Inc.

settled in to conduct a protracted siege, firing about 100 artillery rounds daily into the approximately 30 acres manned by about 2800 U.S. forces. Each side conducted combat patrols into no man's land throughout the month-long siege. Finally, on 17 September, a U.S. sortie forced the British to end their siege and withdraw northward. Modern investigators suspected that the burials at Snake Hill were somehow connected to this mayhem.

The 1987 discovery of the Snake Hill Cemetery Site provoked numerous unanswered questions. For example, it had long been known that in the summer of 1814, the U.S. Army had established a semi-permanent hospital at Williamsville, New York, northeast of Buffalo. Its vestige is a marked burial site near the modern airport containing separate British and American mass burials. Was the site at Snake Hill a similar "mixed" burial site? Furthermore, why were the Snake Hill casualties not buried at Williamsville; and who were they? In order to answer these and numerous related questions posed by archaeologists, pathologists, and the public, it was necessary to provide a comprehensive, systemic understanding of the military forces under study.

A first step to understanding the nature of the military forces in question was to ask how they functioned. Secondary archival sources such as general histories will often identify the principal personalities involved in an action. This is helpful in establishing a list of military organizations and leaders associated with the event. Concurrently, a review of contemporary army/military regulations, personnel registers, manuals on tactics, and orders on procedures and policies can assist in creating a concept of how the organization was expected to function, at least in theory. Learning what the leaders and staff of the military units involved were reading and whose principles they were attempting to apply can contribute substantially to anticipating and understanding evidence of their actions, particularly as they may have conformed with, or deviated from, the theoretical. For example, at Buffalo, New York, the shortage of blue cloth required one brigade of U.S. regulars to resort to wearing gray militia uniforms when it crossed the

Niagara River into Canada in July 1814. Identification and interpretation of the artifacts of the regiment without knowing this situation could be very misleading to a modern archaeologist. This sort of information can also provide ideas on the sources and topics to seek out for developing a research plan for excavation and a context for data interpretation.

Vast amounts of raw, unprocessed, primary documentary material sit on the shelves of numerous public and private institutions, archives, and libraries. In the case of Snake Hill, while the soldiers died on British soil, much of the information about their final weeks was found housed in the files held by the Old Army and Navy Records Branch of the U.S. National Archives and Records Administration (NARA). Although broadly catalogued, the overwhelming mass of material can only become fully productive if the researcher has a grasp of how the military unit under study functioned and who was included in its membership, thus, having an idea of what to look for. The National Archives, with repositories in Maryland and Washington, D.C., contains the primary archives and raw data of a substantial and evolving military bureaucracy of the United States. When these data are searched out and unraveled through the art of the historian, much of the information relevant to the military action in question can be revealed. Official

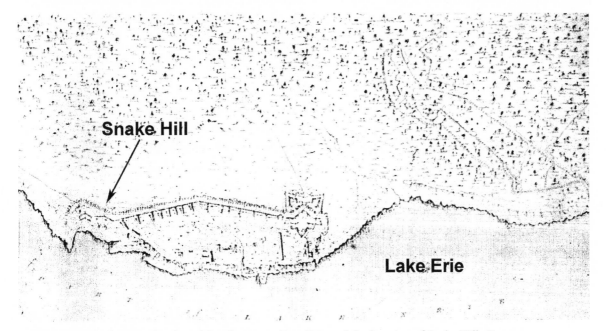

FIGURE 1.2. Map showing the altered fortification at Fort Erie and the location of Snake Hill. Courtesy National Archives and Records Administration.

military records typically document the necessary but prosaic areas of financial and personnel accountability. Occasionally, a commander's report or marginal comment injects some humanity. However, except for the Library of Congress, and the Army's Military History Institute at Carlisle, Pennsylvania, the bulk of personal papers and private letters must be sought in repositories such as historical societies, state and academic archives, and newspaper files. Indeed, as illustrated by the growing volume of firsthand accounts of the American Civil War, many significant documents are in the hands of families and private collectors. The accumulated exposure to this wide variety of sources, often attained only by years of experience, should contribute to the historian's growing feel for the organization in question.

Knowledge of how an army operates and how responsibilities are assigned within it is crucial. Without these facts, it is difficult to develop a successful research approach that will give meaning to information that is recovered from an archaeological site by researchers from various disciplines working on the site. At sites such as Snake Hill, that include a large number of human remains, this broad understanding helps guide the search for the data necessary to answer the questions raised by the material and medical findings.

The so-called "paper chase" is formed by combining the systemic knowledge with the issues raised by material discoveries. In the absence of a defining document or photograph that explains a find, everyone at the excavation works toward building such an overwhelming body of circumstantial evidence that the final conclusion about what is under study is reasonable. The historian with his specialized knowledge and sources often plays a decisive role in this search.

There are certain functions in an armed force that are constant, regardless of the era. Men must be recruited, trained, and accounted for. They must be clothed, fed, sheltered, and paid; and they must be cared for when they are sick or injured. Since the eighteenth century, authorities have frequently been concerned with the respectful treatment of the dead. No single commander can perform all these functions without the help of some sort of staff. It is the role of the historian to learn how a particular staff was structured and what the responsibilities of each of its

members were. This is where familiarity with rosters and regulations pays off. Additionally, it is essential to know what the support system was that served each function in the chain going all the way back to the War Department or its equivalent. Finally, it is important to determine how local commands were structured and organized in relation to each other, the so-called "order of battle," or "table of organization." All this helps follow the various trails of communication between and within the military organization in question.

The most promising official document collections to consider are those usually generated by personnel and pay officers, purchasing quartermasters, different contemporary commands from the smallest units upward, and finally, the post-war claims of veterans. These latter can provide interesting narrations of events while also corroborating details on medical and dietary conditions. Like all armies, the forces on the Niagara in 1814 left a wide variety of personnel registers, purchase orders, supply requisitions, financial records, commanders' reports, and War Department correspondence. These provided the framework for finding answers posed by the archaeologists at Snake Hill and their teams of medical and other specialists. These records also identified numbers of historical participants in the action whose personal papers, such as memoirs and articles, mostly in private locations, also proved helpful in expanding the historic database.

The perusal of quantities of relevant primary documents and accounts can give an excellent picture of the routine operations of a unit—often so mundane that they are cited nowhere else, and hence, are ultimately forgotten. Since many of these records deal with some type of accountability on the part of those making them, they are probably accurate statements. However, even primary sources should be cross-checked before being accepted. The official reports of commanders are less detailed and critical, but still give a reasonable picture of events. Memoirs are less reliable when dealing with matters outside the experience of the writer, and may have their own agenda. But, they often are useful for documenting personal experiences and impressions. In the case of the War of 1812, these included professional military and literary journals.

Modern secondary sources, as interpretations of primary records, in some cases may report and perpetuate errors of fact and observation made in the primary sources. In other cases, the brevity of treatment of actions may leave an incorrect impression of their nature and import. However, it is often beneficial to start historical research with secondary overviews that only can be provided by reputable modern general studies. Scholars of the War of 1812 have also generated several excellent published bibliographical and archival guides that help accelerate research.

Given the presence of human burials at Snake Hill, many showing indications of medical intervention, it seemed reasonable to begin with the medical function and examine contemporary military and other burial customs. This required research also in nineteenth century views on death and burial. The question asked was, "If I was the commander's surgeon, what would I tell him about his medical support, how it was working, and how it linked with larger systems?" Answering this question led to connections with aspects of the other military staff functions, ultimately attaining some firm conclusions as to the probable nationality of the 28 persons in the Snake Hill graves.

Medical treatment began at the regimental aid stations with the unit surgeons and their assistants (called "mates" in 1812–14). Two regimental hospitals served throughout the Fort Erie siege and were joined by a third at the time of the 1814 sortie. The reports and memoirs of the surgeons revealed that the 23rd U.S. Infantry facility stood to the rear of Snake Hill. A reasonable picture of medical operations could be formed from surgeons' after-action reports, unit muster rolls indicating the status of soldiers, hospital returns and records of purchasing officers. Since the purchasing and procurement officers had to account for 100% of their disbursements or suffer personal liability, these latter records were viewed as the most comprehensive and accurate. All the sources revealed that the regimental aid station treated the wounded and sick as quickly as possible, sent them by boat to the equivalent of evacuation facilities in Buffalo, New York, where they were further stabilized. They were then sent to the semi-permanent facility at Williamsville, New York. Patients expecting a long convalescence were transferred to the general hospital at Greenbush, New York. Persons buried in the hasty graveyard behind the 23rd Infantry aid station must have died while undergoing treatment there or were

dead on arrival at the regimental facility. Thus, it was reasoned, they had not entered into this system.

Quartermaster records and family memoirs indicated that the remains of U.S. officers were repatriated for burial in Buffalo or at their homes elsewhere in the United States. It followed, therefore, that the remains at Snake Hill were those of soldiers—but, were they only U.S. males of European ancestry? Through period reports and memoirs it was known that units of Native American warriors participated in the battle on both sides. The issue was answered unequivocally by project forensic specialists when none of the remains showed Native American physical traits.

Discovery of a delicate tibia in a surgical waste pit raised the question of a possible female casualty. Research of pay vouchers and ration requests revealed that five women served as nurses in the Fort Erie hospitals. Conversely, the same records indicated that these individuals continued to draw pay long after the battle, thus eliminating them as casualties. The tibia later proved to belong to a young male. Thus, in this case, science raised the question, history provided a possibility, and science concluded the issue.

Artifacts found with the remains were exclusively American, except for a few souvenir British buttons recovered from what once were inside uniform pockets, leading to the view that all the burials were those of U.S. soldiers. This conclusion needed further verification because the United States and Canadian governments had agreed to pay archaeological and exhumation costs pro-rata based on the numbers of soldiers from each nation that were found at the site. Consequently, research was conducted into the origins of the members of each military unit involved, their diet during the 1814 operations, and their medical complaints reported during that period and as revealed in post-war claims. Each of these topics could help further corroborate a soldier's nationality as well as add information on their physical condition during the time of the campaign.

Exhumation of the remains of soldiers occurred in the late fall of 1984 during brisk stormy weather. Consequently, heated tents were set up over the grave pedestals to allow their careful excavation. As the skeletons emerged, artificial light inside the tents highlighted the whiteness and sparkle of many exposed teeth. Ultimately, it was determined that there were

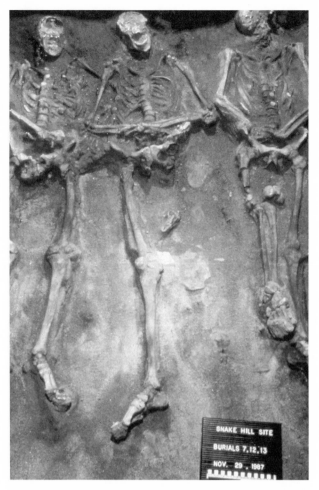

FIGURE 1.3. Burials 7, 12, 13, all showing severe trauma. Note the distinct whiteness of the teeth. Courtesy Archaeological Services, Inc.

few cases of caries or dental abscesses in the 28 subjects (fig. 1.3). This tended to confirm the enlisted status of the men as their wealthier officers would more likely be using refined sugar in their diet with the consequent problems of decay. Additionally, it was found that two of the U.S. units engaged at Fort Erie came from parts of New York and Vermont where there is an unusual amount of natural fluoride in the water supply. The whiteness of many of the soldiers' teeth increased the likelihood that some burials were men from those units. Oxygen isotopic analysis of the remains indicated that the men had spent most of their lives in the same geographic area, most likely the northeastern United States, not Ontario—providing further circumstantial evidence of origin.

Correspondence on file in the National Archives produced during the siege by U.S. commanders at

Fort Erie and Buffalo revealed their growing concern over the adverse health effects of the monotonous military diet available to the troops. The lack of Vitamin C and the threat of scurvy threatened to critically deplete unit strength. In response, the commanding general ordered the quartermaster to purchase potatoes at any price to head off the crisis. Commissary purchase vouchers indicate that adequate supplies were procured across Lake Erie at Ashtabula, Ohio, and became a part of the troops' diet by the end of August. Oxygen isotopic and lead analysis indicated the presence of minerals consistent with consumption of northeastern Ohio tubers.

Post-war pension claims revealed several health problems such as rheumatism, hernias, and stress fractures incurred by the veterans while at Fort Erie. Osteobiographical studies of the remains indicated the traumatic injuries and surgical care cited in medical reports (fig. 1.3). They also reflected the physical and nutritional stresses that contributed to the later claims of the veterans. For example, unit records and reports document months of extensive, arduous training of the U.S. forces before the invasion. They also recount the use of the troops as an intensive labor force used in modifying the defenses of the fort during the siege. Excessive biomechanical strain of this sort can be manifested by osteoarthritis and fatigue fractures. These symptoms were common among the disinterred skeletons along with Schmorl's depressions and benign cortical defects that also indicated extensive exertion. This correlation of the physical evidence with the documentary claims added further to the accumulating circumstantial evidence confirming the identity of the soldiers.

The need to reduce any questions of nationality to the minimum, required research into the uniforms and accouterments issued to the men. For example, 221 identifiable U.S. buttons in several different patterns were found among the remains. Unit records indicated clothing issues that included the various types of buttons. New York militia records and published official correspondence further noted that every arsenal between Albany and Buffalo had issued everything it had in stock. This included ammunition and personal equipment dating from the American Revolution. Very few objects were found in the graves. This is in keeping with hospital practice of collecting personal and official property before burial. Those items that were found were consistent with the supply picture presented by the documents. Added to the other data, everyone was satisfied that all 28 of the remains were those of U.S. soldiers.

Many people, including the scientists on site, hoped at least some remains could be personally identified, or that, at least, regimental affiliation could be determined. Unit muster rolls, a detailed form of roster, noted individual deaths and how many soldiers died at different times. Their precise use of language was helpful: "died" meant death by disease or accident; "killed" indicated an artillery fatality; and "killed in action" signified a soldier who had fallen in close combat. They also provided various physical details to include height, hair color, and other distinguishing characteristics such as scars.

It seemed plausible that some or all of this information could be cross-referenced with the skeletal remains. However, data such as hair color was long gone and insufficient button evidence precluded determining unit affiliation of individual soldiers. Additionally, the muster rolls were not always reliable. Some soldiers were reported dead but appeared in other documents generated months later as having been paroled as a POW or returned from long periods in the hospital. This shows that even some categories of primary documents need to be cross-referenced with other sources before being accepted. As a result, the best that could be done was to draw up a list of 60 men known to have died in Canada but who had no known graves anywhere and leave it at that, much to the disappointment of the archaeologists.

Despite this setback, the nationality of the remains was sufficiently conclusive that they all could be presumed to have been U.S. soldiers. Their remains were sent to the Royal Ontario Museum in Toronto for final studies. Then, on 30 June 1988, they were returned to Fort Erie. In a moving ceremony, Canadian forces transferred the 28 flag-draped coffins to a U.S. contingent. The Americans, in turn, transported the coffins to the national cemetery in Bath, New York, where they were buried with full military honors, each under a headstone simply stating "Unknown Soldier, War of 1812." Documentary, medical, and archaeological evidence indicated that, for most of them, they finally were back in their home region.

The work on the Snake Hill Site was expedited and enriched by the close collaboration of representatives from all of the disciplines required to provide data on the discoveries being made—archaeology, medicine, forensics, anthropology, and history. Thanks, in part, to historical support, the work was able to proceed more quickly than it might have otherwise, a matter of practical concern to those footing the bill. Based on the findings in each discipline, researchers asked questions that stimulated researchers in the other disciplines to consider hitherto unthought-of aspects of their own field. This "turbo effect" resulted in greatly improved, richer products that supported and synchronized the final report in a relatively short period (Pfeiffer and Williamson 1991). The close association with the other disciplines also influenced the historical methodology. This led to a comprehensive product specifically addressing the questions of other disciplines, while providing a far more nuanced historical overview. The Snake Hill experience speaks strongly for making similar interdisciplinary approaches a matter of routine when working on such sites. Sometimes a shard does not a tea party make, and you need a historian to point this out.

CHAPTER TWO

Geophysics

Some Recommendations and Applications

WILLIAM F. HANNA

INTRODUCTION

Historical archaeologists are well-schooled in the traditional methods of visual walkovers, shovel test pitting, trenching, and cutting sharply defined excavation units and using rake, hoe, brush, screen, and trowel. While these traditional methods remain important, tools for remotely sensing the presence and placement of subsurface objects and structural features can greatly reduce the time required to plan and expedite an excavation. Some archaeologists broadly include the bulbous-tipped steel probe (Richardson 2002) and the spoon-tipped soil auger as tools of remote sensing. Such minimally invasive probing involves sensing, by feel and sound, mechanical resistance or vibrations that indicate soil compactness and the presence of soil disturbance. Among all remote sensing tools available, geophysical tools are the least invasive and are the most efficient in terms of saving time.

The purpose of this chapter is to comment on a few geophysical tools and techniques recommended for shallow terrestrial archaeology, to provide brief

examples of historical projects in which we have used these tools, and to summarize a few conclusions, specifically about soldier gravesites, a principal focus of our work. Because we refer to specific sites later, some of the sites in northern Virginia and adjacent areas, mostly associated with the Civil War, where we have conducted geophysical work are shown in fig. 2.1.

MAPS, PHOTOGRAPHS, IMAGES, AND COORDINATES

The geophysical toolbox initially includes maps and aerial photographs (Wilson 2000), many of which can be downloaded at no cost from the Internet, and remote-sensing images (Sever 2000), which can be purchased through the website of the Earth Resources Observation and Science (EROS) Data Center of the U.S. Geological Survey. Field coordinates can be established using combinations of compass, measurement tapes, theodolite, electric distance measurement device (the last two embodied within a single "total station"), or differential Global Positioning System

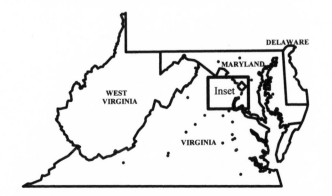
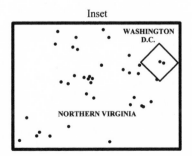

FIGURE 2.1. Map showing archaeogeophysical sites, mostly centered in northern Virginia and connected to the Civil War.

(GPS) device updated via radio signals (Weymouth and Huggins 1985). Positioning coordinates from the air is possible, but expensive, using gyroscopically-stabilized accelerometers, updated by laser tracking and ranging, and integrated with a laser altimeter (Brown et al. 1987). The datum and baseline of the survey should be marked as permanently as possible with iron spikes, or other identifiers that can be recovered later using a magnetic locator or metal detector.

For small areas of an acre or less, we usually lay out a grid of as many as fifty parallel 100-ft measurement tapes for mapping above-ground features and for defining transects along which we can drag a ground-penetrating radar (GPR) antenna without disrupting the tapes. The tapes are then photographed from high above, offering, when zoomed, a detailed, point-by-point picture of our grid for future use.

GEOPHYSICAL TOOLS FOR ARCHAEOLOGY AT MILITARY SITES

Nearly a hundred geophysical tools and techniques are available to archaeologists working at shallow depths in military settings. They can be classified by (1) whether they are "active" (involving manmade signals) or "passive" (involving natural signals); (2) sensor location (e.g., spaceborne, airborne, terrestrial-surface, subsurface [borehole or cave], water-surface, or sub-aqueous); and (3) physics involved (e.g., gravity, magnetic, geo-electric, electromagnetic induction, seismic, sonic, radar, thermal, and radioactivity). A complete list, with its attendant jargon and acronyms, is almost overwhelming to workers outside mainstream geophysics, physics, hydrology, or engineering, thus no attempt is made to offer a comprehensive list here.

A prodigious amount of information about these techniques, including those most suited to archaeogeophysics, can be obtained from journal articles, books, applet applications, and Internet sites of companies, universities, and government agencies. One exceptionally informative, extensive, in-depth, graphics-rich, website is maintained by Professor Kevin L. Kvamme, who heads the University of Arkansas Archeo-Imaging Laboratory and who also supports a North American Database of Archaeological Geophysics.

Special attention is called to the National Park Service (NPS) workshops on archaeological prospecting techniques, coordinated annually by Steven L. De Vore. Recommended textbooks on shallow geophysical techniques include, but are not restricted to: Parasnis (1996), Reynolds (1997), Sharma (1997), Telford, Geldart, and Sheriff (2003), Burger, Sheehan, and Jones (2006), and Stefano and Piro (2009). The last of these is especially designed for student computer interaction. Recommended textbooks on archaeogeophysics include, but are not restricted to, Aitkin (1974), Scollar et al. (1990), Bevan (1998), Clark (2000), Williamson and Nickens (2000), Kvamme (2001, 2005), Gafney and Gater (2003), Garrison (2003), Johnson (2006), and Witten (2006). Also recommended are the compilations of Wynn (1986), Linford (2006), and Campana and Piro (2009). Keywords for an Internet browser include both spellings of "archaeology" and "archeology."

Three Geophysical Tools Recommended for Archaeologists

For terrestrial archaeological work, three relatively inexpensive and easy-to-use, handheld instruments are recommended for the practicing archaeologist:

1. A sensitive metal detector, a traditional nemesis to those protective of areas illegally searched, but an indispensable tool for those authorized to use them (Corle and Balicki 2006). Most detectors currently used are of the single- or multi-frequency phase-shifting type, though others of the pulse-induction type are especially useful in an environment rich in magnetic mineral or saline content. Both types are manufactured by Fisher, White's, Garrett, Minelab, and Tesoro. Metal detectors for deep sensing and landmine clearing are much more costly and some are restricted to military use.

A vast amount of literature exists on the history, design, and operation of metal detectors (Connor and Scott 1998) since Richard J. C. Atkinson (1953) predicted their increased use at the end of World War II. Of great importance to military archaeology, the metal detector was key to deciphering patterns of artifacts in the prototypical, intensive archaeological study of the open battlefield at the Little Bighorn Battlefield

National Monument (Scott and Fox 1987; Scott et al. 1989). Since that time, metal detectors have been successfully used on dozens of battlefields throughout the country despite the fact that many have been relic-hunted previously. Thus, of all of the available geophysical instruments, the humble metal detector sparked the explosion of interest in battlefield and military archaeology more than two decades ago.

2. A magnetic locator, which is a flux-gate, magnetic gradiometer having its two sensors mounted co-axially inside a slender rod. Although this instrument detects only ferrous materials, such as iron, steel, brick, fired soil, and mafic rock, it does so with amazing sensitivity—much greater than any metal detector. While the frequency-type of metal detector in standard "all metal" mode can detect induced magnetization, the magnetic locator senses both induced and remanent (or permanent) magnetization, thereby increasing its effectiveness. Because sensors are mounted inside a slender rod, they can be poked into very narrow spaces where entry by a metal detector coil is precluded, an advantage for forensics work. One important use of the locator is to help clear an area of near-surface ferrous trash prior to conducting a metal-detector survey or magnetometer survey. This trash otherwise would appear as anomaly "spikes" that would obscure or mask anomalies of archaeological interest. Magnetic locators are manufactured by Schonstedt, Chicago Tape, Fisher, CST/Berger, and Dunham & Morrow.

3. A susceptibility meter, a small, palm-size device that is placed next to soil or rock to sense its relative magnetic susceptibility. Magnetic susceptibility is a measure of induced magnetization; remanent magnetization will not be detected except for its slight influence on susceptibility anisotropy (Hanna 1977; Ellwood 1978). This device has a digital readout with memory that can immediately distinguish two or more rocks or soils that visually appear to be identical. It can be used to make a local ground surface survey ("topsoil magnetic susceptibility mapping") or can be used to quickly identify whether or not a rock, brick, or soil contains an appreciable amount of magnetic iron oxides. Susceptibility meters are manufactured by Exploranium, ZH Instruments, and Scintrex.

Magnetic susceptibility mapping became of interest to archaeologists when it was discovered that topsoil susceptibility can be enhanced via several mechanisms.

These mechanisms remain subjects of current research (see Thompson and Oldfield 1986; Reynolds et al. 1990; Maher and Thompson 1999; Evans and Heller 2003). Various processes for this enhancement of a physical, chemical, and biological nature were initially proposed by Le Borgne (1955) and later by Fassbinder, Stanjek, and Vali (1990) and Dalan and Banerjee (1998). There is agreement that susceptibility of soil is usually increased by heating as a result of, for example, ancient campfires, burning of low wooden structures, and wildfires.

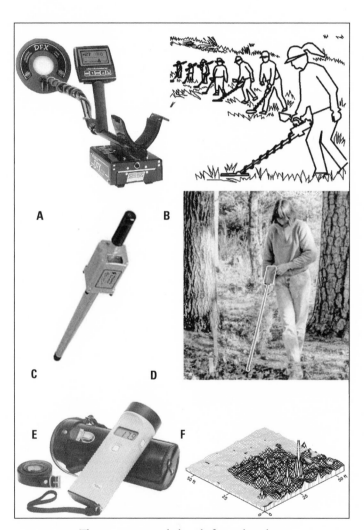

FIGURE 2.2. Three recommended tools for archaeologists: (A) typical metal detector; (B) authorized metal detectorists advancing in a line on a battlefield; (C) typical magnetic locator; (D) magnetic locator in use at Monticello; (E) typical magnetic susceptibility meter; and (F) magnetic susceptibility meter anomalies at a brick clamp (Strutt and Hanna 1998:40), Jefferson's Poplar Forest. Photographs (E), (C), and (E) by author; (D) and (F) courtesy M. A. Strutt.

FIGURE 2.3. Practical uses of the three recommended tools: (A) using a metal detector in a search for the 1793 cornerstone, U.S. Capitol sub-basement; (B) using a magnetic susceptibility meter on a sample of the "found" cornerstone; and (C) using a magnetic locator to detect ferrous buttons, New Market battlefield burial. Photographs (A) courtesy J. H. Polk; (B) courtesy N. V. Hanna; and (C) courtesy C. E. Petrone

Three Geophysical Tools Recommended for Specialists

My favorite geophysical tools—namely, ground-penetrating radar (GPR), electromagnetic induction (EMI) or, alternatively, galvanic resistivity, and vertical magnetic gradiometry are identical to the ones used for many years by those with an archaeological background (e.g., Bevan 1991). Because much information about GPR, EMI, and magnetic gradiometry is available from the internet and from references previously cited, only a few remarks will be offered on each technique.

1. GPR usually entails pulling a ground-based, shielded antenna that transmits pulses of electromagnetic energy downward. These energy pulses are partly backscattered by reflection (and occasionally by diffraction) from objects in the subsurface upward to a ground-based receiver antenna where they are displayed and recorded. For reflections to be seen, sub-surface objects must possess physical properties, such as dielectric permittivity, electrical conductivity, and/or magnetic permeability, which contrast with equivalent properties in surrounding soil. A great advantage of GPR over most metal-detecting devices is its ability to sense nonmetallic as well as metallic targets.

Because the energy is transmitted downward in the approximate shape of a cone, the antenna effectively "sees" a certain distance forward and backward as well as to either side. Signals usually appear as hyperbolic echoes or lateral discontinuities on records that show distance on the horizontal axis and two-way travel time on the vertical axis. Travel time can be converted to approximate depth by multiplying by a velocity of one-third foot per nanosecond (one nanosecond is one-billionth of a second), a reasonable average for most soils. For large areas (>1 ac), it is prudent to use a digital system that can quickly provide maps of amplitude "time slices" of GPR reflections.

Bruce W. Bevan pioneered the use of GPR for archaeological purposes in the United States (Bevan and Kenyon 1975) and James A. Doolittle, a soils specialist, was also an early adopter of the technique (Barker and Doolittle 1992). Good references for archaeological applications of GPR include books by Conyers and Goodman (1997) and Conyers (2004); a multi-authored, more technical book edited by David J. Daniels (2004); and the "GRORADAR" website of Gary R. Olhoeft. GPR systems for archaeological applications are manufactured by Sensors & Software,

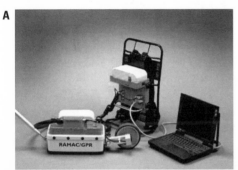

FIGURE 2.4. Ground-penetrating radar (see text for details): (A) typical portable GPR system; (B) van-based GPR control unit and monitor with video recorder; (C) GPR antenna and cable during survey; and (D) GPR record showing burial at Little Fork Church. Photographs (A) and (B) by author; and (C) and (D) courtesy C. E. Petrone

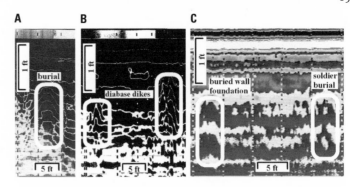

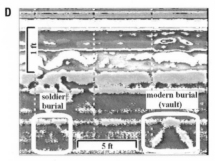

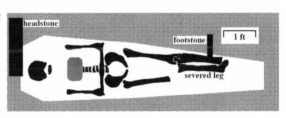

FIGURE 2.5. Examples of GPR echoes on or near battlefields: (A) burial, Mumma Cemetery, Antietam battlefield; (B) geologic features detected where soldier burials were expected, Brawner Farm, Second Manassas battlefield; (C) comparison of echoes associated with a buried wall foundation and a soldier burial, Mt. Zion battlefield area; (D) comparison of echoes associated with a soldier burial and a modern vault, new Market battlefield area; (E) first re-interment of Confederate Captain William Downs Farley; and (F) sketch of Farley's shadow remains, including his cannonball-severed leg. Images and sketches by author.

Inc., Geophysical Survey Systems, Inc. (GSSI), and Mala Geoscience. Figure 2.4 illustrates alternative GPR systems in use. Figure 2.5 illustrates multiple examples of GPR echoes identified on or near battlefields.

2. The EMI conductivity meter, consists of a transmitter coil mounted at one end, and a receiver coil mounted at the other end about 3 feet away. A data logger is attached to the meter so that data can be stored digitally for later transfer to a computer for processing. The EMI meter is usually oriented with its two fixed coils aligned in the same plane (co-planar) with their axes vertical. The transmitter coil generates

an alternating magnetic field, which can induce magnetization if magnetically susceptible material, such as iron or magnetite, is present or which can induce eddy currents within electrically conductive material, such as metal or moist soil. The secondary fields associated with the induced magnetization or eddy currents are then detected by the receiver coil and separated into in-phase or quadrature-phase components relative to the transmitting signal. The strength of the received signal is occasionally enhanced by galvanic "current channeling" if a metallic object is embedded within conductive soil (McNeill 1985).

Both in-phase and quadrature-phase signals can range from negative to positive values. In-phase signals for this low-frequency instrument are generally associated with induced magnetization (positive) or very highly conductive metal (negative). Quadrature-phase signals are generally associated with low to moderate-conductivity of soil (positive) or with magnetic viscosity (negative). Such viscous magnetization is caused by the inability of microscopic magnetic domains inside magnetic iron oxides to shift their walls or to rotate as rapidly as the frequency of the excitation field (Dabas and Skinner 1993). EMI devices are manufactured by Geonics, Geophex (a more expensive multifrequency device), and GSSI. Figure 2.6 shows a typical EMI device consisting of a conductivity meter with polycorder digital storage unit (upper) and an inexpensive, in-field, galvanic resistivity system (lower) in use at the Mumma Cemetery, Antietam battlefield (Creveling et al. 1995).

Figure 2.7 shows a comparison of elongate in-phase and quadrature-phase EMI anomalies at Lord Fairfax's "Ash Grove" Plantation similar to elongate anomalies that are sometimes found to mark buried trenches or wall foundations in a battlefield setting. Two elongate in-phase anomalies (upper) and two elongate quadrature-phase anomalies (lower) dominate the maps. One elongate anomaly of each data set, which is the one directed toward the mansion, have a common subsurface origin. The others have distinctly different sources. This figure demonstrates that the two phases of EMI sometimes give contrasting results, one more sensitive to metal and induced magnetization and the other more sensitive to soil moisture.

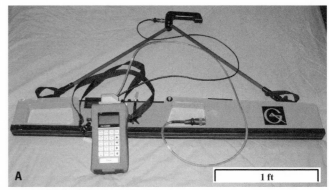

FIGURE 2.6. Electrical archaeogeophysical instruments (see text for details): (A) typical EMI conductivity meter with data logger; (B) inspecting anomalous areas during an electrical resistivity survey using the Wenner configuration (ellipses mark electrode locations), Mumma Cemetery, Antietam battlefield. Photographs (A) by author; and (B) courtesy C. E. Petrone.

An alternative tool to the EMI technique is galvanic resistivity. In this technique, four or more electrodes are placed into the soil. The current passing through two of them is measured while the voltage between or among the others is measured. Four equally spaced and aligned electrodes comprise the so-called "Wenner configuration," a favorite among many archaeogeophysicists. The electrodes can be either loosely or rigidly attached to a frame. Resistivity lows, which are proportional to conductivity highs, often mark subsurface regions of moisture, such as subsurface trenches; resistivity highs can result from relatively dry regions, such as subsurface foundations.

Some of these devices are called resistivity meters

whereas others are called resistance meters. Modern systems are often capable of producing tomographic images. Manufacturers of turnkey electrical resistivity equipment include Geoscan Research, Advanced Geosciences, Inc., Bison, GMC Instruments, Oyo, Scintrex, Zonge, and Syscal. Some offer multichannel capability that allow several simultaneous recordings to be made and provide measurements of self-potential (SP) and induced polarization, a form of complex resistivity.

Galvanic resistivity and magnetic gradiometry were our choices of use (GPR was not immediately available) when my colleague from the U.S. Geological Service, John T. Hack, and I were summoned to the White House, two weeks prior to the presidential inauguration. Officials were concerned about the disappearance of a hedgerow outside the East Wing. In the process of investigating this subsidence, we discovered a previously unmapped oyster-shell carriage path leading diagonally to an unknown iron-gate foundation. We also discovered that the hedgerow had fallen vertically into an old, unmapped tunnel that probably pre-dated construction of the once-secret, tube-like bunker known as the Presidential Emergency Operations Center that was hidden beneath the East Wing.

Many inexpensive, homemade, resistivity devices have been successfully used in archaeological work. More recent capacitively-coupled resistivity systems, which are of interest because they are non-intrusive, have yet to be tested extensively for archaeological purposes.

3. The third of the type of geophysical equipment is the vertical magnetic gradiometer. This array consists of two sensors mounted a fixed distance apart on a vertical staff. The sensors are connected by cables to a computerized console viewed by the operator and may be of the proton precession, proton-electron coupling (Overhauser), fluxgate, or optically pumped types. A typical proton type instrument simultaneously measures and records the total magnetic-field intensity of the lower sensor and the vertical gradient of the total magnetic-field intensity between the two sensors, assuming that the staff to which the sensors are attached is held upright.

Total magnetic-field intensity shows the local behavior of the earth's magnetic field and is especially convenient for numerically modeling magnetic objects that may cause magnetic anomalies. The vertical gradient is valuable for highlighting the shallowest buried magnetic objects or anomalously magnetized soil and is critical for canceling time-varying regional magnetic fields that would otherwise appear as noise. Proton, proton-electron, and optically pumped sensors measure the total magnetic field (combination of vertical and horizontal components). Fluxgate sensors measure the vertical component of the field, if positioned upright.

Manufacturers of magnetometers and gradiometers

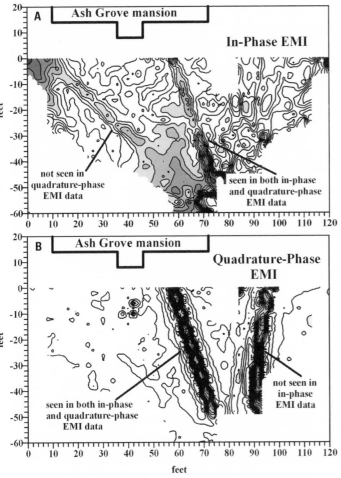

FIGURE 2.7. Comparison of in-phase and quadrature-phase EMI anomalies at Lord Fairfax's "Ash Grove" plantation: (A) Two elongate in-phase anomalies; and (B) two elongate quadrature-phase anomalies. Note that because only one of the anomalies of each data set is coincident, both phases are needed to form a complete EMI anomaly picture. Images by author.

include GEM Systems, GeoMetrics, Scintrex, Barting-ton Instruments, and Geoscan Research. The instruments manufactured by Geoscan Research include fluxgate-sensors and are widely used by archaeogeophysicists here and abroad. The student's bible for magnetic interpretation is the frequently updated applications manual of Sheldon Breiner (1973). More advanced archaeogeophysicists will likely be interested in the excellent summary of the historical development of the magnetic methods in exploration by Nabighian et al. (2005).

Figure 2.8, referring to field research at Gunston Hall, demonstrates the effectiveness of using a single-sensor instrument if a gradiometer is not available. As noted above, however, the preferred tool is the two-sensor gradiometer that provides both total-field and vertical gradient data, the latter of which offers a sharpening of anomalies and requires no diurnal corrections. In general, maximum overall sensitivity is achieved by using the shortest supporting staff possible. The optimal amount of sensor separation depends on the average magnitude of the vertical magnetic gradient.

The Gunston Hall map (fig. 2.8) shows one moderate amplitude anomaly and one large amplitude negative anomaly (known by geophysicists as "magnetic lows" if not referenced to a standard datum) on the left-hand side. The moderate-amplitude magnetic low associated with marked burials in the lower left of the map may be caused by the destruction of viscous remanent magnetization in the process of disturbing the soil. Most viscous soil magnetization is acquired over a period of hundreds to thousands of years, through alignment of the magnetic domains of the constituent iron oxides. Subsequent soil disturbance would tend to spatially randomize the aligned domains, thereby decreasing the magnetic effect.

The large-amplitude magnetic low in the upper left corner (fig. 2.8) was at first as puzzling, as it was surprising. The answer was discovered in a 1938 National Park Service memo. This communication described findings by Assistant Historian Joseph Mills Hanson, while visiting sites of the "battles of Manassas" with local farmer, W. A. Henry. During the in-field reconnaissance, Henry noted that " . . . there are, or there were, the bodies of soldiers along the sides of the ravine just north of this woods. A number of years ago

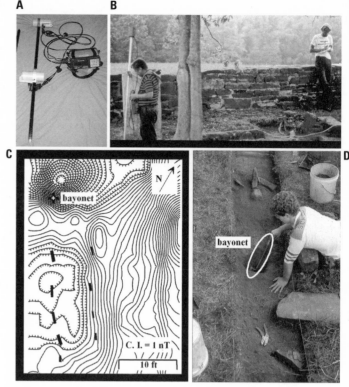

FIGURE 2.8. Magnetic surveys: (A) Proton-electron magnetic gradiometer of the Overhauser type; (B) early magnetometer survey using a single-sensor proton-precession magnetometer at the Ball Family Cemetery, Manassas battlefield; (C) the resulting total-field magnetic anomaly map; and (D) excavating a bayonet from an anomalous region. Photographs (A) and (C) by author; (B) courtesy C. E. Petrone; and (D) courtesy M. A. Strutt.

the bones of 16 were removed from here and reburied within the stone wall of the Ball family graveyard." The large-amplitude magnetic low is probably associated with deep soil disturbance and possibly, with components of reversed remanent magnetization of ferrous metal as well; it almost certainly reveals the approximate location of this mass reburial, which extends beyond the corner of the present wall.

Figure 2.9 shows a comparison of magnetic and EMI anomalies measured at Gunston Hall, home of George Mason IV. Note that both the in-phase and quadrature-phase maps show the same high amplitude circular anomaly in the lower right corner. The total-field magnetic anomaly map, derived from the lower sensor of the vertical Overhauser gradiometer, shows a positive circular anomaly attached to a larger negative anomaly. This is associated partly with the dipolar

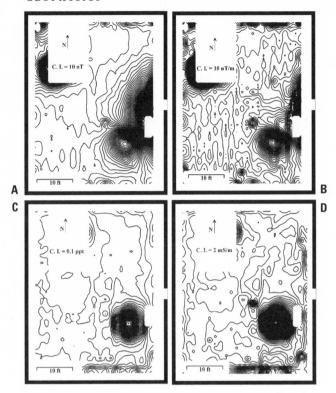

FIGURE 2.9. Comparison of magnetic and EMI anomalies measured at Gunston Hall: (A) total-field magnetic anomaly map; (B) vertical magnetic-gradient anomaly map; (C) in-phase EMI anomaly map; and (D) quadrature-phase EMI anomaly map. Note that, unlike the EMI data of figure 2.7, both the in-phase and quadrature-phase data provide nearly the same information about the location of the sole prominent anomaly. Images by author.

effect of the subsurface source and partly with an iron gate at the wall entrance. The vertical gradient map shows the circular anomaly somewhat sharpened, with a narrowing of the same attached anomaly associated exclusively with the iron gate. The in-phase EMI circular anomaly coincides spatially with the quadrature-phase circular anomaly, somewhat similar to the coincidence of the elongate anomalies of fig. 2.7 noted above. This circular anomaly feature indicates an unmarked, unknown burial within the Mason Family Cemetery. The source is tentatively inferred, on the basis of anomaly data and exploratory probing, to be a brick domed vault containing one or two nineteenth century iron coffins.

The top of fig. 2.10 shows the Little White Church of Annandale, Virginia, and GPR echoes associated with the burials of Union Sergeant Elhanan

Winchester Wakefield and family members who were interred a short distance from the church entrance. The original church was burned during the Civil War by Sergeant Wakefield and his 2nd Massachusetts Cavalry colleagues. Sergeant Wakefield, a carpenter by trade, returned after the war, led the reconstruction of the Little White Church, and became a Methodist minister, preaching to the mostly pro-southern Virginia congregation. Sergeant Wakefield often officiated at services and gave sermons to Confederate veterans that he had shot at in anger during the war.

The bottom of fig. 2.10 shows an in-phase EMI anomaly map within the Mount Zion Church cemetery near Aldie, Virginia, and iron gate posts of the

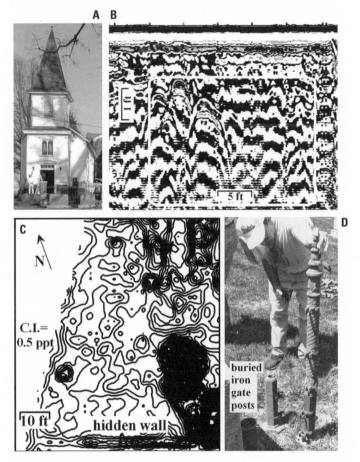

FIGURE 2.10. Geophysical data at historic locations of military interest: (A) Little White Church of Annandale, Va; (B) GPR echoes of Wakefield and family members in the church yard; (C) in-phase EMI anomaly map at Mt. Zion Church near Aldie, Va.; and (D) iron gate posts associated with the hidden wall revealed by EMI data. Photographs (A) and (D) courtesy C. E. Petrone; and images (B) and (C) by author.

buried foundation of a former wall discovered using GPR data and shown vividly in the EMI data. Mount Zion Church is renowned as the initial rendezvous location of Colonel John Singleton Mosby and his partisan rangers from where they launched their first raid. The church is also known for its use as a field hospital, accommodating both Union and Confederate soldiers. It was the location of the "Battle of Mount Zion Church" on 6 July 1864, which is considered Mosby's greatest victory.

CONCLUSIONS

I recommend that the tool chest of the archaeologist includes a sensitive metal detector, a magnetic locator, and a magnetic susceptibility meter. GPR, EMI (or alternatively, galvanic resistivity), and vertical magnetic gradiometry should also be part of the arsenal of archaeogeophysicists and archaeologists, using equipment more affordably owned by groups of workers or institutions. Because the decision whether or not to use geophysics at a site often reduces to cost, it usually is not possible for the individual to own or use the "latest and greatest" equipment available. What is important is that whatever equipment is available should be used with as much skill and attention to detail as possible (see Balicki, chap. 6).

Our work in a military context has been largely confined to searching for soldier burials in cemeteries or potential interment sites on or near battlefields and skirmish locations. To that end, it has been determined by my colleagues and I that a grave-site can be detected directly by sensing some combination of buried human remains, objects buried with the interred, and the burial container, or indirectly by sensing the disturbed soil mixed with objects in shaft backfill. Thus, reflected signals can be weak or strong, shallow or deep, and emanate anywhere from center to edges. It has also been determined that, where eighteenth

and nineteenth century graves are marked in some fashion, the markers often are misplaced; that some burial sites no longer contain the originally interred remains because of re-burial elsewhere; and that burials (a combination of burial container and remains) in acidic soil have often been dissolved to silhouettes or shadows only a fraction of an inch thick. In addition, the graves of children, although small as geophysical targets, sometimes host containers that are substantial and detectable. Also, the fabric of burial shrouds and clothing in some coffin burials may be well-preserved by proximity to copper and cupric alloys that act to inhibit fungal and bacterial decay and that can be sensed by a metal detector. Few burials approach the legendary 6-foot depth to top of coffin or shroud. Most are found at a depth of 30 inches or much less and many on sloped surfaces at a depth of only a foot or less because of hillside erosion.

ACKNOWLEDGMENTS

I was fortunate in 1958 to be an Indiana University student studying under Judson Mead (geophysicist) and professor Georg Karl Neumann (anthropologist), when Mead collaborated with Glenn A. Black to make some of the first galvanic electrical measurements in archaeology in the United States at Angel Mounds. I helped test the Varian magnetometer leased by Black and used by Richard B. Johnston (Black and Johnston 1962). In 1964 Sheldon Breiner of Varian Associates, already an established archaeogeophysicist, but a beginning doctoral student, introduced me to optically pumped magnetometers In the 1980s, I joined my colleague Claude E. Petrone in archaeogeophysical investigations here and in Mexico (Robertson 2001). I owe my experience with and fondness of a broad spectrum of geophysical techniques mainly to my former Stanford professorial colleagues and to more than a hundred of my fellow geophysicists at the U.S. Geological Survey.

CHAPTER THREE

Military Medicine in the Pre-Modern Era

Using Forensic Techniques in Archaeological Investigations to Investigate Military Remains

DOUGLAS D. SCOTT

INTRODUCTION

The history of medical theory and practice is evolutionary and mirrors the greater culture in which it exists. Between the 17th and 19th centuries, American and European medical training evolved from essentially an apprenticeship form of education to a highly scientific and university-based process (Bonner 1995). Like all scientific practice during that time, medical training was in constant flux, responding to changing scientific, social, and cultural stimuli that included attitudes concerning the study of the human body. Military physicians were often among the most well-trained and educated, and their real-world experiences treating disease and battlefield casualties contributed to the development of new and sometimes innovative diagnostic and treatment regimens by those in academia (Gillett 1987, 1991, 1995).

Evidence of military medical practice and the care of the deceased can survive in the archaeological record, and be expressed in several different artifact and feature forms. Features may include remains of permanent or temporary hospitals, medical waste pits, latrines, and camp and hospital cemeteries. Individual artifacts can range from instrument fragments to medicine containers to human remains. Recovered human remains can often provide significant new insight into the lives and health of soldiers during their military tenure, and sometimes their deaths, from acquired disease or battlefield action. The application of modern forensic techniques to the study of the bones of soldiers is building an interesting osteobiographical profile of the men who served their country. They were mostly young, lived incredibly rugged lives as evidence by their early back problems and arthritis, and some met very violent ends. This chapter illustrates the value of studying sites and human remains associated with military medical practice through time.

MILITARY MEDICINE

Archival and documentary research can yield a plethora of information on military medical practice, and hospital plans and organization over time. Despite the rich historical database that exists for many eras, archaeological data and features can reveal undocumented insights into how specific medical practices were implemented and how facilities constructed in the field conformed to or deviated from the standard plans suggested in recognized military guidelines (Gillett 1987:289–93; Soubier and Brown 1989).

The archaeological investigation of the 1776 Continental Army hospital at Mount Independence, New York, that was destroyed by the British in 1777 illustrates this point (Starbuck 1999:144–56). In general, hospitals of the nineteenth century are poorly documented. The excavation of the Mount Independence Military Hospital has added a new depth of understanding of how an army hospital of that era was constructed and organized and how wounded and recuperating men were fed and cared for.

Historic accounts described the hospital as a long, linear building, two stories tall, of wood frame construction, and heated by fireplaces. When excavated, the recovery of a thousand nails confirmed that the building had been of wood frame construction, but without glazed windows (Starbuck 1999:148–52). Fireplace remains were also found, including one that appeared to be unfinished, suggesting the hospital was a work-in-progress and was never finished during its short usage.

Hundreds of wine bottle fragments were recovered during the excavation. This meshed well with historic records that documented ample supplies of wine in the hospital, used not only for drinking, but also as an eigthteenth century medicinal supplement to fortify the sick and wounded. Other artifacts included personal items like pipe stems, buttons from clothing, and military ammunition components typical of the military function of the hospital treating and supporting wounded and recuperating soldiers. Not atypically, little specific evidence of medical apparatus or medicine containers were found during the excavations although some had been collected at the site by an avocational excavator some years earlier.

One surprising find at the site was the array of faunal remains recovered from around the foundations of the medical facility as well as in a separate trash pit. These faunal remains are interpreted to reflect meat fed to the wounded and sick soldiers during their hospital confinement. While the remains of the domestic cow dominate the assemblage, the diversity of the faunal material is interesting. Mutton, fish, pig, deer, and a bird were identified.

By the last half of the nineteenth century, medicine had made huge strides in knowledge and practice. The principle of asepsis (the need to keep a sterile environment) was known, and anesthetics were in wide use. The germ theory of disease was just becoming known, and some of that scientific knowledge and practice can be seen in an archaeological collection from a frontier army site. A latrine excavation at Fort Larned, Kansas, a military installation connected to the history of the Santa Fe Trail (1859–78) (Unrau 1957; Stinson 1966; Sheire 1968, 1969) yielded insight into a the lifestyle of a surgeon and the state of medicine on the western frontier.

At Fort Larned, a latrine associated with an officers' quarters was excavated (figs. 3.1, 3.2). The latrine pit contained glass medicine bottles, liquor bottles, tumblers or common drinking glasses, fragmentary and complete examples of a set of stemmed goblets, and ceramic plates, cups, saucers, serving platters, and a gravy boat (Scott 1989). A hunting knife, military firearms cartridges, men's and women's shoes, toys, toothbrushes, a clothes pin, and a pair of poorly preserved cavalry uniform trousers were also among the finds. Scraps of bone indicated that beef, turkey, chicken, and catfish were eaten by the residents of the quarters. Eggshell, peach pits, coffee beans, tomato seeds, and green pepper seeds also attested to the variety of other foodstuffs consumed by the residents.

FIGURE 3.1. An 1878 view of the South Officers' Quarters, Fort Larned, Kansas. Courtesy Fort Larned National Historic Site.

FIGURE 3.2. Excavation in progress at the Fort Larned officers' quarters latrine pit. Photograph by D. D. Scott.

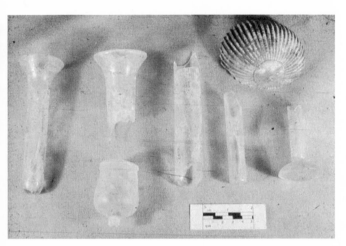

FIGURE 3.3 Scientific and medical apparatus found in the officers' quarters latrine at Fort Larned. Photograph courtesy Midwest Archeological Center, National Park Service.

One of the more remarkable groups of artifacts in the latrine assemblage was a set of scientific and medical glassware (fig. 3.3). The items included glass stirring rods, test tubes, a graduated measuring cylinder, a cupping device for bleeding medical patients, a breast pump, and a variety of medicine bottles, some embossed "U.S. Hospital Department." One medicine bottle still contained some liquid that, upon analysis, proved to be a common nineteenth century medical remedy, laudanum, which is an opiate in an alcohol base (Rich 1976).

While available historical records do not absolutely identify the inhabitants of the officers' quarters, it seems reasonable from the artifacts recovered that the post surgeon or doctor resided in the building and perhaps a married officer and his wife and children.

The food remains suggest they ate well, and consumed a wide variety of foods. Even though they were on America's western frontier, 800 miles from St. Louis, Missouri, the nearest large city, the domestic artifacts recovered indicate that they served and ate their meals on good quality dishes and drank from good quality glasses.

The scientific apparatus recovered are interesting in two ways. First is the presence of laboratory type glassware that may have been used to conduct various scientific experiments or formulate medicines. The scientific apparatus, with the exception of the marked army hospital bottles, is typical of what was routinely available in the civilian market (Viet 1996). The second point is the presence of the glass bleeding cup that was in good condition when deposited in the privy. In the late 1870s when it was thrown out, bleeding had gone out of favor with medical professionals and military surgeons (Gillett 1995).

Jointly, the scientific apparatus and the bleeding cup suggest that whoever deposited the artifacts was a person with a scientific bent, and perhaps one who kept up with the latest scientific and medical theories and practice. Of the three army surgeons known to have been stationed at Fort Larned during the period the latrine was in use (circa 1868–78), two, William H. Forwood and Alfred A. Woodhull, later joined the staff of the Surgeon General and conducted medical research that led to new innovations in the practice of military medicine (Gillett 1995).

HUMAN REMAINS

Around the world today, the remains of soldiers are constantly being recovered from ancient to recent battlefields and reburied (Russell and Fleming 1991; Holyoak and Schofield 2002; de Meyer and Pype 2006; Silverstein et al. 2006). The remains recovered from battlefield sites, camps, and hospital sites, are being studied using the latest available physical anthropological and forensic methods and techniques. Such human remains, as evidenced by skeletal completeness, age, sex, stature, antemortem injuries, diseases, habitual behaviors, perimortem injuries, and personal identification, have individual tales to tell.

By studying groupings of contemporaneous

skeletons, as well as the groups as a whole, a greater understanding of how the individuals related to the larger military organization can be achieved. In addition, information may be gleaned about the domestic populations from which the soldiers originated. (see Whitehorne, chap. 1). To interpret the remains found in certain military settings properly and as individual people, it is not only necessary to know the circumstances of their military affiliations but their ethnicity or place of origin, how they were recruited, and what history has to say about how they led their domestic and military lives.

One of the most thoroughly studied assemblages of the human remains of soldiers using modern techniques comes from Towton, York, England, a medieval battle site of the Wars of the Roses. At Towton on 29 March 1461, Yorkist and Lancastrian armies were involved in possibly the largest battle ever fought on English soil. A mass grave attributed to this action was discovered in 1996 and was excavated by archaeologists and physical anthropologists (Fiorato et al. 2000). The bodies appear to have been placed side-by-side and roughly aligned in an east-to-west orientation.

The Towton work addressed the ages, statures, sexes, and causes of death of the skeletal remains. It also included detailed studies of the weapons of the era, the role of archery and armor, the social background of medieval warfare, and the status of knight or warrior within society. The results of the wide-ranging analyses and studies created a picture of the men themselves set in their own culture and time period. The men were of average height and their average age was 30 years. Some men had well-healed wounds that are presumably from previous battles, others simply displayed the stresses of everyday medieval life, such as arthritis, back injuries, healed fractures, and muscle development indicating work that involved carrying heavy loads. The men died from multiple wounds received while fighting at close quarters. Many men had multiple incapacitating or fatal injuries, including 13 wounds inflicted on one individual. Most injuries were inflicted by handheld weapons, such as swords, pole arms, and halberds that had been wielded by right-handed opponents. The men varied in age and height and appeared to have come from every walk of medieval life.

In 1757, during the French and Indian War, in the American Colony of New York, a British fort, Fort William Henry, surrendered to the French and allied Native Americans. As the British garrison marched out of the fort, they were allegedly massacred by the Native Americans. During 1950s excavations of this "massacre" site, human remains attributed to some of the British soldiers were found (Starbuck 1999). However, it was not until the 1990s that physical anthropologists had the opportunity to apply modern analytical techniques to those bones (Liston and Baker 1995). They recorded the usual age, stature, and sex information, but studying the remains for pathologies, anomalies, and injuries provided a remarkable insight into the lives of these eighteenth century soldiers. They found inter-vertebral anomalies that indicate many suffered from herniated discs, probably from carrying heavy loads over a long time. One individual exhibited pitting of the skull that is consistent with the bony expression of anemia, and others exhibited bony changes consistent with arthritis. Some even exhibited evidence suggesting that they suffered from tuberculosis even though they were relatively young men. These men did not die of disease, however. Rather, the range of perimortem injuries show they died violent deaths, ranging from gunshot trauma to artillery fire. One man had evidence of scalping, and others of cut marks in the bony structure surrounding the abdomen suggesting disembowelment. Two men showed evidence of medical intervention because each had had a leg amputated. The Fort William Henry remains graphically illustrate physical evidence of the rugged life and violent death of soldiers of the eighteenth century colonial frontier.

JOINING THE ARMY

The historic paper trail and medical record of the individual U.S. soldier started with his induction. Policies and practices of recruitment are significant in establishing the baseline medical state of individuals and troop populations as they entered the military. In the 1870s, and at the onset of the Indian Wars, the recruit presented himself to a recruiting depot located in one of the larger cities. After providing two recommendations attesting to his character, the recruit was examined by a military surgeon to determine his fitness for service (Ewing 1894:167).

The physical examination was conducted by a surgeon who followed written regulations concerning inspection and acceptability of recruits. The examining surgeon was caught on the horns of a dilemma, however (Ewing 1894:168). On one hand, the surgeon was to ensure that only the best quality men were selected. On the other hand, he hoped to please the officer, to whom the recruiting service, then as now, was more one of numbers and quotas than of quality.

The recruits were to be examined individually during daylight hours in a well-lit room (Bartholow 1863). The sober recruit was to enter the room stripped (if dirty he was to be bathed before entering the examination room) where he would walk briskly around the room several times. Then he was to hop around the room first on one foot then on the other. After this bit of acrobatics, the examining surgeon placed his hand on the prospective recruit's chest and checked for an abnormal heartbeat. The stethoscope was a relatively new instrument in the 1870s and was not generally utilized.

The prospective recruit was then made to stand at attention while the surgeon examined his head, eyes, ears, mouth, and nose. The surgeon looked for abnormalities such as fractures, depressions, diseases, deafness, unintelligible speech, and poor eyesight. Next, the recruit stretched out his arms at right angles to his body and was then required to touch his shoulders with his hand, place his hands together over his head, and to turn his head and cough while the surgeon checked for hernia.

The surgeon also checked the fingers and thumbs for their dexterity. The doctor checked the chest capacity and looked over the legs to determine if they were sturdy and could carry the man's weight. Finally, the recruit was made to bend over and grab his buttocks while the surgeon checked for piles or hemorrhoids. Hemorrhoids were a cause for rejection, but not outright, absolute rejection. If there was more than one old pile and it was larger than a marble or if one old pile was ulcerated, or if one pile—whatever its size—was associated with a varicose vein, then and only then, was the applicant rejected (Bartholow 1863; Ewing 1894:187). This requirement, nonetheless, would have been especially critical to recruits slated to become cavalrymen and who would find themselves spending long hours riding. Passing all these health and other requirements, or at least being waived

through them, the recruit was found fit for service, sworn in, placed in uniform, and sent for three months training before joining his regiment (Ewing 1894:167).

Age was also a consideration for enlistment. In 1874, the minimum enlistment age was 16 years, although those between 16 and 18 were accepted only as musicians. Recruits between 18 and 21 years needed parental or guardian consent (Ewing 1894:174). Consequently, to be able to enlist in the usual manner, without a note from home, the recruit needed to be 21 years of age or older. Considering that some recruits joined the military to escape home and many others were recent immigrants who had left their parents in the "old country," such consent may have been difficult—if not impossible—for many under-aged recruits to provide honestly.

The reason for establishing and enforcing a minimum enlistment age was twofold (Bartholow 1863:34–37; Ewing 1894:175–79). The first concern was the ability of youths to endure the physical hardships which military life entailed while, at the same time, still being able to provide adequate service. A second, more humanitarian concern was for the growth and developmental well-being of the youth. During the mid-1800s there was a belief that overwork, including military life, drained the energy required for normal development, stunting growth, and leading to smaller, deformed adults (Tanner 1981).

In his consideration of minimum age, Ewing (1894:177–78) cites anatomical evidence that most 20 year olds then were still growing skeletally and should be excused from military duty, presumably until their next, or 21st birthday. However, it is now known that nearly all of the principle growth centers of most people are closed by age 20. This is partly explains why the minimum enlistment age today is several years younger. The maximum age for first enlistment was more rigidly adhered to than the minimum age. It was 30 years for the cavalry and had remained that age for decades (Ewing 1894:178); the maximum age was 45 during the Civil War (Bartholow 1863:178). Once enlisted, however, re-enlistments could occur well past the age of 30.

Height was also a potential reason to dismiss a recruit. The lower limit was set "to exclude such as lack the physical strength necessary to endure the hardships of a soldier's life" (Ewing 1894:179). The minimum stature requirement had changed frequently since it was first instituted in 1790, and was omitted altogether during various wars, such as the War of 1812, when the requisite strength to die in combat—or statistically more likely from disease—apparently saw no minimum height barrier. Following those wars, however, the minimum height requirement was re-established, and such was the case following the Civil War. During the decade between the end of the Civil War and the Battle of the Little Bighorn (1876), there were no fewer than nine changes in minimum stature requirements, so the requirement fluctuated from year-to-year and even month-to-month within a single year (Ewing 1894:179–80). For most of the decade preceding and up to the time of the Little Bighorn, the minimum height for cavalry enlistees was 5 feet, 5 inches.

Maximum stature, just as maximum age, was more rigid than the minimum. It was 5 feet, 10 inches for cavalry recruits in 1876 and had been that height since 1872 (Ewing 1894:180). This maximum was true only for the cavalry; infantry recruits could be taller than a long rifle. Height is correlated with weight: taller people usually weigh more than shorter people, but at induction, weight was another, separate consideration.

The cavalry had a maximum weight of 165 pounds with no minimum weight, unlike the other branches that had a 128-pound minimum, at least by 1890 (Ewing 1894:183). During the Civil War there was no lower weight limit although a rule-of-thumb held that anyone shorter than 5 feet and weighing less than 110 pounds should be rejected (Bartholow 1863:188). There was a common belief that men of medium build and height were more active, cheerful, and capable of enduring the hardships of army life (Bartholow 1863:190) than those taller, shorter, leaner, or heavier. The general rule for height-to-weight ratio was 5 feet and 120 pounds, 5 feet, 5 inches and 125 pounds, and five additional pounds for each inch above 5 feet, 5 inches. Generally, men were rejected if they weighed more than 200 pounds; they were considered too heavy for service (Bartholow 1863:190). The common reasoning for the cavalry needing smaller, lighter soldiers was that the hard-worked horses could carry these soldiers and about 50 pounds of equipment further and faster than they could the larger, heftier enlistees.

Nativity or ethnicity for the army in 1876 was around 50% U.S. born, another 20% from Ireland, 20% from Germany. The remainder came primarily from other European countries. The high percentage of immigrants from Ireland and Germany, and lesser numbers from the remainder of Europe, reflects the immigrant composition of the United States for the same time period. Remember all those John Wayne movies where the sergeant spoke with the heavy Irish accent? They may not be far off the mark.

Despite the raising of African American units during the Civil War by the Union, the U.S. military was a highly segregated entity until after World War II. The vast majority of soldiers were white and of western European background. There were only four black units in the army of the 1870s.

THE LITTLE BIG HORN

As noted earlier, the discovery of human remains in military cemeteries or on the field of battle (fig. 3.4) provides a significant opportunity to assess medical, pathological, and ethnic features of soldiers. An example of this can be taken from the Little Bighorn Battlefield that yielded complete and partial remains of 44 soldiers, approximately 16% of the 268 killed on 25–26 June 1876. These remains were recovered from several contexts: the battlefield itself, reburials in the Custer National Cemetery, isolated finds turned in by visitors to the park, and unauthorized private collections. This disparate assemblage was analyzed and studied over a ten-year period using the latest available physical anthropological methods and theories as well as current forensic investigation techniques. The main focus of the analysis was to determine age, gender, stature, pathologies, anomalies, and manner of death. The physical data was compared to records of enlistment, medical records, and enlistment regulations to build an osteobiographical profile of each soldier represented by their bones (Scott et al. 1998).

The ages of the soldiers derived from the skeletal remains in the set indicated a greater percentage of non-regulation enlistees under 21 years than the enlistment records for Custer's 7th Cavalry indicated. These skeletal age estimations are supported when the ages of troopers with known birth date are employed. The skeletal and the birth date ages of the youthful troopers are comparable and both differ from the ages based on enlistment records alone. On the other hand, the skeletal ages also indicated there were many more oldsters

FIGURE 3.4. An 1879 photograph by Stanley Morrow of scattered horse bone and early wooden markers on Last Stand Hill at Little Bighorn Battlefield National Monument. Photograph courtesy Little Bighorn Battlefield National Monument.

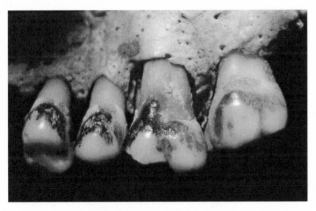

FIGURE 3.5. Little Bighorn Battlefield upper jaw or mandible exhibits staining on the teeth consistent with sustained and regular tobacco use. Photograph courtesy Midwest Archeological Center, National Park Service.

in the battle than the enlistment documents record.

Observed skeletal stature for the troops studied is similar to those recorded on the enlistment records of the casualties. Both sources indicate short (average 67.68 in) men and that the shortest and the tallest potential enlistees were probably excluded from the regiment. On the other hand, the presence of troopers who were shorter and those who were taller than the regulations permitted demonstrate the flexibility of the examining surgeon's discretion.

The skeletons also revealed the active lives the troopers lived. Some forms of degenerative change had occurred early in their lives, especially degeneration of the spine and arm. When compared with the historic documents and comparable contemporary groups, the skeletons demonstrate similar health problems and diseases. Available historic accounts "flesh-out" the picture the skeletons provided with more details on diseases that plagued the 7th Cavalry, yet do not affect the skeleton. The poor dental health of the troopers (fig. 3.5), clearly demonstrated by the skeletons, is hardly mentioned in available historic accounts on the 7th Cavalry. Information on the frequency of tobacco use among the troopers was available from muster rolls but had not been investigated until dental stains and other marks of tobacco use were found on the skeletons. The study amplified and elaborated their day-to-day lives by showing that many men consumed tobacco in one form or other, leaving the telltale stains and pipe stem abrasions on their teeth.

Perimortem injuries and mutilations were often mentioned in the historic documents of the battle and were shown in ledger art done by victorious Native American warriors. The reality of those injuries was clearly shown on many bones. There were gunshot wounds, blunt force trauma, and sharp force trauma on many of the skeletons, although the frequency and severity of the skeletal changes may be less than expected from historic accounts.

DEATH UNDER THE COLORS/CARE OF THE DEAD

Certainly in the twentieth century, those who died in battle often fell far from the home, at least in the worldview of those living in preceding centuries. War dead were typically of two types, those dying of disease or exhaustion and those dying in combat. The soldiers, and sometimes their camp followers, were buried in local cemeteries or near hospital sites. Combat dead were seldom buried in local cemeteries, but were interred where they fell, or were gathered and placed in often hastily dug mass graves. Thus, if the dead were to be honored, it became necessary to memorialize them with monuments near their home and not necessarily where they fell (Mosse 1990:40–49; Scott et al. 1998).

The monuments in the town square became representative of the dead while their souls were at peace in heaven. Their bones, on the other hand, were assumed to be resting in quietude on or near the field of battle. This perception contributes to the modern idea of battlefields as sacred landscapes. Nonetheless, this was often not the case. The phenomena of bodies lying unburied or placed in shallow battlefield graves was fairly common practice prior to the advent of the twentieth century and was particularly commonplace during the American Civil War.

Throughout most of recorded history, soldier dead were nearly always buried on or near the battlefield, a fact still reflected in the vast American military cemeteries in western Europe and England. They were left where they fell in some cases, but most were buried at, or near, where they fell or in trench graves quickly dug by the enemy or by their fellows.

Following, and as a result of the Civil War, formally identified cemeteries were established (Steere 1948; Smythe 1981). These cemeteries often included secondary and even tertiary burial of remains gathered indiscriminately, and often incompletely, from the field years after the battle. The story of the national cemetery at Fredericksburg is a particularly good example. This cemetery includes the dead from at least three battles occurring between 1862 and 1864. Approximately 80% or more of the disinterred battlefield dead have lost their identity because of the faulty recovery and identification procedures employed at the time.

During the Civil War and earlier, families who could afford it had remains of friends and loved ones who could be identified, disinterred, and sent home for reburial in an appropriate family plot. Not until the Spanish-American War of 1898 did the U.S. Congress appropriate funds to allow the next-of-kin to choose the final resting place for soldiers who fell in that war. This authorization was the genesis of the American Graves Registration Service.

By World War I, the armed services were charged with identifying the dead, properly interring them, and marking the graves so the remains could be returned to the next-of-kin. With this charge and the institution of the individual identification tag (dog tag) in 1910 only about 5% of the dead from that war were not identified as opposed to nearly all the dead from the Mexican-

American War, 42% from the Civil War, and 13.6% of those who fell in the Spanish-American War (Steere 1948; Smythe 1981; Wood and Stanley 1989).

The Mexican-American War marked a turning point in U.S. military burial policy. In 1850, Congress appropriated funds to create a cemetery in Mexico City to serve as a final resting place for those who died in or around the city. No other battle sites elsewhere in Mexico or the United States received such treatment (Steere 1948).

Among the many reasons for the establishment of national cemeteries during the Civil War was the recognition that, without them, graves of the fallen were outside military control. There was no way to ensure a grave was maintained if there was no direct control over the ground in which the honored dead lay. Because of the overwhelming impact the war had on all U.S. citizens, there was a sense that the dead should be treated with respect and concentrated in national cemeteries for perpetual care. The military, as well as civilians, recognized that a battlefield grave or an isolated grave of a soldier who died of disease or wounds along a campaign route could easily disappear as the earth compacted and the headboard weathered and rotted away. By 1870, a grateful nation had established 73 national cemeteries that contained nearly 300,000 remains of Civil War soldiers. The first national cemetery was Gettysburg, which was consecrated in the eloquent speech of President Abraham Lincoln in 1863 (Linenthal 1991).

At many battlefields, Antietam for example, it was not uncommon to find exposed bones and even complete skeletons after the bodies were believed to have been moved to the national cemetery. Unrecovered or unburied bodies were occasionally found at Antietam into the late 19th and 20th centuries. In 1989, relic hunters found exposed human bones attributed to soldiers of the New York "Irish Brigade" at Antietam. These incomplete remains suggested that only the long bones and skulls had been recovered for reburial. This pattern of leaving bones behind in recovery efforts was also identified at the Little Bighorn. Those who have castigated Little Bighorn reburial parties for being slovenly in their efforts (King 1980) fail to realize that the recovery of all bones of a body was not as important in the cultural context of the nineteenth century as it is today. The lack of total recovery is not an indication of a lack of respect, only a different cultural perception of what is important. The detailed recovery of the bones of a body only became important with the rise of forensic methods necessary to conduct identifications from DNA and identifying attributes exhibited by the bones. Otherwise, the bones themselves were only symbolic of the person and so a symbolic representation was all that was necessary.

MEMORIALS

Men die in military service from disease, accident, and as a result of combat. Cultural tradition identifies death in action as a heroic death and is honored and bereaved. It is held in high esteem because there is a social dimension to death that requires war-related deaths to be held as heroic (Jackson 1977:4). There is a pervasive concept of the "Myth of War Experience" as ennobling; a patriotic duty that creates adventurers, and nourishes nationalism and the longing of youths to become heroes in the next war. Although Mosse (1990) argues that this "myth of war" in the U.S. psyche arose as a result of the slaughter of World War I, it has probably been with us for centuries.

For most of history, soldiers who died and were buried on the field of battle were rarely memorialized. Usually only the triumphs of their generals received recognition. The American Civil War instituted the concept of the "national cemetery" where the dead could lie in peace. Monuments placed on battlefields usually commemorated the feats of those who died and those who survived. It was the conflicts of World War I and World War II however, that gave the world the cemetery conceived of as an architectural landscape to commemorate the fallen. It is this convergence of the cult of the heroically fallen merging with national sentiment arising from two World Wars that created the cultural mindset through which we, today, view the treatment of the dead (Aries 1982:550). In the case of the military dead, no real mourning period could be allowed due to the press of the war. Thus, the ritual was born of removing the dead to places where formal memorial gardens, the national cemeteries, could be created. The dead, even if initially hastily buried, were recovered and moved to lie beside other heroically fallen comrades-in-arms.

CONCLUSION

It is obvious that skeletal analyses cannot replace the historic documents, though in many instances they may be the only evidence for a human life. As noted, the skeletons provided the material evidence of the lives and deaths of 7th Cavalry troopers. The nature and placement of the skeletons helped clarify, amplify, and correct the historic documents and drawings of the military action. The two data sources may conflict in some areas but by using both, they become a means of cross-correlation that aids in identifying the most reliable elements of both datasets. Clearly, history and archeology are adjuncts needed to build a more complete story of the past. The archeological data and the study of human skeletal remains at military sites have illuminated many details of the lives and deaths of those whose living flesh once surrounded the bones. Many details seen in the bones were too mundane to be written down or were only casually mentioned in the historic record. Archeological and physical anthropological data fill in some of the missing pieces from the past lives of individuals who fought and died, but just filling in details is only a minor part of what anthropology can do. Anthropology is the study of culture and its role in defining society as we know it. The bones of military personnel retain the evidence of how they lived and how they died. The contexts in which their bones were found, on the field of battle, in a camp or hospital cemetery, buried in the national cemetery, set on museum shelves, and even stashed in personal collections, all tell us how societal attitudes about the proper treatment of the dead have changed and evolved over the last century. Memorializing the dead reflects how cultural values have changed regarding views about death and how battlefields have changed in meaning from a place where an event occurred to a place where heroic sacrifices were made on the field of honor. The battlefield has also changed from a place where a battle was fought between combatant groups and where the battle dead were laid to rest to a place that has achieved sacredness. This sacredness is derived not only from the remains of our honored war dead, but because it is the place where there occurred what is now perceived as a momentous and culturally symbolic event in history.

CHAPTER FOUR

When the Site is a Scene

Battlefield Archaeology and Forensic Sites

MELISSA A. CONNOR

INTRODUCTION

Archaeologists are continually stretching the time limits in which they can effectively examine battlefields. Initially, a domain of historic archaeology, more and more prehistoric archaeologists are identifying and examining fields of conflict created before the historic record. Other archaeologists are working on the other end of the time continuum, examining evidence from ever more recent fields of conflict. This latter research is the subject of this paper.

On historic battlefields, archaeological work is completed for many reasons, but mainly for the purposes of generating information in greater detail than exists in the historic record or verifying that record. While work on modern fields of conflict is also conducted to add greater detail to and verify the existing historic record, more importantly it is often conducted to create a legal record that serves as a key part of a forensic criminal investigation.

The techniques used on modern battlefields grew from archaeological techniques developed to explore historic battlefields. The differences between the two are both paradigmatic and methodological. They are significantly different, in fact, allowing some to argue that forensic battlefield archaeology is a sub-discipline unto itself. This paper will explore these similarities and differences.

THE HISTORY OF FORENSIC ARCHAEOLOGY

Clyde Snow once said that ". . . having a policeman excavate a skeleton . . . was a bit like having a chimpanzee perform a heart transplant" (Snow 1995:17). Snow insisted on having archaeologists, not just archaeologically-trained physical anthropologists or investigators, complete forensic exhumations. In 1983, Morse et al. (1983) wrote a guide to archaeological field techniques for the non-archaeologist that was aimed at criminal investigators who were exhuming skeletons. The publication of this guide was a statement of the interest in the use of archaeological techniques in investigation. However, the role of archaeology was limited to the use of field techniques, and was taught as something easily learned by non-professionals.

The concept of archaeological context in forensic work was emphasized by Brenda Sigler-Eisenberg (1985). She expanded the use of archaeology from techniques of recovery only to include the theory directing the process. She called attention to the idea that it is difficult to work under an archaeological paradigm without the entire constellation of skills and abilities gained through an archaeological education and extensive field experience. She stressed that archaeologists do not work alone in a forensic investigation, but are team players who need to know the overall picture in order to understand their role.

In the last two decades, the need to conduct recent mass grave exhumations has greatly expanded the role and use of archaeology and archaeologists in forensic investigations, moving forensic archaeologists onto modern battlefields. The excavation of complex masses of co-mingled individuals in Latin America, Rwanda, and the former Yugoslavia extensively required and used sophisticated archaeological techniques. This trend began with the appointment of Dr. Clyde

Snow by the American Academy for the Advancement of Science Committee on Scientific Freedom and Responsibility, to train Argentine medical and archaeological students in forensic investigation (Snow et al. 1984, 1985; Stover 1985; Joyce and Stover 1991; Stover and Ryan 2001). The Argentine forensic team, Equipo Argentino de Antropologia Forense, works in a number of countries in addition to Argentina and trains others in forensic investigation. They have assisted forensic investigations not only in Argentina, but also in Bolivia, Brazil, Columbia, the Democratic Republic of Congo, Ethiopia, the former Yugoslavia, French Polynesia, Guatemala, Haiti, and the Republic of South Africa (Equipo Argentino de Antropologia Forense 2005).

In the beginning of this new millennium, forensic archaeology is a small, but growing, subfield of archeology. International teams sent to investigate human rights abuses now routinely include archaeologists or anthropologists with archaeological training. In 2001, Steadman and Haglund (2005) estimated that between 1990 and 1999, 134 anthropologists from 22 countries were involved in human rights investigations in 33 different countries around the globe. Between 2004 and 2006, archaeological teams assisted the Iraqi Special Tribunal in investigating charges of war crimes against the regime of Saddam Hussein. The field is growing and can both learn from, and contribute to, anthropological battlefield archaeology.

Paradigmatic Difference: The Legal Context

In North America, archaeologists are trained first as anthropologists and work within an anthropological paradigm. This means that the reason they are examining a site is so they can understand the people who created the site and answer questions about the way they lived. In forensic work, the skills of an archaeologist are usually brought into play when a body needs to be exhumed. Often, archaeologists are working within the context of a criminal death investigation. In both cases, the archaeologist tries to reconstruct what went on at the scene. The archaeological concepts of stratigraphy, feature, activity area, and assemblage are important building blocks in reconstructing the forensic scene as they are in reconstructing the

activities at an archaeological site. But there are differences that are important.

In both modern battlefield archaeology and domestic forensic archaeology, the archaeologists are exhuming recent human remains. In both cases, there is an ongoing investigation as to whether laws have been violated and, if so, who did it. The forensic archaeologist needs to be familiar with those laws to understand the physical evidence that is relevant. Relevant evidence might include material that would lead to identification of individuals or that could be used to argue intent or motive.

In the United States, cases including a dead body can result in different charges, including murder, manslaughter, justifiable homicide, and accidental death (Kurland 1997:44–46). Murder in the first degree is the willful, deliberate, and premeditated killing of one person by another. Murder in the second degree is a killing where there is malice before hand, but premeditation is absent. A homicide committed during a felony other than those specified by state statute is frequently second-degree murder.

Manslaughter in the first degree is intentional killing without either premeditation or malice. Killing another person in a fit of anger or jealousy may be manslaughter in the first degree. Manslaughter in the second degree, also called involuntary manslaughter, is killing someone as a result of gross negligence or a reckless act that carried a high probability of killing another. Killing a person while driving drunk may be manslaughter in the second degree.

Justifiable homicide is generally used in self-defense cases where the defendant themselves would have been seriously injured or killed unless they killed the deceased. Accidental death is death as the result of an accident without premeditation, malice, negligence, or a reckless act.

One difference between murder and manslaughter is intent and premeditation. One difference between accidental death and murder or manslaughter is malice. The forensic archaeologist needs to be sensitive to physical evidence that may show these differences. Bindings, ligatures, blindfolds, or gags attached to the deceased can be used to show intent and malice. Natural rope fibers may decay, but the position of the body (for instance the arms behind the body with the wrists crossed) may suggest that the body was originally bound. Objects associated with the deceased and found outside of their usual context may be used to show intent (for instance, a kitchen knife found in the woods). The perpetrator would have to have thought ahead in order to have this object available.

Generally, an archaeologist in a conflict situation is investigating violations of international law. The three major types of international crimes are crimes against humanity, genocide, and war crimes (Groome 2001:13–16). These crimes involve individual groups of people violated in a systemic manner. Genocide requires the intent to destroy, in whole or in part, a national, ethnical, racial, or religious group. Crimes against humanity consist of widespread attacks against civilian populations, including murder, rape, torture, deportation, imprisonment, and other inhumane acts that intentionally cause great suffering or serious injury (physical or mental). War crimes are serious violations of international humanitarian law, such as the use of gas, treatment of civilian population and prisoners of war in violation of the law, weapons outlawed by treaties, etc. (Robertson 1999; Schabas 2000; Ratner and Abrams 2001). Building a strong case means understanding the strengths and weaknesses of the evidence relative to the definition of the crimes.

The coming of age of forensic archaeology is reflected in the publication of a number of recent textbooks (Hunter and Cox 2005; Dupras et al. 2006; Connor 2007; Gould 2007). Two of these (Hunter and Cox 2005; Connor 2007) discuss excavating mass graves and, thus implicitly, work on modern battlefields.

THE FORENSIC TEAM

Archaeologists will never work at a forensic scene by themselves. Sometimes finding human remains is the start of an inquiry, but more often it is the result of long-term, painstaking investigation. The investigator in charge of the case usually has the responsibility for determining who will work on the case, whether specialists like archaeologists are warranted, and for making an arrest when there is enough evidence for an arrest warrant.

In the United States, the criminal investigator works with the attorney who will prosecute the case for the state. Depending on the legal system, either the judge or the prosecuting attorney may be on site during the investigation. The criminal investigators know their protocols for photography, mapping, labeling, and collecting evidence, as well as the chain of custody, discussed below. Archaeologists need to become integrated with the scene investigation teams and ensure that police protocols are followed.

Whether the remains are skeletal or fleshed, a forensic pathologist will have the responsibility of establishing the identity of the remains and determining the cause of death. If the remains are skeletal, a forensic anthropologist may be called in for consultation, but the pathologist has the legal responsibility of signing the death certificate. Uniformed police officers will also be present who may not be part of the scene investigation team. The scene should be cordoned off and, usually, a uniformed police officer will note who arrives and when, and who leaves the scene and when. The police may also have a media officer present who will talk to the media for the team.

There are a number of other forensic specialists, any of whom may be contacted if warranted by the case. There are groups that specialize in the location of remains and graves (e.g., NecroSearch) that have specialized remote sensing equipment and technicians qualified in their use. Cadaver dogs and their handlers are extremely useful in finding graves. Forensic entomologists specialize in the sequence of insects that inhabit and feed on remains and may be able to determine how long a body lay in the open, if it was moved, or whether a buried body lay on the surface for a while before burial. Forensic soil scientists may be able to look at decomposition stains in the soil and tell if there had ever been a body in a particular area. As with other types of archaeology, the forensic archaeologist needs to know enough about these specialties to realize when an expert is needed.

Artifacts and Evidence

An artifact is a manmade, portable object. Evidence, on the other hand, is anything a judge permits to be offered in court to determine the question at hand (Osterburg and Ward 2004). Evidence can be physical, testimonial evidence given orally by a witness, or documentary/written evidence. Each type of evidence can also be direct or circumstantial. Thus, while the archaeologist gets to decide what is and is not an artifact, the judge for a forensic case will ultimately decide what constitutes evidence.

Depending on the crime scene, there may be many forms of evidence with which archaeologists have little experience. Body fluids, such as blood, saliva, and semen can be found at homicide sites. Depending on the age of the site, the investigator needs to be aware of presumptive methods of finding these. DNA can be found on materials such as cigarette butts, pop cans, and skin found under fingernails. Impression evidence, such as fingerprints, footprints, or marks from the tool that made the grave, is also a type of evidence that archaeologists have little experience with. As with any sub-discipline of archaeology, there is a material culture distinct to the time period and type of site that the archaeologist needs to be familiar with before attempting to work a forensic site.

Generally, it is the investigator and lawyer assigned to the case who will combine physical, oral, and documentary evidence into an argument to put to a judge. The archaeologist will testify only to work with the physical evidence, and needs to confine their conclusions to that. The historical archaeologist, in contrast, is expected to synthesize the physical evidence and the documentary sources.

The Investigation

The investigators need to determine: (1) if a crime was committed; (2) if so, what crime was committed; and (3) who was responsible. At the time a body is exhumed, the investigators may still not know if a crime was actually committed, and this is where the archaeological evidence may be useful.

In addition to the physical evidence that archaeologists deal with, the investigators will work with two other classes of evidence, witness testimony, and written documentation. They will interview witnesses who may include the suspect, or people related to the victim, suspects, or scene, accomplices, informers, and experts other than the archaeologist. Each interview will be meticulously documented and potential leads outlined so they can be investigated further. The

investigators will examine the potentially voluminous documentary evidence—any records that may pertain to the case. These can include telephone records, computer disks, email records, and video, as well as paperwork such as bills, letters, and notes that document the minutia of our everyday life.

All evidence, whether physical, witness, or documentary, must be obtained legally to be admissible in court. So, in addition to the other aspects of the case, the investigators will be working within the complicated parameters of the legal system. For instance, in the United States, to obtain entry to private property for a search (including a search for human remains) the investigators must either obtain a search warrant, the owner's consent to search the property, or there must be an exigent circumstance that requires immediate action. In most buried body cases, they will need a search warrant which requires them to have probable cause that there is evidence related to a crime on the property. Usually a warrant will be specific as to the places that may be searched. If the warrant specifies that a specific property may be searched for a buried body site, the adjacent property may not also be searched without probable cause and obtaining a second warrant.

The Chain of Custody

As a rule, archaeologists keep good track of the artifacts they find. However, the forensic archaeologist must help ensure that there is a paper trail for every piece of material related to the case from the time that piece is found to the time the case goes to court. Anyone who had the item in their possession may be called on to testify that the item in court is the same one they recovered and bagged on the scene. Any disruption in this chain of evidence or chain of custody may result in the evidence not being admitted in court.

Most police departments have protocols that specify how physical evidence should be marked, transported, and stored. Archaeologists should, whenever possible, use these protocols on a forensic case, rather than their own artifact procedures. There should be an evidence technician on site, or one archaeologist should act as the evidence technician, who will take custody of each artifact, as it is uncovered, ensure that the provenience is documented, and enter the artifact into the evidence log under the proper protocol. This begins the chain of custody. When the evidence technician turns the material over to a specialist to study or to a secure facility, that action needs to be documented on a chain of custody form. On many archaeological sites, artifacts are gathered together at the end of the day or when the excavation unit is finished and entered into the artifact log. This is not appropriate on forensic sites. Items need to be entered into the evidence log immediately when they are found.

Many archaeologists and forensic anthropologists have amusing stories about officers bringing bones into their offices and the anthropologist storing the material in their university office, in the back of their car, etc. This is not an acceptable practice in modern law enforcement. All materials should be brought to a secure crime lab and examined there. It is better to lug reference material to the crime lab than to have to answer in court for a break in the chain of custody.

Expert Witness Testimony

Anyone who works on a forensic site needs to be prepared to testify in court as to what they did and how they did it. Any notes taken about the case can be requested by the defense during the discovery period of the trial. These will be minutely examined by defense lawyers for inconsistencies that they can use to create doubt that their client is tied to events at the gravesite. The first important implication about this is that all notes should be solely about the single case. If using a notebook, rather than forms, then that case should be all that is in that notebook, so that the lawyer does not obtain information irrelevant to the case, but which may be used to make the archaeologist look less than expert. Tearing pages out of a notebook will lead the defense attorneys to suggest that something incriminating was deleted before the material was handed over, so that is also not an option. Use forms on independent sheets of paper or a new notebook for each case.

Archaeologists need to learn the applicable rules for expert testimony in their jurisdiction. In the United States, the expert testimony criteria are decided by state and fall under two criteria. The 1923 Frye criteria for expert testimony are based on the Supreme

Court decision *Frye v. United States* (293 F 1014 [D.C. Cir 1923]). The Frye criteria allow expert testimony if there is proof the proposed testimony is generally accepted in scientific publications and by prior judicial decisions. The professional is usually accepted as an expert if they are generally accepted by their peers as an expert and have scientific publications based on the techniques used.

However, in 1993, the United States Supreme Court handed down an opinion in *Daubert v. Merrell Dow Pharmaceuticals, Inc.* (509 US 579, 589 [1993]) that changed the way that courts look at expert testimony. Daubert requires judges to decide whether the reasoning or methodology underlying the proposed testimony is valid and can be applied to the facts of the case at hand. This shifts the focus of the legal decision from accepting the credentials of the expert to the type of reasoning used in reaching the determination as given by the expert in testimony. In the Daubert opinion, the Court stated, "Ordinarily, a key question to be answered in determining whether a theory or technique is scientific knowledge that will assist the tryer [*sic*] of fact will be whether it can be (and has been) tested. Scientific methodology today is based on generating hypotheses and testing them to see if they can be falsified; indeed, this methodology is what distinguishes science from other fields of human inquiry."

The opinion then turns to four criteria for evaluating the admissibility of expert testimony:

1. Whether the methods on which the testimony is based are centered on a testable hypothesis;
2. The known or potential rate of error associated with the method;
3. Whether the method has been subject to peer review; and
4. Whether the method is generally accepted in the relevant scientific community.

The Daubert criteria require that investigations must be framed in the scientific method. Investigators must understand induction, deduction, and hypothesis testing. Investigators are required to have the statistical sophistication to understand error rates and the difference between errors of false positives and false negatives. To use a particular method, the investigator must be familiar with the professional literature and know how that literature reflects on the methodology. The archaeologist may have to tell the law enforcement personnel that they need more time, personnel, or equipment to meet professional standards. If they make such a request and it is denied, this needs to be clearly stated in the archaeologist's notes.

If called on to testify, the archaeologist will undoubtedly receive advice on how to present themselves. However, honesty is the basic criterion. The archaeologist should report their findings accurately and never go beyond the limits of their evidence or experience. The scientist represents the physical evidence and should not be drawn into testifying beyond the physical evidence.

CASE STUDY—RWANDA

In 2004, political instability in Rwanda peaked in a series of massacres committed by the Hutu ethnic group on the Tutsi. The prosecutions for these massacres resulted in the only convictions for genocide in an international tribunal as of this writing. The killing started on 6 April 1994 when President Habyarimana of Rwanda died after his helicopter was shot down. Before dawn the next day, members of the elite Presidential Guard began killing members of the political opposition, and a wholesale massacre of Tutsi and moderate Hutu began (Gourevitch 1998). Thousands of Tutsi and members of the Hutu opposition began seeking refuge in churches, stadiums, and other public places throughout the country.

The killings continued until 17 July, when a Tutsi-led army, the Rwandan Patriotic Force, took control of the country and announced the formation of a new government. It was estimated that at least a half million people were dead. On 8 August, the new government agreed to an international tribunal to try those accused of genocide (des Forges 1995:13). The United Nations established the International Criminal Tribunal for Rwanda (ICTR) to investigate the claims of genocide and crimes against humanity arising from the mass slaughter.

The ICTR chose to investigate the Catholic Church and Home St. Jean Complex in Kibuye Town, Gitesi Commune, Kibuye Prefecture, as part of the prosecution of allegedly responsible individuals

under Indictment ICTR-95–1-I (ICTR 1995). The events at this church and school complex appeared typical of the events at similar complexes throughout the country. The Physicians for Human Rights, under the direction of Dr. Robert Kirschner, completed the forensic investigation in cooperation with the ICTR, whose overall forensic effort was headed by Dr. William Haglund. Kibuye is a small town on the east side of Lake Kivu. The indictment charged that from approximately 8–17 April, individuals were directed by officials to congregate in the Roman Catholic Church and Home St. Jean Complex.

By 17 April 1994, thousands of men, women, and children from throughout Rwanda had sought refuge in the Catholic Church and Home St. Jean Complex (fig. 4.1). These people, according to the indictment, were unarmed and predominantly Tutsis. According to witnesses, on or about 17 April, members of the Gendarmerie Nationale, the communal police of Gaieties Commune, Interahamwe, and armed civilians surrounded the Roman Catholic Church and Home St. Jean Complex. The individuals in the complex were attacked with grenades, guns, cudgels, machetes, spears, and other blunt and sharp force weapons. The attack on the complex and the individuals within continued throughout the day. Survivors of the attack were tracked down and killed during the following days. The indictment alleged that thousands of men, women, and children were killed and injured in this attack (ICTR 1995).

Burial of many of the victims took place in a minimum of four mass graves on the peninsula. According to witness statements, a bulldozer was used to dig a large grave behind the church. Human remains removed from the church and surrounding area were placed into this grave. As with many other churches around the country, the church itself was cleaned. The remaining evidence of the conflict was the shrapnel holes in the roof resulting from grenades tossed through the windows into the church. Evidence of the conflict was still seen in 1996 in the scorched areas by the doors where burning tires were pushed into the structure to try to force people out or asphyxiate them.

The forensic investigation was carried out in three phases (Haglund et al. 2001). In the first phase, three archaeologists arrived in Rwanda in mid-December

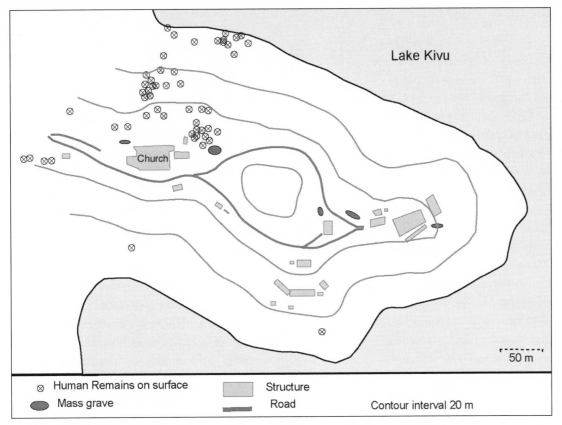

FIGURE 4.1. Catholic Church and Home St. Jean Complex in Kibuye Town. The large grave east of the church is the one excavated for the Tribunal. Redrawn from Haglund et al. (2001).

1995 to begin mapping and initial site documentation. The investigation began by photographing and mapping each of the buildings on the site. There were 22 buildings in all, which showed varying evidence of the conflict.

The archaeologists next walked transects around the entire peninsula, locating surface skeletal remains throughout the area and flagging them when found. This was completed as a standard archaeological inventory, spaced about 10 m apart and walking with the contours of the peninsula. In several areas, the archaeological team found trash dumps and went through these to insure than no human remains or other evidence of the conflict were in them. The team located 39 groups of remains and began to map them.

In early January 1996, six forensic physical anthropologists arrived, beginning the second phase of the forensic investigation. With their arrival, the team went back to the areas located earlier and recovered the remains. The vegetation around each was carefully removed using hand clippers, to expose all the bones in the area. Each skeleton was assigned a number,

mapped, and photographed in place then carefully removed. The anthropologists set up a field laboratory on the outside of the church and analyzed the skeletal remains for gender, age, race, and trauma (Haglund et al. 2001:61).

Following study of the surface remains, one of four mass graves (Grave 1) was excavated using standard archeological and forensic methods, the third and final phase of the forensic investigation. A total minimum number of 493 human remains were examined from the properties of the Kibuye Roman Catholic Church based on the number of crania recovered (Haglund et al. 2001:62; ICTR 1999:Para 325–26). This total is the sum of the minimum number of 454 individuals removed from the excavated grave and the minimum of 39 individual skeletal remains recovered from the surface of the north and south slopes between the church and Lake Kivu. The dead were men, women, and children, suggesting that at least some of the killed were non-combatants.

The spatial distribution of the surface remains can also be broadly interpreted as well. If the refugees were initially clustered in the church and other buildings, then the initial attacks may have occurred there. The scatter of surface remains north of the church, between the church and the lake, may reflect either people fleeing the church building or people going to the lake for water for the wounded. The town of Kibuye is south of the peninsula and is more heavily populated. That may be why the surface remains located are to the north side of the peninsula, opposite the side where they could be more easily seen from the road. The physical evidence collected included the condition of the structures, which showed clear signs of aggression. It also included the spatial distribution of the human remains on the peninsula, which were clustered around the church.

The investigation showed that the killings involved large numbers of people, both in terms of killers and the deceased. That there were so few firearms involved in this case strongly suggested that large numbers of killers must have been involved, or the victims would have overwhelmed the attackers and escaped. The investigations also clearly showed that non-combatants were involved. Nizam Peerwani testified that the grave included a large number of elderly and children (ICTR 1999: Paragraph 326). This could be interpreted as suggesting that killers were not killing in either a combat situation or in self-defense.

Indictment ICTR-91–1-I was issued against eight indictees for four massacres, including the Catholic Church and Home St. Jean complex in Kibuye Town, the massacre at the stadium in Kibuye town, the massacre at the church in Mubanga, and the massacres in the area of Bisesero. Of these, the Kibuye Catholic Church and Home St. Jean Complex was the only

area in which well-controlled forensic evidence was collected.

As of 2007, three indictees were not yet arrested. Of the five who stood trial, one was acquitted on all charges. A second was found guilty of one charge of crimes against humanity (extermination), but not of genocide. Three of the indictees stood trial and were found guilty of genocide.

CONCLUSION

Forensic science is science applied to the law. The science of battlefield archaeology can be applied to the law with some modification. The major difference is the paradigmatic switch from an anthropological perspective to a legal perspective. The forensic archaeologist working on a battlefield is not interested in the development of agriculture or state-level society, but rather whether a crime was committed, what crime it was, and who did it.

On a forensic site, the archaeologist is part of a team and is not in charge of the investigation. Artifacts need to be treated as evidence and the chain of custody respected. Conclusions need to be limited to only what is directly supported by the evidence and no supposition made. Finally, the work has to be professional enough that the archaeologist can defend it in a courtroom against challenge by the defense attorneys. While many of the methods used are the same, forensic archaeology is an exciting application of the methods of battlefield archaeology with an immediacy and relevancy unique in the historical disciplines.

CHAPTER FIVE

Maritime Archaeology of Naval Battlefields

DAVID L. CONLIN AND MATTHEW A. RUSSELL

INTRODUCTION

Battlefield archaeology is fundamentally about looking beyond individual sites and small-scale activity areas to larger contexts. These larger contexts encompass a series of events and human behaviors that may have a very short time span but that typically involve larger areas than most archaeologists consider when looking at sites. This fact is particularly interesting when looking at the archaeology of naval battlefields, since underwater archaeologists have traditionally focused on the tightly constrained "time capsule" nature of individual shipwrecks instead of looking at broader patterns of wrecks considered as groups.

For centuries, seas, rivers, and lakes were the primary avenues of commerce, communication, and military control. China, Holland, France, and England are but a few of the empires that arose partially or wholly due to their mastery of the marine environment. Thus, it is not surprising that contesting this control has been a significant part of human conflict for millennia. Naval battlefields are common but only recently have the two relatively new sub-disciplines of underwater and battlefield archaeology been joined together to produce new insights into human conflict.

As the technology of warfare grew increasingly sophisticated following the industrial revolution, many combatants lost the ability to manufacture what they needed for effective military operations. In this situation, blockade became a viable strategy for winning a war. During the American Civil War (1861–65), the Union naval blockade of Confederate ports contributed significantly to eventual victory. In the waters off the southern states, hundreds of naval engagements of varying scales raged during the four years of conflict. These battles produced wrecks and debris that, when carefully examined by archaeologists, can offer new insights into human actions that are otherwise inaccessible to us today. In the waters off Charleston, South Carolina, one of the most intriguing of these battles occurred between a blockading ship and a new form of naval vessel—a submarine.

The attack of the Confederate submarine *H. L. Hunley* (*Hunley* was a licensed privateer, not a "CSS" ship) on the Union blockade ship USS *Housatonic* was the first time a submarine sank an enemy combatant vessel and produced an archaeological site with two principal features. The first component is the wreck of *Hunley* that mysteriously disappeared after sinking the Union vessel and was not rediscovered until 1995; the second is the wreck of *Housatonic,* the location of which was well-known and marked as a navigational hazard for decades after the Civil War. Underwater archaeologists from the United States Naval Historical Center, the National Park Service, and the South Carolina Institute of Archaeology and Anthropology, investigated and documented the two wrecks and associated outlying materials (Murphy 1998; Conlin 2005). What resulted was the archaeology of a naval battlefield with both sides represented, offering the opportunity to analyze the progression of the attack and the tactics involved by carefully documenting the material remains—directly comparable to similar archaeological studies at the Mexican-American War battlefield of Palo Alto (Haecker and Mauck 1997), the Civil War battlefield of Monroe's Crossroads (Scott and Hunt 1997), and the Indian War battlefield of the Little Bighorn (Fox and Scott 1991; Fox 1993).

In this chapter, we discuss the unique potential of naval battlefields and highlight what maritime archaeology can offer battlefield archaeology. We begin by outlining a methodological framework for studying naval battlefields and discussing the challenges involved. We then offer an extended case study on the *H. L. Hunley*/USS *Housatonic* Naval Engagement Site to illustrate how our methodological framework works in practice.

MARITIME ARCHAEOLOGY OF NAVAL BATTLEFIELDS

Battlefield archaeology can give unique insight into the anthropology of war, one of the most pervasive aspects of human behavior, and can provide data on how decisions are made in the heat of battle. Archaeological study of battlefields is based on the premise that warfare is ". . . one of the most organized, premeditated, regimented, and patterned forms of human behavior . . . the actions of military units on a battlefield are based on the tactics of the prevailing military wisdom of the day; they are not random. Therefore, one should not expect the debris of battle to be distributed randomly over a battlefield. The tactics employed on a battlefield do leave their traces in the archaeological record. Subsequently, if natural forces or human activities do not significantly disturb, mix, or mask all or parts of the battlefield, it should be possible to identify and define artifact patterns created by the tactical positions and movements of individual military units" (Potter et al. 2000:13).

One of the first to recognize the potential for battlefield archaeology was Snow (1981). Innovative methodology allowed Snow and his students to identify the remains of both British and American lines, fortifications and earthworks at Saratoga Battlefield. This methodology was advanced and referenced by Scott et al. (1989) in their pioneering work at the Little Bighorn Battlefield. They used unique characteristics (or "signatures") of different artifact classes to trace individual and unit movements across the battlefield as the structured behavior of the battle unfolded (Scott et al. 1989:146–47). They also proposed a "Post-Civil War Battlefield Pattern," that traced individual movement patterns based on artifacts bearing

unique signatures, such as shell casings (Scott et al. 1989:145–50). From these artifacts unit patterns could be discerned and, when taken as a whole, the progression of a battle is represented in its entirety; what Scott et al. (1989:148–49) refer to as "dynamic patterning." They then analyzed the resulting patterns and compared those to historical accounts that not only described the specifics of the battle, but more generally, the cavalry tactics followed by the U.S. Army at the time. Comparison to contemporary accounts and tactics allowed researchers to evaluate the archaeologically recorded patterns in terms of expected patterns referenced in historical documents, and provided a baseline for comparison to other Indian Wars battle sites (Scott et al. 1989:150).

Like their terrestrial counterparts, naval battlefields are not rare. Less common are archeological studies designed to explicitly determine the progression of a naval engagement and the naval tactics practiced by the combatants. While there are a variety of naval battlefields whose components have been examined individually (e.g. Veyrat and L'Hour 1994; Bratten 1996, 2002; Rodgers et al. 1998; Jeffery 2004; Papatheodorou et al. 2005), few have employed a battlefield framework in these investigations (but see Conlin and Russell 2006). In this chapter, we focus on those specific sites where material remains from both sides of the conflict are available for study. We do not consider here archaeological investigations of individual warships sunk in battle (e.g., Spirek 1993; Olson 1995; Peebles 1995; Delgado 1996) or those lost as a result of non-combat operations (e.g., Arnold et al. 1992). Nor do we consider vessels scuttled for defensive or other purposes (e.g. Broadwater 1980, 1992; Broadwater et al. 1985; Gould 1990; Delgado et al. 1991; Delgado 1996; Riess and Daniel 1997; Hunter 2004), or non-combatant vessels lost during military support operations (e.g. Arnold et al. 1999, 2001a, 2001b; Birch and McElvogue 1999). Rather, we examine the potential for maritime archaeology, using an explicit battlefield approach, to illuminate how the practice of naval warfare unfolds during engagements at sea.

The potential for maritime archaeology to inform on larger social processes associated with preparation and conduct of naval warfare has been demonstrated (Gould 1983, 1990, 2000; Delgado 1992). As part of a search for broader patterns of human behavior,

Gould used maritime archaeology to illuminate universal tendencies in the practice of warfare, such as "defensive recycling" and "trend innovation" (Gould 1983:140–41, 1990:161). Like Scott et al. (1989) above, Gould demonstrated that material signatures representing particular human behaviors associated with naval warfare are often preserved in underwater archaeological remains, and that these can be used to make cross-cultural generalizations (Gould 1983:105–06). This is important, but at the same time, the nature of battlefield data, including naval battlefields, lends itself to not only universal generalizations, but also historical understanding of particular events. As Trigger (1989:375) notes, "Nomothetic generalizations and historical explanations are indissolubly linked processes, neither one of which can make progress without the other or be reduced to the other." Battlefield archaeology, including the maritime archaeology of naval battlefields, is a prime example of such a multi-scalar explanatory approach. The precise movements and battlefield behavior preserved in the archaeological record can be compared to historical accounts from combatants on both sides to accurately establish the sequence of events. In addition, the specific practices gleaned from these studies can be linked to larger cultural structures that influenced overall military strategy and tactics. Wylie (1999:28) calls this type of analysis "generalizing within the case," and she notes that it can effectively overcome the opposition between particularism and generalization.

Our methodological approach is rooted firmly in an historical archaeological framework, combining multiple lines of evidence from both archaeological and historical sources into a cohesive whole that points towards an unbiased view of the past. The holistic approach offered by an historical archaeological framework strengthens archaeological inferences and statements about cultural processes because one source of data is not privileged over another—the various datasets emphasize different viewpoints and create a more balanced account of the past. Using this approach, it is important to critically evaluate each line of evidence separately, examining all sources for logical, internal consistency before combining and synthesizing data sets (Feinman 1997; Kepecs 1997; Keegan 1998; Wylie 1999). Archaeological data relevant to the maritime archaeology of naval battlefields includes fine-grained spatial patterning within sites, as well as detailed evaluation of both natural and cultural site formation processes. Historical sources important for a naval battlefield approach include firsthand observations and accounts from combatants on both sides of the conflict, as well as tactical manuals, official records and primary source documents.

Although we advocate employing multiple lines of evidence in our methodological approach, archaeology provides the foundation for our study. Archaeological data contained within a naval battlefield include both spatial relationships preserved in the archaeological record and environmental data relevant to site formation. Examining relationships between site components, most typically individual shipwrecks, can provide gross patterning about how the engagement unfolded and inform on large-scale strategy. Fine-grained analyses of individual sites, on the other hand, can demonstrate how individuals acted during the course of the battle and illuminate more specific tactics. In the latter case, it is especially important to distinguish material patterning caused by actors and events during the course of the battle (similar to Souza's [1998:47–48] "pre-depositional formation processes") from those caused later by natural deterioration or human intervention (such as salvage activities). Unlike terrestrial battlefields, remains from naval battles will not typically consist of individual artifacts distributed across a landscape. However, multi-scalar analyses of individual site components and the site as a whole can illuminate the progress of the battle and be used to evaluate overall patterns.

Although critical in all archaeological investigation, analysis of natural and cultural site formation processes affecting submerged naval battlefields is particularly important given the dynamic nature of the forces at work underwater. A variety of recent literature reviews the fundamentals of formation processes on submerged sites (Stewart 1999; Ward et al. 1999; O'Shea 2002; Gibbs 2006; Quinn 2006). In our approach to naval battlefield archaeology, not only is it necessary to control for formation processes to make valid archaeological interpretations, but natural processes themselves are used as independent lines of evidence to support particular explanations. For example, one of the key pieces of evidence used to understand post-engagement events is the burial history of

H. L. Hunley, which was synthesized from analysis of coral colonies on the hull of the submarine and radiometric sediment dating of the site matrix, as well as other lines of evidence.

Use of historical documents is a key component of the maritime archaeology of naval battlefields, but it is important to keep in mind that archaeology is much more than a check on historical facts. Within a battlefield framework, each source has its own biases, interpretive problems, and analytical constraints, but each contributes distinct historical perspectives from different points of view. According to Lightfoot (2005:16), historical documents are ". . . not so much biased representations of history as culturally constructed texts that present eyewitness accounts from the vantage point of elite, literate, Western males. . . . These sources are particularly helpful in constructing policies and practices." He goes on to note the documents ". . . present a necessary . . . perspective on events and encounters that unfolded" and that they illuminate the "colonial structures" in which particular practices were situated. In our case, we might substitute "military" or "naval" for "colonial," but the point remains the same—properly contextualized, historical accounts are a vital line of evidence for accurately understanding past events. Similarly, in an anthropological perspective on ethnographic history, Sahlins (1992:14) notes ". . . the so-called distortions of firsthand observers and participants are more usefully taken as values than as errors. They represent the cultural forces in play." Each alternative source must be carefully compared and balanced against the others resulting in a more complete picture of the past.

The basis for a maritime archaeology of naval battlefields is found in the combination of natural and cultural data available as part of the archaeological record, and contemporary historical accounts and documents. Rigorously separating multiple strands of evidence during evaluation stages is vital before synthesizing the data into a coherent whole.

THE H. L. HUNLEY/USS HOUSATONIC NAVAL ENGAGEMENT SITE

The American Civil War shipwrecks *H. L. Hunley* and USS *Housatonic* have been the focus of intensive archaeological investigations since the discovery of *H. L. Hunley* in 1995. This study focuses on what the authors term the *H. L. Hunley*/USS *Housatonic* Naval Engagement Site. Researchers considered both wrecks as complementary components of a single archaeological site, a battlefield affected by similar cultural and natural processes. A series of projects initiated before the recovery of *Hunley* in 2000 gathered maximum information with minimum impact to the archaeological resources. Project principals from the U.S. Navy's Naval Historical Center (NHC), National Park Service's Submerged Resources Center (SRC) and South Carolina Institute of Archaeology and Anthropology (SCIAA) planned and conducted a number of multi-disciplinary and science-based investigations. In 1996, initial investigation of *H. L. Hunley* sought to verify the identity of the wreck as the ill-fated submarine and assess its condition and state of preservation (Murphy 1998). As a follow-up to the 1996 *Hunley* assessment, an extensive field project was conducted in 1999 to evaluate the remains of *Housatonic* and their archaeological potential (Conlin 2005). In both cases, site-formation processes were a primary focus of investigation. Beyond specific questions answered about each wreck, the multi-component site was analyzed as a naval battlefield, following the theoretical and methodological research orientation pioneered at the Battle of the Little Bighorn (Scott and Fox 1987).

To date, most research on *H. L. Hunley* has focused on the substantial conservation issues yet to be resolved (Gonzalez et al. 2004; Mardikian 2004) and on the skeletal remains recovered during interior excavation (Stevens and Leader 2006). Investigation of the *H. L. Hunley*/USS *Housatonic* Naval Engagement Site from 1996 to 1999, however, provided the opportunity for systematic, methodical study of the material remains from a naval engagement with both participants represented. The type of "dynamic patterning" documented by Scott et al. (1989:148–49) cannot at this time be easily applied to naval engagements; however, the general approach to an investigation of material remains from both sides of a naval engagement can allow us to identify tactics and the results of specific actions. After accounting for natural and cultural site formation processes, specific damage identified on the remains of *Housatonic* can be directly attributed to the attack by *H. L. Hunley.* Based on these observations, naval tactics can be hypothesized and historical accounts correlated or refuted. This is similar to what Scott et al. (1989:146–47) refer to as "gross patterning," or a static interpretation of events independent of temporal variables.

The first step in using a battlefield approach was to document the relative position, orientation, spatial organization, and level of integrity of both major site components. Next, site formation processes were identified and controlled for—this was especially significant for the remains of *Housatonic* because we could not isolate and recognize potential battle damage inflicted by *H. L. Hunley* until we understood the considerable natural and cultural formation processes that created the site in its present form. Finally, we compared archaeological data to historical documents to illuminate specific events documented by participants and observers during the course of the battle. Another important site component was also documented during this project: a large, iron buoy that probably marked the wreck of *Housatonic* as a navigational hazard for many decades after the Civil War. Although not directly related to the battle, the buoy is part of the complex human interaction that produced the site as a whole.

Historical Context

On the evening of 17 February 1864, the tiny Confederate submarine *H. L. Hunley,* under the command of Lt. George Dixon, slipped from its dock at Breach Inlet on the outskirts of Charleston, South Carolina, and began its historic voyage to attack the Union blockade. Almost three hours later, under a bright moon and in calm seas, the submarine and its crew of eight rammed a 60 kg (135 lb) black-powder charge into the side of the Union blockade ship USS *Housatonic.* Backing away, *H. L. Hunley* tripped a lanyard and detonated the charge. As pieces of the decking of *Housatonic* blew high into the night sky, *H. L. Hunley* disappeared and remained lost for 131 years. The world's first successful submarine attack had been precisely planned and successfully executed by the Confederate States of America, though with the loss of the submersible and all on board.

The American Civil War was, with the possible exception of the Crimean War, the first conflict in which both sides reaped the dubious benefits of the industrial revolution. Faced with the overwhelming industrial capacity of the North, the South sought an advantage through application of tactical and technological ingenuity. In broad terms, Confederate naval actions took both offensive and defensive forms. Offensively, unable to build a fleet to match the Union, the Confederacy focused its efforts on the construction of fast, well-armed, technologically-sophisticated commerce raiders such as CSS *Alabama* and CSS *Florida* to carry out a *guerre de course* against Union shipping worldwide. Defensively, the principal concerns of the South were breaking the blockade to maintain international commerce and defending its ports. For harbor defense, the Confederacy turned to the relatively cheap but effective use of torpedoes (mines) and the construction of ironclads such as CSS *Virginia* and CSS *Palmetto State.* The South also had a small but vigorous program of innovative new technologies used for offensive operations against the blockade—notably the semi-submersible and submersible. In short, submarine warfare during the Civil War emerged largely as a Confederate response to the Union blockade of Southern ports. Within the narrowly structured context of the blockade emerged a remarkable drama of actions and reactions, strokes and counterstrokes, and technological innovations and responses that culminated dramatically in naval combat off Charleston, South Carolina, in mid-winter, 1864.

USS *Housatonic* and *H. L. Hunley* represent two sides of a naval engagement that, 50 years later, would become a regular feature of war at sea—submarine against surface ship. Writing about events two years previous to the *Hunley/Housatonic* engagement, former First Sea Lord Winston Churchill noted (1995:398), "The combat of the *Merrimac* and the *Monitor* made the greatest change in sea-fighting since cannon fired by gunpowder had been mounted on ships." Churchill, like most naval historians, saw the 9 March 1862 engagement between the Union ironclad USS *Monitor* and the Confederate ironclad ram CSS *Virginia* at Hampton Roads as a pivotal moment in the development of modern naval technology and tactics. Although few would deny that the obsolescence of wooden sailing warships was effectively demonstrated the day before, many fail to appreciate that another profound development in naval warfare—the first successful attack on a surface ship by a submarine—occurred just two years later in the contested waters off Charleston, South Carolina.

The era of armored battleships peaked in the first half of the twentieth century, but by 7 December 1941, the devastation of the U.S. Pacific Fleet by Japanese naval airpower at Pearl Harbor, Hawaii, established the looming strategic irrelevance of the ironclad legacy. In contrast to battleships, although the success of the *H. L. Hunley* was not repeated for another 50 years, the implications of that first submarine attack continue to affect global geopolitics and strategic thinking today.

Project Background

On 3 May 1995, archaeologists sponsored by author Clive Cussler's National Underwater and Marine Agency (NUMA) successfully located the wreck of *H. L. Hunley,* 6.4 km (4 miles) off Charleston, South

Carolina, using a combination of magnetometer survey and test excavation (fig. 5.1) (Hall and Wilbanks 1995; Wilbanks and Hall 1996). In 1996, at the request of the NHC, SRC, SCIAA, and archaeologists from the NHC Underwater Archaeology Branch, archaeologists returned to coordinates furnished by Cussler's team to: (1) confirm the identity of the object located as the wreck of *H. L. Hunley*; (2) assess the condition of the wreck and document the site to the extent conditions permitted; and (3) evaluate the feasibility of excavation and recovery of the vessel remains based upon scientific study of the site and its surroundings (Lenihan and Murphy 1998:15; Neyland and Amer 1998:12). Following the 1996 assessment, that recommended recovery of the *H. L. Hunley* as the preferred management alternative, the same agencies returned to investigate the remains of *Housatonic* in 1999. Goals were to evaluate the integrity of the wreck and evaluate the spatial organization of the site, recover representative artifacts for interpretation and, if possible, delineate battle damage inflicted by *H. L. Hunley*.

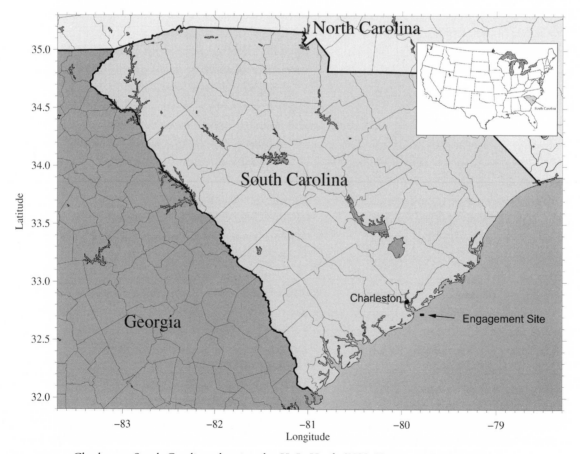

FIGURE 5.1. Charleston, South Carolina, showing the *H. L. Hunley*/USS *Housatonic* Engagement Site.

Pre-disturbance Survey

From the outset of the 1996 assessment, the wrecks of *Hunley, Housatonic,* and associated remains have been considered as different components of a single, multi-component site. Systematic remote sensing with towed instrumentation produced a synoptic overview of known and potential cultural remains and relationships within the study area and was a key first step in the battlefield approach (Murphy et al. 1998:45–62). The 1996 pre-disturbance survey produced a comprehensive data set that was immediately accessible for planning and aided interpretation during excavation. The survey design was based upon the wide-area archaeological survey methodology developed during the National Park Service's System-wide Archaeological Inventory Program (SAIP) survey of Dry Tortugas National Park, which began in 1993 (Murphy and Smith 1995; Shope et al. 1995; Murphy 1997). Remote-sensing instrumentation used for the 1996 pre-disturbance survey included deployment of a portable base station to provide differentially-corrected GPS positioning for magnetometer, side-scan sonar, survey depth-sounder, sub-bottom profiler, and Rox Ann bottom classification device (Murphy et al. 1998:45). Using these sensors concurrently provided a multi-parameter natural and cultural resource hydrographic survey to address goals set forth in the 1996 research design (Lenihan and Murphy 1998:15).

The 1996 high-resolution pre-disturbance survey located cultural materials and characterized the environmental context of both *H. L. Hunley* and *Housatonic.* These data were used to assist operational and interpretive objectives. Location of outlying ferrous masses possibly associated with the *H. L. Hunley,* or perhaps related to the *Hunley/Housatonic* engagement, was also an objective (Lenihan and Murphy 1998:15–16; Murphy et al. 1998:45).

The magnetometer data were contoured on a 2-gamma (nanotesla) interval using the gradient method. This method allows correction for diurnal changes and facilitates locating the physical object responsible for the magnetic anomaly. Magnetometer survey results indicated four main concentrations of ferrous material within the survey area and several smaller concentrations (less than 10-gamma). One of the main anomalies was identified as *H. L. Hunley,* a

second as *Housatonic,* while the third and fourth ferrous concentrations, located between the other two, were unknown until they were investigated in 1999.

Fieldwork

Site verification for *H. L. Hunley* relied on congruence of key features from historical descriptions of the submarine. Definitive verification depended upon location of particular features unique to *Hunley,* including the forward hatch, aft hatch, snorkel-box, dive-plane, cutwater, screw, rudder features, keel ballast, and bow spar or fittings. Verification would be established if five or more of the attributes were located (Russell and Murphy 1998:67). Because there was approximately 1 m (3 ft) of sediment above the suspected *Hunley,* the general strategy was to first uncover the limited area disturbed by the 1995 NUMA investigation to refine excavation methodology before removing previously undisturbed sediments. After opening the first excavation unit in the forward hatch and snorkel-box area, a second excavation unit was opened toward the stern of the vessel to locate the aft hatch; the two excavation units proceeded toward midship to join in the middle.

The after end of the submarine was left undisturbed until the end of the project when a narrow trench along the top hull centerline was carefully excavated to the aft-most point of the hull to establish accurate overall hull length. The bow and its potentially fragile spar attachments were also avoided until the end of the project when, as in the stern, the centerline was excavated forward to finish overall length measurements and determine whether any portions of the spar or spar attachments remained on the hull top (Russell and Murphy 1998:67–8).

Key features located during the course of the excavation, including the forward and aft hatches, cutwater forward of the forward hatch, snorkel-box, dive-plane and keel ballast, together confirmed the wreck as *H. L. Hunley* (Murphy, Russell, and Amer 1998a:76–85) (fig. 5.2). Archaeologists then focused on mapping and documenting the exposed remains, and began the condition assessment, which primarily involved investigation of site-formation processes and a corrosion study of the hull of the *Hunley.* Corrosion studies are not new to archaeological evaluations

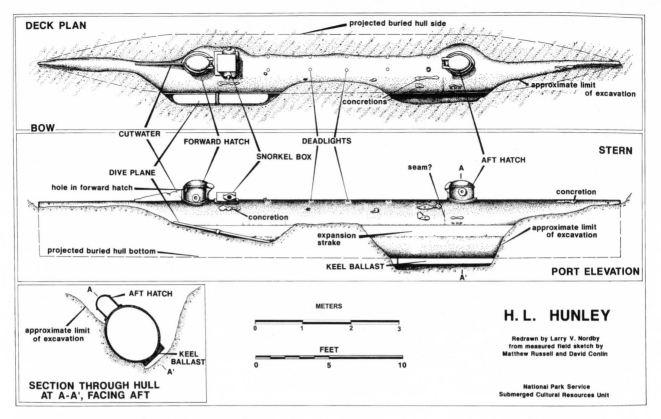

DECK PLAN — projected buried hull side — concretions — approximate limit of excavation

BOW — CUTWATER — DIVE PLANE — hole in forward hatch — FORWARD HATCH — SNORKEL BOX — DEADLIGHTS — seam? — A — AFT HATCH — **STERN** — concretion — concretion — expansion strake — projected buried hull bottom — KEEL BALLAST — **PORT ELEVATION** — A'

AFT HATCH — A — approximate limit of excavation — KEEL BALLAST — A' — **SECTION THROUGH HULL AT A-A', FACING AFT**

METERS — 0 1 2 3 — FEET — 0 5 10

H. L. HUNLEY
Redrawn by Larry V. Nordby
from measured field sketch by
Matthew Russell and David Conlin

National Park Service
Submerged Cultural Resources Unit

FIGURE 5.2. *H. L. Hunley* site map generated during the 1996 assessment.

of submerged metal-hulled vessels (Baker et al. 1969; Lenihan 1989; Arnold et al. 1991; McCarthy 2000, Russell et al. 2004). The goal in the case of *H. L. Hunley* was to determine the state of preservation, and by implication, the strength of the metal in the hull, to make management recommendations for long-term preservation and possible recovery (Murphy, Russell, and Amer 1998b:108).

Close examination of the entire exposed hull revealed *Hunley* was encrusted with a very tough, strongly adhering layer resistant to mechanical impact and abrasion. This layer was presumed to significantly reduce hull corrosion rates, as had been demonstrated on other sites (North 1976:253). Overall, the hull and hatches appeared solid, relatively sound and strong; the only observed damage was a hole in the forward portion of the forward hatch that may have been damage inflicted during the attack. At this level of investigation, based on observations and measurements taken as part of the comprehensive corrosion study (Murphy, Russell, and Amer 1998b:107–17), the hull appeared likely able to withstand recovery and conservation. Due to the potential threat of unauthorized removal of portions of the submarine because of

intense public interest, recovery became the primary management recommendation instead of the more usual option of long-term in situ preservation (Murphy, Russell, and Amer 1998b:117).

Separate and convergent lines of evidence investigated during the 1996 assessment, including analysis of biological organisms on hull of *H. L. Hunley* and radiometric sediment dating of the matrix encasing the submarine, indicated sediments completely covered *Hunley* soon after its loss, most likely within 25 years (Bell and Martore 1998; Moore 1998). The evidence indicated the vessel had not been periodically exposed to seawater through episodic burial and reburial events. Because evidence supported a single burial event and continued burial since 1864, *Hunley* was inferred to be stronger than it would have been if exposed, which indicated vessel recovery was feasible. The 1996 *H. L. Hunley* site assessment generated critical information about the submarine and site formation processes following its sinking in 1864. The location of *Hunley,* approximately 300 m (1000 ft) from the wreck of *Housatonic,* corroborated testimony delivered by Union sailors at the court of inquiry convened following the attack (Bak 1999: Appendix A).

A small hole in the forward hatch might be damage sustained during the attack, but at present, the loss of the submarine is not attributable to any definitive physical damage. While the technology of the submarine itself was impressive, a broader understanding of the historic import of the engagement between the two sides necessitated an examination of the victim of *H. L. Hunley;* the USS *Housatonic.*

1999 USS HOUSATONIC PROJECT

The research design for 1999 archaeological work on USS *Housatonic* built directly upon productive lines of enquiry completed on *H. L. Hunley* in 1996. The 1996 remote sensing survey indicated the *H. L. Hunley*/USS *Housatonic* Naval Engagement Site consisted of *Hunley, Housatonic,* and two smaller anomalies (referred to as "Third" and "Fourth" anomalies).

Research in 1999 focused primarily on *Housatonic,* although a broad, science-based methodology produced data relevant to each site component and placed *H. L. Hunley* in a larger historical and archaeological context whereby *Hunley* derived some significance from *Housatonic* and vice-versa. An initial characterization of USS *Housatonic* evaluated the archaeological integrity of the wreck and potential eligibility for the National Register of Historic Places. Goals for this part of the survey were to identify the key features of the ship, site extent, and vessel orientation through minimum-impact techniques. Following an assessment of archaeological integrity, research to interpret the construction of the ship, spatial organization, and possible battle damage followed.

Fieldwork

As with *H. L. Hunley,* the entire wreck of *Housatonic* was buried under sediment and could only be located through an examination of the magnetic signature of the wreck. Diving conditions were difficult and visibility low, which hampered productivity and made photographic documentation of the site impossible.

Adhering to the minimum-impact investigation strategy of the 1996 *Hunley* assessment, only small, precisely-located test-excavations were conducted on

Housatonic. Researchers selected initial test-excavation locations through interpretation of remote-sensing data derived from the 1996 wide-area survey. These initial locations were refined with a jet probe used to delineate wreck areas not deeply buried by estuarine sediments. Archaeologists probed into the seabed to characterize archaeological elements of the site buried beneath the modern bottom. When the probe hit something, listening to the sound the pipe made while hitting the object gave the operator an idea of the composition of the material struck—metal made the pipe ring, wood produced a dull 'thunk,' and coal produced a characteristic scratching sound. In the zero visibility conditions, 50 m (165 ft) transects of polypropylene line laid out in cardinal directions over the site and knotted at 1 m (3 ft) intervals provided spatial control. Through-water communications allowed a surface tender to immediately record spatial data and observations from the archaeologist working on the seabed.

Once a test excavation area was located, an archaeologist used a standard induction dredge to remove overlying sediment until features were distinguishable or, until it became clear that continued excavation would prove unproductive. As data accumulated that clarified the orientation of the wreck, excavation activities turned to the stern area to investigate evidence of the attack and post-depositional processes such as salvage and obstruction clearing. Primary features of interest were the boilers and engine, the starboard stern quarter, and the propeller and propeller shaft assembly. Historical accounts record that the *H. L. Hunley* attack damaged both the starboard stern quarter and the propeller area. Once the layout of the wreck was determined and post-depositional processes understood, the ultimate research goal was to document the effects of the attack. Of the 321 holes documented during site probing, 43 contained coal, 23 wood, 108 metal, and 147 had no contact. The shallowest probe return was 1 m (3 ft) below the seabed, and the maximum depth for probe returns was 2.4 m (8 ft). Materials buried deeper than 2.6 m (8.5 ft) below the seafloor were not detectable by the probe.

Researchers excavated three test trenches in an area of relatively shallow sediments to recover some diagnostic artifacts and to refine site delineation. One, Trench 2, was immediately above two water tanks identifiable on the plans from a sister ship, an *Ossipee-*

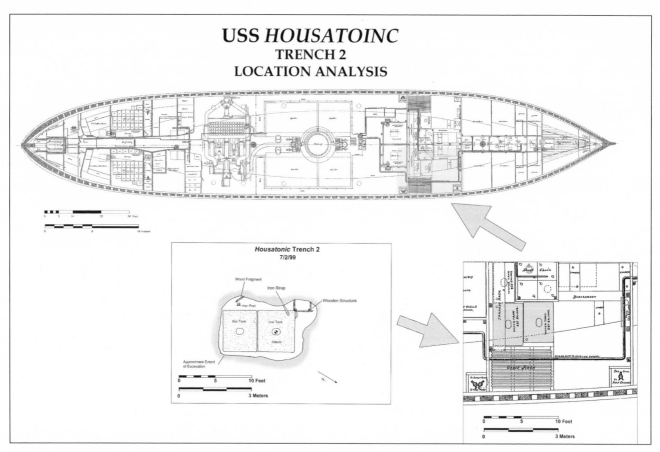

USS *HOUSATOINC*
TRENCH 2
LOCATION ANALYSIS

FIGURE 5.3. The water tanks of USS *Housatonic* provided data necessary to determine the wreck's orientation and a specific, identifiable location within the ship that could be used to geo-rectify the original plans.

class, sloop-of-war like *Housatonic* (fig. 5.3). By scaling and geo-rectifying the plans of the ship in the GIS database based on the location and orientation of the water tanks, team members were able to generate real-world coordinates for other areas of the wreck and ascertain where probe lines would fall when overlaid on an intact *Housatonic* deck plan (fig. 5.4). Overlaying probe lines in this way also indicated where other extant ship structure should be encountered with the probe had *Housatonic* been undamaged and unaffected by post-depositional formation processes. As data developed, it became clear that, although the probe encountered structure where the plan overlay indicated it should be, the area of the starboard stern quarter produced no contacts at all. This meant that the wreck was either below the maximum 2.4 m (8 ft) probe depth or that the area of the wreck was not present under those probe lines. Our interpretation is that negative contact with the jet probe in the starboard stern quarter is the result of that portion of the wreck being absent. This corroborates historical testimony concerning the nature of the attack and

damage sustained by the Union ship recorded at the Court of Inquiry following loss of the *Housatonic* (Bak 1999:Appendix A).

Probing and excavation of the *Housatonic* wreck indicates superior preservation of even relatively small organic artifacts and intact structural fragments in some areas. Assuming the magnetic contours are congruent with site extent, the *Housatonic* wreck encompasses more than 11,891 m² (128,000 ft²). The area of contiguous probe contacts on the wreck is approximately 678 m² (7300 ft²) or 5.7% of the total area of the magnetic anomaly caused by *Housatonic*. The hull plans for the *Ossipee*-class sloop-of-war show the original hull area, before the attack and post-depositional scattering, as approximately 550 m² (6000 ft²) or about 4.6% of the area of the 2-gamma anomaly contour. Total excavation area for the *Housatonic* assessment was approximately 31 m² (336 ft²) that amounts to 0.02% of the total area surveyed during 1996 or 5.6% of the original hull area before the attack and post-depositional scattering. In summary, a systematic, but extremely minimal impact examination of a large and difficult site produced artifacts in a superior state of preservation, critical data pertaining to wreck orientation and degree of preservation and information directly pertinent to understanding the *H. L. Hunley* attack and the damage it inflicted.

Third Anomaly

The Third Anomaly sits approximately 130 m (430 ft) east of the *Housatonic* wreck. Archaeologists documented the object producing the magnetic anomaly in a preliminary manner largely by feel in nearly zero visibility conditions, and uncovered only a portion of it. Although only a few observations could be made, they were sufficient for identification. The object

producing the 160-gamma magnetic anomaly is large, roughly bullet-shaped, hollow, and made of ferrous metal. It is flat at one end and tapering to a blunt point at the other. The object was found with a section of the round side and part of the large diameter flat end protruding above the seabed approximately 22 cm (9 in). Attached to the side of the object is an approximately 20 cm (8 in), semi-circular piece of round iron bar stock 38 mm (1.5 in) in diameter. Attached to the bar stock are at least two links of open-link chain 22 cm (9 in) long. The chain disappears into the sediment and was not excavated to its full extent; though an examination of the magnetic contours derived from the 1996 survey indicate additional ferrous material present.

The Third Anomaly is almost certainly a buoy that

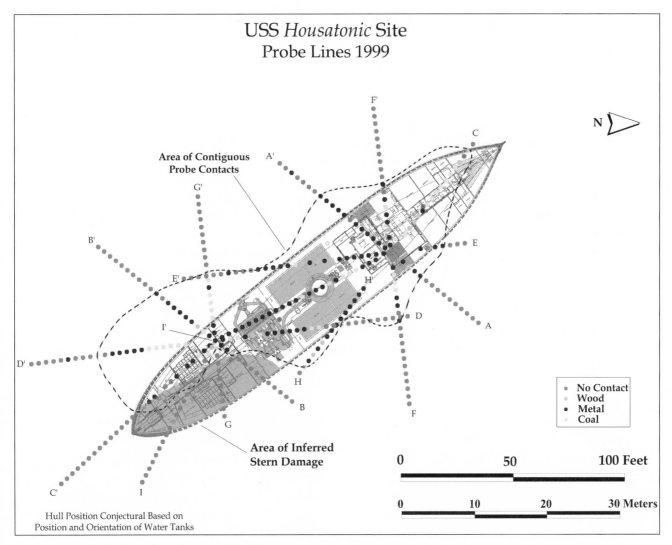

FIGURE 5.4. Probe lines from the 1999 USS *Housatonic* assessment.

probably marked the wreck of *Housatonic* as a hazard to navigation soon after its loss. The 1870 Coast Survey chart of Charleston Harbor shows a buoy marking the wreck. When this chart is geo-rectified to bring it into accordance with the 1996 and 1999 survey data, the charted position is 131 m (430 ft) from the present location of the Third Anomaly and 278 m (915 ft) from the present location of *Housatonic*. Historical documents report that salvagers dragged the wreck to the silt-line in 1909 to remove the hull as a navigational hazard, after which there was no reason to keep the buoy in place. Because the buoy was nearly 40 years old by this time, it was probably at the end of its use-life and consequently was not recovered but probably sunk at or near its original position.

Fourth Anomaly

The Fourth Anomaly is located approximately 137 m (450 ft) northeast of the *Housatonic* wreck. It is a 6-gamma anomaly produced by a small Admiralty-type anchor connected to a length of open-link chain buried 1.5 m (5 ft) under the seafloor. Although the bearing of the shank of the anchor points toward the wreck site of *Housatonic*, it is not known whether this anchor is associated with that vessel or was lost in some other event.

Burial Sequence

Burial sequence data from *H. L. Hunley* were originally sought in multiple lines of evidence because they were important for interpreting hull-corrosion data relevant to hull strength. Evidence collected in addition to the visual examination of hull encrustation characteristics discussed above included biological indicators, historical evidence, sedimentary analysis, and additional sediment-bound radioisotopes measurement. Historical evidence for the burial sequence begins soon after the engagement. *Housatonic* was investigated in detail in November 1864. In the nine months since sinking, the vessel hull had "settled in the sand about 5 feet [1.5 m]" and salvage divers reported that it was "very much worm-eaten" (O.R.N. Series 1:15:334). A specific search was

conducted for the submarine at that time. Investigators dragged "an area of 500 yards [450 m] around the wreck, finding nothing of the torpedo boat" (Lieutenant Churchill in Official Navy Records, cited in Kloeppel 1987:93). By April 1870, six years later, divers reported that the "wooden sheathing inside and the flanking [*sic*] outside are eaten by worms down to the copper" (Miscellaneous Wrecks, 1871–1888). In 1872, the Army Corps of Engineers contracted for work on both wrecks: clearing *Housatonic* wreckage to 6 m (20 ft) below mean low water and removal of *H. L. Hunley*. But they were unable to locate the submarine using grappling hooks. The hull of *Housatonic* presented a navigation obstacle until 1909 when salvagers removed an additional 2 m (6 ft) of hull by dragging, blasting, and removing the boilers of the ship (Kloeppel 1987:93).

The 1996 *H. L. Hunley* assessment demonstrated the archaeological relevance of sediment analysis and sequencing for determining site formation processes for the area. Researchers collected additional vibracore samples surrounding *Hunley* and *Housatonic* during the 1999 fieldwork to answer additional questions not addressed in the 1996 fieldwork. Cores from the vicinity of *Hunley* allowed for shear-strength analysis of the sediments (data vital for developing a safe and successful recovery methodology for the submarine), while coring in the vicinity of *Housatonic* allowed additional dating of depositional sequences for sediment overlying the two principal site components. ^{210}Pb isotopic dating of upper-level sediments in two of the nine vibracores provided age data for sedimentary layers in the site within approximately the last 100 years. Sediment ages for the layers differed between the two cores, with the core taken closest to *Hunley* showing older dates shallower, and the core taken closest to *Housatonic* having older dates deeper. These data indicated an overall higher sedimentation rate near *Housatonic* (8.9±3 mm/yr) and a lower sedimentation rate near *Hunley* (7.4±2.5 mm/yr). The generally exponential decay of ^{210}Pb as a function of depth below modern bottom in the vibracores indicated that sediment accretion over both *Hunley* and *Housatonic* was not punctuated by episodes of erosion. This helped explain the superior preservation of *Hunley* as well as the numerous small and delicate artifacts recovered during fieldwork on *Housatonic*.

Sedimentary deposition was probably episodic with relatively large amounts of sediment deposited on site in short periods of time due to events such as storms and, as discussed below, changes to coastal sedimentation dynamics caused by human actions.

In addition to direct analysis of sedimentary stratigraphy with vibracores, high-resolution remote sensing with two different sub-bottom profiling instruments was accomplished. The sub-bottom profiler characterizes deeper strata at a lower resolution, and the CHIRP depicts shallow strata, which are of primary archaeological interest, in higher resolution. Combining data from both instruments provides a comprehensive depiction of seabed strata that correlates with strata documented in the sediments recovered in the vibracores. Correlating core strata and reflectors allows very accurate stratigraphic interpretation from sub-bottom data and facilitates reliable projection of core strata analysis over a large area. Geostar CHIRP data revealed numerous paleochannels buried by marine transgression throughout the *Hunley/Housatonic* site. Of particular interest to an understanding of site-formation processes is a distinct reflector in CHIRP images at approximately 1–1.3 m (3–4 ft) below the modern bottom. Based on sedimentation rates derived from ^{210}Pb data, as well as comparative historical bathymetry, this stratum marks the position of the seafloor before construction of the Charleston jetties. Strata between this layer and the modern bottom are the result of post-jetty sedimentary deposition and partially explain both observed variations in burial of *Housatonic*, *H. L. Hunley* and other elements of the site as well as the superior preservation of many fragile artifacts recovered.

Geological characterization of the vibracores produced evidence of a stiff greenish-gray stratum of clayey sediments at a mean depth of approximately 1.8 m (5.8 ft) below the modern bottom. Based upon similarities with regional sediment sequences, this layer is Pleistocene marl from the regional Daniel Island Bed (Weems and Lemon 1993). The result of sediment deposition in estuarine and lagoonal environments during periods of lower sea levels approximately 1.6 million to 730,000 years ago, the relatively high cohesive strength of this Pleistocene layer, particularly in comparison to the muddy, shelly Holocene sand that lies on top of it, has an important effect on site-formation processes for the *Hunley/Housatonic* site.

An analysis of vibracore stratigraphy, sedimentation rates indicated by ^{210}Pb, historically documented changes in bathymetry and coastal geomorphology (corrected for sea level change), an analysis of offshore sediment transport patterns, and a uniform reflector in CHIRP sub-bottom data at about 1 m (3 ft.) below the modern bottom all point to the fact that the *Hunley/Housatonic* site has experienced recent and rapid sediment deposition. The primary reason for this sediment accumulation is the construction of the Charleston jetties, completed in 1895, which disturbed the dynamic equilibrium of coastal sedimentation and transport and caused extensive sediment deposition over all elements of the site. Before construction of the Charleston jetties, the entrance to Charleston Harbor lay several kilometers south of its present location. Under the combined influence of ebb tidal flow and northeast-to-southwest longshore sediment transport, several large sand bars extended more-or-less due south across the mouth of the harbor and impeded maritime commerce. In February 1857, work began to dredge a deep channel directly into the port. With the onset of the Civil War in 1861, however, these efforts halted (Moore 1981:18–20). Following cessation of hostilities in 1865, plans began again. In 1876, Gen. Quincy A. Gillmore of the U.S. Army Corps of Engineers finalized a comprehensive plan for harbor improvement incorporating dredging and construction of two large stone jetties beginning in 1877 (Moore 1981:32–33). By 1895, jetty construction was completed and deemed a success. Jetty construction, however, interrupted prevailing patterns of long shore sediment transport. Before construction, waves from the east and northeast intersecting with the northeast-southwest oriented coastline resulted in a net southward transport of mobile sediments. The north jetty diverted the southwest-moving sediment further offshore into deeper water where current speeds rapidly diminish. As current speeds reduce, increasingly finer sediment drops out of suspension. This process has resulted in a net sediment accumulation offshore from Sullivan's Island over the *Hunley/Housatonic* site (fig. 5.4). The bottom sediments have accreted at least an additional meter since jetty construction began in 1877, which is consistent with all other lines of evidence pertaining to burial sequence.

Summary

Cumulative sedimentary data derived from vibracoring operations, including sediment dating, sedimentation dynamics and geotechnical characteristics, explain site-formation processes for the wreck of USS *Housatonic,* and by extension, *H. L. Hunley.* Muddy, shelly sediments starting at approximately 1.2 m (4 ft) below the modern seabed mark the original bottom as it was before jetty construction. This was the approximate position of the bottom that *Housatonic* landed on following its sinking on 17 February 1864. By 26 November 1864, 10 months later, divers reported that *Housatonic* had settled in an upright position and had scoured into the sand about 1.7 m (5 ft), forming a bank of mud and sand around it (O.R.N. Series 1:15:334). This initial settling put the keel just into a cohesive Pleistocene marl layer. The settling rate of the *Housatonic* decreased dramatically once the hull bottom contacted the firmer Pleistocene layer. Reduction of the hull cross-sectional area exposed to the current caused by the 1873–74 salvage activities probably further decreased the scouring and settlement rate. In February 1909, additional salvage activity to remove the remaining hull as a navigation hazard, which included dynamiting and dragging the wreck with chains to the mud-line, presumably halted any further settling.

Sedimentation in the area of the *Housatonic* wreck accelerated following the 1895 completion of the Charleston jetties. Jetty construction diverted dominant southwestwards longshore sediment transport offshore and, as the currents moved into the deeper waters, they slowed and dropped their sediment load.

^{210}Pb data analysis from vibracores established a consistent chronology for sedimentary accretion occurring over *Housatonic* following its sinking. Sediment accumulation was episodic, sometimes proceeding at a faster rate than at other times, (probably due to storm activity) but was not interspersed with erosional periods.

The *H. L. Hunley* settled and scoured in the same way as *Housatonic,* though in the case of *Hunley,* differences in sedimentation rate due to a location further offshore resulted in overall shallower settling and burial. As with *Housatonic,* on the night of its sinking, *Hunley* settled onto the rather loose, unconsolidated sand that overlay the marl. Judging from the rate of scour and settling for *Housatonic,* the *H. L. Hunley* settled rapidly through the approximately 60 cm (2 ft) thick sand layer until it encountered the firmer marl below it. Supported by the more resistant layer, scouring and settling eventually slowed and then stopped. Following scouring to the Pleistocene marl layer, upper portions of the submarine remained exposed and served as a substrate for coral colonization, as discussed above. After a period of exposure, longshore sediments diverted by the Charleston jetties buried the exposed upper portions of the *Hunley.* Ultimately, approximately 1 m (3 ft) of diverted sediments buried the previously exposed upper surfaces of the submarine, and the entire wreck remained buried without subsequent exposure until its rediscovery in 1995.

While the superstructure of *Housatonic* rotted, was salvaged, and then dragged to the mud line, the *H. L. Hunley* was not discovered and may not have been directly affected by human actions following sinking. Sediment accumulation completed the burial processes initiated by scouring, and explains the burial depths of both wrecks observed in 1995, 1996, and 1999. Multiple lines of scientific evidence point to rapid burial following sinking, which accounts for the superb preservation of site components. The Third Anomaly is the sole feature not completely covered by sediments. The buoy scoured through the relatively soft Holocene sands to the firmer Pleistocene layer below and was partially buried by displaced long shore sediment, but a portion of it remained exposed above the present mud-line because of its large diameter (2.6 m or 8 ft, 7 in). Sediment accumulation is continuing, however, and it is likely that sediments will bury this final component of the site.

DISCUSSION

The *H. L. Hunley*/USS *Housatonic* Naval Engagement Site consists of four principal components: the wreck of the Union blockade ship USS *Housatonic;* the wreck of the Confederate submarine *H. L. Hunley*; the iron buoy that marked wreck of the *Housatonic* as a navigational hazard from at least 1870 to 1909; and a small, Admiralty-style anchor that may or may not be related to either the *Hunley* or *Housatonic.* Historical accounts from the Court of Inquiry convened to investigate the loss of *Housatonic* paint a detailed picture of a well-planned and directed attack that placed the black powder "torpedo" of the *Hunley* at the precise location that would deliver a killing blow. By the time the lookouts on *Housatonic* saw the approaching submarine it was already too late—*Hunley* had closed to the point where the larger guns of the Union ship could not be trained on the submarine. Because the submarine did not become visible to the crew of *Housatonic* before it was at close range, there was insufficient time to slip anchor and maneuver out of the path of the attacking *Hunley*. Barring failure of the torpedo, the success of the attack was already assured by the time the Union sailors on *Housatonic* became aware that something was wrong.

Fundamentally, the skill and precision of the attack of the *H. L. Hunley* on *Housatonic* mirrored the sophistication of *Hunley* as a weapon and as a piece of technology. As *Hunley* attacked, both Master's Mate Lewis A. Corinthwait and Lt. F. J. Higgson

from *Housatonic* reported that the submarine changed course and steered parallel and towards the stern of *Housatonic* before moving in for the final run into the starboard stern quarter (Bak 1999:161,162). Testimony by both Acting Master John Crosby and John Saunders at the *Housatonic* Court of Inquiry stated that *Hunley* slammed home the torpedo in the area of the mizzenmast (Bak 1999:154). The mizzenmast was a convenient aiming point for the attack—easy to see from the small, water-level view port on the forward hatch of *Hunley*. Assuming the *Ossipee*-class plans are representative of the interior arrangement of *Housatonic*, aiming at the mizzenmast would place the torpedo directly between the powder magazine and the guncotton room (fig. 5.5). Secondary explosions in either the guncotton room, the powder magazine, or both could result in sympathetic detonations in the port powder magazine multiplying the effect of the torpedo fired by *Hunley* more than a hundred-fold.

Observers aboard *Housatonic* reported that there

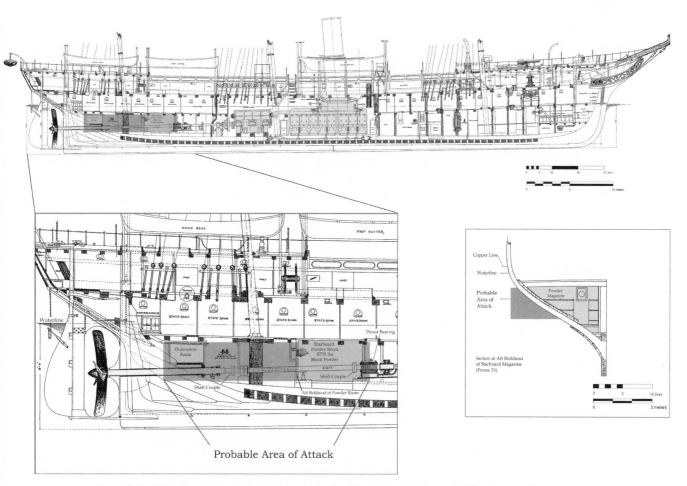

FIGURE 5.5. Area of the USS *Housatonic* where the torpedo fired by *H. L. Hunley* probably detonated.

was no water plume from the torpedo explosion—evidence that the hull of the ship and the water depth dampened the explosion. The explosive force did not dissipate upward, but instead was directed into the interior of *Housatonic*, indicating a precise charge placement well below the waterline beneath the hull where it would have maximum effect. On 20 February 1864, just three days after the attack, Union observers of the wreck reported the after part of the spar deck of *Housatonic* appeared to have been entirely blown off (O.R.N. Series 1:15:331). Ten months later, on 27 November 1864, salvage divers reported that all bulkheads aft the mainmast were completely demolished—further evidence of the effectiveness of the explosion and the manner in which it propagated through the ship (O.R.N. Series 1:15:334). In addition to the tamping effect of water over the explosive charge from *Hunley*, by attacking towards the stern of *Housatonic*, the crew of the *Hunley* was able to take advantage of the relatively sharp turn of the stern dead rise, which would channel any upward explosive force into the hull. The sharp deadrise would also have the net effect of creating a blind spot where the *Hunley* could place its charge in relative safety shielded from small arms fire from the Union crew.

Data relative to torpedo delivery and the precise charge placement were indirectly observed in the archaeological record during the 1996 investigation of the *H. L. Hunley*. During the excavation, only the upper surface of the bow of the *Hunley* was uncovered, but researchers did not find any indication of a top-mounted spar for torpedo delivery. Although all historical documentation indicated the *Hunley* was equipped with a spar mounted on the upper surface of its bow, the lack of any indication of a spar or attachment features led archaeologists at the time to speculate the *Hunley* likely had a bottom-mounted spar (Murphy, Russell, and Amer 1998b:104–05). This speculation was supported by magnetic data from the *Hunley* site, which indicated a ferrous mass extending northwest of the hull of the *Hunley* (this bottom-mounted spar hypothesis was later proven correct during recovery operations on *Hunley* in 2000). At the time when *Hunley* attacked *Housatonic*, Confederate naval forces had considerable experience with spar torpedoes, including the near sinking of USS *New Ironsides* by CSS *David* in 1863. Although *New Ironsides* was damaged during that attack, it was not sunk, likely because the torpedo was not delivered far enough below the waterline. Since *Hunley* was to be used only on the surface, its crew would have undoubtedly considered the failure of *David* as they prepared to attack the Union blockade and moved the spar torpedo location to the bottom of the submarine to deliver the torpedo as far beneath the waterline as possible.

The physical layout of the material remains at the *Hunley/Housatonic* site can provide insight on how the attack unfolded. Before recovery of *Hunley* in 2000, the remains of both *Hunley* and *Housatonic* lay about 300 m (1000 ft) apart on the seafloor outside Charleston Harbor; *Hunley* nearly due east of *Housatonic*. The bow of the *Hunley* faced 297° magnetic (Murphy, Russell, and Amer 1998a:76), while the projected orientation of the bow of the *Housatonic* remains is 316° magnetic (Conlin 2005:185). Both are oriented roughly north-northwest, or directly into the ebb tide flowing out of Charleston Harbor at the time of the attack. *Housatonic* was at anchor when the attack occurred, with its bow into the ebbing tide, and it came to rest on the bottom in nearly the same orientation. Historical records indicate that *H. L. Hunley* was on the surface for at least 50 minutes after the attack—witnesses both on shore and aboard *Housatonic* reported seeing a blue light (signal for a successful mission from *Hunley*) about 50 minutes after the *Housatonic* sank. With an ebb tide flowing, it is likely that after *Hunley* backed away from *Housatonic* and detonated the torpedo, the crew would have had to expend significant effort to maintain a position near *Housatonic*, or they may have anchored themselves in place. In either case, after at least 50 minutes or more, *Hunley* succumbed to whatever forces eventually caused it to sink. The answer to what ultimately sank *Hunley* will have to await further investigation by archaeologists and conservators during their ongoing research and analysis of the submarine.

Careful archaeological documentation and analysis of physical processes on the *Hunley/Housatonic* site have allowed us to reconstruct the sequence of events during and after the attack, and isolate and identify damage to the remains of *Housatonic* that can be associated with the attack by *H. L. Hunley* rather than the significant salvage and obstacle clearing activities on the site. This is analogous to what Scott et al. (1989:146–47) refer to as "gross patterning," or the "composite of battle events exclusive of or poorly understood in time." Based on the gross patterning and the historical record, we can recognize specific battle preparation and tactics employed by the crew of *Hunley*, and offer reasonable speculation about events after the attack.

Explicitly delineated research designs led to a field-work methodology that produced observations concerning *H. L. Hunley*, *Housatonic*, the Third Anomaly, and the Fourth Anomaly with minimum impact to the site. These data were augmented with historical research and an understanding of the environmental context of the *H. L. Hunley*/USS *Housatonic* Naval Engagement Site to set the stage for a broadly-based analysis of the attack by *Hunley* on the USS *Housatonic* and events occurring to the different site components after the battle. Archaeological data derived from probe lines and test excavations support historical accounts of a massive explosion caused by the torpedo fired by *Hunley*, which destroyed the starboard stern of *Housatonic*. Despite multiple episodes of salvage and obstacle removal, the wreck of *Housatonic* displays a high degree of integrity and superior preservation of portable artifacts illustrative of daily life on the Union blockade. Following its sinking, *Housatonic* scoured and settled rapidly down through relatively loose, sandy sediments and then stopped at the firmer layer of Pleistocene marl. Following construction of the Charleston jetties, redirected sediments began burying the wreck, and in 1909, salvagers leveled the wreck to the silt line. The Third Anomaly, most likely the buoy that marked the *Housatonic* wreck as a navigation hazard, also scoured and settled to the Pleistocene marl layer and then experienced partial burial. The Fourth Anomaly, a small anchor not conclusively linked to any of the other engagement site components was also buried by diverted sediment flow. By understanding and accounting for post-depositional changes to the wreck of *Housatonic*, we were able to account for them in the archaeological patterning and thereby delve deeper into the damage caused by *Hunley* that resulted in the sinking of the Union vessel.

The *H. L. Hunley* apparently survived the attack for at least 50 minutes—long enough to shine the blue signal light for success to waiting Confederate sentries

at Breach Inlet. The location of *Hunley*, as discovered in 1995, matches a reported sighting of the blue light quite well by a member of the crew of *Housatonic* and may indicate that signaling a successful attack was the one of the last things the crew of the submarine did. Following sinking, *Hunley* experienced the same dynamics of scour, settling and burial that covered and preserved the other components of the engagement site. An analysis of testimony delivered at the Court of Inquiry convened following the destruction of the Union blockader, combined with an examination of the internal arrangement of the ship, paints a picture of a skillful and precisely executed attack that delivered a single, killing blow.

As a naval battlefield, the two principal components of the site, *H. L. Hunley* and *Housatonic*, derive a large measure of their importance from their relationship to each other. The tactical mode of the attack by *Hunley*—specifically the nature and placement of the torpedo—left physical traces that were discernable even after 131 years, multiple episodes of salvage, and complete burial. As a significant event in world history, the first-ever engagement between a submarine and a surface ship deserves evaluation in the broadest possible historical and archaeological context. Treating the linked shipwrecks as a naval battlefield is the beginning of that process.

CONCLUSION

Naval battlefields, the patterned result of human conflict acted out in a marine environment, are worldwide phenomena that stretch from deep in the past to the present day. Although these battlefields are common, an archaeological investigation of them using an explicit battlefield framework is not. The reasons for this are varied, but are essentially the result of a general preoccupation of underwater archaeologists with single shipwrecks as isolated "time capsules" to the detriment of a broader examination of the context and inter-site relationships that a battlefield approach demands.

When the Confederate submarine *H. L. Hunley* rammed its explosive charge into of hull of the USS *Housatonic*, it was the result of a series of human actions and intentions that continued to affect both vessels long after they settled into the murky waters off Charleston. Illuminating the specific human behavior and general naval practice that contributed to creation of the *H. L. Hunley*/USS *Housatonic* Naval Engagement Site—the ultimate goal of the research discussed above—came to light only after researchers had teased out multiple strands of archaeological pre- and post-depositional evidence preserved in the site, and then braided them back together with the historical record to illustrate the strategies and tactics of both sides. To illuminate this remarkable drama of naval warfare we drew heavily on multiple data sources—archaeological, historical, and environmental—to present the same event from multiple viewpoints. In doing this, we examined fine-grained spatial patterning within the wreck of *Housatonic* and combined it with coarse-grained spatial analysis to situate the site in a larger context of marine sedimentary deposition driven by long-shore currents and the construction of the Charleston jetties. Historical accounts, unfortunately not including those of the *H. L. Hunley* crewmembers, were cross-referenced and provided interpretive guidance for the archaeological patterning we inferred from probing the buried remains of *Housatonic*. In these and other instances, we were acutely aware that only the most broadly based, problem-oriented archaeology could produce a coherent and nuanced account of this otherwise poorly understood, yet historically significant, naval battle.

While the fundamental precondition for a battlefield approach to underwater sites is conceptual, it bears mentioning that relatively recent advances in marine remote sensing technology and data presentation/visualization such as GIS make implementation of this approach both easier and more compelling. As these technologies advance and simplify the job of the archaeologist, we fully expect that analytical and interpretive frameworks will likewise advance, allowing more nuanced naval battlefield interpretations.

In the muddy water off Charleston, South Carolina, archaeologists were able to demonstrate the patterned behavior of one of the most famous naval engagements of the Civil War despite extreme diving conditions, multiple episodes of salvage and post-wreck alterations to components of the site, and the passage of more than 130 years in a dynamic marine environment. Researchers were able to filter through intervening processes and illuminate the manner and tactics of the attack by *H. L. Hunley* on *Housatonic,* thus illustrating some of the conceptual and methodological prerequisites for a maritime archaeology of naval battlefields. Perhaps more important, it also illustrates the potential for future and better archaeological examinations of this fascinating aspect of human history.

ACKNOWLEDGMENTS

The 1996 *Hunley* assessment was directed by Daniel J. Lenihan (NPS) and Christopher F. Amer (SCIAA); Larry E. Murphy (NPS) was field director. The 1999 *Housatonic* assessment was directed by Robert S. Neyland (NHC) and Christopher F. Amer (SCIAA); David L. Conlin (NPS) was field director. Research on *Hunley* and *Housatonic* has been generously supported by the Department of Defense Legacy Resources Management Fund and Friends of the *Hunley*. Research drew on many organizations and both authors apologize to those left out here. For updates on the remarkable work that is ongoing on *H. L. Hunley* go to www.hunley.org. All errors of fact or reasoning are the sole responsibility of the authors.

CHAPTER SIX

Watch-Fires of a Hundred Circling Camps

Theoretical and Practical Approaches to Investigating Civil War Campsites

JOSEPH BALICKI

INTRODUCTION

During the five years of the American Civil War (1861–65) there was a dramatic shift in the cultural and physical landscapes in much of the United States. Where armies where present, landscapes were drastically altered and archeological sites created. These sites range from monolithic fortifications and battlefields to small artifact scatters denoting a lone soldier's picket duty. As a depositional process, armed conflict created fewer archeological sites than processes associated with the most ubiquitous site type of the war: the military camp. A soldier's moments in battle were brief compared to time in camp where daily events formed the core of an individual's military experience. Establishing camps, maintaining camps, constructing buildings, training, and just plain living in camps is what soldiers did most.

The experiences of J. C. Williams, 14th Vermont Infantry, are typical (Williams 1864). Williams spent the majority of his nine-month enlistment in an approximately 175 square mile area of Fairfax County, Virginia. In the 87 days before settling into winter quarters, William's diary contains entries for 12 different camps, and the construction of winter quarters on five separate occasions. On average, not counting overnight marches, a new camp was established every seven days. After 63 days in winter quarters, the 14th was assigned to a permanently garrisoned fortification.

It is impossible to estimate the number of archeological sites created by the armies of the North and South, but clearly soldier encampments are a common site type. Civil War camps are increasingly recognized for what they are: archaeological sites that have the potential for containing significant information to address research questions on a wide range of topics relevant to archaeologists and other Civil War researchers.

This chapter presents an overview of camp types, their archaeological signatures, common features, and methods and procedures with which they may be investigated, interpreted, and recorded. Research designs should include a combination of background research, informant interviews, subsurface testing (shovel testing), metal detection, and mechanical stripping. Field procedures should be based on research questions, the nature of the deposits, and potential effects to the site. Fieldwork should be flexible enough to respond to the nature of the archaeological site as it unfolds. For example, one of the most effective methods for locating and investigating campsites is mechanical stripping combined with metal detection; but this is a very heavy-handed approach not appropriate in all cases, particularly where preservation of the site is an option. Viable field methods such as ground-penetrating radar and soil testing are not included only because the author has no firsthand experience with their use on an encampment. There is no one best set of methods and procedures for investigating a camp.

CAMP TYPES

In general, Civil War camps consist of permanent camps, winter quarters, and surface camps. This oversimplification provides a beginning framework that can be expanded to include differences between

Federals and Confederates, period of war, location, time of year, availability of materials, response to threat, level of training, officer experience, and, possibly, cavalry and infantry camps. The archaeological signature of each camp type varies.

Permanent camps are associated with long-term occupations, for example a garrison at a fort. In general, when stationed at permanent camps soldiers lived in barracks or modified their domiciles to be more permanent and hospitable (McBride and Sharp 1991; McBride 1994; Balicki 2000; McBride, Andrews et al. 2003; McBride and McBride 2006).

Winter quarters are characterized by the construction of "huts" or "shanties" by the soldiers. Photographic evidence suggests that by the winter of 1863 at least some Federal winter quarters included standardized cabin architecture. Hut architecture shows variability and was not an aspect of soldierly life prescribed by military regulation although established military doctrine dictated camp layout. Nelson (2006) presents an overview of the vernacular forms these domiciles took.

Typically, in an effort to gain more protection from the weather, soldiers dug in. By digging shallow depressions and banking earth against the sides of their domiciles, soldiers created better shelter from the elements. Frequently stone, brick, or earthen hearths and fireplaces were constructed. As a result, the archaeological signature of Civil War winter quarters often includes surface features seen as mounds, depressions, platforms, or combinations of the three (Balicki 2006a). These telltale features, regularly laid out in rows, greatly increase the chances of this type of site being found and investigated by archaeologists. The surface features also make these sites targets for relic hunters, which in turn impacts the probability of finding metallic artifacts.

When not in a permanent camp or in winter quarters, soldiers obtained shelter as they could. In general, camping in the field was not an enjoyable experience for the Civil War soldier. George Benedict, 12th Vermont Infantry, wrote "Some of the men look a little blank as they saw the cheerless surface of Virginia clay, on which they were to pitch their tents, and some blanker yet when they took in the length and breadth of the little strips of canvas, which were to be our only shelter from sun and storm. These 'shelter tents'

are made of a couple of strips of light cotton duck, about five feet long and four feet wide, which button together at the top or ridgepole of the concern. They are pitched by straining over the muzzles of a couple of muskets set upright, and so form a little tent, with both ends open, until closed at one end . . ." (Ward 2002:38).

Surface camps were generally temporary, and include summer camps, short-term occupations, and camps that are not "dug in." This is likely the most common site type and the most difficult to identify. Their archaeological signature will primarily be a scatter of artifacts and occasional small features such as hearths. The absence of surface features and the inherent difficulties in locating these sites by field methods currently employed by the majority of archaeologists has resulted in many sites going unrecorded.

ENCAMPMENT IDENTIFICATION

Military encampment archaeology is challenging. The indistinct nature of artifact and feature distributions coupled with the cultural processes affecting these distributions results in archaeological signatures that are difficult to identify and interpret. Presently, archaeologists are not very successful at developing and implementing successful field methodologies for these camps. Successfully investigating military encampments requires a departure from the minimum standard operating procedures accepted by many governmental agencies, and implemented as a set of formulaic boilerplate steps by many archaeologists in the Cultural Resource Management (CRM) industry.

Corle and Balicki (2006) present several factors that will improve chances of locating encampments. However, the most effective, quickest, and most cost-efficient method is to ask where the encampments are. This may seem simplistic, but it involves a dialogue with the relic hunter community. Recently, Legg and Smith (2007:227) put forth that "With rare exceptions, all reasonably accessible battlefields, field fortifications, and campsites in North America have been collected for several decades by numerous individuals. This condition extends to even the most obscure skirmishes and bivouacs, thanks to the rigorous historical research conducted by thousands of

TABLE 6.1. Metal detection verses shovel testing as a recovery technique for military artifacts on military sites.

Site	Area tested	Number of shovel tests	Artifacts found in shovel tests	Artifacts found by metal detection	Source
44FX195	2.5 ac (10,118 m²)	101	1	635	Balicki (1995)
44FX199	0.62 ac (2,509 m²)	36	3	222	Balicki (2006b)
44PW917	0.11 ac (464.5 m²)	25	0	58	Sterling and Slaughter (2000)
Blenhiem	0.9 ac (3,642 m²)	38	0	522	Reeves (2001)
44AX200	0.67 ac (2,712 m²)	46	0	79	Balicki et al. (2002a)
44AX198	1.87 ac (7,568 m²)	32	0	146	Balicki et al. (2005)
Antietam	75 ac (303,515 m²)	292	2	1,679	Balicki and Corle (2006)
Manassas	7.7 ac (31,161 m²)	479	3	1,698	Balicki et al. (2006)
C.F. Smith	10 ac (40,470 m²)	349	5	1	Seigel et al. (2006)
Valley Forge	15 ac (60,705 m²)	829	1	140	Balicki et al. (2007)

collectors." Archaeologists who develop relationships with local historians, collectors, and relic hunters are the most successful at locating and investigating military sites.

HOW NOT TO FIND A CAMP

Systematic shovel test surveys as the primary method of locating archaeological sites are the standard procedure for most CRM archaeologists. Excavating small (50 cm or less) pits at standard intervals has gained such acceptance that it is often believed to be the most cost efficient and most effective field method. In reality, this methodology almost guarantees that military sites will not be found (Jones 1999; Buttafuso 2000; Sterling and Slaughter 2000; Espenshade et al. 2002; Corle and Balicki 2006; Jolley, in review).

A comparison between metal detection and shovel testing methodologies clearly illustrates the deficiency and irrelevance of a field strategy relying solely on shovel testing (table 6.1). None of these sites would have been recognized had the field methods relied only on shovel testing.

In table 6.1, Fort C.F. Smith is atypical and this reflects both the nature of the site and the metal detection methodology. The site was a maintained landscape. The soldiers policed the camp as part of their garrison duties so artifacts were not distributed evenly across the site because trash and refuse were deposited in two dumps on a steep hillside. The refuse dumps account for all the positive shovel tests containing Civil War material. Metal detection was used in an effort to locate the support buildings of the fort, but not on the dumps themselves. To sample and evaluate the dumps, 11, 1 m² test units were dug and, on average, artifact density was 179 artifacts/m² in one dump and 701 artifacts/m² in the other; such artifact densities are more than high enough to be found by shovel testing.

Negative results based solely on shovel testing bias interpretations. For example, a systematic shovel test survey was conducted on the yard adjacent to the Blenheim House, an antebellum residence near Fairfax Courthouse, Virginia. Gardner et al. (1999:34) concluded that much of the backyard was disturbed and that it was unlikely that additional archaeological work would produce significant results. Their investigation in the front yard identified intact deposits but these were interpreted as having little research potential. Gardner et al. (1999:33) indicated that "Although the use of a metal detector was initially planned for the property to attempt to recover Civil War materials, this was not conducted because of the extent of the disturbance in the yard area. In addition, large numbers of relic collector's holes were noted which would also preclude effective metal detector results." During a subsequent metal detector investigation, however, Balicki (2006b) identified a spring 1863 cavalry camp in the front yard as well as the location where the guard stood next to the back door. It is noteworthy to point out that if relic hunters were actively risking searching the site, then in all likelihood there were still objects to be found; in this case 522 Civil War artifacts.

Background Research

Detailed descriptions of camp life and battles aid interpreting the archaeological record. This is especially true for the writings of recent recruits as well as writings from the early years of the war when military experiences were new and novel. Early in the war, camp descriptions were in-depth, but as the war progressed, these descriptions often were less detailed. Writings from after the war often contain inconsistencies and contradictions based on incomplete memories or personal agendas. In many cases, these inaccuracies can only be addressed through archaeology. The Official Records (O.R.) of the War of the Rebellion (O.R. 1997; O.R.N. 1999) and The Official Records Supplement (Hewett 1994) are starting reference points. From these references, names, locations, and units can be obtained. A more thorough search of records can then be initiated through letters, newspaper accounts, regimental histories, and personal papers.

At the Confederate cantonment at Evansport, historic documents assisted in interpreting camp occupation and features among camps. Rows of depressions denoting company streets of the 35th Georgia Regiment camp were found (Balicki 2006a). These depressions were consistently smaller than corresponding features from three other nearby regimental camps. A letter from the commander of the 35th indicated that his regiment continued to live in tents throughout the winter. The soldiers of the 35th attempted to gain more shelter by digging shallow depressions beneath their tents. The nearby winter quarters of the 22nd North Carolina contained evidence for well-constructed domiciles. Period newspaper accounts of this camp describe the Christmas decorations of the camp and uniquely constructed fireplaces. Some hearths were excavated archaeologically and found to match historic accounts. The features, coupled with records, allowed examination of how living conditions affected the health of the troops; disease killed 145 men in the 35th, but for the better-housed 22nd only several dozen died (Irvine 1891; Wilson 2002:155).

Informant Interviews

Professional scholars and amateurs alike have written on topics ranging from sweeping overviews of the war and battles (Foote 1974; Bearss 2006) to specific minutiae such as the sex lives of the soldiers (Lowry 1994) or the humble shelter tent (Gaede 2001). A large body of information on the war and its locations exists in the form of notes, memories, and recollections of people who do not have the means or do not see the relevance of synthesizing their material for others.

Local historical societies and Civil War Roundtables are organizations where contacts can be developed. During a survey of Civil War sites in Fairfax County, Virginia, members from the Bull Run Civil War Roundtable donated their time, taking researchers to locations they had identified in over twenty years of personal research (Balicki et al. 2002a). It would not have been otherwise possible to replicate the depth of research provided by the Roundtable within the confines of the survey.

Collecting Civil War artifacts as souvenirs and remembrances is nothing new, beginning almost with the first shots at Fort Sumter. The scavenging of Civil War sites and the removal of objects is a cultural process that affects artifact deposition (Legg and Smith 2007). During the war, individuals picked up items for reuse and as "relics" and governments paid salvers to recover material from battlefields (Silvia and O'Donnell 1996; Toomey 2004:68). After the war, many people survived by collecting and recycling objects from battlefields and camps, and within the last 50 years relic hunting as a pastime and hobby became popular (Silvia and O'Donnell 1996).

Sylvia and O'Donnell (1996) have chronicled the history of relic hunting in the United States. In most cases collecting Civil War artifacts, or for that matter any object, is not illegal. While archaeologists can never reconcile taking objects from archaeological sites, they need to understand that many other individuals enjoy this activity as a hobby and as a way to commemorate the past. The ever-increasing price of Civil War artifacts and an active artifact market also is a consideration. Most relic hunters know more about Civil War history and the investigation of Civil War camps than the majority of archaeologists. Although secretive and generally distrustful of archaeologists, relic hunters donate large amounts of their time to archeological projects (Reeves, chap. 8; Reeves 2001; Balicki et al. 2002b; Beasley 2005). It is unlikely that these projects would have been so successful if not for the time and knowledge donated by relic hunters. Breaking through the layers of distrust and cultural bias can be difficult but worth the effort.

Metal Detection

Mainstream archaeologists have been slow in adopting metal detectors as an essential tool for the examination of historic sites. Metal detection, however, is a complimentary method of information collection applicable to most historic sites (Conner and Scott 1998). Conner and Scott (1998:83) suggest that metal detectors are "easy to learn to use and operate, although using experienced hobbyists is usually preferable. . . ." It is likely that metal detection on the open grasslands of the West is an easy skill to acquire, but under the drastically different site conditions on Civil War military sites, effective metal detection is far from easy. It takes years of experience under varying conditions to become proficient with metal detection. Few professional archeologists are skilled in metal detection and fewer still acknowledge that metal detection results depend on more than just knowing how to use an on/off switch. Archaeological investigations where metal detection has been successful tend to rely on relic hunters for assistance (Scott and Fox 1987:21;

Buttafuso 2000:15; Geier and Potter 2000; Sterling and Slaughter 2000; Reeves 2001; Espenshade et al. 2002; Geier et al. 2006; Reeves, chap. 8).

Metal detectors work by emitting a magnetic field as described in Hanna (see chap. 2). Several factors, including soil composition moisture, temperature, and humidity, ground cover, and number of metallic objects in the soil alter instrument effectiveness. In an effort to improve instrument performance, metal detector manufacturers often add adjustments that will aid in reducing the background noise caused by soil mineralization and modern metallic trash (Silvia et al. 2006:45). Discrimination comes with a price; in addition to selecting against an artifact class, discrimination reduces the sensitivity and depth at which objects register. Thus, the type of instrument and the settings to use need to be adjusted to site conditions and the recovery strategy, and these factors should be recorded, just as one would explain the diameter and interval of shovel tests, in the report of the investigations.

The nature of the ground cover should be considered when undertaking a metal detector survey. Thick grass, overgrown lawns, crops, leaf litter, a thick modern A horizon, pasture, or a thick understory are enough to reduce the effectiveness of metal detection by increasing the distance of the instrument from potential targets. Simply mowing the grass or raking the leaves can greatly increase metal detector performance. Late fall to early spring is the best time to conduct a metal detector survey because of less vegetation.

During his investigations on the 3rd Battle of Winchester, Virginia, Robert L. Jolley undertook detailed recording of a variety of attributes to evaluate and quantify metal detectorists and metal detection results (Jolley, in review). He states:

Fifteen different metal detectorists participated in the survey and twelve different detectors were used. Information on the metal detectorists (years of experience and frequency of metal detecting), the detector(s) they used and the time spent metal detecting was recorded. The three key variables to successful metal detecting proved to be: 1) number of years experience, 2) frequency of detecting, and 3) the type of metal detector. Metal detectorists with over 30 years experience who frequently detected recovered the greatest number of artifacts. These were also the detectorists with the state-of-the-art metal detectors. The three top ranked detectorists expended 32% of the total man hours metal detecting but recovered 68% of the artifacts. They were also more successful in recovering percussion caps (90%), a small artifact difficult to detect and recover. The results of the survey would have been far different without their involvement.

Among historic archaeologists, those investigating battlefields have employed metal detection most extensively (Scott and Fox 1987:21; Scott et al. 1989; Geier and Potter 2000; Sterling and Slaughter 2000; Reeves 2001; Espenshade et al. 2002:43; Beasley 2005; Geier et al. 2006; Jolley, in review; Reeves, chap. 8). Investigations at Antietam National Battlefield used a variety of metal detection procedures, which resulted in a successful investigation (Sterling and Slaughter 2000:305–22). In general, Sterling and Slaughter (2000) affirmed the ineffectiveness of shovel testing, developed a collection sampling strategy, and made observations on metal detection. An effort at setting instruments to discriminate against "junk" signals was viewed as unpromising. When operators are allowed to choose which targets to investigate, "experienced operators will miss a significant portion of military artifacts if operator discrimination is allowed" (Sterling and Slaughter 2000:318). Only one type of metal detector was reported to be in use during this survey (Sterling and Slaughter 2000:311).

Metal detector survey methodologies vary between non-systematic surveys to metal detection along standardized transects (see Reeves, chap. 8). Whether all targets are investigated or a sampling strategy is employed is a variable dependent on the research design, site, and monetary concerns. No one method is better than another under all conditions. The experience of the metal detectorists, quality of the instruments, and the amount of time devoted to actual metal detection are the most important factors. In some cases, such as a project area to be developed, it is essential to maximize coverage in order to find archaeological evidence. In this case, an unsystematic survey focusing on discriminating metal detection targets may provide the quickest method of site identification. However when a site will be preserved, it may be more prudent to sample the site along transects. Regardless of the method the detectorist uses to sweep a site, it is

fundamental that sweeps be made by several detectorists utilizing different types of metal detectors.

Mechanical Stripping

Removing vegetation and modern stratigraphy overlaying camp deposits through controlled mechanical stripping has been proposed as an efficient and effective field method (Legg and Smith 1989; Jones 1999; Espenshade et al. 2002). Prior to mechanical removal of deposits, it is imperative that the investigators understand the stratigraphic sequence of the site, its depositional history, and the distribution of artifacts. Faced with limited funding and time constraints, mechanical stripping may be the most reasonable excavation strategy to investigate a camp. If it is employed carefully and judicially, mechanical stripping greatly increases the effectiveness of a metal detector survey and the chance of finding features. Several investigations have employed the stripping of large areas to assist in identifying Civil War sites (Legg and Smith 1989; Bentz and Kim 1993; Espenshade et al. 2002; Balicki et al. 2005).

An example of this approach is the investigations at 44AX195, Alexandria, Virginia, (Balicki et al. 2005). Initial CRM investigations included shovel testing and metal detection. The fieldwork resulted in the recovery of one round ball from a shovel test, 21 Civil War artifacts from metal detection, and an observation that a remnant buried ground surface was present beneath a modern yard surface. The metal detector survey also found that the roofs of the residences had been replaced several times, refuse disposal and incineration had taken place in the rear yards, and the project area was being used as a modern dump. Further, the rear yards were overgrown. Based on an assessment of the stratigraphic sequence of the project area, artifact deposition history, and vegetation, investigators recommended additional investigations that included mechanical stripping, metal detection, and examination of the exposed surfaces for camp-related features.

Two stages of mechanical stripping were undertaken using a backhoe equipped with a flat-bucket. The first stripping removed only the thick overgrown vegetation and modern A horizon, the top 0.2–0.3 ft of soil but greatly increased the effective depth of the metal detectors. Further removal of most modern refuse reduced time expended investigating modern signals. Once the stripped area was metal detected, artifacts mapped, and the surface cleaned and examined for features, the area was stripped again to the subsoil interface, and the exposed surface metal detected and examined. This strategy resulted in the identification of a scatter of Civil War artifacts, seven Civil War hearths, and a brick feature (Crimean Oven) associated with heating a hospital tent.

CAMP MAINTENANCE AS A DEPOSITIONAL PROCESS

The strengthening of Federal military authority and its imposition on the troops is reflected in the way troops maintained their local environment. As this authority grew and was imposed upon the troops, it was expected that camps would be more orderly and well maintained. Civil War camps are often highly-maintained landscapes so the manner in which artifacts are deposited on this landscape must be considered. Policing is a site depositional process that grew in importance as the war progressed and that can be investigated through fieldwork. Research questions that include examination of camp policing can provide insight into health, sanitation, discipline, and emerging military procedures. By 1863, "the importance of police, general and personal, cannot be too highly regarded. The blankets and bedding of the men should be removed from the tents and exposed to the sun and air daily when the weather will permit. Every tent and the grounds in and about and between the camps should be thoroughly policed daily, and all refuse matter or filth of whatever kind be buried at least 3 feet under ground" (O.R. Series 1:20(2):492).

This does not mean all camps were policed. Several factors including period of the war, proximity to officers, and training influence how well a camp was policed. There may also be a difference between Federal and Confederate camps and between the eastern and western war theaters. At the beginning of the war, conditions in the Federal camps near Washington, D.C. were deplorable. United States Sanitary Commission inspections of some camps found them unclean, unhealthful, not well maintained, and

soldiers surrounded by "pestilential influences" (Stillé 1866). Partially through the influence of the Sanitary Commission, conditions in permanent camps changed for the better, as the commission called on the military to comply with stated regulations governing camp maintenance. Further, the 1861 revised regulations dictated that officers maintain order and cleanliness using a fatigue detail or prisoners, if available (United States War Department 1861:85).

Site 44AX195 is an example of a short-duration surface camp dating from the fall of 1861 when the Sanitary Commission and Federal Army were just beginning to address the issue of camp cleanliness (Balicki et al. 2005). By the fall of 1861, the Federal command was exerting control over the volunteer units that constituted the majority of the army. This control included stricter enforcement of regulations for fatigue duty and policing of camps, which not only instituted discipline but also improved the health of the soldiers (Stillé 1866:93–99). At 44AX195, it is likely that the reason few artifacts were found adjacent to the hospital area is that this location was kept free of debris.

Artifact distributions observed at Fort C.F. Smith reflect policing after camp cleanliness and regulations for policing had become established protocols (Balicki 1995, 2000). Fort C.F. Smith, Arlington, Virginia, a permanent installation occupied from 1863–65, and one of 68 forts defending Washington, D.C. also displays patterning indicating that the site was policed more intensely than a camp, like 44AX195, from the beginning of the war. Artifacts were thinly scattered over the location of the former support buildings, which had been built on footers. The majority of artifacts were recovered from refuse dumps located away from the fort and habitation area.

Camp Layout

The 1861 Revised Regulations for the Army of the United States (United States War Department 1861) was the primary set of regulations used by both the Federal and Confederate Armies. These regulations present the official manner in which regimental camps were to be laid out (United States War Department 1861:76–82). Archaeological research has demonstrated that the armies from both sides followed these regulations when laying out and maintaining camps (Balicki et al. 2002a; Balicki et al. 2004; Balicki 2006a; Reeves 2006; Whitehorne 2006).

The degree to which discipline, training, stress from campaigning, orders, topography and other factors created variance in camp layouts and the distribution of different types of artifacts are topics that can be addressed through examination of the archaeological record. The surface camp at 44AX195 was probably laid out according to the regulations, even though the camp was an early war volunteer camp. At other Civil War sites, summer tent camps contain drainage and tent-platform features that assist in determining of camp layout (Jensen 2000a, 2000b). These features were not present at 44AX195. While only a small portion of the regimental camp was investigated, some general observations can be made based on the feature and artifact distributions.

At 44AX195, the camp contained a hospital area, camp kitchens, and possible evidence of company streets. The hospital area is located on the east side of the camp near a historic road and contains the remains of a hospital tent feature. The area around the hospital tent had few artifacts. The kitchen area contains five hearths arranged in a row and an associated artifact scatter, and is located 250 ft west of the hospital tent.

We could not identify the type of occupations between the hospital and kitchen areas. It is clear that some activity occurred in this area, as evidenced by the presence of artifacts. This area may have been camp, cook houses, non-commissioned officers quarters, or retained as open space and functioning as a reception area and transfer point for goods and invalids.

The enlisted men's camp is located 75 ft west of the kitchen area and includes two small hearths. Here the distribution of artifacts suggests organization into company streets. The area between the interpreted enlisted men's camp and the kitchens was relatively free of artifacts. The 1861 regulations for the arrangement of infantry camps include guidelines for the placement of kitchens as well as a map showing camp configuration (United States War Department 1861:76–79). The kitchens were placed "20 paces behind the rear rank of company streets" (United States War Department 1861:76). The use of a soldier's pace to lay out a camp is inherently variable. As a test,

the field team paced off the 75 ft between the cooking hearths and the area interpreted as soldier habitation. The number of paces varied from 19 to 21, so it is reasonable to conclude that the distance is within the range of 20 paces and reflects the regulations.

The artifact scatter denoting the enlisted men's camping area hints of organization, but what this organization signifies is not readily apparent. While the distribution of ammunition types and melted lead could reflect company organization within a regimental camp, this is not certain. The small hearths in this area may be individual fireplaces used mainly for heating tents.

The process soldiers went through to set up their camps can reflect training, the experience of the officers, discipline, tactical situations, orders, and to a degree health and sanitation. Viewing camps in relation to the landscape allows interpretations on choice, orders, and strategy.

Investigations at Evansport, Virginia (now Marine Base Quantico), documented a 193 ac winter cantonment (Balicki 2006a, 2007). Mapping of surface features resulted in the identification of four main clusters of features representing two infantry regimental camps (Camps French, 35th Georgia Infantry and Camp Holmes, 22nd North Carolina Infantry), the winter quarters of troops under the command of Confederate Navy officers (Camp Mallory), and a camp whose designation is unknown. Identified features include depressions, mounds, platforms, and combinations. Based on the distribution of features, adherence to military doctrine varied between camps. This variation reflected the training of army and navy officers (Balicki 2006a). Placement of the camps was interpreted as, in part, reflecting the perceived threats caused by Federal artillery and the desire for concealment from aerial observations (Balicki 2007).

Domicile Features

Tangible evidence for the domiciles of soldiers can be found archaeologically. Several different types of rectangular tents were available for soldiers including wall, A, or wedge, and shelter tents (Jensen 2000b). In September 1862, George G. Benedict related that "the regiment will be supplied on its arrival at Washington, with the little 'shelter tents,' so called—strips of duck, which, laid over some suitable sticks, make a shelter for a couple of men a-piece, lying on the ground, at night or in a storm, and are packed and carried on the shoulders of the men on the march. Of course, if we remain stationary for any length of time, we shall have huts, or at least sheds of brush to cover us" (Ward 2002:21). Archaeological evidence for tents can be postholes, drainage features, platforms, and depressions. The depressions at Camp French probably reflect use of A-tents (Balicki 2006a).

Soldiers wrote about "stockading" their tents. Stockading refers to the construction of a base on which the tent is set. Period photographs show that soldiers trenched around their tents to improve drainage. Evidence for drainage trenches denoting tent locations was found at Fort Pocahontas (Jensen 2000a:106; 2000b).

One of the most distinctive temporary shelters of the war was the conical Sibley (Bell) tent (Nelson 2006:183) with its distinctive teepee shape (Lord 1965:280). A typical Sibley tent could accommodate upwards of 20 men, stood 12 ft high, and had a footprint 16–18 ft in diameter (Lord 1965:280; Nelson 2006:183). In the winter or, apparently, when used in semi-permanent camps, Sibley tents were stockaded by erecting the tent on a prepared "foundation" of earth or wood (Nelson 2006:183). The day after Christmas, the 5th New Hampshire at Camp California, Alexandria, Virginia, ". . . curtailed drilling so the regiment could prepare true winter quarter. The men felled pine trees, cut them in four-foot lengths, and then split the logs. These were placed on end in a trench matching the circular base of each Sibley tent, with an opening for a doorway. Gaps between the logs were filled with mud, and the tent was erected again on top of its new wooden base, creating a much more spacious home. The stove was placed in the middle of the tent, with a chimney made of mud and stone or even barrels" (Price and Travis 2001:59–60).

Evidence for constructing a "wooden base" for a Sibley tent has been found at an 1862–1865 Federal camp at Gloucester Point, Virginia, where mechanical stripping revealed the feature outlines of three stockaded Sibley tents (Higgins et al. 1995). The archeological signature for each Sibley tent was an approximately 18 ft diameter circular trench containing numerous

FIGURE 6.1. Circular feature outlines of Sibley tents. At the top of the photograph, a California Stove pattern crosses the center of the tent feature. Photograph by William and Mary Center for Archaeological Research; courtesy Virginia Department of Transportation.

smaller postmolds (fig. 6.1). Soldiers had dug a narrow trench, set upright wooden posts into the trench, and then backfilled around the posts, compacting the soil to reinforce the base (Higgins et al. 1995:52).

Nelson (2006) and Jensen (2000a) provide in-depth discussions on huts built primarily by Federal troops. Balicki (2006a) provides information on the 1861–62 Confederate winter quarters in northern Virginia. Early in the war in northern Virginia, winter quarters for both armies were constructed more like cabins rather than the unique vernacular huts built by soldiers in following winters. The variety afforded by the vernacular designs coupled with availability of materials, provides ample fodder for archaeological comparisons. Often soldiers used their tents as roofs for their huts. Hut size should reflect which type of tent was used. At Evansport, "the size and square footage of the hut footprints varied. Platforms tended to range around twelve feet by twelve feet or 144 square feet, while features with mounds ranged from fourteen by fourteen feet or 196 square feet to as big as sixteen by sixteen feet or 256 square feet" (Balicki 2006a).

The foundation of a hut may have been made from logs, stone, or bare earth. "Where timber is scarce and the ground dry the boys dig down and settle the floor below the surface, leaving the walls partially a solid bank of earth, and the rest is made up of logs and mud. A fire-place is easily excavated in this bank of peculiar soil, and there is no need of brick or mortar to make it firm and solid" (Fisk 1992:57). Hut floors received a variety of treatments including compacted earth, wooden planks, brick, and slate.

Like hut design, chimneys and hearths within huts vary (fig. 6.2). Civil War period accounts, photographs, and drawings show chimneys could be located on the ends or along one side of the hut, and that a particular location was not prescribed but varied from camp to camp, and even between adjacent huts. Chimney design incorporated building materials like scavenged brick, stone, logs, the use of empty boxes and barrels, and wattle and daub contrivances. Reeves (2006), Balicki (2006), and Nelson (2006) include discussions on hut fireplace and chimney configuration.

A unique chimney/hearth configuration in many huts, and often written about by the soldiers, is the "California" stove, oven, or furnace. The terms "California" stove, oven, or furnace are colloquial terms for a variety of heating devices and fireplaces and does not refer to a specific configuration. All California stove designs included a buried air passage or passages that drew air to the fire or vented smoke to a chimney.

In October 1861, Elisha Hunt Rhodes wrote: "We have finished our so-called California oven to warm our tent. It is a large hole in the centre [*sic*] of the tent covered over with stone with one canal, or passage, to

FIGURE 6.2. Chimney architecture. Note individuals on left admiring a California stove (Leslie 1896:508).

carry off the smoke and another to let in a draft of air. The passageways are under ground, and we left off the top stone of the oven to put in wood. It works well and keeps us very warm" (Rhodes 1985:36). The winterized Sibley tents at Gloucester Point were heated by a variant of the California stove (Higgins et al. 1995) that conforms to the pattern described by Rhodes.

Another variant of the California stove was investigated in the winter quarters of the 22nd North Carolina Infantry at Evansport (Balicki et al. 2004). Here shelter construction included digging into the hillside, necessitating the use of only one air channel rather than two. A newspaper correspondent wrote "Our camp is upon the side of a hill; the men remove the dirt from the upper side of their tents, making the floor level. This gives from two to three feet of dirt wall on the upper side of the tent; in this they cut out a fire-place, and for a chimney cut and cover a trench some six to ten feet to the rear, capping it with a flour barrel, or a few stones set upright, or a little pen of daubed sticks. It is astonishing how well these chimneys draw the smoke, and how small a fire it requires to keep the tent perfectly warm" (Jarrell 2004:17). The archaeological signature of one domicile consisted of a very indistinct depression with an associated pile of rocks on its upslope side. Excavations exposed a stone firebox, a stone and sheet-metal lined vent, and chimney base. The indistinctness of the depression and the shallow depth of the deposits indicate that the occupants did not dig-in and, as the newspaper account relates, lived in a tent. The fieldstone firebox is approximately 2 ft wide and 1.5 ft deep and its interior height is about 1 ft, the entirety built in a shallow hole. The interior of the firebox contained ash and charcoal, and the subsoil was thermally altered within the firebox. Whether the firebox was located within the domicile or the hearth front was set flush against the exterior side of the wall is unclear. Extending 3 ft from the back of the firebox is a 1 ft wide stone and sheet-iron vent that connects to the remains of a 2 ft wide chimney. The vent is about 1 ft deep.

At permanent installations the types of features found will reflect a more traditional architectural construction. Investigations at Fort C.F. Smith and Fort Nelson show that at these locations the Army constructed permanent buildings with foundations or erected temporary buildings that were periodically moved (Balicki 1995; McBride and McBride 2006). The archaeological signatures of these buildings are similar to civilian buildings and include post holes, foundations, and ground sills.

Hospital Feature (Crimean Oven)

A Crimean oven, also referred to as a California furnace or a California plan, is a Z-shaped radiant heating system used to heat tents. The radiant system was simple: a heating source was located on one side of the tent, the Z-shaped flue for the heating source was buried just below ground level, and a tent was placed over it. As the hot air flowed through the flue, the adjacent ground was heated, warming the tent. In the historic documentation, this type of heating device appears to have been adopted primarily by the hospital corps. This heating device differs from the California stoves used by the soldiers in scale and in the consistent placement of the tent over the flue for radiant heat.

In 1864, future poet Walt Whitman visited a hospital in Culpepper, Virginia, and described the use of the oven. "They heat them [the hospital tents] there by digging a long trough in the ground under them, covering it with old railroad iron and earth, and then building a fire at one end and letting it draw through and go out at the other, as both ends are open. This heats the ground through the middle of the hospital quite hot" (McElroy 1999:85).

The remains of two Crimean ovens have been discovered at sites (44AX193 and 44AX195) in Alexandria, Virginia (Jirikowic et al. 2004; Balicki et al. 2005). Whitehorne et al. (2000:160–61) found a similar but smaller feature while excavating an 1864 field hospital in Winchester, Virginia. Army correspondence indicates that the Alexandria Crimean ovens were built in November 1861 as prototypes for the army (Jirikowic et al. 2004; Balicki et al. 2005). In the fall of 1861, Charles S. Tripler, Surgeon and Medical Director, Army of the Potomac, reported: "For warming the tents and drying the ground a modification of the Crimean Oven, which has been devised and put in operation by Dr. McRuer, the surgeon of General Sedgwick's brigade, appears to me to be the cheapest and most effective. Dr. McRuer has submitted to me a report on this subject" (O.R. Series 1:5:664–65).

FIGURE 6.3. Chimney base (on left) and flue of a Crimean oven. Photograph by author.

The Crimean oven at 44AX195 was disturbed and only a section of the flue about 29 ft long and the base of the chimney survived (fig. 6.3). Its construction included a builder's trench in which a brick flue lined with sheet tin was set. The flue is about 1.5 ft wide to its exterior side. The interior sheet-metal lined chamber is about 0.8 ft wide and ends at a 2 X 2.5 ft brick chimney base. Since the heat signature was present at the base of the chimney, about 50–60 feet from the firebox, the heat source produced a high heat and the draft of the flue in the Crimean oven was well maintained.

The second oven, located about 600 ft north of 44AX195, consisted of a 50 ft long brick and sheet-tin flue attached to a 4 X 11 ft brick box (Jirikowic et al. 2004:56). The box held the heating source and, presumably, fuel. The feature followed the north-south slope of the hillside on which it was situated, with the heat source on its downslope side. The chimney end of the feature was disturbed.

Although both features were disturbed, a comparison of both the Crimean oven remnants and Tripler's

report allows an understanding of how Crimean ovens are configured. Both ovens are placed on gently sloping terrain, with chimneys upslope. This aided the creation and maintenance of a draw within the flue. Using the natural lay of land eliminated the need to bury the heating source deeply underground to lower it below the chimney. If there was not a slope between the heating source and the chimney, hot air probably would have had to be forced through the flue. At 44AX193, the heating source was located within a 4 X 11 ft brick structure. The half of the structure that contained the flue entrance also contained some type of heating device (presumably a stove), and the other half was used for storage and drainage (Jirikowic et al. 2004:56).

Crimean ovens have z-shaped flues, but the wings off the body of the flue are curved and not acute angles. Jirikowic et al. (2004:62) suggest that the curve functioned to prevent the feature from collecting water. This does not appear to be practical, since the curves were laid parallel to the slope and would have provided a larger exposure of the flue to water runoff than a straight run of flue. Based on Tripler's account, the curves acted to regulate the movement of air and heat through the feature. The curves in the design are also related to camp layout or to the tents that were used. The curve in the ovens placed the chimney and the heat source away from the entrances of the tent or adjacent tents minimizing the amount of smoke and cinders blowing into the tents.

It is unknown which type of tent would have been placed over the Crimean oven. The regulation- issue wall tent had a 14 X 14.5 ft rectangular footprint (Jensen 2000a:52–56). The 1862 Revised Regulations for the Army of the United States state that tents must be constructed in a fashion to allow two or more tents to be "joined and thrown into one with a continuous covering or roof" (United States War Department 1861:290–91). If standard-issue hospital tents were placed over the Crimean ovens then up to four may have been joined to form one large connected space as Tripler suggested. Since each hospital tent could accommodate eight people, it is possible that 32 soldiers may have been sheltered over the Crimean oven.

Ammunition Impact Areas

While troops were trained at or in close proximity to camps, tangible evidence of this training is not easily identified. An exception is impact areas and possible firing lines associated with target practice. However, it is not clear how prevalent live fire training was. There are more accounts of the absence of weapons training than actual accounts of target practice. In camp, troops also discharged their weapons when they returned from picket duty and armed patrol, presumably at a designated location. Therefore, when interpreting a cluster of fired ammunition, care should be given to considering both activities.

Target practice, like many other mundane activities (camp policing and fatigue duties) was not recorded in detail by army chroniclers. However, examination of camp activities such as target practice allows for insight into the experiences of the combatants, participation in militaristic institutions, and training. In the overall study of conflict, an understanding of these topics allows for meaningful interpretations of the experiences and reactions of the participants when under fire.

The Official Records of the Union and Confederate Armies (O.R. 1997) contains few detailed entries on infantry target practice. In 1862, one entry from the Headquarters, Department of the Pacific discusses target distances. Col. James H. Carleton ordered Maj. D. Fergusson to "Have your men drill at target practice with the carbine, commencing at seventy yards and progressing upward ten yards per day to 150 yards, three shots each distance" (O.R. Series 1:50(1):949). In 1864, Col. George Bowie, Commanding the District of Arizona, wrote, "Have careful and systematic target practice to the extent of twenty rounds per man with musket and carbine and eighteen rounds with revolver, and have careful drills at skirmishing at least two hours a day for all troops on the river" (O.R. Series 1:50(2):820). Based on these entries and other scant mentions of target practice and infantry training in the O.R., it is clear that target practice was a part of the activities soldiers undertook while at camp.

Unlike most Civil War campsites, where the majority of ammunition is dropped, extracted from weapons, or altered (carved or melted) by the soldiers themselves, the majority of Civil War ammunition from one site in Alexandria, Virginia (44AX198), was fired (Balicki et al. 2007). From 44AX198 (located 1 mi northwest of 44FX195), only two of the Minié balls show evidence of extraction from weapons and the absence of large numbers of dropped, altered, or extracted ammunition as well as other typical artifacts indicates that this location was not a camp. Investigations sampled an approximately 40 X 50 ft concentration of fired ammunition and recovered 72 pieces of fired ammunition (Balicki et al. 2007). Also, numerous fired projectiles were found away from the concentration, and reflect ricochets or extremely poor aiming. Historic research clearly shows that this location was not the scene of a battle. The only possible explanation for the amount of fired ammunition is that this location was used as an impact area for target practice or a location designated to discharge loaded weapons upon return to camp. In contrast, investigations at Site 44AX195 found 231 pieces of ammunition and all but two were intentionally discarded (Balicki et al. 2005).

Target ranges and firing ranges/impact areas have not been extensively investigated. The only other known Civil War era target range is from the 1861–62 camp of the 35th Georgia Infantry stationed at

Evansport, Virginia (Balicki et al. 2002a). However, at that site investigations were restricted merely to identification of the resource. Other target ranges investigated archaeologically include a Revolutionary War target range at Valley Forge, Pennsylvania (Catts et al. 2006) and one at Fort Fred Steele, Wyoming, dating to 1868–86 (Hanson 2005:45–58).

Hanson (2005:49) characterizes firing ranges as locations that (1) possess one or more firing positions, represented by cartridge cases and (2) possess one or more target positions, represented by fired bullets or target architecture. This probably also holds true for locations where weapons were discharged after patrol or picket duty. In the case of a Civil War-era target range, the firing position would not be marked by cartridges, but by a combination of dropped or unfired Minié balls, round balls, other types of ammunition, percussion caps, and possibly cartridges. Fired ammunition will be found perpendicular and downrange from the firing line with the target position as the focal point of an elliptical distribution representing the distribution of undershots, overshots, shots through the target, and direct target hits (Hanson 2005:49). Target ranges share some characteristics with battlefield artifact distributions, such as the use of small arms, the establishment of firing and target positions, and order (the military formation: individual, platoon, company, battalion, brigade, etc.) that created the artifact signature (Hanson 2005:48). The cluster of fired ammunition recovered from 44AX198 matches the distribution of artifacts suggested by Hanson (2005) as characterizing a target range impact area.

Surface Fireplaces

Regardless of camp type, there exists the possibility for a wide range of hearth features. Often these features have been dug into in the past. Investigations where surface fireplaces were studied include Balicki et al. (2005) and Bentz and Kim (1993). Three types of surface fireplaces were encountered at 44AX195. Two small fires built in shallow pits were found in the area occupied by the soldiers, and were used for heating or for cooking methods that required direct heat. One of the small features was a firepit 2 ft in diameter and 0.4 ft deep that was filled with sandstone cobbles and surrounded by 0.5 ft halo of thermally altered soil. The sandstone cobbles were

not burned. Rather, it appears that after the hearth was used, the cobbles were placed in the hearth. It is likely that this activity reflects policing.

The kitchen area at 44AX195 has a row of five hearths, representing two fireplace types. Although simply constructed, these hearths were complex cooking areas containing sub-areas where specific types of cooking occurred. Evidence for diversified cooking techniques is an indication that the soldiers had variety, at least in terms of preparation, in their meals. The soldiers may have used boiling, broiling, frying, baking, and roasting techniques (Balicki et al. 2005).

All five hearths had fires contained in shallow depressions but one type had three divisions and the other type had two. One kitchen fireplace configuration (Features 6 and 7) was approximately 3 × 7 ft and consists of a shallow linear depression interpreted as a location where coals were raked and gathered for cooking. On one end was a shallow pit where wood was burned. On the other end of the linear depression was a concentration of charcoal. The use of a combination of direct fire and coals allowed for diversified cooking methods. On one side, the fire would have been kept burning and used where a high heat was required, such as boiling, broiling, and frying. For other types of cooking, such as baking and roasting, coals were raked from the fire into the depression and opposite end of the fireplace. Fragments of a cast iron skillet and spider-pan, commonly used for cooking over coals, were found in these fireplaces.

Early in the war, the Federal government printed a pamphlet on cooking aimed at assisting new troops who were not used to preparing their own meals. In *Camp Fires and Camp Cooking; or Culinary Hints for the Soldier* (Sanderson 1862) soldiers were instructed on preparing a fire. "The usual and most simple mode is to dig a trench 18 inches wide, 12 inches deep, and from four to six feet long. At the each end plant a forked stick of equal height, with a stout sapling, from which to suspend the kettles, extending from one to the other" (Sanderson 1862:3 and Plate 1). This description is similar to Features 6 and 7.

The second kitchen fireplace type (Features 3, 4, and 9) consists of a shallow depression containing a fire pit on the south side, and an adjacent shallow depression on north side, containing a concentration of charcoal. The fire pit was used for direct fuel burning and cooking, and the concentration of charcoal used for other cooking activities. The different functions of the divisions within these three hearths can be inferred from examination of the thermal signatures left in the subsoil. The two separate divisions within the depressions are not evidence for sequential burning episodes because the thermal alteration of the soil surrounding the pits is different from the charcoal areas. Within each feature the pits are surrounded by a halo of thermally altered soil, but the thermally altered soil halos associated with the charcoal depressions were less pronounced. This suggests separate internal sub-areas where different cooking techniques were employed.

Material Culture

The material culture from campsites provides information on military units, armament, chronology, provisioning, decision-making, ethnicity, foodways, personal choice, and a host of other topics relevant to archeologists. For the most part historians, relic hunters, and amateur historians have conducted exhaustive research on the military objects, from buttons to bullets, used during the war (Albert 1976; Thomas 1981, 1997, 2002, 2003; McGuinn and Brazelon 1988; Katcher 1989; Coates and Thomas 1990; McKee and Mason 1995; O'Donnell and Campbell 1996; Tice 1997; Johnson 1998; Jones 2001; Campbell and O'Donnell 2004). Archaeologists should utilize this body of work to identify material culture found on camps. In general, few studies have addressed non-military artifacts recovered from camps and comparative material is limited (Balicki 2000). While kitchen ceramics, container glass, and faunal remains are common recoveries, analytical and comparative analyses of these materials have not been extensive. Balicki (2000) presents a preliminary comparison of material culture between field camps and permanent installations based on ceramics, glass, camp type, and access to urban centers. Much work remains to be done. Future studies have the potential for examination of ethnic food choice, regional food choice, procurement, foraging, origins of supply, and the supplementing of army supplied rations.

The following discussion is only one example of the types of information artifacts carry and is restricted to ammunition. Examination of ammunition provides insight into troop identity, camp maintenance, leisure activity, and adherence to regulations. It is likely that melted lead, modified ammunition, and extracted ammunition, when found together, is the clearest archaeological signature of a Civil War military camp. Within a camp, dropped and discarded unfired ammunition is common. While in camp, a popular pastime for the troops was modifying lead by carving it into shapes for art pieces, gaming pieces, or just whittling to pass the time. In camp, weapons were kept unloaded. Patrols and picket guards needed to unload by extraction or firing their weapons upon return to camp. Extracted ammunition was rendered useless once removed from the weapon and the process left distinctive marks on the lead (fig. 6.4). A gun tool alternatively known as a ball-screw, wiper, worm, or ball-puller was used and each left a distinctive mark (Crouch 1841:98; United States War Department 1863; Coates and Thomas 1990:69). Lead ammunition was also melted intentionally or coincidentally when trash was burned.

More than any other object, melted lead is closest to being a signature artifact for a Civil War camp. The majority of this lead is not, as commonly interpreted, from the manufacture of ammunition. Although the making of bullets sometimes occurred, the majority of melted lead was the result of discard or the melting

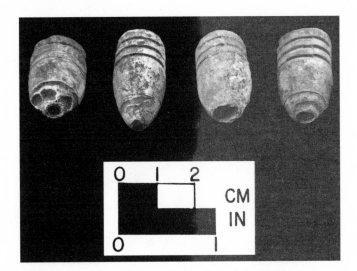

FIGURE 6.4. Extracted ammunition. From left, .58 Williams cleaner (type III) extracted using a combination bull-puller/wiper tool; .577/.58-caliber Minié ball extracted using a wiper tool; .577/.58-caliber Minié ball extracted using a ball puller; and .577/.58-caliber Minié ball extracted using a combination bull-puller/wiper tool. Photograph courtesy John Milner Associates.

of lead ammunition to make objects. Wet cartridges were discarded by soldiers and resulted in lead ammunition scattered across campsites. During policing of camps some of this lead would have been burned and the lead melted. As a result, melted lead is ubiquitous. Additionally, soldiers often entertained themselves by melting lead and making objects. For example, at 44AX195 melted lead conforming to the base of a pot and evidence of troops making fishing weights was found, whereas at Blenheim carved lead gaming pieces were recovered (fig. 6.5).

Dropped ammunition can provide information on whether Federal or Confederate forces were present, what types of weapons were being used, and period of occupation (fig. 6.6). In general, smooth bore rifles using buck and ball ammunition were prominent in the early part of the war but became less common towards the end of the war. Over the course of the war manufacturing techniques for .577/.58-caliber Minié balls changed resulting in slight morphological variations

that may assist in dating occupations (Jolley, in review). Many new types of ammunition were introduced and their identification can help date occupations and the service branch present. For example, Williams Cleaner bullets (there are three varieties issued at different times) are distinctively shaped and designed to remove powder from the bore of a rifle. Williams Type I bullets were issued along with regular ammunition after December 1861, with Type II issued in May 1862 and Type III after December 1863 (Lewis 1960:124–25; Thomas 1997:211–37). Williams-type bullets are common finds because many troops distrusted the bullets and simply discarded them (Smith 1994:71–74).

The types of ammunition found can also narrow the possibilities for the identification of specific troops occupying a site. At Blenheim, the cavalry troops dropped Sharps and Merrill Carbine ammunition (fig. 6.6). The Quarterly Summary Statements of Ordnance and Ordnance Stores in the Hands of Regular Army and Volunteer Artillery Regiments

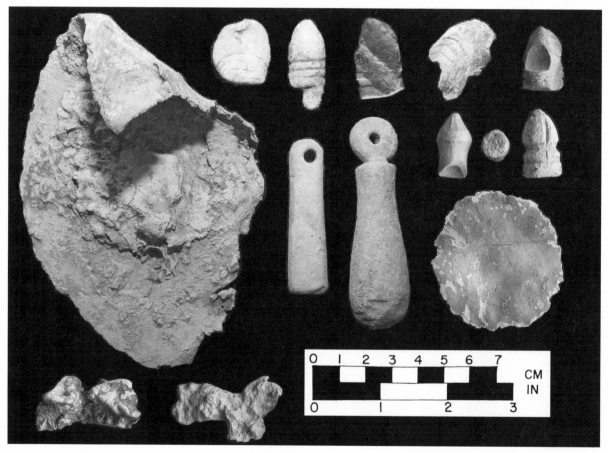

FIGURE 6.5. Melted lead, cast fishing weights, carved game pieces, and modified ammunition from Civil War camps. Photograph by author.

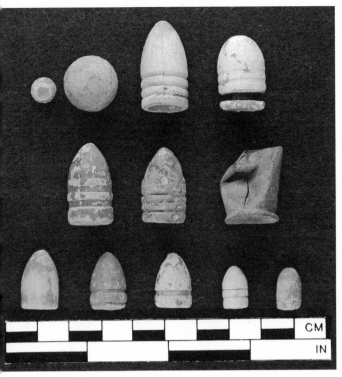

FIGURE 6.6. Sample range of ammunition for Blenheim. From top left: buckshot; .64-caliber round ball; .577/.58-caliber Minié ball; .57 Williams cleaner (type III); .54-caliber Sharps carbine bullet; .54-caliber Merrill carbine bullet; .52-caliber Spencer carbine cartridge; .44-caliber revolver bullet; .44-caliber revolver bullet; .44-caliber revolver bullet; .30-caliber revolver bullet; and .29-caliber revolver bullet. Photograph by author.

(Ordnance Department 1861–1865) assisted in the possible identification of the specific cavalry troops that were present (Balicki 2006b). Based on the graffiti in the house, the cavalry units occupying the camp may have been the 4th New York, 18th Pennsylvania, 1st West Virginia, and/or the 1st Michigan. For cavalry troops stationed at Fairfax Courthouse in 1863 and who left their signatures on Blenheim's walls only the 18th Pennsylvania was issued ammunition for the Merrill carbine. However, the recovery of Sharps carbine ammunition indicates that any of the other four cavalry units may also have camped at this location.

SUMMARY

Civil War campsites are likely to be the most overlooked, least investigated, and most poorly interpreted archaeological sites. As discussed above, application of archaeological methodologies and anthropological theories to the information obtained from these sites can be used to address research questions on adherence to military doctrine, tactical positioning, group identity, ethnicity, foodways, vernacular architecture, differences in Federal and Confederate settlement pattern, settlement pattern differences in western verses eastern war theaters, and material culture. Camps often have detailed historic accounts written by the actual participants, and contain numerous features and artifacts distributions that display distinct patterning that reflect activities of the occupants. Civil War campsites are routinely found, investigated, and their artifacts collected by relic hunters who have no training in archaeological method and theory.

Identifying, evaluating, and investigating Civil War camps requires the use of innovative field methods. Unfortunately, as funding sources decrease and the cost of labor increases, innovation and thinking "outside the box" are disadvantageous qualities within the CRM industry. The continued emphasis on field methods that will not lead to the identification of Civil War campsites and the reluctance to adopt procedures that will continues to hamper efforts to advance our knowledge of these sites. This chapter specifically focused on using examples from CRM studies to illustrate that compliance archaeology can add significant contributions to Civil War encampment archaeology once the practitioners employ realistic methods of information collection that will result in a good faith effort to investigate these site types.

ACKNOWLEDGMENTS

The author thanks John Milner Associates, Inc., Bob Jolley, Mike O'Donnell, Bryan Corle, Charles Cheek, Kerri Holland, Alexandria Archeology, Steven Shephard, Fran Bromberg, the Northern Virginia Relic Hunters Association, the Virginia Department of Transportation, EDAW, William and Mary Center for Archaeological Research, Bull Run Civil War Round Table, the Natural Resources and Environmental Affairs Branch (NREAB) at Marine Corps Base Quantico, and Mary Jane, Arielle, Jenna, and Corinne.

CHAPTER SEVEN

Mapping Early Modern Warfare

The Role of Geophysical Survey and Archaeology
in Interpreting the Buried Fortifications at Petersburg, Virginia

DAVID G. ORR AND JULIA STEELE

INTRODUCTION

Since the early 1970s, the now invisible trench lines and fortifications at Petersburg have been successfully revealed through broad applications of geophysical prospecting followed by selected excavation. Other still extant earthworks have been mapped and explored archaeologically. This chapter builds on these achievements and places the Petersburg campaign within the context of "modern" trench warfare. How "modern" was it? The impact of the rifled musket, for example, in the development of tactics during the Civil War is controversial and needs to be firmly contextualized in the light of new analysis (see Hess 2005, 2008, 2009a, 2009b). For their part, the Petersburg fortifications need to be carefully scrutinized and their locations firmly plotted. As more research is accomplished on the nature of the origins and use of Civil War fortifications, the material evidence of the forts will play an increasingly critical role. The interpretation of these highly significant remnants can proceed in a more holistic manner as the archaeology is physically linked to the present cultural landscape. This chapter will discuss the above issues and make recommendations for future research and management at the battlefield (see Babits, chap. 10 for details of earthwork construction over time).

From 5 May 1864, when Federal troops steamed up the James River and secured landings at City Point and Bermuda Hundred, Virginia, until 3 April 1865 when Lee maneuvered westward toward the eventual surrender at Appomattox Courthouse, the Petersburg region was subjected to bombardment and assault. Union and Confederate troops endured months of

trench warfare that altered between sporadic but deadly assaults and long periods of relative calm. After the war, many fortifications were obliterated by the returning landowners anxious to restore agricultural activities to their shattered landscapes.

BACKGROUND: PETERSBURG, THE GATEWAY TO RICHMOND

At the time of the war, Petersburg was the second largest city in Virginia (Henderson 1998:1). In the first quarter of the eighteenth century it emerged as a shipping point for tobacco and conversely served merchants receiving European goods (fig. 7.1). By the nineteenth century, its location on the fall line of the Appomattox River allowed waterpower to be harnessed, which in turn encouraged tobacco and cotton processing, using the labor of free and slave African Americans. Petersburg also had an important flour milling industry that subsequently became vital to the Confederate war effort. Petersburg also ranked just below Richmond in iron manufacturing, clearly important in military terms (Henderson 1998:8).

Equally significant in terms of the strategic location of the city, were its important links by water, rail, and road to the nearby James River and ultimately to the Chesapeake Bay and the Atlantic, and to the south (Henderson 1998:1–4; Trudeau 1991:4–6). The city was the nexus for five rail lines (fig. 7.1) that tied the coast and the interior to its larger neighbor Richmond, approximately 25 miles to the northwest. One rail line, the Weldon Railroad, connected Petersburg to the important cotton and tobacco producing regions of

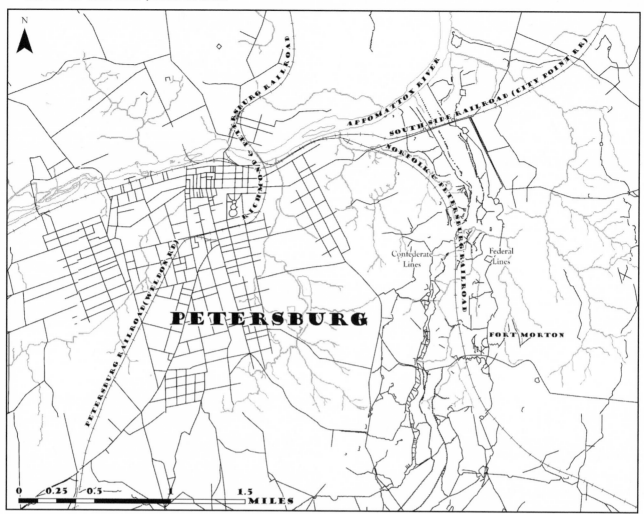

FIGURE 7.1. Petersburg was a vital industrial center and transportation hub where five railroad lines converged. The city was also located 20 miles south of the Confederate capital, Richmond. Courtesy Jonathan Mitchell, Petersburg National Battlefield.

North Carolina. Conversely, the Southside Railroad led to the west and the grain producing areas of the James River valley. Combined with Richmond, the Confederate capital, the two cities became a highly desirable target for the Union. Throughout the four years of the war, the North tried many approaches to gain this prize. From March through August 1862, the Union army under George McClellan tried to fight its way west towards Richmond along the peninsula between the York and James rivers. The Peninsula Campaign failed and military action shifted to other theaters of war. However, both Confederate and Union military planners understood that the James River provided a convenient invasion route into the heart of Virginia, and that Petersburg was a gateway to Richmond. The Confederacy decided to encircle the town with a ring of partially enclosed forts, connected by

trench lines. Over 4000 troops aided by as many as 1000 conscripted slaves from Virginia and North Carolina, took part in the construction. The initial design was done by Lt. Col. Walter Stevens and Col. J. F. Gilmer. Because the project was completed under the supervision of Capt. Charles Dimmock, who was originally assigned to construct obstructions on the Appomattox River, the completed fortifications were known as the Dimmock Line (Henderson 1998: 54–56).

When the Confederates began work, the Army of the Potomac was at Harrison's Landing on the Virginia Peninsula, and some Federal troops actually crossed the river into Prince George County, east of Petersburg. No doubt because of the immediate threat, initial construction of the defenses proceeded rapidly, but once the Army of the Potomac withdrew to northern Virginia, work slowed down. As late as

March 1863, Dimmock was still conscripting slaves and free blacks to work on the line.

The finished line consisted of 55 numbered batteries connected by entrenchments, completely encircling the town south of the Appomattox River. In the spring of 1864, the Confederate Gen. P. G. T. Beauregard inspected the Petersburg defenses. His comments indicated an unfavorable opinion of the work. "Too many gun positions had been designed for barbette gun mounts instead of embrasure mountings which were more protected from enemy rifle fire and shrapnel. Trees and brush should have been cleared for at least 1200 yards in front of the fortifications . . . The general design, a continuous series of trenches with interconnected forts in the rear, required too many men" (quoted in Henderson 1998:105–106). Additionally, the forts were open to the rear, leaving them vulnerable to enemy attacks. Beauregard preferred a system designed for limited manpower—a series of enclosed redoubts within firing range of each other with no intervening trenches (Henderson 1998:106).

There was a significant gap between Battery 24 and Battery 25, just east of the vital Jerusalem Plank Road. Several projecting salients were vulnerable to enemy attack, including the obvious path of any Federal advance from the James River. Too many guns were exposed above the parapets, and insufficient fields of fire were cleared in front of the line. None of the forts were completely enclosed; they were all open to the rear, which meant they were vulnerable to assault. Beauregard, who would be tasked with defending the line in June 1864, thought a better design would be to enclose the forts and provide only minimal entrenchments between them.

By 1864, Lincoln had an aggressive new general in Ulysses S. Grant. Grant came east to take command of the Army of the Potomac and the Army of the James. After the armies had battled inconclusively in northern Virginia during the spring at the Wilderness and Spotsylvania, Grant decided to try to turn the Confederate right flank to the east of Richmond. Advancing to the east assured him of uninterrupted supplies via Union-controlled tidal rivers of Virginia. The Federal drive south was finally checked at Cold Harbor, where Union forces sustained about 13,000 casualties in the first three days of June (Trudeau 1991:16; Kennedy 1998:294). At this point Grant

concluded, "The key to taking Richmond is Petersburg" (Kennedy 1998:352). On 9 June, a small Federal contingent already located at Bermuda Hundred crossed the Appomattox River and probed the Dimmock Line in several locations. The Federal infantry decided the defenses were too strong to assault, unaware that they were lightly manned. Federal cavalry, attacking south of town, was repulsed by Confederate artillery and cavalry in an action known as the "battle of old men and young boys" (Kennedy 1998:352). Meanwhile, north of the James River, Grant brilliantly led the movement of the main Union army away from Richmond toward Petersburg. Lee was momentarily unaware of this shift and remained defending the northern and eastern approaches to Richmond as Grant's forces converged on Petersburg. On 15 June, the vanguard of the Union Army under General William "Baldy" Smith attacked Confederate batteries 5–11 and pushed the Confederates back to Harrison's Creek, capturing more than a mile of the Dimmock Line north and east of the city (Kennedy 1998:353). Smith believed the Confederates had reinforced the line and did not push on, thereby squandering an opportunity for a decisive victory. Over the next few days, newly arrived Federal divisions captured more of the line, but the Confederates were able to reinforce, fall back, and prevent the total collapse of their defenses. Over the next few weeks, other battles and skirmishes were fought as Grant tried to feel out weaknesses in the Petersburg defenses and destroy railroad lines as both sides strengthened their lines. The Union forces squandered another promising opportunity when they failed to capitalize on the breach of the Confederate line made by exploding a mine excavated from Union lines underneath Confederate Elliott's salient. After this disaster, the troops settled in for another eight months of trench warfare (Kennedy 1998:355–56). As historian Earl Hess (2009b:45) states in his recent work on Petersburg: "Petersburg saw the longest period of close contact of any campaign in the Civil War and produced the longest, most sophisticated system of field defense as well."

Hess (2009b:284–85) concludes that in the 292 days of continuous contact at Petersburg, the use of field works enabled Lee to "extend the life of his army by helping it fend off repeated attacks" but that the Federals "gained more from their use of fortifications" as they maneuvered westward, securing their gains with newly extended earthworks.

NATURE OF THE EARTHWORKS

By late summer 1864, the two armies faced each other along a front about 10 miles long, that snaked around the city, from the Appomattox River near Harrison's Creek northeast of town, south to Hatcher's Run and the Boydon Plank Road. The opposing works were generally about a mile apart, but in places, especially in the northern section where the Union forces had overrun the original Dimmock Line, they were only a few hundred meters apart. In the area discussed here, the picket lines of were only 75 m apart in places. From rear to front, the typical trench layout was as follows: reserve camps, rear trenches, forts connected by covered ways front rifle trenches, traverses and bombproofs, small rifle pits for vedettes and inter-line pickets at night, and then a no-man's-land of scarred fields (Trudeau 1991: 288–89).

According to Trudeau (1991:289): "The forts were the pillars of Petersburg's trench system. The Confederates were more sparing with this designation than the Federals, and their lines, though bristling with fortified batteries and salients, boasted comparatively few forts. . . . Federal engineers took advantage of the Petersburg siege to test a wide variety of designs. There were forty-one forts constructed along the inner and outer Union trench lines, with an additional eight protecting City Point."

The covered ways and communication trenches were deeply cut, designed so men could walk upright under cover between positions and between the front and the rear. They were sometimes wide enough that a supply wagon could pass through. On the 9th Corps front "troops dug in securely because they were very close to the enemy . . . The rank and file placed traverses every 20 feet, forming bays with protection on three sides" (Hess 2009b:51).

Bombproofs were found within the fortifications as well as throughout the main trenches. These were enclosed spaces of many dimensions and designs, fortified by timbers and earth, to protect men and munitions from artillery. Forts, batteries, and main trenches were additionally protected by a welter of wooden entanglements in this pre-barbed wire, pre-mechanized

vehicle world. Abatis were dense concentrations of felled trees, oriented so their bushy tops were facing the enemy, presenting an impenetrable thicket of small branches. Fraise were sharpened stakes set side-by-side anchored in the ground and angled upwards towards the enemy. Chevaux-de-frise were even more elaborate portable constructions bristling with sharpened stakes and meant to fend off horses as well as troops. These defensive entanglements had been in use and under development for centuries (see Babits, chap. 10).

Official records exist that describe the living conditions of the troops in this hellish landscape but soldier's letters describe it most graphically: "It was endurance without relief; sleeplessness without exhilaration; inactivity without rest; constant apprehension requiring ceaseless watching. . . . Not the least of the evils encountered was the unavoidable stench from the latrines" (a Confederate officer quoted in Trudeau 1991: 289). Another Confederate veteran recounted "For eight months and more [his regiment] lived in the ground, walked in wet trenches, ate its cold rations in ditches, and slept in dirt-covered pits." The nearly year-long siege took the troops through the extreme temperature changes typical of Virginia. Summer photographs show tents of the soldiers sheltered from the sun under pine branch bowers. Winter photographs exhibit tents insulated with cabin-like log, mud, and sod walls, with brick and barrel chimneys providing warmth. Letters, journals, and newspaper reports describe troops of both sides constructing camps and winter quarters near the lines. In fact, some quarters seem to have been incorporated into the earthworks and fortifications while others were laid out on the classic military model of company streets.

THE ARCHAEOLOGY OF THE SIEGE

The besieged landscape around Petersburg was subject to great devastation and never quite recovered from the war. Partly as a result of this, and also because preservation efforts began soon after the war and culminated in the establishment of Petersburg National Battlefield in the 1920s, many military features discussed above still survive. The landscape was altered as farmers reclaimed their land and continued agricultural pursuits while in other areas trees grew up and obscured fields of fire, modern roads sliced through earlier works, grass grew over once raw earthworks, and wooden cribbing and wicker gabions rotted away, leaving works susceptible to erosion. Farmers also had access to large scrapers that leveled the earth. Despite these processes, the vast scope of Civil War construction and destruction is still visible around Petersburg at the present time. Less visible, but equally dramatic, is the archaeological record of the siege that focused one of the greatest concentration of troops and war materiel ever known on U.S. soil.

Very little archaeological exploration or excavation has been done within Petersburg National Battlefield. The earliest professional work was done to establish the preservation status of the Union mine shaft leading to the Crater explosion. Other early work was geared toward locating two dwellings that were destroyed during the siege, the Hare House and the Taylor House, (see Blades 2001). Modern projects have been designed to avoid impacts on historic resources, so compliance archaeology has mostly confirmed the presence of ordnance throughout most of the battlefield and not uncovered features. Three projects did, however, directly address the archaeology of earthworks.

Fort Morton, a large, eventually D-shaped, fortification containing 14 guns was initially constructed in June and July 1864 (fig. 7.2). This Union fort was placed on high ground opposing Confederate Elliott's salient near the site of the Taylor House, which was destroyed in the June 1864 fighting. The fort was connected to Union secondary defenses by a zigzag communications trench. Fort Morton faced the Confederate sector that was undermined and blown up on 30 July 1864, in what is known as the Battle of the Crater, and its artillery contributed to the massive bombardment that supported the Union attack.

Ironically, the Union stronghold of Fort Morton was not vanquished in the war. Its earthen walls were leveled as the landowner, William Taylor, reconstructed his farm and reclaimed his fields after the war. When the site of Fort Morton came under National Park Service ownership in 1936, it was a flat, featureless field that exhibited no visible traces of the events of 70 years earlier. The site was shielded from view of the Crater by trees that had grown up in the no man's land between the positions of the two armies.

In 1979, the National Park Service contracted the services of Bruce Bevan, a noted geophysical researcher,

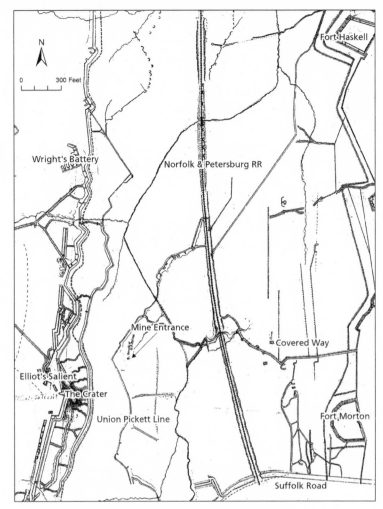

FIGURE 7.2. This map of the Union and Confederate trenches and works in the vicinity of Fort Morton was redrawn from the 1865 Michler map. Today there are no visible surface indications of the existence of Fort Morton. Map by Bruce Bevan.

in an attempt to reestablish the precise locations of the Taylor House and Fort Morton. Bevan first investigated the site of Fort Morton during the fall of 1979. He continued to explore the site throughout the 1980s and early 1990s, using ground-penetrating radar, proton magnetometry, and resistivity to refine his initial results, which indicated that remnants of the large fort still existed beneath the surface. Bevan was able to generate a map of buried features that match almost precisely with war era plans of the fort (fig. 7.3).

This testament to the power of non-destructive remote sensing was verified archaeologically in 1998 and 1999 when archaeologists from the National Park Service, Valley Forge Center for Cultural Resources, assisted by Virginia Military Institute cadets during

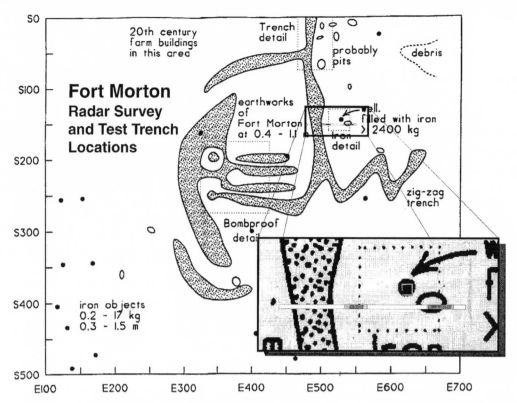

FIGURE 7.3. Geophysical exploration conducted by Bruce Bevan located the distinctive traces of Fort Morton and related Union earthworks and trenches under the present day featureless field. Archaeological testing verified the presence of intact Civil War structures. Maps by Bruce Bevan.

1999, excavated portions of the buried trenches identified by Bevan. Mechanical excavation was first used to open a trench bisecting the probable fort on an east-west axis. The bottom of the main Union trench, running behind the gun emplacements, was easily located in the position predicted by Bevan despite the deceptive surface. Standard excavation units were opened there. Finds in this small portion of the trench included brick, coal, nails, unidentifiable iron, a full panoply of fired and unfired ammunition, redwares and stonewares, and a variety of bottles and other glassware. These artifacts have not yet been analyzed in depth. Additionally, a feature identified by Bevan as a possible well containing a massive ferrous concentration was also partially excavated. A square brick shaft feature was uncovered, stuffed with large quantities of cast iron decorative fencing! It is difficult to explain this feature in terms of the war or its aftermath.

As a result of these studies, the superintendent and staff of Petersburg National Military Park believed that the location of Fort Morton had been reestablished. In order to more clearly interpret trench warfare between the opposing forces and elucidate

the battle of the Crater, the park has delineated the outlines of the fort by a band of crushed oyster shells and the placement of cannon. This sensitive treatment preserves the real material fabric of the past in a way not possible with a reconstruction, yet clarifies the siege and battle terrain for those who want a precise understanding (fig. 7.4).

As bad as conditions may have been within Fort Morton, they were no doubt worse for those on picket duty in front of the main trench lines on either side. In 1978, National Park Service archaeologists undertook an archaeological survey of the Confederate picket line near the Crater. "The excavations were designed to reveal the original profile of the trench behind the earthwork and in the process reveal data which may be utilized to more completely and accurately comprehend the experience of picket line duty. . . ." (Blades 1981:1).

Written records, however, show how dynamic the constructions were. On 24 September 1864, Gen. Bushrod Johnson wrote: "I would respectfully recommend the following improvement in the line of defense now occupied by my command. The connection of the line of rifle pits from the pickets in front of

Wise's Brigade, extending from the river to the right, with the abatis ten paces in front, the line of rifle pits will thus be made continuous. They should be sloped to the rear, so as to be fired into from the main parapet, if ever carried by the enemy, and the earth thrown up in front should be sloped to the natural surface like a glacis" (O.R. Series1:43(2):1287). A later report indicated chevaux-de-frise had also been placed in front of the line (Blades 1981:7).

The location of the Confederate picket line is visible today as an eroded earthwork east of the Crater, with a steep face on the western side of the earthwork and a fairly wide depression and a sloping face on the western side of the trench. It appears to be continuous, rather than a linked series of rifle pits. A 7 X 20 ft test unit was excavated through the trench west of the earthwork (Blades 1981:23–41). The trench was approximately 12 ft wide and the final compacted trench floor was buried 1.0–1.3 ft below modern grade. An earlier compacted floor was located 2 ft below modern grade. The multiple floors and the presence of two building episodes of narrow drainage ditch construction are testimony to the erosion and filling that occur especially when earthworks are new and raw. An excavated firepit, with three distinct levels of coal ash was found near the eastern embankment. Another hearth lay on the trench surface, also near the eastern trench wall. This seems to have been used to melt and recast spent ammunition by evidence of lead grains and lead sprue. A post mold was located between the sunken hearth and the drainage ditch, suggesting the presence of some sort of shelter.

Civil War artifacts were recovered from both levels of the excavation: the occupation level where artifacts were found in situ, and the post-occupation fill layer where artifacts were washed in from their original location on the surrounding earthworks but which are clearly associated with the Confederate occupation (Blades 1981:42–57). Percussion caps made up the largest artifact category found in the occupation strata. A total of 47 complete caps were found (all but four had been fired) and 67 cap fragments. Only nine fired bullets and one unfired bullet were found. The excavators attribute this to Confederate efforts to melt and recast lead due to severe shortages. The hearth mentioned above seems to support this theory. However, it is also clear that the earthworks were performing as designed

FIGURE 7.4. As a result of geophysical and archaeological research, Petersburg National Battlefield is currently able to interpret Fort Morton in its true setting. The outlines of the fort are delineated in oyster shell. Photograph courtesy National Park Service.

to shield troops from fire. It is likely that most fired ordnance would be found on the enemy side of the earthwork, which was not excavated. Other artifacts from this level include iron fragments, a fragment of an iron entrenching tool, a brass bayonet scabbard tip, and brass trigger guard. Only eight personal items were found, fragments of two different pipes, a small porcelain button, and five brass brads that may have been from a boot sole. Although it is not entirely clear, almost all the artifacts attributed to the occupation level were found in features located on the forward side of the trench. It is not surprising that most activities took place in the safest location, although discarded material might be swept to the rear to keep the trench clear.

In 1999, a comparable 7 X 20 ft archaeological excavation was placed through the nearby Union picket line by University of Maryland graduate students (Brown 2000:14). Unlike the Confederate line, the Union trench had been nearly obliterated by post-war filling and plowing. This line is very significant in the history of the Petersburg Campaign because it demarcates the closest position the Federal troops had to their opponents after the initial battle of June 1864. It also was the work from which the 9th Corps launched their attack on the Confederate lines breached by the mine explosion on July 30th (see Cavanaugh and Marshall 1989; Slotkin 2009).

Archaeologists chose the excavation location using maps, slight breaks in the hill slope, and extrapolation from locations where the trench is visible. Researchers were able to find the filled Union trench, identified as Feature 1, just beneath the plow zone and extending to approximately 2.0–2.5 ft below the modern ground surface (fig. 7.5) (Brown 2000:30–35). The trench is approximately 7 ft wide. The southern portion of the trench may contain some in situ trench deposits, identified as Feature 4 and trench floor in the south wall profile (Brown 2000:33), but this needs to be clarified by further excavation. The excavators concluded the trench was filled during one short episode, probably by landowner William Griffith pushing the earthwork parapet into the trench. This fill contained a large number of pebbles and clay, which is very consistent with the underlying subsoil of the area. The material probably came from both the trench excavation and the mine tunnel excavation (Brown 2000:36).

In terms of artifacts, large amounts of leather and canvas were preserved in the trench fill. The leather pieces came from cap boxes, cartridge boxes, and haversacks. The source of the canvas was less clear. It may have come from haversacks, "but could also have been tent halves used as shelters over picket trenches" (Brown 2000:36). It is unclear whether this material was lying on the surface or incorporated in the earthwork parapet later used for fill or if the landowner gathered up detritus from the battlefield after the war and buried it.

Feature 4 underlay Feature 1 near the forward side of the trench and trends towards the Confederate lines. Brown (2000:41) speculated that, "the feature appears to be an early expansion of the picket trench, and may be associated with the Battle of the Crater." It may be related to either a breach in the trench to allow Union troops to scale the wall as the battle began, or a documented attempt to dig a hasty covered way to rescue troops trapped in the Crater after the Federal attack failed. Military artifacts recovered from this feature, which appears to have been filled in one episode, include a canteen half, tin cups, a food tin, stoneware beer bottle, more preserved leather, bullets and percussion caps (Brown 2000:42).

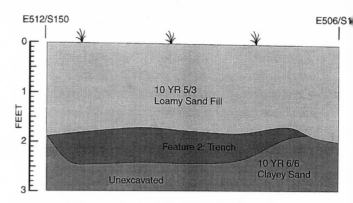

Feature 2: Trench, South Section
Fort Morton
Petersburg National Battlefield, Virginia

Valley Forge Center for Cultural Resources
October 23, 1997

FIGURE 7.5. The lowest levels of the Union trench at Fort Morton were well preserved under about 2 ft of fill. Diagram courtesy National Park Service.

CONCLUSIONS

The small amount of archaeological work done on the earthworks at Petersburg National Battlefield—only 14 linear feet of excavation into the literally miles of trenches and little more than that in one fortified position—is more tantalizing than conclusive. The work at Fort Morton and the Union picket line succeeded in establishing the subsurface presence of lost features and the preservation of intact Civil war deposits. Working in tandem, archaeology and geophysical prospecting enabled the park to more confidently interpret these lost features to the public. It also explains the post-war processes, both natural and cultural, that dramatically transformed the siege landscape. In addition, all three projects had the explicit intent of adding to the understanding of life in the trenches. They succeeded in vividly exposing the tangible reality of mud, dirt, exposure to the elements, and the constant reworking of the positions. Less can be said about other aspects of siege life—supply, amusements, living conditions—because so little of the lines on either side have been sampled, and none of the camps and other support areas to the rear have been explored. Much has been preserved, and there is the promise of much to be learned.

Topics in the Historical Archaeology of Military Sites

CLARENCE R. GEIER, LAWRENCE E. BABITS, DOUGLAS D. SCOTT, AND DAVID G. ORR

As the first set of articles introduced the reader to certain methodologies inherent in the current application of historical archaeology to military sites, the second set of twelve papers introduces the ever-widening topics that serve to define the field. As noted earlier, there is a direct interplay between technique and research question. As new tools have been added to the tool kit of the archaeologist, areas of research that were previously impractical have become more accessible. This can certainly be seen in the application of geophysical techniques to terrestrial archaeology (see Hanna, Orr and Steele, and Balicki, Section I) as well as in the technologies that have revolutionized underwater archaeology (see Conlin and Russell, chap. 4; Broadwater, chap. 15; Cantelas and Babits, chap. 16). As students of military history studied military events, non-traditional questions concerning the lives of the soldiers as individuals, army social and political structure, and the impact of both the military establishment and the individual soldier on indigenous have entered the discussion and become important. Building on and including

the seven papers already presented, the papers that follow introduce the reader to a selection of research topics that define modern military history. These papers also continue to build an understanding of new field methods, techniques, and strategies, because each paper, while addressing a specific topic, also considers the strategies with which it can be addressed.

In each case study, one theme holds true. The quality of the historical data provided by multiple project historians has a direct bearing on the specific questions that can be addressed and the extent to which the available archaeological record can be meaningfully and accurately interpreted. This issue is further developed in Phillip Freeman's discussion of the reliability of the historic record and oral histories in interpreting events associated with the "Charge of the Light Brigade" during the nineteenth century Battle of Balaclava (chap. 13).

The value of the diverse strategies of historical archaeology for analyzing and interpreting troop deployments, tactics, and strategies in the course of specific battles is of ongoing interest. Matthew Reeves illustrates modern approaches to

these issues in his analysis of the Matthews Hill fighting during the Battle of Manassas (chap. 8), while Tony Pollard applies similar approaches to analyses of the Jacobite Rebellion battles of Killikrankie and Culloden in Scotland (chap. 9).

Military earthworks, fortifications, and the manner in which these often extensive and sometimes permanent features establish lines of defense have also been a long term focus of study within the realm of military history. Larry Babits (chap. 10) presents an introduction to the tools needed to identify, describe, and interpret defensive features of military earthworks including the manner in which they exploit natural terrain circumstances. Stephen and Kim McBride (chap. 11) expand on this by providing discussions of the strategies they have developed in identifying and interpreting Colonial era fort sites on the Virginia-West Virginia line, many of which were engaged in the French and Indian War.

Advancing in time and confronting the phenomenal technologies of the early twentieth century, Mathieu de Meyer (chap. 12) introduces readers to the problems and patterns of historical archaeology on the vast World War I battlefields of France, in particular the Ypres Salient in "Flanders Fields." Lines of entrenchments played a key role in defending troops on both sides and de Meyer discusses the problems of preservation in areas where such features appear commonplace. He also discusses the role of period cartography and the use of aerial photographs in interpreting military lines.

While Joe Balicki (chap. 6) raised the important issue of studying the lives of encamped soldiers, Clarence Geier and Kimberly Tinkham (chap. 14) draw the reader's attention to the notion of collateral damage and the impact of a battle on civilian populations and economic systems on landscapes over which battles were fought. The reader is introduced to the ideas of natural and cultural landscapes as features defining the setting in which military actions take place and as features that often shaped occurrence and flow of the action. As devastating as a battle can be to the troops involved, as evidenced by the situation of Fredericksburg, Virginia, the impact on the domestic communities that have the misfortune of being in the way can be just as devastating and can take decades to recover from, if at all. Physical destruction of property, fields churned into cemeteries, civilian deaths from combat and disease, economic depression, depopulation, and the occupation by hostile victors, are only some of the factors that can shape local histories.

The new technologies that are revolutionizing underwater archaeology (see Conlin and Russell (chap. 5) are further developed in chapters 15 and 16. In chapter 5 Conlin and Russell draw attention to the fact that individual shipwrecks are often singular features indicative of a larger naval battlefield. In this context, the nature and condition of a set of contemporary ships is a key to delineating that action much as the physical remains on and in the earth are invaluable in interpreting land actions. John Broadwater (chap. 15) broadens this discussion. He points out that with reference to concepts of cultural and natural landscapes, naval engagements are not isolated events in space or history. Instead, they can only be understood in terms of the far broader cultural-political events of which they are a part and which give them historical context and meaning. In many, if not all, instances, the interpretation of sea battles must be considered in terms of contemporaneous military/cultural actions on land, some of which may be a part of the same action, i.e. naval battles do not necessarily end at the shoreline. After a discussion of the modern field of maritime archaeology and methods applied in the conduct of underwater research, Broadwater provides the 1781 Battle of Yorktown as a case study, to illustrate his thesis.

In chapter 16, Cantelas and Babits addresses the considerable value that excavating well-preserved shipwreck sites can have for interpreting the material culture of a particular time period. As virtual "time capsules," ships, and the often dramatic array of material artifacts that they contain, can provide insights into the nature of life and lifestyle of communities of common people that might otherwise be lost in time. Cantelas and Babits provide several examples of this use and then focus attention on the excavation of the *Maple Leaf,* a side-wheel paddle steamer under contract to the Union Army in 1864. This ship, designed as a Lake Ontario freighter, was the first ship sunk as a result of the Confederate mining of the St. Johns River, Florida. At the time of its demise, the ship was carrying the personal and field supplies of three Union regiments, a Union brigade headquarters, and the goods of two sutlers. The rediscovery and excavation of the wreck provided a nearly unprecedented view of military life and supply at the most personal level. While celebrating the historical value of this and other ship discoveries, Cantelas and Babits also discuss critical problems of conservation that can, if not dealt with in a timely manner, result in the loss of both the wreck and its contents.

Stewart (chap.17) addresses an issue of growing interest to historians and anthropologists, the manner in which military events and the lives of the deceased are commemorated and remembered. While introduced briefly by Doug Scott earlier (chap. 3), Stewart focuses attention on one set of commemoration, that involving losses at sea. His discussion considers the manner in which differing personal and societal interests at the time of the event, and over time, can choose to recognize or interpret it.

Following the topic of commemoration and the recognition of the dead, Scott (chap. 3) and Geier and Tinkham (chap. 14) address issues having to do with the care of those who fall in battle or when encamped. In a modern era when recovery of the dead for identification and "proper burial" is of such great concern, these chapters address the reality of earlier times when there was little responsibility given to securing the remains of those who died on battlefields and in camps. Referencing mid-nineteenth century examples, they consider how, in some instances, and particularly in circumstances where armies hurried to disengage, the battlefield dead would be placed in shallow graves, often where they fell, sometimes individually, sometimes in mass graves. In some instances they may not have been buried at all. Subsequently, efforts at recovery and reburial may have been attempted, but these were often inadequate, incomplete, and in many instances resulted in the loss of identity of the individual remains resulting in the legions of "unknown soldiers" in Union and Confederate cemeteries established during and after the Civil War.

A significant point in the study of warfare presented by Whitehorne (chap.1) lay in the fact that accurate interpretation of military features, policies, and strategies can and will vary in providing any historic context for the analysis of adversarial groups. As military technology evolves and as the scope, magnitude and length of military actions change over time, it becomes impractical to use standards in play at one point in time as a basis for analyzing later actions. In addition, the technologies, policies, and guidelines for competing groups of differing histories and ethnicities will not necessarily be the same. Whitehorne cites similarities and differences in the procedures and recording patterns of the English and American armies on the Niagara Frontier in 1812 which, though similar, were not the same. In a like fashion, differences in the nature and strategies of war between the Scottish Jacobites and the English armies advancing against them were dramatically different (Pollard, chap. 9). Freeman (chap. 13) provides another example of the capabilities of a cavalry charge against entrenched infantry and artillery at Balaclava.

In chapters 18 and 19, these differences and their challenges to historians focuses on the fact that relatively modern armies (i.e., Iraq, Afghanistan) often fought with, or against tribal groups of dramatically different military capability and with very different military motivations. Ron Williamson (chap. 18) provides insight into the circumstances of the American northeast in the 18th and 19th centuries. In particular, he addresses the military interplay of the powerful members of the Iroquois Confederacy or League as they interacted with their Native American and European neighbors. Starting with a discussion of traditional patterns of warfare, Williamson discusses changes in Iroquois strategies.

From the French and Indian War through the War of 1812, these tribes served as valued and aggressive allies of the English or American troops. The chapter highlights the difficulties and situations that arose as attempts were made to integrate these "tribal" groups as allies within the more structured and regimented European modeled armies. Turning to the archaeology of such joint actions, Williamson notes the difficulties associated with the archaeological record in defining the place of Native allies in larger military actions.

In the concluding chapter (chap. 19), Scott continues to explore the asymmetrical interplay that existed between military forces representing societies at different levels of social complexity. Scott draws the reader's attention to the American northwest and 1877 hostilities between the U.S. Army and the Nez Perce tribe that resulted in Chief Joseph's surrender at Snake Creek, Montana. Scott discusses the cultural differences that created problems and then interprets events associated with the Battle of Big Hole, Montana, fought on 9–10 August 1877. After a comprehensive discussion of the military and Nez Perce accounts, Scott illustrates how archaeology has clarified and validated the episodes of the battle. This discussion is particularly interesting in that it reveals how modern forensic methods that allow bullets to be attributed to specific weapons can be used to document the movement of individuals across a battlefield.

CHAPTER EIGHT

Civil War Battlefield Archaeology

Examining and Interpreting the Debris of Battle

MATTHEW B. REEVES

INTRODUCTION

The ground at Civil War battlefields is filled with patterned debris from infantry and artillery engagements. As such, the deposits found at these landscapes are ripe for archaeologists seeking to decipher the material signature of warfare. What belies this seemingly easily harvested cache of information is the process of moving from artifacts to actions, i.e. the combat that resulted in the creation of the material record. The notion is that human behavior, in this case military behavior, is patterned and the artifacts left behind should also be patterned and reflect the actions that produced them. The archaeological materials recovered from 1998 surveys of Matthew's Hill at Manassas National Battlefield exemplify the potential for deciphering patterned battle-related debris. These investigations are presented as a case study to illustrate the process of recovery, identification, and interpretation of battle-related debris.

The archaeological record of a mid-nineteenth century battlefield is made up of a wide variety of artifact types including dropped and fired bullets, hardware sheared off uniforms, packs and weapons, shrapnel from exploded shells, and canister. Making sense of battle debris necessitates a thorough grounding not only in the specific events of the battle under study, but an in-depth knowledge of Civil War material culture and military tactics. Analysis involves separating assemblages into types including bullet types by form and caliber, shrapnel, and lost personal items with their additional subtypes. Each data subset is plotted and examined for patterning within topographic space. Spatial patterning might include concentrations, a uniform scatter across the entire site, or linear patterns of artifacts. This fine-grained analysis allows several sets of potential activities to be defined within an area being examined. The next step involves interpreting these patterns.

Critical to interpreting observed artifact patterns is the ability to establish a relationship between the artifacts and specific events that took place on the field of battle. This is often a difficult task because the archaeological record is formed by a series of events separated by minutes, hours, and, more often than not, months and years. Longer time periods are especially relevant to archaeological investigations at sites such as Manassas National Battlefield Park where there is the potential for multiple battles on the same site. All these events form one record that, from the standpoint of the archaeology, is collapsed into a single layer in which the sequence of activity needs to be deciphered. Decoding the archaeological record is accomplished through a series of analytical procedures that combine documentary research with a thorough knowledge of the material culture of the period, and the spatial distribution of artifacts recovered from the field. The process involves three steps: (1) examining the documentary record to gain an understanding of what events transpired in the project area, and what military units (specific regiments or brigades) were involved; (2) obtaining detailed information on the specific weapons and equipment used by the individual units so that associations can be made between artifacts and military units; and (3) a thorough analysis of the recovered battle-related materials that takes into account troop movements, the activities in which they were engaged, and the historic landscape (i.e., location of fences, structures, roads, woodlots, and terrain).

A general knowledge of Civil War tactical maneuvering combined with the known sequence of movements that took place, results in an expectation of what should be found in the archaeological record. However, more often than not this expectation does not precisely match what is observed in the material record recovered in the field, i.e. the patterns of artifacts. The incongruity between the archaeological record and the historical record is where new insights into the sequence of battle events can often be ascertained. New information on unit positions, artillery scatter, and infantry firing zones can reshape how battle sequences are understood.

Using the archaeological record goes beyond augmenting the historical record. The materials recovered from the battlefield shadow individual activities and group behavior. Combining archaeological evidence with documentary data is a didactic process. Insights gained from these comparisons allow examination of the documentary accounts from a different perspective and highlight details that might otherwise be overlooked. Such careful interpretation can reveal much regarding unit activities and the battle experience of soldiers. By combining the information sources of archaeology and the documentary record a more well-rounded picture of these battles is gained.

MATTHEW'S HILL: A CASE STUDY

This article uses the case study of the Matthew's Hill survey at Manassas National Battlefield Park to document the process of archaeological recovery of battle-related artifacts and their subsequent analysis and interpretation (fig. 8.1). By presenting the sequence from the recovery of artifacts to their final interpretation, the various techniques used to recover, identify, and interpret the scatter of warfare are discussed.

The Recovery of Battle-related Materials

Meaningful battlefield surveys require equipment and techniques that are adapted to finding a broadcast scatter of the battle debris. At Matthew's Hill, the project area was surveyed using two methods of subsurface testing. Initially, archaeologists excavated test pits at 25-ft intervals along transects across the hill. This systematic testing was followed by metal detecting to locate and recover metallic artifacts. The combined total of Civil War battlefield materials recovered using shovel test pits was one canister shot. In contrast, close to 900 battle-related artifacts were recovered using metal detectors on the same terrain. While the survey results made it clear that systematic test pit surveying is not effective in recovering and identifying battle-related deposits, the question of why demands some explanation.

The primary reason test pits are not effective is the depositional patterning of battlefield debris. Deposits such as trash middens tend to cluster in dense concentrations that can effectively be located using interval-based testing. Battle-related debris, on the other hand, is often scattered in relatively low densities over a large area. Even with dense concentrations of battle-related materials, more often than not, test pits fall between military features such as battle lines—making interval-based testing procedures, such as test pits, unreliable for locating battle-related deposits.

Unlike shovel test pits, metal detector surveys allow for continuous ground coverage and allow scattered concentrations to be deciphered. Using metal detectors makes it possible to recover numerous battle-related resources ranging from isolated artifact concentrations to rather diffusely scattered material. If metal detectors were not used in the survey of Matthew's Hill, none of the artifact patterns examined in this article would have been discovered.

While metal detectors provide an effective means of finding metal objects, their successful use is complicated by three factors. The identification of metallic hits can only be carried out by excavating each individual target signal. Often, this is a laborious and time consuming task when large quantities of modern debris are intermixed with historic materials. Second, metal detectors are sophisticated pieces of electronic equipment. Successful use in a systematic survey is dependent on the operator understanding the nuances of the machine and their ability to identify the often subtle readings these machine provide (see Hanna, chap. 2; Balicki, chap. 6). Finally, non-metallic artifacts are not identified unless in association with metallic material.

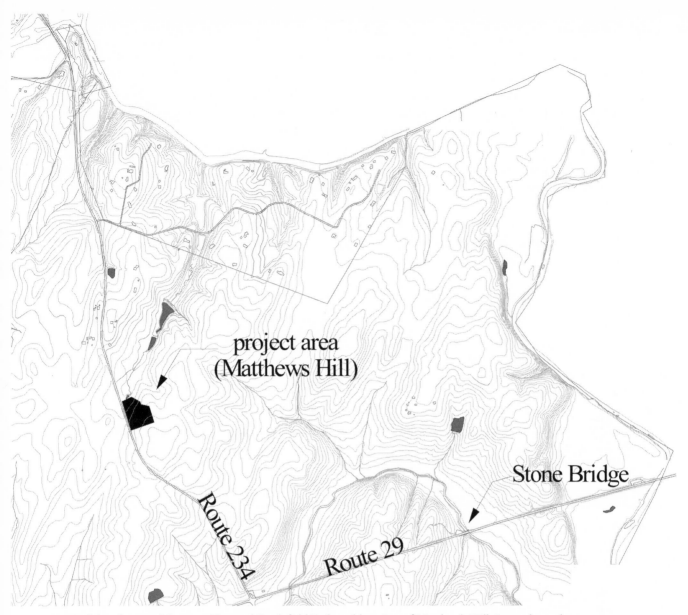

FIGURE 8.1. Map showing Manassas National Battlefield Park and location of Matthew's Hill. Image by author.

In resolving these complications, we were fortunate to enlist volunteers from one of the largest and oldest Civil War relic hunting associations in the country, the Northern Virginia Relic Hunters Association (NVRHA). Members from the NVRHA volunteered hundreds of hours for this survey, brought the finest metal-detecting equipment on the market, and provided detailed knowledge of Civil War material culture that went far beyond any books available today.

The survey at Matthew's Hill demonstrated that 100% coverage did not equate to 100% recovery of metal artifacts. Repeated metal detector sweeps in areas previously surveyed, revealed additional targets masked by earlier signals. In an effort to determine the recovery rate of materials, 12, 50 X 50 ft quadrants on

Matthew's Hill were re-swept after completing the initial survey. The second metal detector sweep provided a measurement of the reliability of various volunteer machine operators and the degree of data recovery entailed by a single sweeping of an area. The overall results revealed that a single pass resulted in finding less than half of the materials present.

In areas containing high artifact densities (n>20), the secondary sweep revealed roughly the same amount of materials as the initial search. Possible reasons for the high rate of recovery in the second effort might relate to close proximity of metallic artifacts masking neighboring signals. In areas containing lower artifact densities (n<20), the recovery rate in the secondary search was approximately 50% of the initial sweep.

The higher success rate during the initial quadrant sweep might relate to metallic objects being spaced further apart, thus reducing chances that stronger, or shallower, targets masked weaker signals. As with the quadrants containing higher densities, factors contributing to missed hits include random factors such as targets falling between metal detector transects, ground noise, and ground cover (see Pratt 2006a).

USING SMALL ARMS AMMUNITION TO INTERPRET BATTLE ACTIVITIES

Some 854 battle-related artifacts were recovered at Matthew's Hill, including 600 bullets, 72 artillery projectile fragments, 23 military buttons, 70 attachment items (buckles, rivets, and knapsack hooks), gun tools, and other pieces from uniforms, packs, and clothing. Small arms ammunition provided the most telling evidence due to high numbers and evidence gained from their associated weapon, scarring, and caliber.

Small arms ammunition was analyzed for identifiable manufacturing characteristics and then measured and examined for scars and wear indicating use. In this analysis, artifacts were examined for: (1) identification of any manufacturing characteristics that could tie the ammunition to a particular weapon, or unit; and (2) clues as to how the ammunition entered the archaeological record, i.e., accidentally dropped, intentionally rejected, or fired.

The firearms represented by the ammunition recovered at Matthew's Hill are muzzle-loading shoulder arms (186 round balls and 342 conical bullets), breech loading carbines and rifles (11 carbine bullets and two cupric cartridge cases), and pistols (27 bullets) (McKee and Mason 1980). By far, the majority of the small arms ammunition recovered during this survey consisted of ammunition from muzzle-loading, rifled muskets and smooth-bore muskets. Most of this shoulder-arm ammunition is round balls and 3-ringed conical bullets. While these bullets generally do not contain any identifying features that suggest their manufacturing origin, the wear marks on and dimensions of these bullets provide important clues to their history and use on the battlefield.

Ammunition for muzzle-loading rifled arms typically is conical-shaped bullets with a basal cavity. The basal cavity creates a thinner wall at the rear of the bullet that expands upon firing. The expansion of the base drives the bullet into the rifling of the barrel and also serves as a gas seal. Rifling is the spiral grooves running the length of the interior of the gun barrel. Bullets fired through rifled barrels are given a spin that stabilizes the projectile in flight. The combination of confined gas expansion in the barrel and spin provided by rifling resulted in a marked increase in bullet velocity and accuracy (Coates and Thomas 1990).

Along with identifying bullet types, several measurements were taken to determine caliber, length, and weight. Measurements were made with calipers to the nearest thousandth of an inch. Measurements of diameter and length were often important in distinguishing different calibers and for denoting differences among revolver bullets (McKee and Mason 1980). Measuring conical bullet diameters allowed determination of caliber, and also helped define subtle characteristics such as oversize bullets that were possibly rejected during the loading process.

Unlike round balls, conical bullets used in rifle muskets were produced with diameters very close to the caliber of the barrel (Thomas 1997). While rifling necessitated that bullets be produced to close tolerances, bullets were often cast oversize during manufacture (Babits 1995). For example, while most 3-ring conical bullets designed for the .58-caliber rifle were intended to be manufactured to a .575-caliber, many were cast in the range from .575 in to .59 in (Thomas 1997:135–38). As the range for .54-caliber bullets was specified at .537 in by the U.S. Ordnance Department (Thomas 1997:124), the range used for determining oversize .54-caliber bullets at Matthew's Hill fell between .538 in and .55 in.

During surveys at Manassas National Battlefield Park, archaeology and relic hunter teams recovered several concentrations of dropped bullets whose diameters fell in the range denoted as "oversize" (Reeves 2001:15). Based on the spatial patterning of these bullets and their quantifiable presence within many project areas, it was hypothesized that such bullets represent intentional rejects of oversize bullets on the battlefield. The rationale for interpreting these bullets as rejects is based on the loading procedures for muzzle arms.

The presence of an oversize conical bullet would not be known until the soldier attempted to load the bullet into the gun. Soldiers received these bullets wrapped in cartridge paper containing both the gunpowder charge and the bullet. Only upon tearing open the paper cartridge, loading the powder, and then placing the bullet in the muzzle would the oversized bullets be discovered. In such circumstances, the oversize bullet was possibly rejected for fear of its jamming the rifle and necessitating the time-consuming process of pulling the projectile. As a result, such bullets were potentially dropped prior to ramming them home in the weapon.

Further complicating the loading process was barrel fouling that occurred during heavy fire. Fouling occurred from powder residue accumulating inside the barrel. Fouling begins to interfere with the loading process after about seven to eight shots (McKee and Mason 1980:64). This buildup effectively decreased weapon caliber and made ramming the bullet to the breech more difficult. This likely caused even more bullets to be rejected for fear of jamming (Thomas 1997: 137).

MATTHEW'S HILL HISTORICAL BACKGROUND

The historical background for the First Battle of Manassas provides important context to understand the actions at Matthew's Hill. In July 1861, a Federal army of more than 35,000 men, led by Union Gen. Irvin McDowell, advanced from Washington, D.C., to take the Confederate capital at Richmond, Virginia. Confederate forces, under Gen. P. G.T. Beauregard, positioned themselves at Manassas Junction and the northern fords of Bull Run. The combination of Confederate forces in the Manassas area and westward troop movement of the Federal army set the stage for the First Battle of Manassas.

On the morning of 21 July, Union troops began their westward movement to cross Bull Run. With most Confederate troops being massed along fords closest to Manassas Junction, this left a single brigade, under Col. Nathan Evans, to defend the northern crossing of Bull Run, known as Stone Bridge. With previous knowledge of the position of Confederate troops, Union commanders detailed a small detachment to engage Evans's troops at Stone Bridge and moved the majority of their troops to the north on a flanking attack (Johnston 1996; Hennessy 1989:49). When the Confederates realized that the Stone Bridge skirmish was only a diversion, Evans moved to meet the Union flank attack (Moore 1983:49).

Evans sent a company from Maj. Roberdeau Wheat's Louisiana Battalion and two companies from Col. J. B. E. Sloan's 4th South Carolina Regiment as skirmishers to contest Union movements. By spreading his small force over a wide area, Evans succeeded in creating the illusion of a large Confederate force that not only covered the Federal flanking movement, but also held a strong position at Stone Bridge (Moore 1983:49–51). Evans soon realized that the Union troops had moved to his northwest and would soon turn south and outflank his position (O.R. Series 1:2:559). In advance of this action, Evans moved troops west towards Sudley Road and sent two, 6-pounder guns, under Lt. George Davidson, to be positioned on a suitable eminence to confront the enemy.

Evans was well-informed about the local terrain as his scouts had been moving through the area for the past several days (Moore 1983:48, 51). Evans arranged his regiments on the southern portion of Matthew's Hill (south of the project area) with Wheat's Louisiana Tigers formed to the right and Sloan's men on their left (O.R. Series 1:2:561). Once established, Wheat sent skirmishers to the north for the initial confrontation with the Union army (fig. 8.2). Meanwhile, Davidson positioned one six pounder, under Lt. Clark Leftwich, just north of Stone House on Buck Hill, and his other gun north of the Robinson House (O.R. Series 1:2:488, 563).

Shortly after 9:30 A.M., Union Col. Ambrose Burnside's Brigade arrived at the Sudley Road crossing of Bull Run. Upon receiving news that the Confederates were to his front with considerable force, he sent Col. John Slocum's 2nd Rhode Island Regiment to advance southward along Sudley Road. Slocum's skirmishers "were soon confronted by the enemy's forces" (O.R. Series 1:2:395), most likely skirmishers from Wheat's Battalion who had moved down the northeast slope of Matthew's Hill (O.R. Series 1:2:489) (fig. 8.2). Wheat's skirmishers were soon badly outnumbered and forced to fall back to their regiment at the base of Matthew's Hill (Hennessy 1989:50).

After Wheat's skirmishers withdrew, the remainder of the 2nd Rhode Island "debouched from a wood

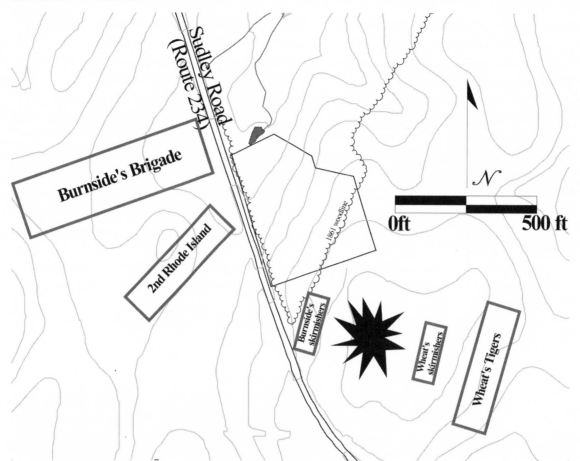

FIGURE 8.2. Map showing details of initial clash between skirmishers of Wheat's Tigers and the 2nd Rhode Island. The relative position is based on historical records of this portion of the battle. Image by author.

in sight of Evans' position, some five hundred yards distant from Wheat's Battalion" (O.R. Series 1:2:489) and deployed along the ridge of Matthew's Hill. After arriving at this position, they withstood heavy fire from Evans's brigade positioned between Buck Hill and Matthew's Hill (Hennessy 1989:51) and Confederate artillery fire from Lt. Leftwich's six-pounder located on Buck Hill (O.R. Series 1:2:563). Soon after the 2nd Rhode Island deployed on Matthew's Hill, Burnside ordered Capt. William Reynolds's battery of six guns to their right (Bearss 1981:19). While heavy artillery and infantry fire made Reynolds's deployment difficult, his artillerymen were able to fire into Evans's position.

Fifteen minutes after the initial confrontation between Wheat's and Sloan's skirmishers, the remainder of Burnside's brigade arrived at Matthew's Hill. Burnside had hoped the 2nd Rhode Island would be able to clear the hill for deploying his brigade.

However, Slocum's lone regiment remained trapped on the ridge by the intense infantry and artillery fire, which made deployment of the other Union regiments extremely difficult (Hennessy 1989:50).

With the arrival of Burnside's and Porter's brigades, it appeared that Slocum's much needed support was on the way. However, a series of botched orders and lack of cohesion among troops delayed the much-needed support for nearly 30 minutes. Finally, the 1st Rhode Island moved into formation on the right flank of the much-beleaguered 2nd. The remainder of Burnside's regiments, the 71st New York and the 2nd New Hampshire, then formed into line east of Sudley Road.

With the ridge of Matthew's Hill occupied by Union forces, the tactical actions within the project area were brought to a close. For the next hour wounded soldiers fell back into this area to escape the onslaught of bullets and exploding shells before moving towards a field hospital farther north (Barnes 1865). This brief historic snapshot of actions at Matthew's Hill provides the background for interpreting the militaria recovered from the project area.

ANALYSIS OF BATTLEFIELD MILITARIA

The interpretation of battle-related artifacts assumes that the patterning of artifacts found in the ground relates to meaningful activities (Scott and Hunt 1998). At Matthew's Hill, these artifact patterns took the form of concentrations of .54- and .58-caliber 3-ring conical bullets, artillery shrapnel, .69-caliber round balls, and personal items from the uniforms and packs of soldiers. Dissecting such a diverse range of artifacts necessitates being able to attribute particular artifacts to specific military units. For example, at Matthew's Hill, an otherwise scarce bullet, the .54-caliber 3-ring conical bullet, was encountered in relatively high frequencies. These bullets were used in a Model 1841 "Mississippi" Rifle. When ordinance records were consulted, Wheat's Louisiana Tigers were the only infantry unit carrying this weapon in the survey zone (Todd 1978, 1983). The recovery of several Louisiana state buttons found within the zone of .54-caliber bullets supported this attribution (fig. 8.3).

The presence of large numbers of .69-caliber round balls was more difficult to ascribe to a single military unit since many engaged soldiers, both North and South, carried .69-caliber smoothbore muskets. However, the extremely high number of fired round balls made the 2nd Rhode Island (Todd 1978, 1983) the most likely source as they are the only group known to be firing into this particular zone. The attributions of the .54-caliber 3-ring bullets and the .69-caliber round balls allowed the complex interplay between the 2nd Rhode Island skirmishers and Wheat's Tigers to be deciphered.

Once positive associations were made between artifact types and military units, the historical record could be used to assign munitions patterns to battlefield events such as the skirmish between Wheat's Tigers and the 1st Rhode Island skirmishers. Historic accounts identified landscape features such as roads, fence lines, structures, woodlots, and terrain as important landmarks in the engagement. Military maneuvers were often thwarted or enhanced by the landscape, thus rendering otherwise mundane terrain features into items of tactical and thus, historic, importance. Whether a distribution of dropped bullets is located along an edge of a woodlot, near a historic fence line, or beside a road is an important distinction for assigning such artifact groups to specific historic events.

The Matthew's Hill landscape consisted of three main features: Sudley Road bordering the survey area to the west; an oak woodlot in the northern portions; and fence lines. Landscape studies documented the presence of a fence surrounding the woodlot (Dames and Moore 1979; Joseph 1996a). The project area discussed in this report encompasses the southern portion and edge of this woodlot where linear patterns of battle-related materials located during metal detector

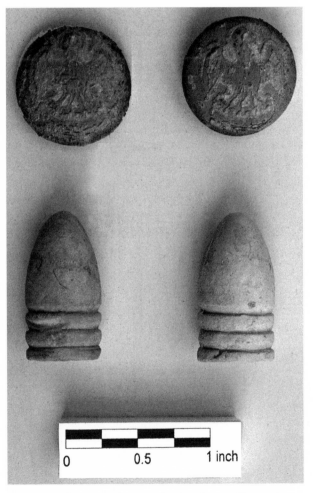

FIGURE 8.3. Louisiana buttons (top) and .54-caliber 3-ring conical bullets (bottom). Photograph by author.

surveys appear to mirror its southern edge. The importance of patterned military scatters being present is that they indicate tactical activities taking place in an area that historic documents do not pinpoint as being a tactical location during the beginning stages of the First Battle of Manassas.

During the battle, the project area was just north of an intense firefight between the 2nd Rhode Island Regiment and Evans's brigade. The combination of archaeological and historical evidence identifies this zone as the site of two stages in the fight between Evans's and Burnside's brigades: (1) the initial fighting between Evans's skirmishers and Burnside's skirmishers, and (2) the deployment of the 2nd Rhode Island followed by the 71st New York and the 1st Rhode Island into battle formation on the ridge of Matthew's Hill. The mature oak forest played a definitive role in both events, because it provided an excellent vantage point and cover for Evans's skirmishers to engage Union troops advancing south along Sudley Road. Later, as the 2nd Rhode Island skirmishers deployed, these same woods provided the Rhode Islanders with cover from both Evans's skirmishers, then located on the top of Matthew's Hill, and, to a lesser extent, from incoming artillery projectiles fired by Confederate Lt. Leftwich's gun on Buck Hill. The analysis of archaeological materials from Matthew's Hill not only provides material evidence for both activities, but also sheds light on how these events played themselves out on the landscape.

Narrative Discussion on Finds from Matthew's Hill

The most telling artifact set consists of the pattern formed by 75 dropped .54-caliber 3-ring conical bullets combined with two Louisiana coat buttons. Both artifact sets are potentially associated with Wheat's Battalion. Documentary sources note the Tigers were located south of the Matthew's farm during the main engagement on Matthew's Hill. The archaeological discovery of these items north of the main engagement provides the sole evidence for locating Wheat's Tigers during the initial fighting on Matthew's Hill. The following discussion summarizes these events as revealed by the archeological findings.

Early in the morning of 21 July 1861, Wheat

positioned his skirmishers in the woodlot on the east side of Sudley Road along the northern base of Matthew's Hill. This location was a prime tactical position because Union troops moving south along Sudley Road would be forced to file between this woodlot and another located directly to the west. Such a bottleneck would make it difficult for troops to deploy if fired upon. As a result, this location served as an excellent position for a surprise attack against Burnside's advancing troops. Forward (north) of this position, other Louisiana skirmishers moved through the woods to prevent flanking fire from Union skirmishers.

Meanwhile, Burnside sent Slocum's 2nd Rhode Island as an advance force to confront any Confederates. Slocum, in turn, sent skirmishers ahead to scout for Confederate troops. Once these skirmishers appeared in front of the woods, Wheat's men opened fire (fig. 8.4). The concentration of dropped .54-caliber conical bullets and two Louisiana buttons reflects their position (fig. 8.5). That 22 of the 29, .54-caliber bullets in this concentration were oversized suggests they were rejected during loading rather than being accidentally dropped. The quantity of dropped bullets here provides evidence that the Tigers engaged Burnside's men for several shots. The Rhode Islanders quickly fired back into the woods at Wheat's skirmishers. The Rhode Island volley is supported by the scatter of fired round balls just inside the wood line (fig. 8.6).

Heavily outgunned, Wheat's skirmishers moved further into the woods, toward the southern edge of the woodlot. Meanwhile, the 2nd Rhode Island moved southward. Unsure of the exact location of Wheat's skirmishers in the woods, Slocum's troops established a firing line along the western edge of the woodlot. While loading their smoothbores during this engagement, the 2nd Rhode Islanders dropped numerous balls, as evidenced by the 37, .69-caliber round balls found in this area.

When the Louisiana skirmishers started crossing the fence on the southern edge of the woodlot, they likely came under fire from Rhode Island skirmishers. The stress of this event likely inspired quick movement on the part of Wheat's skirmishers. The presence of 29 dropped .54-caliber bullets suggests that some members of the Louisiana Tigers lost some

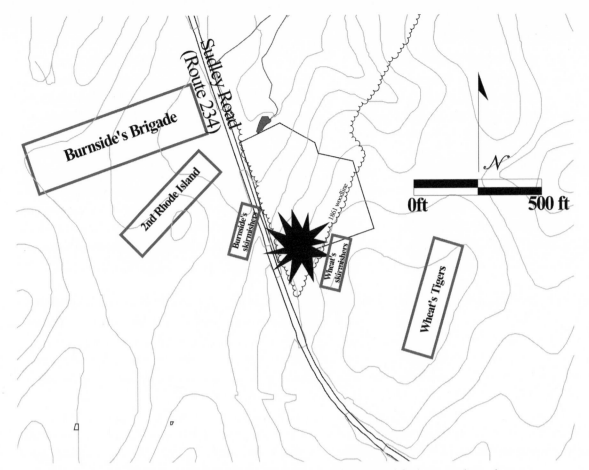

FIGURE 8.4. Map showing location of skirmish units based on archaeological finds. Image by author.

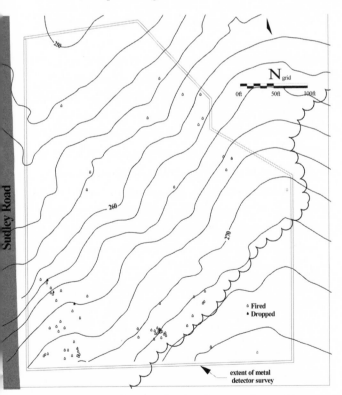

FIGURE 8.5. Map showing the distribution of .54-caliber 3-ring conical bullets recovered from the project area. Note the concentration along the southwestern edge of the wood-lot. Image by author.

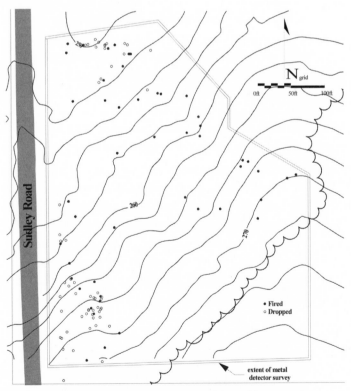

FIGURE 8.6. Map showing distribution of .69-caliber round-balls recovered from the project area. Image by author.

contents of their cartridge boxes while passing over the fence. The presence of only seven oversized bullets within this cluster suggests accidental loss rather than intentional rejection. By this time, the bulk of the 2nd Rhode Island was deploying into the woods (Woodbury 1862:93).

As Burnside's troops rapidly took over the woodlot, Wheat's men withdrew and arranged themselves along the ridge of Matthew's Hill. The 2nd Rhode Island poured into the woods and deployed against the Confederates further south on Matthew's Hill. The absence of fired .54-caliber conical bullets along the southern edge of the woodlot suggests Wheat's skirmishers provided little resistance as the Rhode Islanders occupied the woods.

As the 2nd Rhode Island moved forward, the fence at the southern edge of the woodlot either served as a chance locale to reload weapons or an obstacle to be scaled. Interestingly, a cluster of dropped .69-caliber round balls are positioned at the same location where numerous dropped .54-caliber bullets were found, indicating an obstacle such as the juncture of a fence with the woodlot, a feature suggested by a 1937 aerial photograph.

The documentary record and archaeological evidence suggest that the 2nd Rhode Island rapidly drove Wheat's men from their position on Matthew's Hill. Once cleared of Confederates, the ridgeline became the main Union firing line for the morning fight on Matthew's Hill. The 2nd Rhode Island battled Evans's brigade alone for nearly an hour, despite the presence of other Burnside's brigade regiments on the other side of the woodlot.

Due to a combination of Union division commander Col. David Hunter's poor judgment and the influx of artillery fire from Confederate batteries on Buck Hill, the arrival of Burnside's other troops seems to have been chaotic. Instead of deploying on the east side of Sudley Road to support the 2nd Rhode Island, these men remained in formation west of the road. In the meantime, Leftwich intensified his artillery fire using Borman-fused shells. Evidence for his artillery attack takes the form of 16 rounded shell fragments, four Borman-type fuses, and ten-case shot—with case shot being consistent with the shells that would used for such long distance artillery fire (Dickey and George 1993; Griffith 1986:27).

In this melee of exploding shells, Hunter was struck on the cheek and gave Burnside command (Woodbury 1862:93). Burnside immediately ordered his regiments to deploy to support the 2nd Rhode Island. The 71st New York was the first regiment that moved and, using the woods for cover, they likely encountered wounded and dying skirmishers from Wheat's and Burnside's units. The shock of green troops encountering wounded and dying comrades combined with exploding artillery shells and splintering trees is the likely cause for the loss of all regimental cohesion.

Correcting a potentially disastrous situation, Burnside ordered the 71st New York to allow the 1st Rhode Island to pass through their ranks (Hennessy 1989:53). As the 1st Rhode Islanders moved into the woods, soldiers jostled by one another and had items torn from their knapsacks and uniforms as they maneuvered through the brush. The confusion of this scene is supported by over 200 dropped .58-caliber 3-ring conical bullets, most of which were concentrated in the southern and western portions of the woodline (fig. 8.7). While both the 71st New York and the 1st Rhode Island Regiments carried .58-caliber rifle muskets, it is likely that the 71st New York contributed most heavily to this concentration of dropped bullets. Soldiers seemed more likely to lose cartridges in combat situations if they unfastened their cartridge box flaps to facilitate access. In addition, the overwhelming majority of these bullets were not oversized (as found among the .54-caliber bullets) suggesting these were not rejected during loading. Among the array of knapsack hooks, brass studs, buttons, and other military gear were several New York buttons, most likely from the 71st New York (fig. 8.8).

The scatters of .58-caliber 3-ring conical bullets and heavy concentrations of personal items indicate activities aberrant from what should otherwise be patterned unit behavior (Fox and Scott 1991:92). These dropped bullets are not the result of ordered regimental activities, but suggest a breakdown in structured troop movement. Such a disruption of military order was likely the result of troops, previously unexposed to combat, being seized by panic in their first battle. Given the skirmishing that occurred only a half hour previous to the 71st New York moving into the

wood line, these troops probably encountered dead
or wounded soldiers. Combined with these sights,
the crashing of artillery shells into the woodlot only
added to their apprehension. Such a stressful situation is a classic setting for "fight or flight" syndrome.
Numerous Civil War accounts document soldiers
being seized with panic and fleeing combat situations.
In the case of the 71st New York, historical records
and the archaeological evidence suggest a breakdown
of regimental order. This breakdown immobilized the
regiment and created significant delays for regiments
deploying to their rear.

CONCLUSION

The previous narrative suggests the value that artifact
scatters have for revealing regimental positions and
sequences of military maneuvers. Most deposits dupli-
cate the expected debris of ordered battle and conform
to patterns noted by Fox and Scott (1991) and Scott

and Hunt (1997) as "battlefield patterns." But the artifacts from Matthew's Hill are also particularly revealing of the reactions of green soldiers in the first major
land battle of the Civil War.

It should be stressed that deciphering such patterns of military activity from the archaeological
record is not without its pitfalls. In the case of
Matthew's Hill, there are events that occurred during the Second Battle of Manassas (28–31 August
1862) that potentially contributed many items to
the archaeological record, most especially during 29
August 1862, when the vicinity of the project area
was used as a staging area for troops (J. Hennessey,
personal communication). The only way to confirm the interpretation of the patterns noted in this
paper is the survey of additional areas at Matthew's
Hill to note differences or similarities in artifact
patterning.

The presentation of this case study should be seen
as more than adding a few details to an otherwise
well-documented battle. It shows the methods and the

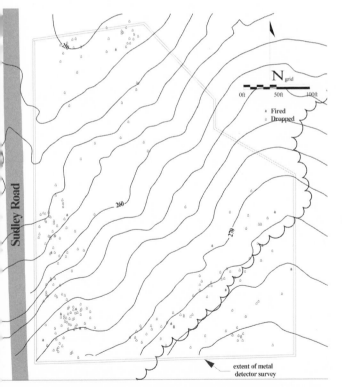

FIGURE 8.7. Map showing distribution of .58-caliber 3-ring
conical bullets across the project area. Note the concentration of bullets along the western and southern edge of the
woodlot. Image by author.

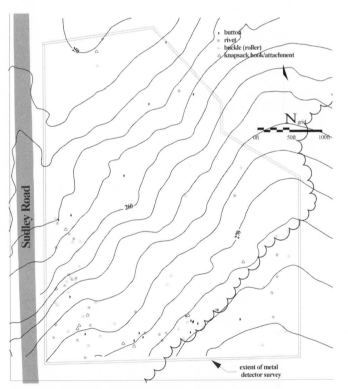

FIGURE 8.8. Map showing distribution of personal items
recovered from the project area. Image by author.

potential archaeological investigations on battlefields have for placing historical data in a fresh perspective. The new perspective is on two primary levels—that of the landscape and that of the individual actors. For the landscape perspective, archaeological discovery of battlefield actions provides a means to ground these events in space. Historical accounts are often sketchy on the precise location of battle events. Exact location is critical since maneuvers were contingent upon terrain and landscape features. The placement of Wheat's skirmishers is such an example of how knowledge gained about battlefield locale has the potential to bring new light to old maneuvers.

The second perspective is that the material remains of battle are a direct by product of human activity. The unfettered material record of individual actions is the realm for which archaeology is unique. The archaeology at Matthew's Hill shows that human behavior has a material signature that can be deduced from the archaeological record. As such, the ever-present element of human agency, choice, and response can be brought back into the trauma of warfare. Given the range of battlefield contexts and preservation of material record of warfare at Civil War sites, the potential for archaeology of battle is just beginning to be tapped.

CHAPTER NINE

Dissecting Seventeenth- and Eighteenth-Century Battlefields

Two Case Studies from the Jacobite Rebellions in Scotland

TONY POLLARD

INTRODUCTION

Given that a survey has identified no less than 358 battlefields and skirmish sites in Scotland (Foard and Perdita 2005:7), it may seem surprising that few of them have been subjected to archaeological investigation, although perhaps not so much so when one considers that the practice of battlefield archaeology in the United Kingdom as a whole is a very recent phenomenon. The first archaeological investigation of a Scottish battlefield took place in 2000 when Culloden was the subject of a limited survey program under the auspices of the BBC television series, *Two Men in a Trench* (Pollard and Oliver 2002, 2003). As part of that project, metal detector survey recovered musket balls, cannon shot, and other metal objects dropped during the battle. Topographic survey provided a better understanding of the terrain, and geophysical survey located buried remains such as building foundations and potential gravesites. In all, 12 British battlefields and other military sites were investigated as part of the series. Four sites were located in Scotland: Culloden, Killiecrankie, Inchkeith, and Bannockburn. Relatively modest in scale, these projects provided the impetus for an upsurge in battlefield and conflict archaeology, while also being almost entirely responsible for laying the foundations for the establishment of the field within Scotland.

This chapter provides an overview of the work carried out on two battle sites relating to the Jacobite rebellions, which took place over more than a half century between 1689 and 1746 (fig. 9.1). Killiecrankie, the first battle of the rebellions or uprisings, followed hot on the heels of the "Glorious Revolution" of 1688, when the Stuart royal house was deposed. Culloden, fought in 1746, was the last Jacobite battle, and also the last pitched battle fought on British soil. As mentioned, the investigations at Killiecrankie and Culloden were carried out as part of the television series, *Two Men in a Trench*. However, work at Culloden has now extended for several years since and has developed into one of the most intensive archaeological research program carried out on a British battlefield.

The aim of this chapter is to highlight the contributions that a variety of techniques can bring to the study of battlefields and the events they represent. It stresses the importance of a multi-faceted approach, using numerous techniques in complementary association. Each of the two case studies is prefaced by a brief historical background and summary of the battle under investigation.

KILLIECRANKIE 1689

Historical Background

In 1688, the Catholic King James II was ousted from the combined thrones of England, Scotland, and Ireland when his protestant son-in-law, William of Orange, arrived from Holland with an army of 15,000 men. James fled to France leaving William and his wife Mary (daughter of James), to occupy the vacant throne. This event was a great relief to the Protestant government that had feared the foundation of a Catholic dynasty with the birth of James's son James

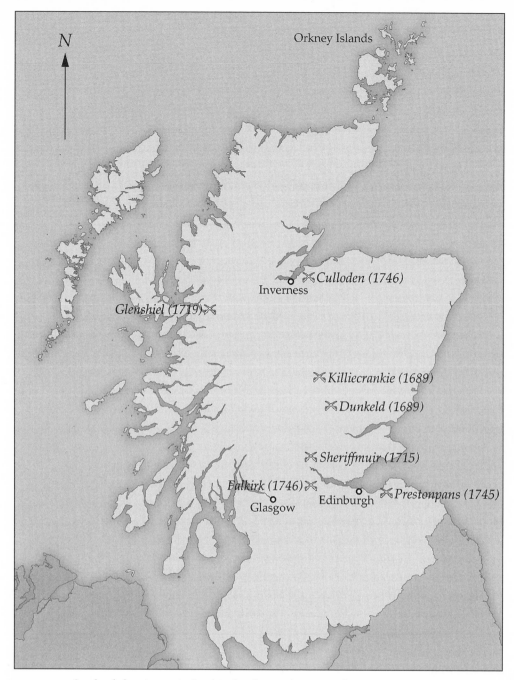

FIGURE 9.1. Scotland showing main Jacobite battle sites (1689–1746).

Francis Edward Stuart. The relatively peaceful character of this episode led to it becoming known as the "Glorious" or "Bloodless Revolution." However, bloodshed followed not long thereafter.

While in exile, James was not totally without loyal supporters, especially among the Catholics of Scotland and Ireland. His cause suited the ambitions of the French king, Louis XIV. The first Scottish Jacobite uprising was led by John Graham, Earl of Claverhouse and Viscount of Dundee (referred to hereafter as Dundee), in 1689. This first uprising climaxed

with the battle of Killiecrankie, in which Dundee was killed. The word "Jacobite" simply means "a supporter of James" and for the next 50 years or so Scotland was periodically torn by Jacobite attempts to put James and, after his death, his son, also called James (the "Old Pretender" to his foes and James VIII to his supporters) on the throne. The Jacobite cause was finally lost for good under the leadership of James's grandson, Charles Edward Stuart (the "Young Pretender" or "Bonnie Prince Charlie") on the field of Culloden in 1746.

The Battle

The Battle of Killiecrankie marked the end of a game of cat and mouse played out between a government army under Maj. Gen. Hugh Mackay and a Jacobite army led by Dundee. Both sides finally came face-to-face just outside the Pass of Killiecrankie on 27 July 1689. The Jacobites, who numbered around 2000, positioned themselves on high ground on the north side of the glen. The government force, which numbered almost 4000 men, extended their line across a terrace downslope from their foe, leaving a baggage train of more than 1200 pack horses along the River Garry. Both sides faced one another through the afternoon and into the evening, taunting and skirmishing before at last, just before dusk, the battle drew to its inevitable bloody climax.

Mackay's men were troubled for some time by a party of Jacobite sharpshooters positioned in buildings part way up the hill. Mackay gave orders for them to be flushed from this position, so a group of musketeers from his own regiment was dispatched on the right flank (fig. 9.2). The operation was a success and the snipers were sent scuttling back to their own lines, losing some of their number in the process. This action seemingly prompted Dundee to move and, at around 8 P.M., the Jacobites charged in three bodies. The government line quickly broke, possibly because the lack of an extended killing ground reduced the effectiveness of their musketry. One eyewitness (MacBane 2001) reported that the enemy was upon them before they had chance to fire more than three rounds apiece. It was a perfect Highland charge and even the experienced Anglo-Dutch troops turned and fled.

Dundee led a charge of the small Jacobite cavalry force (~40 strong) down the center but was shot and killed. Probably unaware of the demise of their leader, the victorious Jacobites chased the routed government troops for several miles, slaughtering many and plundering the baggage train. It is said that when they returned to the battlefield, they were horrified at the terrible carnage they had inflicted. The loss of

FIGURE 9.2. Killiecrankie slope showing right flank of Jacobite army charge; note terraces which would provide temporary cover during advance. Photograph by author.

Dundee to the Jacobite cause was grave and undoubtedly helped seal the fate of the uprising. The Jacobite campaign continued without Dundee but spiraled downward when they were defeated by the Cameronians after street fighting in Dunkeld. Eventually, the rebellion failed and in less than twelve months, the government campaign was brought to a successful conclusion by General Mackay, despite his terrible defeat at Killiecrankie.

The Killiecrankie battlefield is sited around 6 km northeast of Pitlochry and around 4 km southeast of Blair Atholl, in Perth and Kinross (fig.9.3). The battle took place in a picturesque valley forming the eastern limit of Glen Garry. From the east, the location is approached through narrow defile known as the Pass of Killiecrankie, the route taken by the government army prior to the battle. This trackway later became the route of Wade's military road constructed in the late 1720s, which at this point, closely follows the course of the River Garry. In the 1970s, this road was replaced as the main thoroughfare through the glen by the A9 that cuts across the battlefield.

Testing an Eyewitness Account

We are fortunate to have several eyewitness accounts of the Battle of Killiecrankie, which includes a contemporary poem, the *Grameid*—written in Latin by James Philip of Almerieclose (1888). Two eyewitness accounts are government (Mackay and McBane) and one is Jacobite (Ewan Cameron of Lochiel—edited by Drummond 1842). In many respects, the most important is by Major General Mackay (1833), a rare seventeenth century example of a narrative account of an entire battle (in which he writes of himself in the third person). Although the account is obviously one-sided, it appears to be a fairly thorough and

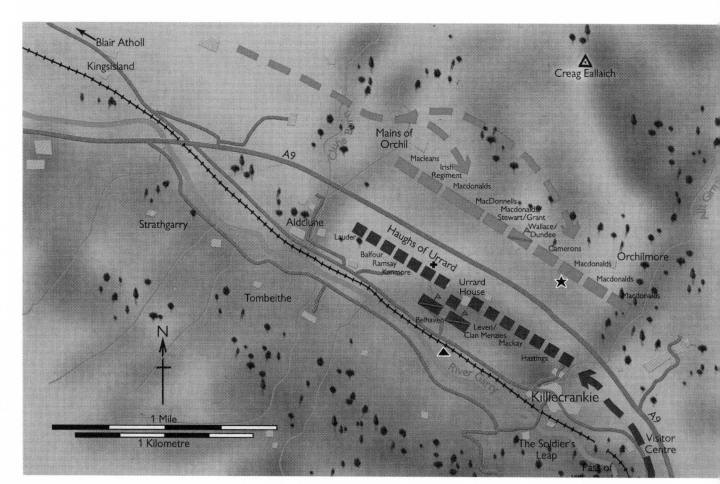

FIGURE 9.3. The Battle of Killicrankie: Jacobites (top), government army (bottom); Symbols: + Grave of the Officers ★ Sniper's cottage ▲ Government baggage train (Pollard and Oliver 2003).

even-handed report, especially when considering the magnitude of his defeat and the temptation to shift blame (which he does to some extent). There are obviously some exaggerations in his favor. For example, in his speech to his men before the battle he paints such a ferocious picture of the Highlander, warning that if they do not stand they are doomed, which comes across a little like a retrospective "I told you so." Bias aside, these written accounts, especially in their descriptions of deployment, location, and landscape, are especially important since no maps were drawn in the immediate aftermath of the battle (Pollard 2009a). A reasonably careful reading is enough to locate the site by referring to them while walking the ground. Despite this, it is surprising to discover that several historians have placed the battle lines in entirely the wrong place (Terry 1905; Smurthwaite 1993).

Mackay begins by describing the movement of the government army through the Pass of Killiekrankie and into the wider valley beyond, where the enemy was spotted some distance away on a hill. At first believing this to be the Jacobite main body, he moved some troops forward along the valley floor, but then a much larger group of the enemy were seen higher up the side of the valley, less than a kilometer away. Fearful that they would move down the hill and take up a strong position in woodland and scrub, Mackay ordered his entire army to perform a *quart de conversion* (quarter turn) to the right and advance up slope to occupy an intermediate terrace before the Jacobites had time to move down. By moving upslope, the government army put themselves in a weaker position because the Jacobites had already taken the high ground and the climb removed a woodland obstruction between themselves and the enemy. This definitely favored the Jacobites, who preferred to charge downhill. Having emerged from the wood, the government troops took a position on a wide terrace, now as then occupied by Urrard House and its walled garden.

In the early afternoon, Mackay supervised his army as it deployed into line, with musketeers taking up the new European practice of deploying in three lines rather than the more traditional six. Mackay (1833:51) described his position thus: " . . . a ground fair enough to receive the enemy, but not to attack them,

there being, within a short musket shot to it, another eminence before our front, as we stood when we were up the lowest hill, near the river, whereof Dundee had already got possession of before we could be well up, and had his back to a very high hill, which is the ordinary maxim of the Highlanders, who never fight against regular forces upon anything of equal terms, without a sure retreat at their back."

The day was drawing on, with afternoon turning to evening as Mackay (1833:55) described the first stages of the fight:

The enemy having full view of our forces, by reason of the height they possessed above us, discerned the General, which drew their fire into all places where he stood or walked, whereby several of our men were wounded before the engagement; and to have so much nearer aim, they possessed themselves of some houses upon the ascent of the height whereon they stood, which the General not willing to suffer, least the enemy should be emboldened thereby, ordered his brother, commanding his own regiment, before whose front the houses were, to detach a captain with some fire-locks to dislodge them; judging withall that skirmish might draw on a general engagement, which he earnestly longed for before the night approached. The captain chased the enemy's detachment to their body with the loss of some of their number; but shortly thereafter, and about half an hour before sun-set, they began to move down the hill.

Clearly, Mackay was a target for Jacobite sharp-shooters as he went about deploying his men. Having failed to provoke a Jacobite attack with fire from his artillery, which collapsed on their carriages after three rounds apiece, Mackay took more direct action. A group of the Jacobite sharpshooters had moved forward from their lines and taken positions in some houses further down the slope. In order to get rid of this menace and in the hope of provoking a full scale attack, Mackay ordered his brother, who was commanding his (Mackay's) regiment, to detach a captain and some men to dislodge them. This operation succeeded on both counts.

The houses in question have never been identified, and one project aim was to locate them to check the accuracy of Mackay's account. From preliminary map analysis, using the first edition Ordnance Survey (OS) map (1867), several possible candidates were identified. The first was a small ruined house, Lagnabuig farmstead, located on a terrace just on the southern side of the A9 road.

Although it appeared to be in front of the Jacobite line and close enough to the government line to provide accurate musketry, there was one problem with its location. Mackay (1833:55) said that the houses (more than one building) were positioned to the front of his own regiment, located toward right flank of the government line, while Lagnabuig sits roughly in the center of the line. Excavation revealed no evidence for occupation predating the late-eighteenth or early-nineteenth century.

The other options for the buildings used by the snipers were two farmsteads, called Stirkpark and Orchilmore on the 1867 OS map, that are situated further east than Lagnabuig, and therefore better candidates for an alignment with Mackay's Regiment. However, the buildings are much further up the slope, 300–400 m away from the level ground on which the government troops were arrayed. That distance would put them out of any sort of effective range. These buildings sit on the 200-m contour and are likely to be on the Jacobite line, not in front of it. The two sites were discounted and the hillside scoured for evidence of a building not present on the first edition of the OS map, perhaps because it had been ruined or demolished prior to the map survey.

A rapid walkover survey revealed the remains of a farmstead some distance below the 200-m contour, on a small hillside terrace in the form of grass covered banks and depressions. At least one building was present, with long walls and gable ends still visible as low banks. Access to the site was via a hollow way, or track, to the west. Unfortunately, the site was found too late in the project for excavation. A localized metal detector survey was done which recovered a pistol ball from the gabled end of the building as well as a brass trigger guard from quite close by. These artifacts are the kind of finds expected at the scene of the fight described Mackay. The pistol ball is suggestive of close range combat and the trigger guard was perhaps broken from a musket in the hand-to-hand fighting as the Jacobite sharpshooters were evicted.

The Charge

To this point, Mackay's account held up pretty well against the archaeological evidence: the discovery of the farmstead not far below the original Jacobite position, opposite and above the government right, and perhaps most importantly, evidence that close quarter fighting had taken place. But how does Mackay's account stand up to the archaeological evidence for the battle proper?

Around eight o'clock in the evening, the Jacobites finally charged and Mackay (1833:58) describes its terrible impact on his own army thus:

> . . . the foot was just plying over all [folding or flying?] tho's sooner upon the left, which was not attacked at all, than to the right, because the right of the enemy had not budged from their ground when the left was engaged. Balfour's Regiment did not fire a shot, and but half of Ramsay's made some little fire. Lieutenant Colonel Lawder was posted advantageously upon the left of all, on a little hill wreathed with trees, with his party of 200 of the choice of our army, but did as little as the rest of that hand, whether by his or his men's fault is not known.
>
> Having passed through the crowd of the attacking Highlanders, he turned about to see how matters stood, and found that all his left had given way, and got down the hill which was behind our line, ranged a little above the brow thereof, so that in the twinkling of an eye in a manner, our men, as well as the enemy, were out of sight, being got down pall mall to the river where our baggage stood.

In order to verify this picture, which has the left fleeing the field without firing a shot and a stiff fight put up by the center and right, a metal detector survey was carried out in transects across the face of the slope down which the Jacobites charged. To the right and center, across the front of the government line, the slope was peppered with musket balls. Most had been fired by the government musketeers, who were arrayed in three lines and fired in platoon fashion rather than by volley which had been the common practice until then, especially in Britain (Pollard and Oliver 2003). In some cases, the lead balls lay in lines, this pattern mirroring the positions of the men who fired them.

All metal finds were plotted using a Total Station [a surveying instrument], which is vital for mapping and then interpreting the debris patterns of the battle. Heavy fire appeared to have been delivered by the center and right of the government line. However, in front of the left part of the line, which Mackay said was anchored on a little hill that can be seen today, the picture was very different.

Very few musket balls were recovered here, though buttons lie where they fell from Jacobite waistcoats after being torn away in the vigor of the charge. The Jacobites took off their plaids to run faster and fight more effectively in their shirts and waistcoats. The absence of musket balls again matches Mackay's description that some of his most experienced regiments fled the field, barely firing a shot.

Even where the government troops did fire, it is apparent from the study of the terrain that accompanied the metal detector survey, that the Jacobites chose their ground well. The slope they charged down was broken into one or two quite prominent terraces, which provided wide steps on the way down. As the Jacobites ran down onto the back of these terraces, they disappeared from the view of the government soldiers and were immune to their fire until they reached the lip of the terrace. This became very clear when the position was assessed while recovering musket balls. An observer stood on the government line, marked by impacted Jacobite musket balls, and watched a fellow team member walk from the back to the front of a terrace, demonstrating this very effectively.

The government line quickly folded, and despite Mackay's best efforts to rally his men, all was quickly lost. Mackay had little choice but to lead what men he could back down the hill and across the river, where hopefully they would find safety. Fortunately for him, the Jacobites seem to have been more interested in looting the baggage train than pursuing their routed enemy.

CULLODEN 1746

Historical Background

We now turn to the battle of Culloden. Fought on 16 April 1746, it marked the final defeat of the Jacobite Rebellion led by Charles Edward Stuart in his attempt to reclaim the crown from the Hanoverian King George II. Bonnie Prince Charlie, as he became known, arrived on Scottish shores from France in July 1745, raising his standard in Glenfinnan on 19 August. A Jacobite army was recruited, in the first instance largely from the Highland clans, as Charles made his way through the Highlands and enjoyed early success. At Prestonpans south of Edinburgh on 21 September, the Jacobites routed almost the entire British army in Scotland under General Cope (Reid 2004). Flushed with success, they marched into England as far south as Derby, less than 200 km north of London, before returning to Scotland. The Duke of Cumberland, the king's youngest son, followed, leading an army freshly withdrawn from Flanders and war against the French in order to crush the rebellion.

After successfully engaging the government at Clifton Moor, the Jacobite army crossed back into Scotland on 20 December, where it besieged Stirling. There was no time for complacency however, as General Hawley marched from a newly re-occupied Edinburgh with 8000 government troops. A battle took place at Falkirk on 17 January 1746, and after some uncertainty, it dawned on the Jacobites that it had been their victory.

Charles failed to follow up this success, and from that point on the government forces took the initiative. The Jacobite army turned north and by 21 February arrived in Inverness, the traditional Highland capital. Here, the Jacobite army broke into several units that began a largely successful program of engaging Highland forts and garrisons. However, the tide was about to drastically turn in favor of the government forces. The Duke of Cumberland quickly marched north, via Perth and Aberdeen. After crossing the River Spey on 12 April, his force, numbering some 9000 men, rapidly closed on Inverness. In response to this threat, Charles reunited his army and prepared to do battle near his new headquarters at Culloden, on ground then known as Drummossie Moor (fig. 9.4).

The Battle

On 16 April, the Jacobite army, with a good proportion of the troops still to rejoin, was not fit for a pitched battle. The night before had been wasted on

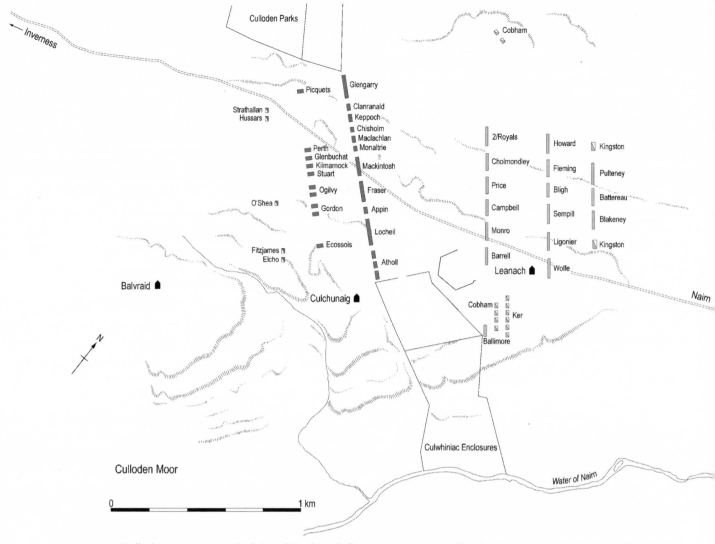

FIGURE 9.4. Culloden: government (right) and Jacobite (left) positions at start of battle. Drawing by G. McSwan after Reid.

a forced march that failed to surprise the government army (Duffy 2003). The Jacobites returned to their starting position, tired, cold, and hungry, and were ordered to form their battle lines. The Highland clans formed the front line with Irish and Scots French troops and others composing the second. What little cavalry the Jacobites stood as a third line. Their artillery was scattered along the front line, but proved no match for its government counterpart. The government troops deployed by regiment in two lines with artillery spaced between the front line regiments. The Jacobite command hoped that that the high enclosure walls between which its own line deployed would prevent any outflanking maneuvers by the enemy.

The battle began with Jacobite artillery taking potshots at one of the government commanders as

he conducted last minute surveillance. Government cannons were quick to reply and a ferocious barrage knocked out the Jacobite guns and then began to cut swathes through the Jacobite infantry. Eventually, when the order to charge was given, the Jacobite center surged forward. The right wing was a little slower off the mark and this staggering of the advance created a diagonal movement, with boggy ground, the slightly sloping topography, and heavy fire further directing the Scottish advance toward the left flank of the government line (Pollard 2009b). The MacDonalds, on the left, were the last to move forward. They did not make good progress over the wet ground and heavy fire from the government line effectively stopped them in their tracks.

As the Highlanders surged forward, government artillery opened up with case shot. At about 100 yards, a volley of well-aimed musketry struck the Jacobite front. The losses must have been terrible, but the momentum and determination of the charge was enough to carry the attackers crashing into the front ranks of the government left. Although they managed to hack their way through the front line, this did not help the Highlanders as they effectively found themselves sandwiched between the bayonets of the front and second lines. It was there that the Jacobite struggle effectively came to a bloody end.

Meanwhile, government dragoons had been able to get behind the Jacobite right, after having passed through breaches made in the enclosure walls south of the battlefield. By this time, all was lost. Partially screened by their horse and the second line of infantry, the Jacobites streamed from the field. The government line advanced in close order, dispatching the wounded and those too slow to escape. The cruel aftermath of the battle entered popular consciousness with stories of Jacobite wounded being dragged from shelter and shot against walls, or the barns in which they sheltered burned after the doors had been bolted (Forbes 1896).

Charles famously went into hiding, and eventually gained passage back to France. Those supporters left in Scotland, and indeed the general population of the Highlands, suffered the consequences of Jacobite defeat, with their lands taken and the clan system effectively demolished. Culloden became a symbol, however misconstrued, for the oppression of Scotland by England, with the romantic image of Bonnie Prince Charlie as freedom fighter and liberator contrasting with the English ogre in the form of the "Butcher Cumberland." In reality however, it was a civil war played out on the periphery of a pan-European conflict.

The Archaeology of the Battle (Combining Techniques)

The Culloden project is one of the most intensive investigations ever carried out on a British battlefield. It is notable for its multi-faceted character, with historic research, a topographic survey, and a metal detector survey augmented by a geophysical survey and excavation. The following brief summary will provide an idea of how these techniques can be combined to shed new light on a subject that has long been dominated by historians. The site is a popular destination for tourists and today much of the site is owned by the National Trust for Scotland, which has gone to considerable lengths to interpret the site through footpaths and signs. The Trust has also attempted to return parts of the site to something approximating the 1746 landscape, cutting down trees and even altering the course of the road that previously ran through the clan cemetery. In 2008, the old visitor center (built in the early 1970s) was replaced by a more up-to-date facility and the results of the archaeological work discussed here were used to provide a more accurate interpretation of the battle.

Culloden is notable for the wealth of documentary evidence in the form of eyewitness accounts and battle maps (Stephen 2009b). This information, in part, reflects increasing levels of literacy and the expanding bureaucracy of the mid-eighteenth century military establishment. Of almost 50 battle maps published in 1746 alone, most originated from around six maps drawn up by people who actually witnessed the event (Pollard 2009a). There is general accord among this small group of maps with regard to the nature of the terrain and the disposition of the armies. The most regularly reproduced is probably that by Thomas Sandby (1746), who served on Cumberland's staff.

Features that appear on all maps are the walled enclosures between which the Jacobite army formed its line. The northern enclosure is known as Culloden Parks and the southern as the Culwhiniac Enclosure. A smaller, horseshoe-shaped area shown northeast of the Culwhiniac Enclosure is known as the Leanach Enclosure. By the mid-nineteenth century, these walls disappeared as the modern field system was established. To fully understand the battle, the location of these structures must be ascertained. The National Trust for Scotland actually went so far as to reconstruct the smaller Leanach Enclosure that it believed was built from turf and earth not stone. Map work carried out at the time (Aitchison 1994) and more recently has established that the reconstructed enclosure is pretty much exactly where the original stood and a metal detector survey shed more light on its role in the battle. A walkover survey also identified the remains of the larger stone enclosure, as foundations of a wall that survive beneath a modern fence line.

The search for the northern enclosure was less successful as ditching and hedging effectively removed any obvious traces. A fragment of what is believed to be the western wall was located as a clear line of stones set into the earth some distance away from the present field boundary.

The enclosures are not the only features surviving from the battle. The most visited part of the site is undoubtedly the clan cemetery, where Jacobite dead, numbering 1000–1500, were buried in mass graves. Low, grass-covered mounds cover the long burial pits, and the ends of most are marked with roughly hewn boulders. Carved into these are the names of the clans for which the dead men fought and died; Camerons, Stuarts of Appin, MacIntosh, etc. However, it is unlikely that the picture is this straightforward. The dead were left on the field for three days. Then, under the watchful eye of government troops, they were buried by local people to whom they would have been strangers. Although tartans had long been worn, their use as rigid regimental and familial signifiers was a largely later introduction and so would not have provided a ready means of identification by unit. In addition, it is not known whether some men charged after taking off their tartan plaids as had been the case at Killiecrankie. Therefore, it is unlikely given the chaotic nature of the fighting, that it would have been possible to identify which corpse belonged to which clan. Some stones simply say "Mixed Clans" and this more than likely applies to every grave. The cemetery as we see it today, with its cairn-like monument dedicated to the "Gallant Highlanders," is in large part the result of a face-lift carried out by the landowner in the mid- to late-nineteenth century. However, there does appear to have been at least an oral tradition regarding the clan-specific nature of the graves. This is just one example of how battlefields can be manipulated in the decades and centuries after the fighting. There are no markers on the graves of the some fifty government soldiers who are reported to have been killed in action and many more died of their wounds (Reid 1998).

A cottage standing at the time of the battle was also rebuilt in the nineteenth century. It is one of three buildings on most 1746 battle maps that show a farmstead called Leanach just behind the government left. "Old Leanach Cottage," as it is known today, is a key feature of the National Trust for Scotland battlefield experience, and until recently it hosted a "living history" reconstruction of a government army surgeon at work. Although the building probably stands on the foundations of the original structure, a drawing made in the mid-nineteenth century and various descriptions of it as a ruin strongly indicate that it was rebuilt in the late nineteenth century and occupied until 1912 (Anderson 1920). It was further renovated by the Gaelic Society of Inverness and presented to the National Trust for Scotland in 1944

Coming off the gable end of the cottage on its south side is a roughly rectangular, low, grass-covered bank. For many years this was believed to be the site of the notorious "Red Barn" which, as accounts (e.g., Forbes 1896) would have it, was where a number of wounded Jacobites were brutally murdered when the doors were bolted and the building set a fire by victorious government soldiers. One objective of the project was to test this story using archaeological excavation as a forensic tool in a search for evidence of the barn and its burning. The structure proved to be the wall around a kitchen garden, which did not pre-date the early-nineteenth century. A photograph taken in the 1890s clearly shows this kitchen garden in use. There was no trace of a burned building.

Old Leanach Cottage was one of only three buildings, the other two having been demolished some time before the first map surveys by the Ordnance Survey in the 1860s. In order to relocate these lost buildings, a geophysical survey was carried out over level ground surrounding the surviving building. A number of anomalies were identified, one of which could be interpreted as a rectangular structure. In order to establish its true character, or "ground truth" it, this anomaly was subjected to an exploratory excavation (Pollard 2009b). The small trench revealed a slot cut into the subsoil that contained a possible posthole. This appears to be the foundation ditch for a wattle and daub (timber and clay) wall. This obviously differs from the dry stone construction of the standing cottage but ties in with a nineteenth century description of the building which stated that it was built from clay and turf (Anderson 1920). It is hoped that a more extensive excavation will allow a thorough investigation of this feature and its relationship, if any, to the story of the Red Barn.

FIGURE 9.5. Metal detector survey at Culloden. Photo taken from in front of Jacobite position toward left flank of government line, with reconstructed Leanach enclosure in middle distance. Photograph by author.

Metal Detecting

The preceding case study has shown how metal detector survey can be used to accurately locate battle sites and also how it can be used to identify smaller actions within the main battle. Culloden also proved to be a very suitable case for this treatment. The metal detector survey not only established that the battle covered a much larger area than previously believed, or at least portrayed, but also that certain actions did not necessarily take place where sign posts and display boards would have the visitor believe.

One of the most intensively detected areas is the "Field of the English," so-called because of the tradition that the government dead were buried here. This is also the field occupied by the greater part of the reconstructed Leanach enclosure, and therefore its original antecedent. An area about 80 m wide and almost a kilometer long was detected across this field (fig. 9.5). The transect passed through the enclosure, extending from the government line to the Jacobite line, as marked today by flags, and beyond. The effort was rewarded with a large assemblage of battle debris, including musket balls (fig. 9.6), artillery shot (grape and canister), buttons, buckles, coins, personal possessions, and pieces of broken musket. The picture they paint is of a dreadful storm of lead launched at the Jacobites as they charged across the moor.

The greatest concentration of material was found near the government line, but at a point some distance south of where the end of that line is marked by a plaque showing the position of Barrel's regiment. This debris scatter represents the actual point where the Jacobite right hit the government left, the regiments of Barrel and Munro. Pieces of broken musket lay where the weapons were smashed in the vicious fighting, while buttons torn from uniforms and pistol balls add to a characteristic signature of hand-to-hand fighting.

Several contemporary battle maps, including the map by Sandby (1746), show a road passing across the moor, running diagonally between the two front lines. The potential importance of the road was only noticed during the first phase of archaeological research when it was realized that the road may have been used by the Jacobites during their charge. It certainly seems more than a coincidence that the road passes roughly through the center of the Jacobite line and through the government left, where the Jacobite charge hit home. Ironically this road, widened in the nineteenth century and then metalled, was moved about 200 m to the north in the 1990s because it was regarded as an anachronistic intrusion. It seems likely that the clan graves were dug either side of the road because it was used to transport the dead to grave pits close to where the majority of the Jacobites fell (Pollard 2006).

Some musket balls recovered from in front of the government left have been almost severed in two, possibly when they struck the sharp edge of broadswords held aloft as the Jacobites charged home. A brass, Brown Bess trigger guard bears a crescentic scar from the musket ball which carried it away from the wooden stock and possibly killed the man holding the musket. To some extent, it is even possible to tell whether musket balls were fired by the government soldiers or Jacobites. The Brown Bess musket used by the government troops (the British army) was .75-caliber, whereas the French muskets carried by many Jacobites were .69-caliber. This means that the lead balls fired by the Jacobites are slightly smaller than those from government muskets. However, the Jacobites captured large numbers of Brown Bess muskets at Prestonpans and Falkirk, and so not every Brown Bess ball was necessarily fired by a government soldier.

On the basis of these artifacts and their distribution on the landscape, it is apparent that the government line extended across the mouth of the Leanach enclosure, in expectation of a Jacobite assault coming through it. This is clearly indicated by the dense scatter of musket balls, artillery ordnance, dropped coins, etc., recovered from within the enclosure. On the basis of the artifacts, there can be little doubt that Leanach enclosure, mentioned in very few contemporary accounts, did not represent a substantial barrier. Even today, the reconstructed turf banks have been heavily denuded by cattle and sheep and may in places give some idea of their condition during the battle.

The metal detector survey established that the government line extended further south than previously suspected. It also helped extend the distance between the two lines by around 100 m, the distance over which the Jacobites charged to reach the government line. The telling evidence came in the form of musket balls recovered west of the Old Leanach enclosure. Some had been heavily distorted and therefore fired at close range, which meant that they had not been fired from the government line, which at this point is over 400 m away. Historical accounts identify a fire-fight between the Argyll militia and the Jacobite Scots French troops as they retired to their dissolving line after being brought forward to support the

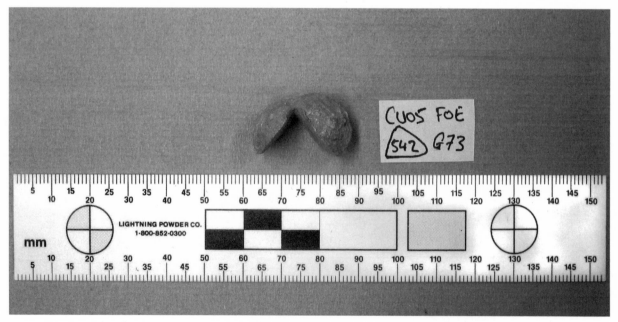

FIGURE 9.6. Lead shot from Culloden: British musket ball possibly cut by striking broad sword. Photograph by author.

Jacobite attack (Pollard 2009b). As they fell back, the Argyll Militia opened fire from behind the northern wall. This position is obviously at odds with the site as it was laid out prior to 2008 since it corresponds with the end of the Jacobite line, when in reality it stood out in the "no-man's-land" between the two lines. This conclusion is bolstered by contemporary maps that show the main Jacobite line well west of this position.

Geophysical Survey

Culloden is a good example of how all the different analytical techniques complement one another to provide an important insight, which at times forced us to question the conventional wisdom about these sites. One last example will serve to demonstrate the validity of this point. In addition to searching for the missing buildings, a geophysical survey was also employed in the "Field of the English," in an attempt to locate unmarked government graves. The survey produced a number of anomalies, some of which may relate to buried archaeological features, which possibly include both prehistoric remains and the graves of the government dead. While it is only possible to establish the character of these anomalies through excavation, metal detecting may provide a clue. During the survey, the area corresponding to one of the most obvious anomalies was noticeably bereft of metal detector finds, which seemed unusual as it was an area of otherwise high concentration where hand-to-hand fighting took place. The one notable exception

was a silver 12 Thaler coin dated to 1752. Obviously not of local origin, this coin came from the Duchy of Mecklenburg-Schwerin, on the Baltic coast, north of Hanover. It is not implausible that the coin represents a casual loss or even an offering by a serving soldier (in Hanoverian service), who was in the 1750s Fort William garrison, then under construction a few miles from the battlefield. It is not difficult to imagine him visiting the graves of fallen comrades at a time when the graves were still marked, perhaps by mounds which have since been plowed way. It is hoped that excavation may be used to ground truth this suggestion; only then will it be possible to mark the graves in a suitable fashion and also to ensure their future preservation.

CONCLUSION

Although inescapably brief, the forgoing case studies hopefully provide some idea of the potential role of archaeological techniques in furthering our understanding of late-seventeenth and eighteenth century battlefields and their associated bloody events. Each technique can be of value in its own right, whether documentary research, topographic survey, metal detector survey, geophysical survey, or excavation. But, when used in combination as a suite of techniques they really fulfill their potential. Battlefield archaeology in Scotland may still be in its infancy, but the projects discussed here have helped ensure that it will go on to take its place alongside more traditional fields of archaeological endeavor.

CHAPTER TEN

Patterning in Earthen Fortifications

LAWRENCE E. BABITS

INTRODUCTION

Earthen fortifications have been utilized for centuries. Anglo-Americans can look to the defenses at Maiden Castle, the Antonine Wall, Offa's Dyke, and the English Civil War for ancestors of pre-1865 American works, albeit with later French influence. More recent examples can be found in World War I trench lines and dugouts, hundreds of foxholes dug by Allied and Axis troops across Europe, U.S.-built firebases in Vietnam, and the 1990–91 "berm" along the Saudi border built by the Iraqis. This chapter provides a synthesis of the earlier earthen fortifications, a look at how they were built, and some things an archaeologist should look for when excavating.

Although most earthworks are seen as temporary, many fortifications constructed in the past obviously had some permanence, because their footprint is still evident on the landscape today. This paper will concentrate on the 1750–1865 era but the terms, methods, and results are virtually the same from 1600 to 2000. Hence, American Civil War photographs provide a valid starting point for accurate imagery to supplant what exists today. From the photographs, it will be obvious that the longer a military force was on-site, the more elaborate the fortifications could be.

INVESTIGATING EARTHWORKS

Any investigation of earthen fortifications should start with the technical manuals of the day. Understanding what was intended and comparing the ideal to actual fieldworks allows better interpretation of the often complex structures. Using the proper, period terminology is also important. Many terms utilized in the manuals have very specific meanings that convey a great deal of information. For example, the meaning of the word "berm," has changed from "a flat space above the scarp" in the eighteenth century, to "an earthen wall" in the twentieth century. There is a key difference between palisade and stockade that relates to gaps between the vertical logs of a palisade, spaces that are not found in a stockade. The glossary, using original text, included in this volume should provide clarification.

Knowledge of local history relative to the site is important. This information can be gleaned from residents, county and town histories, maps, photographs, and paintings. Finally, as Balicki (chap. 6) points out, an archaeologist should never overlook local collectors who often have great knowledge and cultural material specifically related to their locality.

A visual inspection, including map, aerial photographic and terrain analyses can be particularly useful. Crop marks are zones where growth is greener or taller due to disturbed soil, and/or more water and nutrients. The location of such differences can provide clues to subsurface fortification elements. Even in heavily wooded areas, the growth of trees on rectangular or linear mounds can cause shadows that reveal trench and mound lines. Visible remains can include depressions that were once fort ditches, magazines, and bombproofs (Babits 1990). On mounds, a depression can often be a clue to an internal structure.

Although it is not often done, a geological study of the area should be undertaken. The underlying strata can provide key information about the site, indicating why fortifications were successful, or why they were not. An outstanding example of what geology can reveal about fortifications is Doyle's (1998) study of the World War I Western Front. Coupled with the geology, an understanding of the drainage is also essential. Ed Rutsch (personal communication) was fond of saying, "If you understand a fort's drainage, you understand how the fort was built." During the American Civil War, many fortifications were built on prehistoric shell middens because they were on well-drained soil.

Various forms of remote sensing can be helpful (see Hanna, chap. 2). Ground-penetrating radar (GPR) can be useful on sites suspected of having buried fortifications, but "ground-truthing" by excavation will still be required to verify the nature of any anomaly that is observed. Resistivity surveys are time consuming but may well show outlines of buried works because the different soils interrupt electrical currents. A magnetometer that measures variations in the magnetism of the earth might be useful, particularly if large amounts of iron metal are present. Metal detectors can be very useful, but, as Balicki and others in this volume point out, their utility depends on the experience of the operator and the quality of the machine itself

Excavation of earthwork features should be designed to minimize damage to the archaeological resource, while still recovering a maximum of meaningful information. Following historical research, visual inspection, and remote sensing, excavations can be planned to intersect anomalies and obtain cross-section profiles useful in confirming the status and possible function of the feature. Spatial (or areal) excavation, uncovering a wide space, is not recommended unless the site is slated for total alteration (Balicki, chap. 6).

"Ideal" Earthwork Fortifications

The military has long been conscious about providing instruction for the "proper," or ideal, way of doing things. The design and construction of fortifications are no exception. Vauban (1737, 1968) synthesized and published his analysis of current fortification practices in the seventeenth century. His work serves as a baseline for understanding fortifications, both permanent masonry or brick forts and temporary earthen works.

In the eighteenth century, texts by Muller (1747, 1756, 1783), Clairic (1776), Saxe (1756), Diderot (1763), LeBlond (1764) and Vauban (1737, 1968), to name only a few, were available for French, British, and American military personnel. In the nineteenth century, fortification manuals were even more common and include Adye (1804), Hoyt (1811), Duane (1809, 1810), O'Connor (1817), Nesmith (1824), Yule (1851), Gibbon (1860), Halleck (1862), and Mahan (1862), to name some of the more common examples. More works came out following the experience of the American Civil War (e.g., Gilmore 1865; Von Schliha 1868; Corps of Engineers 1868; Wilhelm 1881; Mercur 1889). Most drew heavily from a combination of Civil War experience and earlier writers who, in turn, had drawn from Vauban and his contemporaries. That means there was a published, systematic approach to fortifications.

During wars against Native Americans, there was a continuation of field expedient fortifications and manuals dictating their construction. These one-man fighting positions were also utilized by Native Americans (Scott 1991). Linear trench and one-man fighting positions were also utilized during the Spanish American War and the Philippine Insurrection. Oddly, with all this extensive experience, the basic U.S. infantry manual for NCO's and privates, published in 1917, did not discuss trench warfare. There were attempts to educate Americans about trench warfare while Americans were serving in British and Commonwealth units and at least one book was designed specifically to inform Americans about trench warfare (Empey 1917). More modern fortification syntheses include Robinson (1977), Lewis (1979) and Hess (2005). Specific, detailed studies include Higgins (1985), Babits and Pecoraro (2006). Two of the best fortification studies involving research and limited excavation are Harrington's (1957) examination of 1755 Fort Necessity and Hagerty's (1971) preliminary work on Fort Bull.

More pragmatically, while engineering officers generally oversaw the placement, design, and construction, the vast majority of earthen fortifications, especially during the Civil War, and away from major ports or urban areas, were thrown up by men who knew they needed protection. Even then, tactical and terrain considerations dictated practical construction. Just as some officers knew something about fortifying a position, so too, must an archaeologist have a

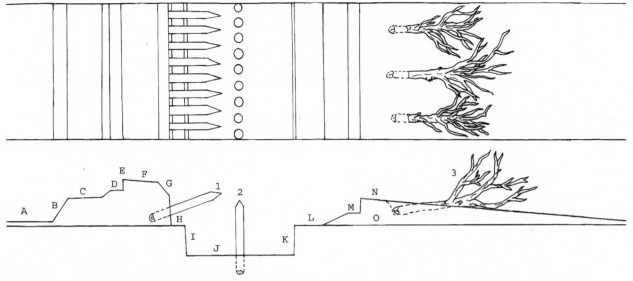

FIGURE 10.1. Cross-sectional view of fortification (after Robinson 1977:113): (A) Parade; (B) Parade Wall; (C) Terreplein; (D) Banquette (sometimes with additional firing step); (E) Parapet; (F) Superior Slope (same plane as glacis); (G) Exterior Slope; (H) Berm; (I) Scarp; (J) Ditch (fosse, moat); (K) Counterscarp; (L) Covered Way; (M) Banquette; (N) Glacis; (O) Original Ground Surface; 1: Fraise; 2: Palisade 3: Abatis. Illustration by author.

reference library of military manuals and knowledge of how terrain affects tactics, especially defensive tactics, for the time period under study. In the absence of such temporally relevant insights, sound analyses and interpretations of the defensive features can be significantly diminished.

During the American Civil War, the large armies created extensive earthen fortification lines. Today these seem to meander over the countryside, but understanding why they were built shows they were not random constructions. The use of any high ground provided an advantage. Where ground was relatively level, or where a fortification continued for some distance, soldiers extended the line forward for a distance as a salient angle. These protrusions, variously called redans, bastions, salients, and other terms, allowed flanking fire, or enfilade, against an attacking force. While a fortification might have a variation that seems quite odd, it was probably sited to cover dead space, where the normal run of the line would not allow weaponry to cover the ground surface. In all cases, Vauban's (1737) basic premise that the front of a fortification should be covered by another part of the fort was maintained.

Whether an earthen fortification was an enclosed work (redoubt, bastioned fort), or an open defensive line, the same terms, and most of the same procedures were followed. Excavating the outer ditch provided earth for the rampart and thus created an inverse stratigraphic sequence inside the earthen wall (fig. 10.2). As the rampart went higher, or was expanded, earth came from further away, resulting in other inverse stratigraphic zones that had topsoil under subsoil. To keep the wall from eroding, it was usually covered with sod (Davis 1981–84; Babits et al. 1987, V:59, Babits 1990), pinned to the bare surface with long wooden pegs, or treenails.

The terminology for any work included a set of terms, but the general cross-section of a fortification from its outer defenses to the place where defenders stood was virtually identical (fig. 10.1). The outer slope beyond the ditch was called the glacis. It was designed to bring attackers onto a plane covered by defensive fire as well as protect the lower portions of the rampart. The glacis might be improved by using intertwined treetops and branches with their ends sharpened called abatis. The next part of the fortification was the ditch (fosse, moat).

The outer wall of the ditch was called the counterscarp, and it might have a place for men to stand and use the glacis as a parapet. The inner ditch face, below the rampart, was called the scarp. At times, the ditch would be reinforced by a palisade. This open log wall was usually erected midway in the ditch, and had

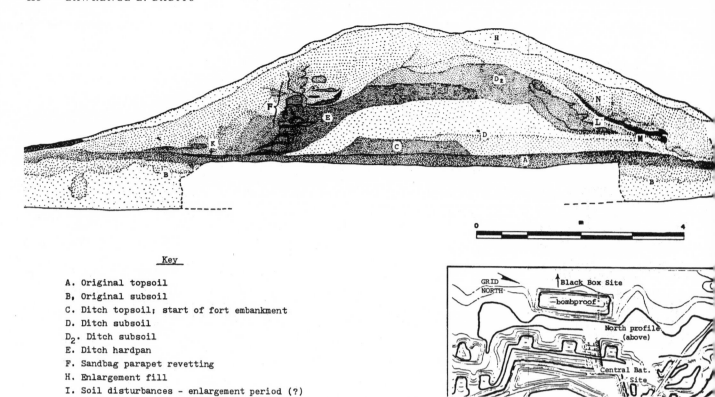

Key

A. Original topsoil
B. Original subsoil
C. Ditch topsoil; start of fort embankment
D. Ditch subsoil
D_2. Ditch subsoil
E. Ditch hardpan
F. Sandbag parapet revetting
H. Enlargement fill
I. Soil disturbances - enlargement period (?)

FIGURE 10.2. Upgraded river face earthen wall; looking north. The constructional sequence shows inverse stratigraphy and two stages of raising the wall at Fort Bartow, Causton's Bluff, Savannah, Georgia (from Babits et al. 1987). Original drawing by Rick Leech.

pointed logs to shed assault ladders. These vertical logs were placed about 6–9 in apart to allow soldiers to shoot between them, but not so wide as to allow attackers to get through. The logs were not linked by cross timbers so the ladders would slip down the log and not permit entry over the palisade.

Above the scarp was a narrow walkway where men could stand during construction to toss earth higher. This berm also allowed access to repair the rampart face. Fraise might be inserted into the rampart. This added defense was a near horizontal palisade that further obstructed attackers, but still allowed defenders to shoot through gaps between the logs.

The top of the rampart was called the parapet. The upper surface sloped down and out to allow firing along the slope of the glacis and into the ditch. Parapet thickness varied but was enough to stop musket balls, if not artillery shot. The inside of the parapet was at least 54 in high to allow men to fire over the parapet. To allow reloading in relative safety, the vertical face of the interior parapet was usually much higher and a firing step, or banquette, was placed on the horizontal surface

so men could step up to fire, and down to reload. A variant of the firing step can be seen in the shallow ditch dug behind the wall of the sunken road at the foot of Marye's Heights west of Fredericksburg, Virginia (Hess 2005:188; Davis 1981–84).

Vertical earthen faces were often revetted, or reinforced, to avoid slumping. Sandbags, logs, wickerwork, or planks (Davis 1981–84) were used to reinforce exposed surfaces. Soldiers often dug into trench walls to create living quarters with greater protection (Davis 1981–84). These elements all leave traces in the archaeological record.

Whatever the time period, regular troops were detailed as pioneers to build fortifications, usually under the guidance of engineers. By the American Civil War, large engineering units often supplemented the line troops, but their most important duty was logistical, building bridges and improving roads. Erecting a fortification required little experience of the men because the final shape of the earthwork was laid out with poles and all that was required was that the empty spaces be filled in as shown in an 1862 illustration

(Bellard 1975:55, 164) noting that as early as April 1862, "Fortifications were built very fast."

One manual familiar to many Civil War officers was written by D. H. Mahan in 1862. This work contains statements about labor, time, and procedures for constructing an earthen fortification wall that are useful starting points: "The ditch should be regulated to furnish the earth for the parapet. To determine its dimensions, the following points require attention; its depth should not be less than six feet, and its width less than twelve feet, to present a respectable obstacle to the enemy. It cannot, with convenience, be made deeper than twelve feet; and its greatest width is regulated by the inclination of the superior slope, which, produced, should not pass below the crest of the counterscarp (Mahan 1862:33). He continues: "Experience has shown that, in ordinary soils, a man with a pick can furnish employment to two men with shovels; that, not to be in each other's way, the men should be from four-and-a-half to six feet apart; and finally, that a shovel full of earth can be pitched by a man twelve feet in a horizontal direction, or six feet in a vertical direction" (Mahan 1862:49).

The directions were amplified by additional commentary about the process:

"The pick commences by breaking ground so far from the counterscarp crest that, by digging vertically three feet, he will arrive at the position of the counterscarp. The excavation is carried on by digging to the depth of three feet, advancing towards the scarp, where the same precaution is observed as at the counterscarp. The earth is thrown forward, and evenly spread and rammed, in layers of about twelve inches . . . (Mahan 1862:50).

The time required to throw up a work will depend on the nature of the soil and the expertness of the laborers. From troops unaccustomed to the use of ditching tools, six cubic yards may be considered a fair day's work in ordinary soils, when the earth is not thrown higher than six feet; but when a relay is placed on an offset in the ditch, from four to five cubic yards may be taken as the result of a day's work for each man. Expert workmen will throw up from eight to ten cubic yards at task-work"(Mahan 1862:51–52).

In an artillery treatise, John Gibbon (1860: 448–49) made an explicit reference to excavating in sandy soil.

He claimed that if picks were not required, a "man can shovel and load on a wheelbarrow from 15 to 19 cubic yards of earth per day" (Gibbon 1860:448). He also stated that sand bags had been used to revet fortifications in sandy soil during the Mexican War (Gibbon 1860:445).

On occasion, existing earthworks were modified by building them higher as seems to have happened at Fort Bartow, on Causton's Bluff, Savannah, Georgia (figs. 10.2, 10.3). At the same fort, space inside the parapet was deliberately filled in with layered soil to raise the wall higher (fig. 10.4). In other cases, when a line of earthworks was overrun and used by the other side, as at Chancellorsville (Hess 2005:194) or Petersburg (Davis 1981–84; Frassanito 1983:239), trench lines were realigned after their capture. To provide support for the new gun platforms, the backside of the new parapet was built up and revetted with posts and logs. Archaeologically, this sort of alternation will manifest itself with a ditch "inside" the existing fortification. The revetting will be seen as a post mold line that is discontinuous inside the ditch.

In many cases, contemporary maps show a sequence of upgrading earthworks on the landscape. While superposition might demonstrate rebuilding and expansion, those key areas might have been subjected to farming and urban renewal. Consequently, any fortification should be looked at with a consideration for time depth because later forts were often built on top of earlier ones (South 1973). The 1862 Confederate use of Revolutionary War siegeworks at Yorktown is one example. More impressive is Kelso's (2006:50) demonstration that Confederate forces built an earthwork over the 1607 Jamestown Fort. Frequently coastal earthworks were built on prehistoric shell middens (Watts et al. 1981:47; Babits et al. 1987; II:1; South 1973).

Overlapping layers of fortifications can also occur during a war. At Ninety-Six, South Carolina, early war fortifications were upgraded on several occasions. Then, in response to a siege by Continental forces that produced trench lines (parallels), approach trenches (saps), and a tunnel (mine), the fortifications were again enhanced (Holschlag and Rodeffer 1976a, b, c; Holschlag et al. 1978). Something similar also occurred at British Fort Watson, where a secondary interior earthwork (a traverse) was erected during a

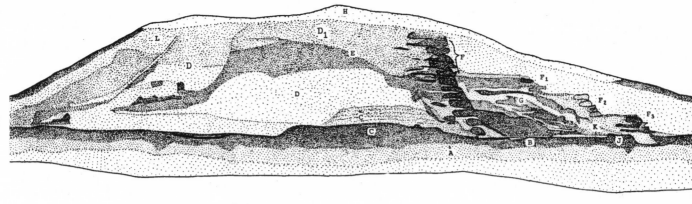

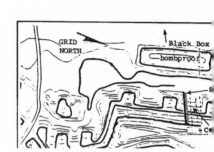

Key

A. Original subsoil
B. Original topsoil with some ditch topsoil
C. Original ditch topsoil and A Horizon
D. Ditch subsoils
D_1. Ditch subsoils
E. Hardpan from base of fort ditch
F. Sandbag parapet revetting
F_1. Sandbag terracing
F_2. Sandbag terracing
F_3. Sandbag terracing
G. Enlargement fill in fighting position
H. Enlargement fill in parapet

FIGURE 10.3. Upgraded river face earthen wall; looking south. Constructional sequence shows inverse stratigraphy and two stages of raising the wall stepped down. F1, F2, and F3 represent traverse footings at Fort Bartow, Causton's Bluff, Savannah, Georgia (from Babits et al. 1987). Original drawing by Rick Leech.

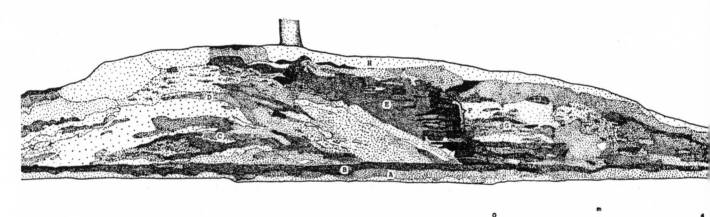

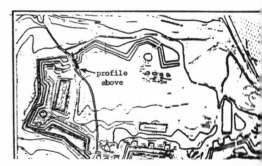

Key

A. Original subsoils
B. Original surface
C. Beginning phase of wall construction with surface and ditch soil
D. Ditch subsoil
E. Compacted soil mixed with reddish hardpan
F. Sandbag parapet revetting
G. Enlargement filling of fighting position
H. Enlargement fill

FIGURE 10.4. Upgraded land face earthen wall at Fort Bartow, Causton's Bluff, Savannah, Georgia (from Babits et al. 1987). Original drawing by Rick Leech.

short siege to protect men from American rifle fire (Ferguson 1973)

Earthworks were not simply long lines of parapets and ditches. Many provided shelter for equipment and men. The Fort McAllister bomproof photograph (Davis 1981–84) shows how sharp and crisp the outline of a sodded earthwork could be. When earthworks collapse, they often preserve the interior structure in compacted form as found at Causton's Bluff outside Savannah (fig. 10.5). The collapse often leaves a depression in the top of the mound providing clues to the structure beneath (Babits et al. 1987, V:18–54; Babits 1990).

At some forts, the protective covering was left open on the interior (rear) side for a variety of reasons including fresh air and a more rapid response to defend the walls. The overhead cover at Fort Fisher, North Carolina (Davis 1981–84, III:177), relied on heavy posts to support the roof and its protective overburden. The support posts are likely to be the only archaeological evidence remaining if the area has been ploughed or eroded. Something similar was found at Jamestown where molds indicating a supporting system were found to parallel palisade postmolds (Kelso 2006:57).

More common, and harder to detect in an archaeological context would be a field-expedient shelter along a fighting line. Many, made of barrels, planking, and logs, with a shallow interior trench excavation, would probably only appear as a pit with a humic layer if excavated. Other trench lines appear only as a shallow ditch after excavation (Braley 1987), the organic nature of the parapet leaving no physical evidence because of deterioration or post-battle removal.

Most archaeologists are familiar with the concept of postmold and posthole or trench, but detecting these is often a lot more difficult than first thought. The vertical angle at which posts were emplaced in the ground should be determined. The angle may well indicate whether the post(s) were intended as a stockade, palisade, fraise, revetting or abatis. Knowing what a timber was used for will provide important clues about the fortification.

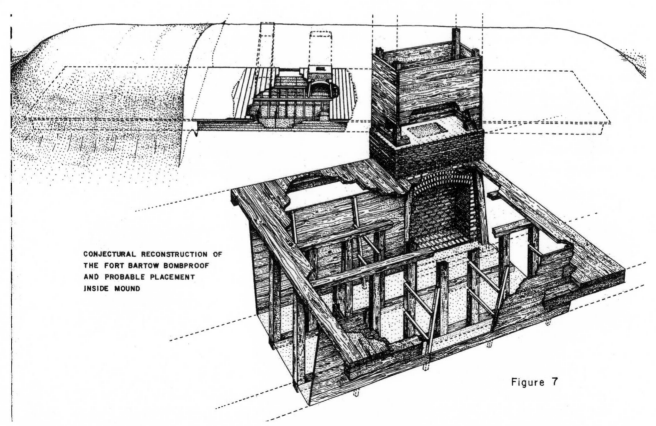

CONJECTURAL RECONSTRUCTION OF
THE FORT BARTOW BOMBPROOF
AND PROBABLE PLACEMENT
INSIDE MOUND

Figure 7

FIGURE 10.5. Bombproof interior reconstruction at Fort Bartow, Causton's Bluff, Savannah, Georgia (from Babits et al. 1987). Original drawing by Rick Leech.

While it is often easy to see a linear soil stain at the surface, it might not be visible in a trench floor that has been worked and trod upon by archaeologists. There may be no telltale postmolds in the ditch floor. Aerial photography may reveal a linear soil stain inside a fort ditch. This might align with a soil stain photographed during an earlier excavation phase. Other views may show a linear anomaly in another part of the same ditch that is also associated with artifacts in linear alignment. Photographs and field drawings can show even more clearly that something interrupted soil lenses and artifact distribution. The shallow ditch, stain, and break in artifact distributions can suggest a ditch may have anchored abatis, or that it contained a palisade.

Trenches were very often reinforced with timbers on vertical faces, raised logs creating a firing port (head log) and sometimes overhead cover. The vertical timbers often leave archaeological traces. Evidence of horizontally placed timbers and iron rails (traversing rings) should be sought at earthwork sites where a parapet for a gun platform was revetted with logs backed by vertical posts, and the gun sat on a wooden platform. At some Civil War fortifications, such as Fort Branch, Hamilton, North Carolina, evidence of both horizontal logs (or planks) and the vertical posts have been recovered (Shiman 1990). At artillery positions, the necessary reinforcement under the gun platform will also leave traces beyond the stringers on which the planks were laid. Despite World War I and World War II scrap iron drives, iron traversing rings often remain, as well as the flooring and stringer remnants or their molds. Obviously, this type of fortification was more common at longer-term earth works. Field works still had the same features but in a less solid state.

As combat grew more intense in the Civil War, steps were taken to avoid enfilade, or fire from the side, by erecting traverses. These mounds prevented an attacker from firing down the length of a trench and also provided a fighting position for defenders. Today, they are often confusing, but photographs show how they once looked. The traverses ranged from log barriers to huge earthen mounds (Hess 2005:191; Davis 1981–84, III:174–75, 178–80). Fort Fisher photographs show fighting positions between traverses (Davis

1981–84, III:175, 179). Earthen traverses will overlap onto the parapet as they were usually built later; this can be seen in profiles of Fort Bartow, Savannah, Georgia, (fig. 10.3).

The massive Fort Fisher traverses and wall (Davis 1981–84, III:178) reflect constant upgrading and reinforcement over more than two years. In contrast, hastily built field works were often small and irregular and were often designed to meet an immediate, and short term, need. A parapet built during the campaign against Atlanta in 1864 (Davis 1981–84, IV:273), consisted simply of horizontal logs with dirt thrown between and over them. Archaeologically, the shallow nature of such remains might result in their evidence being lost if the field were later plowed.

A more obvious trench system is a Confederate work in north Georgia. Here a distinctive feature of the latter part of the Civil War is visible in the horizontal logs that revet the upper interior. Logs were often placed across the trench, perpendicular to, and on top of the breastwork logs. Resting on top of these cross-trench logs, on the "enemy" side, were "head logs" (Davis 1981–84). The head log allowed a soldier to shoot out under the head log without really exposing his head. Archaeologically, a head log would be very difficult to detect.

Even in short-term situations, a tremendous amount of earth could be moved. This is perhaps best exemplified by a portion of the trench systems around Atlanta, Georgia, and Petersburg, Virginia. Here there were revetments, bombproofs, palisades, and exterior defenses such as chevaux-de-frix (crisscrossed timbers) and abatis (the outward pointing tree limbs, the pre-1870 version of barbed wire entanglements). Planks built into the defenses came from nearby frame buildings. Trenches were revetted with any available material that was later abandoned and left to rot in place. The most likely place to find remnants of this material is at the bottom of the trench against the wall.

On many occasions, wooden basketry (gabions, saucissons, fascines) served to create protective barriers as well. Fascines and gabions might not appear in the archaeological record at all, except perhaps as an organic stain. Yet they were very common, and by comparing where they were located in a trench line, it may be possible to identify them, even if only a stain or a mass of burned "twigs."

Finally, within more complex earthen fortifications there were often bewildering mazes of housing for troops. These should be treated carefully as they often contain a variety of material related to the daily life of soldiers, aside from the military activity. This was certainly the case in New York where Calver, Bolton, and their fellow excavators (Calver and Bolton 1966) excavated numerous British and American Revolutionary War camps that now provide a basic understanding of the common soldiers of that war.

Taken as a whole, earthen fortifications can provide a wealth of information about tactics, soldiers, and weaponry if the investigator is armed with a knowledge of what they once looked like and what modern vestiges should resemble.

ACKNOWLEDGMENTS

Matt De Felice created the cross sectional profile of a fortification for fig. 10.1. Rick Leech made the original drawings for the Fort Bartow, Causton's Bluff project, shown as figs. 10.2–10.5. This chapter was materially enhanced by their graphic skills. A great many students and Coastal Georgia Archaeological Society members worked on my projects over the years. This chapter reflects their dedication to accurately observing and recording what they found.

CHAPTER ELEVEN

Methods in the Archaeology of Colonial Frontier Forts
Examples from Virginia and West Virginia

W. STEPHEN MCBRIDE AND KIM A. MCBRIDE

INTRODUCTION

In this article we discuss research methods to locate and further investigate eighteenth century frontier forts in present West Virginia and western Virginia. A background context for these forts illustrates their position in the frontier settlement landscape. These forts were generally built by local citizens, county militia, or provincial soldiers, or a combination of these, and often served as the earliest central places in the landscape. They provided a place of refuge for settlers and a point to garrison troops. In many cases, the presence of a fort and defense prevented total abandonment of a settlement. As such, these forts were an important adaptation to the colonization of a disputed territory.

Unfortunately, historical documentation on these forts is extremely limited. This is particularly the case with questions of fort design and their precise location. Archaeology is the best, and sometimes only, avenue of research. Subsurface remains such as stone foundations, stockade trenches, and postmolds can help us understand the original footprint of a fort and how it was constructed. Artifacts inside these features, such as nails, spikes, and daub (sun-baked clay) provide additional information on construction methods.

The first and hardest part of this type of archaeological research is locating the forts. Since they, or at least their military functions, were ephemeral, there is often very limited artifactual evidence and a lack of reliable military maps. If the fort site experienced later domestic occupation, locating definite fort-period artifacts or features is even more difficult. It usually takes a combination of oral and documentary sources plus creative archaeology to locate these sites, especially ones that have good integrity. Once located, excavation can be further complicated if the sites have lengthy occupations including many non-fort features and artifacts. Methods used to locate and excavate these sites will be discussed following the presentation of a brief historical context.

THE FRONTIER DEFENSIVE SYSTEM

It is impossible to understand the nature and function of frontier forts without background on the defensive system in which they existed. When the French and Indian War began in 1754, local frontier defenses were not well-developed. As a result, Virginia created and administered a frontier defensive system that included fort construction and creation of a military force known as the Virginia Regiment. These initiatives reinforced those residential forts built in 1754 and 1755 and the activities of the poorly organized local militia.

This system was later strengthened, or better organized, by the settlers and militia constructing new forts, during Dunmore's War (1774) and the Revolutionary War (1775–83), and by improving the militia and using a network of scouts ("Indian spies") to observe enemy movements. Local initiatives were aided, at times, by broader offensive military campaigns such as Andrew Lewis's Point Pleasant campaign and the campaigns of George Rogers Clark, Lachlan McIntosh, and by government-sponsored peace negotiations. Still, settlers relied primarily on their own local defensive system for protection.

During the frontier period, the primary local military force was the county militia. During the French and Indian War, the militia was supplemented by the Virginia Regiment. Made up of volunteers and appointed officers, the Virginia Regiment was divided into companies under a captain. Commanded by Col. George Washington after August 1755, the Virginia Regiment constructed numerous forts down the Valley of Virginia in present Virginia and West Virginia. During the Revolutionary War, the militia was supplemented by Virginia State Troops; regular state soldiers who enlisted to serve within the boundaries of the state and who garrisoned forts on the Ohio River.

The Virginia Militia was modeled on an ancient English institution (Cress 1982). All free white males aged 18 to 50, excepting those with vital occupations, were required to serve. Although the governor was the overall commander, the militia was organized at the county level and led by county lieutenants whose staff and company officers commanded the men. Each county had at least one regiment divided into five to ten companies of approximately 20–80 men and officers. The county lieutenant could order the militia to service within the county, but to take his companies outside the county he had to ask for volunteers. This hindered offensive action because creating a sizeable force of more than 200–300 men required volunteers from adjacent frontier counties (Sosin 1967:106; Stone 1977:13). Accounts provided in pension applications suggest that entire companies would guard a fort from a few days to as long as six months. In addition, they participated in offensive campaigns during the 1770s and 1780s. The most notable were Andrew Lewis's 1774 Point Pleasant Campaign, George Rogers Clark's aborted 1781 Detroit expedition, and forays into Kentucky (McBride et al. 1996:A.2, A.17, A.24). Militiamen also protected farmers planting crops and pursued Indian raiding parties. According to militiaman James Gillilan, "in the summer season [we] would all turn out in a body and work each others places by turns—whilst some were working others would be watching and guarding—to give alarm of the approach of Indians" (McBride et al. 1996:A.11).

Scouts, or "Indian spies" as they were usually called, were another crucial element of the frontier defensive strategy. During the French and Indian War, scouts functioned in an offensive capacity, gathering intelligence and attacking enemies in their camps. By the 1770s and 1780s, scouts had become more defensive, roaming the landscape to look for enemy signs. Greenbrier Valley (now West Virginia) pensions show that many men served in this duty. The application of scout Michael Swope, who lived and operated in the Greenbrier Valley, provides an example, "when [scouts] saw signs of Indians they would fly from Fort to Fort and give the alarm so that preparations might be made for defensive operations by the people that were Forted and that those who had ventured out to work their corn might betake themselves to the Fort before the Indians would attack them . . ." (McBride et al. 1996:A:24).

Forts Within the Defensive System

The concept of community forts is ancient and one that settlers of many nationalities brought with them to the New World. Most settlers of the western Virginia regions were likely familiar with both log blockhouses and wooden stockaded forts. This was particularly true during and after the French and Indian War. Interestingly, there is little or no evidence of forts being built between Pontiac's Rebellion (1763–64) and Dunmore's War (1774). Apparently, settlers saw them as unnecessary during times of peace. By the spring of 1774, when Dunmore's War began, both privately built and militia-built forts were constructed in the border country, and some larger, two-story, private dwellings were garrisoned and designated "forts." The national importance of forts is evidenced by their prominence on Fry and Jefferson's *1755 Map of Virginia,* or nearly 30 years later, Filson's *1784 Map of Kentucky.*

Forts were usually located in the approximate center of a settlement cluster or neighborhood. They were often built by, or on the land of, a prominent settler who may have donated land and materials, or supervised construction to gain prestige as well as defense. Sometimes they were built around an existing house, which continued as a residence during and after the fort era. Forts were always near a permanent water source such as a spring or creek and they were usually on a ridge or terrace, high, but not too high for settlers to reach. They were also on or near trails or roads.

Forts were quite numerous. For example, we know of at least 32 privately built or militia-built forts in the Greenbrier Valley of West Virginia by the Revolutionary War, though a few were built there during the earliest (unsuccessful) settlement attempts of the 1750s and early 1760s. The distance between forts varied with population density, areas of cleared land, and exposure to danger. Virginia's official French and Indian War "Line of Forts" were placed every 15–26 miles, but there were private forts in between. In the Greenbrier Valley, forts were located 3–10 miles apart during the Revolution. Randolph County settler David Crouch (1841) stated that "In Tygarts Valley [WV] the forts were not more than 4, 5, or 6 miles apart. There were some 10 or 12 forts. All of the forts were stockaded, with bastions for the sentries to stand in at night."

Forts served as early central places in the landscape. An interesting commentary on a sense of regional attachment to a fort site is provided in the memoirs of the Rev. Joseph Doddridge (1824:94–95), who noted that "My reader will understand by this term [fort], not only a place of defense, but the residence of a small number of families belonging to the same neighborhood . . . The families belonging to these forts were so attached to their own cabins on their farms, that they seldom moved into the fort in the spring until compelled by some alarm, as they called it."

The Structure of Frontier Forts

Fort design could vary considerably, depending on the builder, its purpose, and its location. Documents suggest that many were built of vertically placed logs forming a stockade and with various log buildings placed inside. Other forts, particularly in the French and Indian War, may have been built partially of earth and horizontal logs for extra protection against artillery. The Virginia Regiment forts were supposed to follow strict designs such as laid out by Col. George Washington or the Augusta County Council of War. Forts were typically directed to be from 60–90 or 100 ft on a side, and with bastions. For example, the 1756

Augusta County Council of War ordered that ". . . Fort Vanse [Vause] be made at least one hundred feet square in the clear; and that the stockades be at least fourteen feet long; that all the other forts be made 60 feet square with two bastions in each fort" (Koontz 1925:101).

Two generalized descriptions of typical forts are very instructive. According to the Rev. Joseph Doddridge (1824:94), "The fort consisted of cabins, blockhouses, and stockades. A range of cabins commonly formed one side, at least, of the fort. Divisions or partitions of logs separated the cabins from each other. The blockhouses were built at angles of the fort. They projected about two feet beyond the outer walls of the cabins and stockades. In some forts, instead of blockhouses, the angles of the fort were furnished with bastions. A large folding gate made of thick slabs, nearest the spring, closed the fort. In some places less exposed a single blockhouse, with a cabin or two, constituted the whole fort."

A wonderfully detailed description and drawing (fig. 11.1) was provided by Spencer Records (1842):

> I will for the information of those that never saw a stockade fort, describe one, and lay down a plat thereof. In the first place, the ground is cleared off, the size they intend to build the fort, which was an oblong square. Then a ditch was dug, three feet deep, the dirt being thrown out on the inside of the fort. Logs, twelve or fifteen inches in diameter and fifteen feet long, were cut and split open. The top ends were sharpened, the butts set in the ditch with the flat sides all in, and the cracks broke with the flat sides of other[s]. The dirt was then thrown into the ditch and well rammed down. Port-holes were made high enough that if a ball should be shot in, it would pass overhead. The cabins were built far enough from the stockades to have plenty of room to load and shoot. Two bastions were constructed at opposite corners with port-holes about eighteen inches from the ground. The use of these bastions was to rake the two sides of the fort, should the Indians get close up to the stockades, so that they could not shoot them from the port-holes in the sides. Two gateways were made fronting each other with strong gates and bars so that they could not be forced open. Some forts had a bastion at each corner.

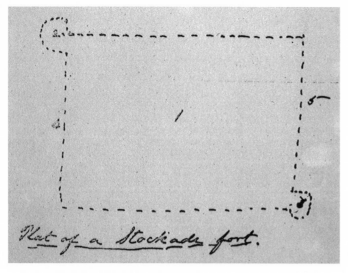

FIGURE 11.1. Plan of a typical fort by Spencer Records (1842). Courtesy Wisconsin Historical Society.

LOCATING THE FORTS

Our research suggests that it is best to begin with a large universe of possible fort sites, and then focus on a smaller sample of the more well-documented and better preserved sites. This will greatly increase the chances of success in locating sites with research potential. Background research on forts is the first step and should include examining primary and secondary documentary sources and interviewing local historians and site landowners. County histories and published primary documents are good starting points. These records often give the names and sometimes a general location of area forts. Next, we talk to local historians and landowners to see if the locations for any local forts are known. Informant interviews have proven to be the most effective way of locating discrete sites and narrowing the search area to 2–5 acres before beginning an archaeological survey.

Land records are important in verifying which fort was in a given location, as well as providing economic information on the property owner of the fort, who was often its builder. County personal property tax records are another good source of information on fort owners/builders. County order books are useful to identify militia officers as well as county officials, many of whom were fort owners or builders.

The most useful primary record groups include the Draper Collection of Manuscripts of the Wisconsin State Historical Society, the Revolutionary War Pension Applications in the National Archives, the Washington Papers (Abbott 1983, 1984), and the Governor Dinwiddie Papers (1884). The Draper Collection of Manuscripts is widely available on microfilm at libraries and historical societies. It consists of period letters and reports, usually by militia officers and other officials, or later interviews of pioneers and their descendants. The collected manuscripts also provide information on fort garrisons, Indian attacks, and supply issues, as well as more general contextual information. Many of the more descriptive Draper Collection of Manuscript letters were published in the early twentieth century (Thwaites and Kellogg 1905, 1908, 1912; Kellogg 1916, 1917). Calendar series to some of the Draper Collection of Manuscripts have also been reprinted from Wisconsin State Historical Society (e.g., Preston and Virginia Papers, 1915; Kentucky Papers, 1929; Frontier Wars, 1991).

Revolutionary War pensions are perhaps the best records for understanding the entire frontier defensive system at this time. Former soldiers and militiamen had to describe their military service during the war to prove they deserved a pension. They typically mention forts they garrisoned and for how long. Some mention spying circuits and guarding settlers as they worked on crops. Interestingly, most militiamen were denied a pension unless they went on larger expeditions or garrisoned Ohio River forts. Excerpts from some frontier Virginia pensioners have been published (e.g., Johnston 1990; McAllister 1913). The published George Washington Papers include letters, reports, and orders to and from Col. George Washington, Commander of the Virginia Regiment 1755–58 (Abbott 1983, 1984). These documents include orders to build forts, some construction suggestions, orders to garrison forts, locational information of forts, battle descriptions, and orders and reports related to supplies. The Governor (Robert) Dinwiddie Papers (1884) also cover the French and Indian War and are similar to the Washington Papers, although not as detailed.

Secondary sources on Virginia frontier forts are limited and of a mixed quality. County and regional histories dating from the 19th and early 20th centuries provide detailed descriptions of Indian attacks and frontier life (Stuart 1820; Doddridge 1824; Withers 1831; Kerchevel 1833; De Hass 1851; Chalkley 1912) and a combination of oral history and documentary research (Hale 1896; Summers 1929). Historical or archaeological studies focusing broadly on Virginia frontier forts are limited (Lewis 1906; Cook 1940; Bond 1974; Morrison 1975; Ansel 1984; McBride et al. 1996; McBride, McBride et al. 2003).

Local oral traditions have been crucial to our success in locating fort sites. We do not typically conduct formal tape-recorded interviews, but rather take detailed notes. Still it is important to be sure the informant gives permission for use of the information given, and to cite them in reports if they consent. County or regional level historians are a good place to start. Our initial research in Greenbrier and Middle New River valleys in West Virginia during 1989–90 included touring known fort sites with local historians. Local historians can introduce you to persons with knowledge of a given locale. Landowners are another good source of information, especially if the property has been in their family for generations or the family has lived nearby. Current landowners may have crucial information from past landowners. Locating descendants of the occupants, or builders of the fort, who might have information, is also important. Once informants are located, be prepared to receive information on other types of local sites, such as mills or general stores. Many informants will assume you are interested in all "old sites" not just forts, and your study could be the last chance to record memories of important community places. Initially, it may help not to use the name of the fort you are looking for, since the informant may have known it by another name. Oral history data must be treated just as archival data, with rigor and realization that errors can creep into the local tradition.

Metal Detecting a Fort Site

Once a probable fort location is identified through historical research and interviews an archaeological survey is conducted to pinpoint the location and provide information on the research potential of the site. Metal detecting is the most effective way to locate and verify ephemerally occupied fort sites (see Hanna, chap. 2 and Balicki, chap. 6).

Our particular method is as follows. Once a signal is received, and pinpointed by multiple scans,

we prepare for the investigation by locating an area nearby that has no metal. This area is covered with plastic sheeting, to investigate the soil from the pinpoint area. The plastic makes for easier and more complete backfilling, which is important to landowners. A cone of earth about 10–12 inches in diameter and about 8 inches deep, hopefully encompassing the signal-generating artifact, is excavated with a shovel and laid on the plastic. The detector is swung over removed dirt to isolate the signal. If no signal is found, the excavated hole is rescanned and the process repeated until the operator has successfully removed the signal-producing artifact. This process of elimination is repeated until the artifact is recovered.

It is important that the operator not wear metal rings or other jewelry that could give misleading signals. Care should be taken to keep trowels and shovels away from the detector. Just because one artifact is located does not mean that others are not present; both the excavated dirt and the hole should be rechecked. Notes should be taken on observed soils and stratigraphy. Middens and features may be discovered, although this is not the main goal of metal detecting.

Wrought nails and cast iron kettle fragments have been the most common diagnostic items found on fort sites during our metal detecting. Other artifacts include iron and pewter utensils, brass and pewter buttons, and musket balls. If a dense midden is found and/or there is a need to collect all artifacts, screening through $1/4$ in hardware cloth can be employed. Systematic screened shovel test pits (STPs) have also been excavated at ephemeral and longer occupied fort sites, with mixed results. On more ephemeral sites, such as militia-built forts with occupations of six years or less, shovel test pits are not effective and will often miss the site. At Arbuckle's Fort, Greenbrier County, West Virginia, excavation of shovel test pits at a 10-ft interval produced only a French gunflint, a wrought nail, animal bone, and prehistoric flakes. The low density of historic material would have inhibited identifying the site during standard survey.

At larger and more intensively occupied sites, such as fortified house sites, shovel test pits are more effective, since artifact density is much higher. In these sites they can be especially useful in locating concentrations from different occupations, as we found at Fort Edwards, Hampshire County, West Virginia (McBride 2001, 2005). Even on domestic fort sites, particularly those with occupations of only 10–30 years, metal detecting is still very useful.

On fort sites with extremely long occupations, particularly those that have late nineteenth or twentieth century occupations, metal detecting is much less useful. Shovel test pits, and perhaps larger unit excavation, are necessary to locate and evaluate eighteenth century deposits. While the longer occupation sites are easier to discover, the fort period within them is much more difficult to isolate.

JARRETT'S FORT, A TEST CASE

Many of these research methods are illustrated in our discovery of Jarrett's Fort, a local residential Revolutionary War era fort in Monroe County, West Virginia. Jarrett's Fort was on our initial list of forts to research in 1989–90, but we did not initially choose it for fieldwork because the only locational information we could find was that it "was at the mouth of Wolf Creek" (Morton 1916:45). The information was too vague so we focused on other forts with better documentation. Years later, our grant sponsor requested that we make another effort to locate Jarrett's Fort; we conducted more intensive archival research, particularly in land records. From holdings of various generations of Jarrett family members, we isolated what we thought was the original 270 acre tract of David Jarrett, who built the fort. But when we drew up the survey following the metes and bounds calls, and attempted to place it on a modern USGS. topographic map, we had little success due to a lack of any geographical features mentioned in the survey calls. We then followed the chain of title forward and noticed that the original survey calls and acreage significantly changed by 1818. The original 270 acres had been reduced to 243 acres; the new tract boundaries included more references to Wolf Creek. The references were sufficient to allow us to redraw and fit this parcel precisely on the USGS topographic (McBride and McBride 2003). This location was not at the mouth of Wolf Creek as reported in local history.

We now had a definite area to search, but the 243 acre plot was still too large to survey in its entirety.

After studying the topographic map, two elevations overlooking the creek looked similar to the settings of other fort sites. Using property valuation assessment (PVA) maps, we identified the modern landowner. After talking with him about local history, he volunteered that an elderly resident had told him about the location for "an old stronghold" on his property. He gave us directions and permission to metal detect. At the described location, and within a short time, we located numerous wrought nails, cast iron kettle fragments, and a two-prong fork. Soil augering helped locate deeper midden-like soils, which were tested in two 50 X 50 cm shovel test pits and found to be as deep as 50–60 cm. They also contained creamware, redware, a brass coin button, wrought nails, and animal bone. The survey suggested that this site deserved more investigation, carried out on two subsequent occasions, excavating many shovel test pits and several larger units. Our most recent season resulted in discovery of the stockade trench, so more work is planned.

Our search for Jarrett's Fort taught us a number of valuable lessons. First, it reinforced combining archival research and informant interviews as the most effective way in locating these sites. More land record analysis was necessary, but that is not unusual with frontier sites. Our initial universe of forts was biased towards ones with a strong local tradition as to their location. The second lesson was to be more careful in talking with informants. They may not be willing to share information until a level of trust is developed. Also, they may not know of a fort, or any site, by the name you give it. In some cases it may be best to pose your questions more generally, such as "did you ever hear about a fort in this area, or on your property?"

Fort Excavation

Excavating at frontier forts is much like other historic sites. The main difference is that the excavation is perhaps more feature-driven, since architecture is often a main research question, and the researcher is often interested in only a small segment of the total occupation of a site. The latter issue can be a particularly difficult problem on sites with extremely long occupations. In both cases, fort-period architectural features

FIGURE 11.2. Stockade gate at Arbuckle's Fort. Photograph by author.

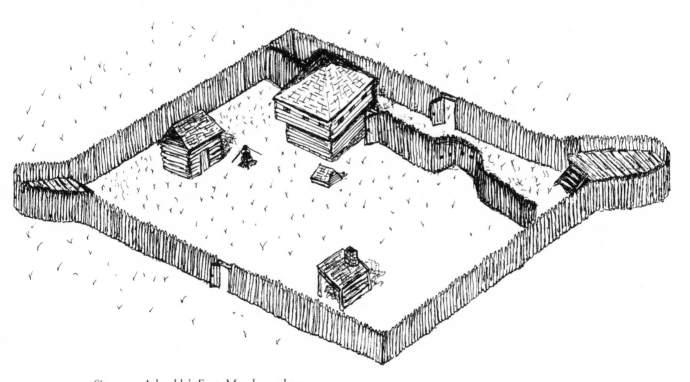

FIGURE 11.3. Site map, Arbuckle's Fort. Map by author.

must be discovered to understand the design of the fort. In the latter case, one also needs to find and excavate fort-period refuse features or strata to learn about fort lifeways. The discovery of fort-period features can be quite difficult on long occupation sites since the sites typically contain more features from later occupations, and sometimes even earlier ones.

The most diagnostic feature of many forts is the stockade trench. This is a trench excavated to support vertical whole or split logs and create the stockade or palisade. We have found these trenches on five West Virginia fort sites, Arbuckle's Fort and Fort Donnally in Greenbrier County, Jarrett's Fort in Monroe County, Warwick's Fort in Pocahantas County, and

Fort Edwards in Hampshire County. The first four are Revolutionary War era and the last is French and Indian War. In all cases, the stockade trench was about 50 cm (18 in) wide and 30–50 cm (12–18 in) deep. It was usually found at the plowzone-subsoil interface at 30–40 cm (12–16 in) below surface. Depending on the soil color and conditions, the stockade trench is usually easy to see, because the trench was excavated into subsoil and backfilled with darker humus and sometimes midden soils. The stockade trench may have

openings for gates (figs. 11.2, 11.3, and 11.4), or otherwise be discontinuous, such as when it connected buildings, as was the case at Fort Donnally (fig. 11.4).

We have found stockade trenches by a number of methods. At Fort Edwards, they were located by excavating parallel backhoe trenches and machine stripping large areas (Gardner 1990; McBride 2001, 2005). At Fort Donnally, hand trenching was used in conjunction with historical documents (McBride and McBride 2006). At Warwick's Fort, soil auguring was

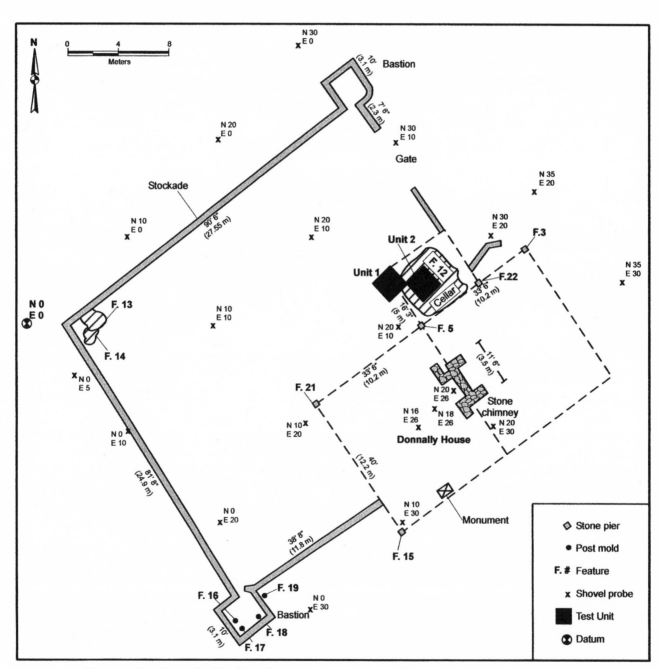

FIGURE 11.4. Site map, Fort Donnally. Map by author.

FIGURE 11.5. Aerial photograph of Arbuckle's Fort stockade excavation. Photograph by author.

employed to find the stockade trench. At Arbuckle's Fort (McBride and McBride 1993, 1998) and Jarrett's Fort the stockade trench was found in test units. We conducted a geophysical survey (resistivity) at three fort sites, but were unable to pick up any definite signs of a stockade footprint, although at Jarrett's Fort remote sensing was successful in delineating the Jarrett house foundation.

Once discovered, the most cost-effective way to expose the entire stockade enceinte (trace) on a fort site is by utilizing mechanical equipment such as a backhoe or trackhoe to remove overlying soil (usually plowzone), (see also Balicki, chap. 6). If a site has not been plowed, or there is sub-plowzone midden, the use of heavy equipment may be precluded. On plowed sites, however, if backhoe excavation and backfilling is done carefully, disturbance is minimal and acceptable given the importance of understanding the layout of the stockade. Following excavation, we recommend aerial photography, as well as detailed mapping, to record the overall fort structure, as shown here for Arbuckle's Fort (fig. 11.5).

Postmolds should be visible in the stockade trench. It is important to document these to truly understand how the fort was constructed. For instance, were whole or split logs used, or large logs, or a combination of large logs with smaller ones filling gaps, the main construction method? Sometimes postmolds are not clearly visible when the stockade is first exposed.

In this case, the stockade trench should be first sprayed with water. If posts are still not visible, the trench may need to be carefully scraped with a trowel to expose them. Once exposed, the stockade trench postmolds should be mapped and a sample excavated or bisected so that their shape and depth can be recorded. Sectioning posts at Arbuckle's Fort showed that they had sprouted roots—a sign the posts were green when placed in the ground. If any fragments of wood or charcoal are recovered in these post molds they should be saved to later determine wood species. Daub may suggest that clay was used to fill gaps between the logs.

Some forts, particularly during the French and Indian War, were constructed with horizontal logs and/or earth, so that their archaeological footprint would be much different from that of a vertical palisaded fort. At Fort Vause, Montgomery County, Virginia, three bastions are clearly visible on the surface as rounded raised earthen areas (fig. 11.6). The fourth bastion was disturbed. We found evidence of thick clay fill in the bastions, but we did not find evidence of the curtain walls.

Other features encountered on frontier forts include building and chimney foundations, cellar pits, probable trash pits, possible privies, and middens.

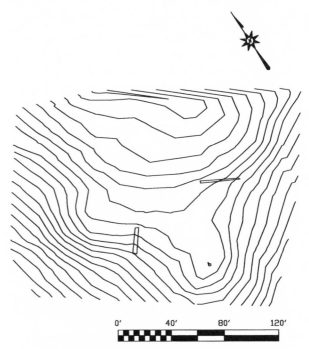

| 0' | 40' | 80' | 120' |

FIGURE 11.6. Topographic map of Fort Vause. Map by author.

Such features are similar to ones found on domestic sites and should be mapped and excavated in the usual fashion. These features were found by systematic shovel test pit excavation, augering with a split spoon auger, larger unit excavation, or by backhoe trenching and stripping of the plowzone.

On forts with both short (8–15 years) and medium (15–30 years) length occupations we strongly recommend unit excavation. Significant fort-period artifacts have been recovered from plowzone contexts. While fort-period features tend to have moderate or even dense faunal remains, other artifact classes tend to be rather sparse. Any sub-plowzone strata should be sampled, and if they date from the fort-period a large sample should be recovered.

On sites that have been occupied longer, the plowzone is generally going to be fairly mixed and the researcher will have to decide how much of this is worth excavating and analyzing. A site can have spatial and temporal variability in refuse disposal practices or activity areas. We have found that systematic shovel test pit excavation is a good method for determining temporal variability across a site. This was especially crucial at Fort Edwards, where after locating eighteenth century artifacts, we were able to document a large cellar from Joseph Edwards's original house (McBride 2005).

During later excavation seasons at Arbuckle's Fort (McBride and McBride 1993, 1998; McBride, McBride et al. 2003), we excavated even more test units and shovel test pits, and continued with metal detecting, soil augering, and investigation of soil chemistry. The shovel test pits, excavated just inside the stockade, helped locate a blacksmithing area and a trash pit full of slag and scrap iron. The augering, soil sampling, and chemical testing, which could only be done in the spring when soils were soft, helped locate another cellar, a large circular refuse pit that may have been a cooking/animal processing area, an angular defensive position known as a redan in the internal stockade, and finally, another short stockade segment west of the blockhouse (fig. 11.3). These features were further investigated with larger test units.

One important aspect of a short-term site like Fort Arbuckle is low artifact density, perhaps accentuated by the fact that this was a militia-built fort and never a permanent residence. By far the most common

historic cultural remains were animal bone and slag. Wrought nails, scrap iron, and gunflints, or gunflint flakes, were the next most common items. A moderate quantity of lead shot, both fired and dropped, was found through metal detecting and in the test units. These and the gunflints suggest that rifles, primarily .45- to .50-caliber, were used by the occupants of the fort as well as by attackers during two known raids. Ceramics and container glass were relatively rare, with lead glazed redware being the most common. Clothing items, including metal buttons and buckles, were recovered, but not in any quantity.

Most larger artifacts and larger animal bone were recovered from features, but a significant amount of material was found in the plowzone. Given the short occupation of Arbuckle's Fort, the plowzone was a critical information bearing component on this site, particularly in terms of spatial questions. We therefore strongly recommend complete screening of as much plowzone as possible.

CONCLUDING THOUGHTS

Frontier forts were important central places within the eighteenth century landscape of western Virginia, and a crucial part of the defensive system that was formed in response to conflicts with Native Americans and other European nations. The forts are often included in local and regional histories, but details of exact locations and physical characteristics are scarce. Few actual forts have survived and archaeology is one of the best methods for understanding their specific structure and construction methods. Investigation and preservation hinges upon precise location of these sites. Detailed research in primary archival records, secondary histories, and use of local oral history traditions are all crucial to locating fort sites. If these resources can be used to narrow down a site location, methods such as metal detecting frequently result in a positive location.

Since forts were often located in strategic locations, and with good access to water, these sites were often subsequently reoccupied. Sometimes forts were located at an existing residence, often a local militia leader or the home of a prominent citizen. In this case, the fort site might be easier to locate, but integrity of fort-era deposits may be compromised or more difficult to sort out.

Fort sites are typically located on private land. We stress the importance of landowners as stewards, and the importance of maintaining positive contacts with the landowners. We surveyed the site of Fort Donnally in Greenbrier County in 1989–90 (McBride and McBride 1991) and verified the fort location but decided against more intensive excavation since the site had a long occupation extending into the twentieth century. In 2004, the landowner told us that cattle wallowing near their feeding trough had exposed foundation-like stones. Subsequent investigations revealed these stones were part of the double chimney of the Donnally house. Since we knew from period accounts that the front of the Donnally house was tied into the stockade, we were able to locate the stockade and eventually excavate it completely (McBride and McBride 2006). This site followed the plan of Arbuckle's Fort in having two opposing bastions, but was quite unique in that the Donnally house formed a third defensive position in a corner (fig. 11.4).

We have tried to distinguish some advantages and disadvantages of sites that have only fort period occupations versus those that also have residential occupations. Fort sites that contain brief, exclusively fort-period occupations are the easiest sites if you want to address fort structure, material culture, and life within the fort, but sites with longer and more complex occupations can also yield important information. Many longer occupation sites represent the more successful or influential sites in terms of their occupational histories, and so should not necessarily be ignored just because they require more effort to separate the varying occupations.

There is support for the study and preservation of fort sites among the general population, but because of their ephemeral nature, they are being lost at a rapid pace in areas of rural development or suburban sprawl. Standard survey methods within the CRM context, such as broad interval shovel testing, will miss most fort occupations because of their low artifact density (see Balicki, chapter 7). Oral traditions are often crucial to locating sites, but with every year the number of potential informants, typically the older citizens, dwindles. We hope our colleagues will look for and promote preservation of fort sites now, while many local informants are still alive and the sites extant.

CHAPTER TWELVE

Great War Archaeology in Belgium and France

A New Challenge for Battlefield Archaeologists

MATHIEU DE MEYER

In Flanders fields the poppies blow
Between the crosses, row on row
That mark our place; and in the sky
The larks, still bravely singing, fly
Scarce heard amid the guns below.

We are the dead. Short days ago
We lived, felt dawn, saw sunset glow
Loved, and were loved, and now we lie
In Flanders fields.

This excerpt from "In Flanders Fields," by Canadian army physician and poet John McRay (1872–1918) is without doubt one of the most famous and moving war poems. "In Flanders Fields" is also the name of a museum in Ypres (Ieper) and the American War Cemetery at Waregem, where 368 Americans who died at the end of the First World War (1914–18) are buried. Ypres lies in the heart of the region that is now called "Flanders Fields." It is located in the province of Western Flanders (West-Vlaanderen), Belgium. The World War I Western Frontline crossed the province from Newport (Nieuwpoort) to Messines (Mesen), from where its course continues through France, ending at the French-Swiss border. The infamous Ypres Salient became one of the worst battle areas along the entire frontline.

John McRay wrote the poem on 3 May 1915, a few days after the second battle of Ypres when a young friend of his had been killed by a shell the day before. It is a lasting legacy of this terrible event. The poppy mentioned in the poem became a worldwide symbol of Remembrance Day (Armistice Day, Veterans Day). The focus in this chapter is the archaeological research that has been carried out on World War I in this area.

THE YPRES SALIENT: A SHORT HISTORY

On 3 August 1914 when France announced war against Germany, Germans invaded neutral Belgium, seeking to reach Paris by the shortest possible route. Britain declared war against Germany because of treaty obligations to defend neutral Belgium. With the entry of Britain into the war, her colonies and dominions abroad offered military and financial assistance. The United States entered the war on 6 April 1917.

The Belgian Army was forced to retreat towards the coast. By 7 October, German troops had crossed the river Lys (De Leie), and moved forward towards northern France. The army of Belgian King Albert I took up position behind the river Yser (De Ijzer) and the Ieperlee-channel (Het Ieperleekanaal). Between this line and the river Lys is a gap of about 20 km. The French, British and Germans brought as many troops as possible to this region, where later that year the Ypres Salient came into being.

The First Battle of Ypres (First Ypres) took place between 19 October and 22 November 1914. French, British, and Belgian troops occupied positions around Ypres to defend a well-defined salient. Both armies suffered many casualties. From then onwards, the Germans began to dig trenches on high ground, particularly the low ridges that surround Ypres to defend themselves from fire by the allied forces. When the Allies realized that a breakthrough was impossible, they also started to dig in. They were at a disadvantage, however, because they had to use the topographically lower areas, closer to the city and beneath the surrounding ridges.

In April 1915, the Second Battle of Ypres (Second

Ypres) commenced (22 April–25 May 1915). This second attempt by the Germans to conquer Ypres is remembered for the first large-scale use of chlorine gas. It was the first chemical gas warfare anywhere in the world. Within the gained territory, the Germans built a new extensive and heavily fortified system of trenches. After this intense combat period, the position of the front line stabilized and remained very much the same for the next two years. The soldiers entrenched themselves again and fortified their positions. From there both sides continuously attempted to win ground but failed, leaving the situation more or less unchanged.

On the first day of the Third Battle of Ypres (31 July–10 November 1917) British soldiers broke the German lines and advanced towards Passchendaele (Passendale). The Third Battle of Ypres cost about 450,000 lives, of whom many are still listed as missing in action. The ground won in Third Ypres was later lost during the Fourth Battle of Ypres, but this fighting did not occur where this archaeological research took place.

In between these major battles, the area provided the backdrop to many more minor actions and skirmishes that left traces on the landscape. The region was totally devastated by the time the Armistice was signed on 11 November 1918. The inhabitants came back and cleared the land, filling in thousands of bomb craters and trenches. But beneath the ground many traces of the war are still preserved.

WORLD WAR I ARCHAEOLOGY IN BELGIUM AND FRANCE

It is only recently that professional archaeologists have become interested in World War I archaeology. Until a few years ago, amateur archaeologists and collectors were the only ones concerned with this heritage. Unfortunately, the so-called "excavations" were not very professional. However, there would be little known about some sites if the amateurs were not there as new industrial and housing areas developed.

Before 2002, when the A19 Highway project began, there had been very few professional investigations of World War I sites in Flanders carried out by the Flemish Heritage Institute (VIOE—Vlaams Instituut voor het Onroerend Erfgoed). In most cases, they were

excavations of deep dugouts; underground shelters dug behind the frontline where soldiers could sleep or rest or the wounded were treated. Many investigated sites were near the Salient. In the same period some trenches were excavated on the future industrial estate of Boesinghe (Boezinge); they were found alongside Roman and Iron Age remains.

An early inventory of World War I sites was carried out in 2001, when the archaeological heritage of some villages near the Belgian frontline was examined using literature, trench maps, and a GIS system. Trench maps were produced by both sides to show trenches, shelters, wire entanglement, etc. Information on the maps was based on ground observation and aerial photographs.

Meanwhile, a group of British archaeologists, the No Man's Land Team, became active in Northern France near the Somme battlefields. Around the city of Arras, French archaeologists also became interested in the subject during major development works.

The situation in Flanders changed in 2002, when plans were revealed to extend highway A19 through the northern half of the Ypres Salient. The Flemish Government asked the Flemish Heritage Institute to carry out archaeological research in the area. Questions were raised about what remains from the war might be found and their condition. Were there human remains? What damage would the highway inflict on the archaeological heritage and human remains? The Institute decided to deal with it like an excavation on a medieval site using all available techniques.

While the research progressed, universities, governmental organizations, and other scientific institutions became more and more interested in the subject and soon it was considered normal archaeological research. The research in Ypres also received support from the Belgian Bomb Disposal Unit (Dienst voor Opruiming en Vernietiging van Ontploffingstuigen—DOVO) and many international specialists and institutions. Finally, a decision was made not to extend the A19, partly due to this report. A new proposed route avoids the battlefields and frontlines almost completely.

One of the main issues concerning World War I archaeology is the question of its usefulness. Some are still not convinced because there is an abundance of resources dealing with the period: regimental and personal, aerial photographs (fig. 12.1), trench maps,

FIGURE 12.1. A fragment of a British trench map with a German aerial photograph projected on top of it in the GIS. This is a part of the Ypres Salient, north of Ypres. Courtesy Flanders Fields Museum.

letters, poems, paintings, pictures, etc. Should World War I sites therefore be examined as precisely as Roman, medieval or prehistoric sites? Are the remains old enough to be conceived as "archaeology"? Should so much attention be paid to the inventory of every single trench, dugout, or shelter? Are they worthy of protection? Should it be UNESCO World Heritage? Which techniques should be used in order to investigate the sites? The excavations that were carried out during several projects, proved the value of research on such recent sites. A great deal of new information about living conditions in the trenches and the material culture in actual use was collected. And of course, human remains were recovered and re-buried in one of the many local war cemeteries.

THE A19 PROJECT

There were two major chapters within the A19 project: the inventory and the excavations. During the preliminary research, it became clear that the planned A19 would impact many important areas of the Ypres Salient. It would cross the frontlines of three major battles around Ypres and threatened to cut through many military structures (fig. 12.2). An example is the frontline of the First Battle near Bixschote where fighting took place between French and German units. The trench system dug after the second battle

was threatened for a stretch of 2 km and was examined at several locales: High Command Redoubt (Mauser Ridge; German trenches), Turco, Forward Cottage, and Cross Roads (British trenches). Between Turco Farm and Wieltje, Third Ypres began on the exact location where the A19 extension was planned. This area was the fighting ground for Belgian, Indian, British, Moroccan, German, French, and soldiers of other nationalities, hence its international importance. Many casualties remained in no man's land. Where possible, the deceased were buried in temporary graveyards near the front.

The Inventory

First, the important trench line systems and infrastructures were mapped in a GIS using British and German trench maps and aerial images. These were used as a guide for the field walking campaign of the entire highway route (length = 7 km, width = 100 m). Several concentrations of material were mapped. These were composed of ammunition (shrapnel balls, shells, bullets, grenades, etc.), wire entanglement, remains of trenches and meter gauge railways, telephone wires, remains of concrete shelters, bottles, rum jars, etc. Depressions in the fields were also registered in the GIS, because they could be the result of a collapsed deep dugout. All farmers who owned

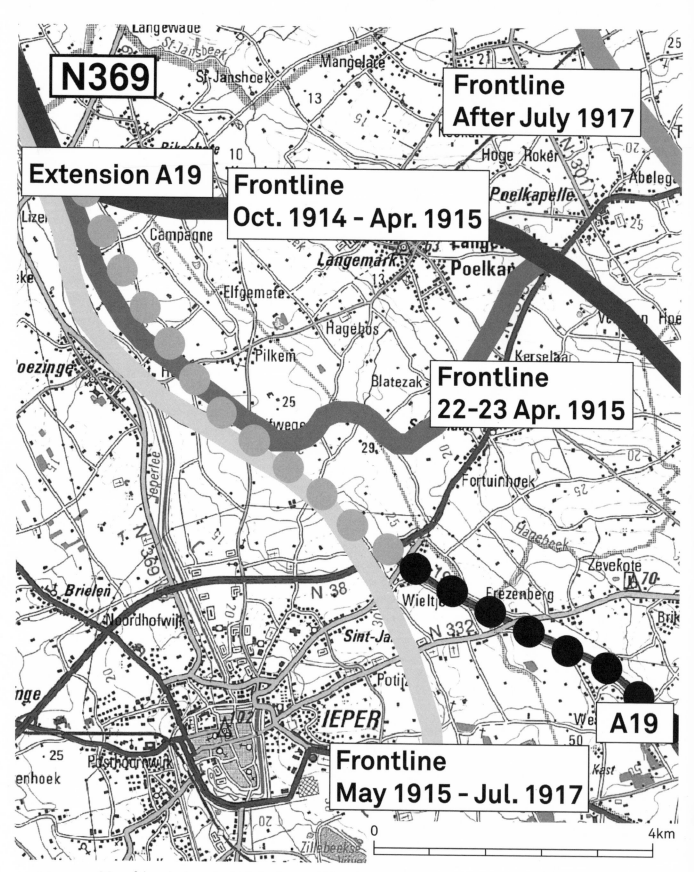

FIGURE 12.2. Map of the area through which the A19 would have been extended. Courtesy ©AGIV.

land on the route were interviewed about the presence of World War I remains on their fields. Some of them came up with important information, especially those who were descendants of farmers living on the same spot during the war. While ditches were being cleaned, it gave us a chance to look at the profiles. In a couple of places, the remains of trenches and meter gauge railways were found.

Later in the project, we discontinued the field walking campaign and interviews. Processing and studying aerial photographs led to better results. Aerial photographs combined with trench maps and some documents are generally enough to get an idea of the site (see fig. 12.1). Some documents, e.g. the "secret" army documents used to locate deep dugouts, were of a great value to the project and history of specific sites. The diaries of the German Maj. Rudolf Lange were also a rich source of information. This officer was quartered in the zone where the A19 would be extended. He made many notes, sketches, and watercolors of life at the frontline including his own and enemy trenches (fig. 12.3). He described the actions, clashes, etc. He did not survive the war. Many other similar sources were used to complete the inventory.

Based on this extended inventory, nine zones were selected where the Institute conducted fieldwork: geophysical research (resistivity and magnetometry) and/or excavations. These zones were examined in even more detail using all available information. The excavation plans and geophysical research results were afterwards geo-referenced in the GIS to compare them with the inventory. Using these techniques, excavated trenches could be dated very precisely and different phases in trench building could be better determined.

The Excavations

Three sites have been the subject of a geophysical survey. One of them proved to be especially successful: the survey of the Forward Cottage site. The private firm BACTEC International Ltd (Explosive Ordnance Disposal & Landmine Clearance) performed a magnetometry search of the site and the results were very good: trenches showed up very clearly and other anomalies became clear (fig. 12.4). The results were later compared with the excavation ground plan for the site.

In general, much more material was found during British trench excavations; the Germans did not

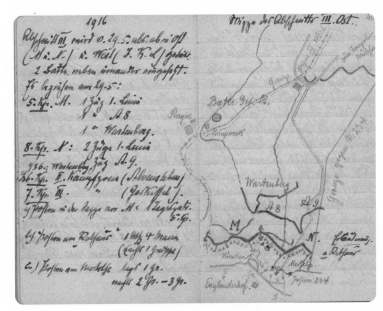

FIGURE 12.3. Drawing of the British and German trench system (Turco/Das Hörnchen and High Command Redoubt/Mauser Ridge) by the German officer Rudolf Lange. Courtesy Flanders Fields Museum.

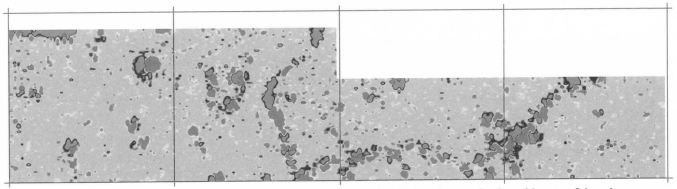

FIGURE 12.4. Results of geophysical research at the Forward Cottage site. The trenches are clearly visible; one of the other patches could be the entrance of a deep dugout. Courtesy BACTEC International Limited.

FIGURE 12.5. British trench with corrugated iron, duck-boards, and inverted A-frames at the Forward Cottage site. Photo by Mathieu de Meyers - VIOE.

of the first excavation, several trenches were excavated. The bottoms of these trenches were overlaid with wooden duckboards. This is not always the case. For example, at Cross Roads the oldest trenches (April–May 1915 in this case) did not contain the remains of duckboards. That means the soldiers stood with their feet in the clay and water, an intolerable situation. Not only were rats and diseases a problem, it was not good for the morale of the troops. An early solution was the use of duckboards to cover the trench bottom. But that was not the best solution either. There was still a lot of mud and water that covered the wood. So, soldiers started to pile up a series of duckboards to keep their feet and legs dry. At Cross Roads, three layers of duckboards were found on top of each other. Later on, a wooden structure with an inverted A-shape form was put in the bottom of the trench (fig. 12.5). The duckboards were placed on top of the structure and the water and mud could run underneath the duckboards. It was still not luxurious, but certainly better than standing in the muddy trench bottom. These phases in trench building were determined during the excavation of Cross Roads and Forward Cottage.

There seemed to be a typology in the duckboards themselves. They were made in standard shapes behind the frontline and brought to the trenches, but three different kinds were noted. At some places where shellfire had destroyed the trenches; duckboards had been repaired using bricks, stones, and even stable doors. The walls of the trenches were covered with sandbags, chicken wire, and corrugated iron or left uncovered. Sandbags could sometimes only be recognized through the textile impressions in the earth. Only fragments of textiles were recovered.

There is also an evolution from unconnected straight, shallow trenches to the typical deeper zigzag pattern trenches, with second and third battle lines and communication trenches. All these changes were introduced to improve the comfort and security of the soldiers. In 1917, starting from the frontline trench at Cross Roads, a sap that led to a jumping off trench was dug toward the German frontline to prepare for Third Ypres. The trench was quite deep and reinforced with expanded metal, inverted A-frames, vertical posts, and horizontal planks.

In the opposite German system at High Command

leave much behind. The only objects found on the German High Command Redoubt site were a bayo-net, the poorly preserved remains of a shovel, and some ammunition. The most important excavated sites were Turco Farm, Cross Roads, High Command Redoubt (Mauser Ridge), Forward Cottage, and Bix-schote. But what kind of traces and material came from these excavations?

The most important features found during the excavation were the trench systems. At Turco, the site

Redoubt, remains of heavily built trenches with inverted A-frames were excavated. They were built from heavier wood beams than the British ones and made a stronger impression. The walls of one trench were certainly covered with branches and twigs as was typical of most German trenches. After the Third Battle of Ypres, the British probably re-used the German frontline system as their own rear support trenches.

At most sites, several kinds of shelters were found. They were used to store ammunition, food, and other necessities. They were also used as shelters for soldiers who had to stay in the trenches. Most British shelters were made from wood, corrugated iron, and sandbags. One of these shelters was examined at Turco. The structural element found was probably the wooden roof, covered with corrugated iron plates. Some sandbags that served as part of the walls of the shelter were preserved in situ. The sandbags covering the walls were gone, but the shape of the bags and the marks of textile could still be recognized. In an ammunition depot on the Cross Roads site, a case filled with cartridges for a standard Lee-Enfield rifle was found.

In the remains of a small rectangular shelter along another trench segment, a dump of 25 empty glass water bottles was found. Another shelter was probably a machine gun post.

One particular kind of structure found at the Cross Roads site was a "mini" deep dugout (fig. 12.6). This underground wooden room was well-preserved. The dugout was reached via a staircase. A brass pump was found at the entrance with a rubber tube leading to the room. The function of the room is yet unclear; it may have been a sump, but was more likely used to store ammunition.

The High Command Redoubt Site, an important German observation post, was protected by many small concrete shelters. All but one was destroyed after the war. Their remains can still be seen scattered in the field and in archaeological test pits.

Artillery was commonly used along the front. At High Command Redoubt, four rectangular wooden platforms were excavated. They were probably used as floors for heavy field artillery. A fifth platform had a more irregular shape. At Cross Roads, several artillery

FIGURE 12.6. A "mini" deep dugout with pump at the Cross Roads site; trenches are connected with this underground depot. The pump was found in situ at the entrance and used to keep the dugout dry. Photo by Mathieu de Meyers - VIOE.

platforms were linked to trenches. A wooden platform was probably used for a Stokes trench mortar as suggested by a nearby dump of 35 unfired Stokes mortar bombs. At another location, a brick floor had probably been used as a platform for an artillery piece, as suggested by depressions in the surface of the bricks, which seem to match the positions of the wheels and trail. On all the sites, many shell holes were noted.

An interesting discovery was the remains of ignition material from a Livens-projector at Turco. This is an early type of mortar to launch chlorine-gas grenades. It was placed in batteries consisting of 20–25 pieces, with tubes inclined at a 45° angle. Sometimes it is possible to determine the type of ammunition that caused the explosion, and the direction from where the shell was fired can be reconstructed by investigating the shape of the crater. Some archaeological features were severely disturbed by the intensity of the shelling. At High Command Redoubt, the traces of shell holes seemed to be the dominant feature.

Many artifacts were recovered but the most obvious was ammunition. The excavation team was assisted by the Belgian Army's Bomb Disposal Unit in recovering unexploded ordnance. Examples included several types of cartridges, shells (or fragments), mortar bombs, shrapnel-balls, rifle grenades, and hand grenades. They were found scattered around the sites or together in dumps. At Turco, two handmade, improvised grenades made from the remains of 18-pounder shells were found.

Another category of artifacts was the remains of the standard equipment from British soldiers: buttons from uniforms, copper buckles, woolen stockings, spoons, blue water bottles, fragments of uniforms and leather web gear, pocket-knives, razors, toothbrushes, parts of shaving brushes, Lee-Enfield rifles, and hair combs. Regimental insignia were also found in the trenches. The East Kent Regiment, Royal Sussex, and others were identified (fig. 12.7). Also noteworthy were the remains of several types of gas masks. Several large and small entrenching tools were also collected. Remarkable finds were the aniline pencils. These were used by the soldiers to write messages or letters. Another find was a small glass ampoule (phial) once filled with iodine to disinfect wounds.

Besides standard equipment, many other objects were recovered. They reflect daily life and are part

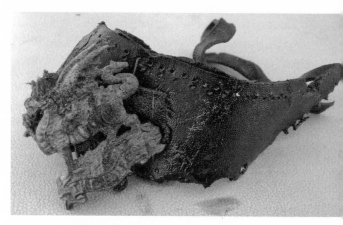

FIGURE 12.7. The Buffs (Royal East Kent Regiment) regimental insignia found at Cross Roads. Photo by Franky Wyffels - VIOE.

of the material culture of trench life. Fragments of ceramic rum jars were found on every site. Rum was consumed in colder periods and used to reinforce morale. The letters "SRD" were written on each jar, meaning Supply Reserve Depot. But soldiers did not only drink rum; bottles for wine, water, beer, and other liquids were also recovered. Glass receptacles were also used for medicines, meat, and oil. Other finds include sniping plates, pickaxes, waders, a watch, coins, screw caps from petrol tins, ceramic pipes, matches, mouth organ parts, some remains of candles, pincers, and fireballs from flare pistols. On Cross Roads and Forward Cottage, dumps were found with metal cans of food and petrol tins.

The most sensitive issue was the recovery of human remains at several sites. At Turco the remains of French and British soldiers were recovered. It was impressive to find remains with preserved uniforms and boots. At Cross Roads, three soldiers were found on top of each other in a shell hole; two of them were still wearing their entire uniform and leather webbing. Other incomplete skeletons on the site remind us of the terrible war that took place only 90 years ago. The families of these missing soldiers still visit Ypres in memory of their grandfathers. Their history is very close giving the archaeology an anthropological dimension. Identification of the remains is not easy and in most cases, it is only possible to determine nationality and regiment. In these cases, uniform buttons are used, but other parts of the standard equipment can also provide evidence. At Turco, one of the soldiers was identified as British because of the buttons and the gloves he was wearing. Even then, you cannot be completely sure, because sometimes they wore parts of uniforms belonging to other soldiers. The location where a body is found is also important. During the A19 project, not one body could be identified; of the more than 150 bodies found at Boesinghe a couple of years before by the amateur archaeologist De Diggers, only one was wearing his name tag.

Aerial Photographs: the Basis for a World War I Heritage Inventory

Along the Western front, thousands of kilometers of trenches were dug along with the construction of other military infrastructure. To conduct an inventory is not an easy task. As mentioned before, the first inventory project was carried out in 2001, when all known data on some villages (Houthulst, Merkem, Klerken, and Jonkershove) near the Belgian frontline were put in a database: prehistoric, Roman, medieval, and World War I traces. The result was a map with over 1000 different sites, from medieval farms to deep dugouts, trenches, meter gauge railways, and bunkers. The main resource for the war period was trench maps. It soon became apparent that this method was not entirely satisfactory. Although the results were useful for obtaining some basic information, there were too many mistakes and inaccuracies on the original wartime maps. This is the reason why trench maps were combined with other sources during the A19 project, especially wartime aerial photographs. All sources used for inventories were processed in a GIS.

As a result of the A19 project, new opportunities were created to continue the inventory of World War I remains in Flanders. The In Flanders Fields Museum and Flemish Heritage Institute began an inventory of the entire Ypres Salient. Besides a vast collection of German, British, and Belgian photographs, there is an incredible collection of photographs in the In Flanders Fields documentation center which were made by Lieutenant von Kanne, a German officer who died in 1916 when his plane was brought down during an exploration flight. Additional images were obtained from the Imperial War Museum in London (Box Collection).

The In Flanders Fields Museum continued the inventory to re-create the landscape as the last witness

of the Great War. Most of the veterans have passed away and few who were born during the war remain. Visitors to the museum and the area in general have lost all direct personal contact with the subject. They are in search of another way to remember the war and that is the landscape. To compare the new landscape with the war landscape the entire Ypres Salient was re-created using the aerial photographs. This re-creation can be used to help visitors visualize the historical context of the present day landscape that exists today.

Not only are the geographical features important, so is the time. As many phases as possible of the war between the Second Battle and Third Battle of Ypres were examined and illustrated with aerial photographs. The different large and small engagements, with their different trench systems, were reconstructed. During the excavation of Cross Roads, eight different phases of trenches were identified that were constructed over a two-year period. With the GIS we can now overlay images of different eras, and show to the meter where events took place. These layers of geo-referenced aerial photographs allow us to create a reanimation of the current landscape with the tragic events of the war.

The pilots and observers from the different warring parties took thousands of aerial photographs of the Western Front during the war. Aerial reconnaissance and photographic interpretation reinvented the way modern battle was envisioned, planned, and executed. It became the primary information source behind most battlefield decisions on the Western Front and provided a permanent photographic record of the results of those decisions. Initially, the quality of the photographs was not very good. But as the war dragged on, techniques were improved, and better results were achieved. Today, these very sharp pictures allow us to tell a remarkable tale.

The thousands of pictures enable us to study the Ypres Salient, and all the smaller movements on the frontline, in a very thorough manner. It is impossible, unnecessary, and too time-consuming, to use every single picture that exists. Therefore, we select them based on historical research. All the information about available photographs are first put into a database, before selecting the most qualitative and representative images of different phases of combat in the area.

The pictures are then put in a GIS using the "image

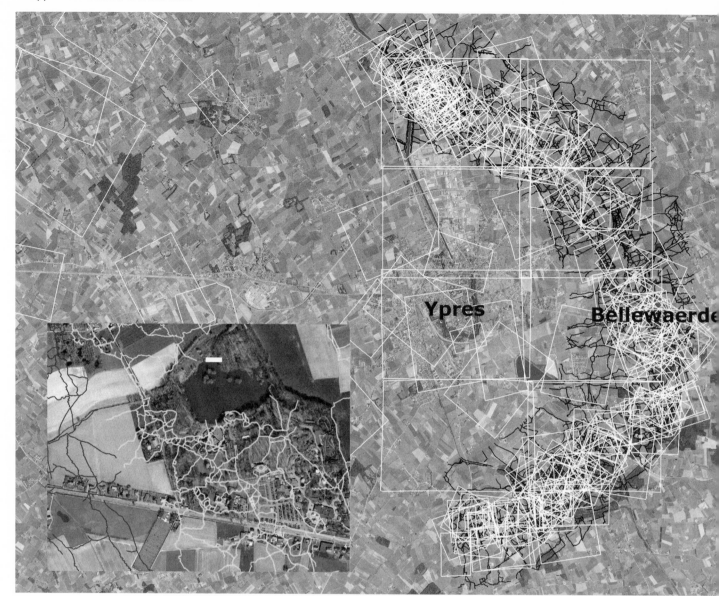

FIGURE 12.8. An overview of the geo-referenced aerial photographs in the Ypres Salient, with trenches drawn in. Inset: Detail of the map (area of image 12). Courtesy © AGIV.

warping" technique which allows the images to be projected on top of modern maps and aerial photographs (see fig. 12.2). Comparisons between old and new images are interesting, not only to study the battle, but also to study the evolution of the "war landscape." Next, polygons, lines, or dots are drawn on modern maps to indicate structures visible on the aerial photograph. Trenches, barbed wire, tracks, old-field boundaries, battery positions, and other structures can be located exactly. This technique is applied to aerial photos from different periods and the results can be placed on a series of overlays (fig. 12.8).

From a historical perspective, the images revealed

hitherto unknown mine craters and frontline shifts which could be linked to specific actions. Then there are the less obvious domains in which the pictures have proved useful. Ancient and forgotten medieval sites, complete with ramparts and moats, show up clearly on the pictures. Natural history and landscape interpretation information is an added bonus that may explain the origin of specific ponds, and shed light on deforestation and land divisions. In many cases, these are the oldest known photographic records of villages, cities, houses, and streets. In some cases these are the only known records.

Although this technique may be modern, similar

methods were already in use during the war to produce trench maps, discuss tactics, and observe the frontlines on an ongoing basis. Obviously, the newly obtained information is far more accurate and contains fewer errors. This in no way detracts from the fact that the results obtained during the war were very impressive as well. A new medium was being developed and fine-tuned there and then, paving the way for modern aerial photography and its processing into geographically correct cartographic material.

The inventory project also contained areas under heavy threat of development. In some cases, we collaborated with a team of the provincial administration specializing in the inventory of World War remains that are still visible above the ground (cemeteries, monuments, bunkers, etc.). For a basic inventory of Zonnebeke, it was possible to compare the "disappeared" archaeological remains with sites that are still visible. In that manner, maps could be created that show how many bunkers and cemeteries have disappeared since the end of the war. The majority of bunkers seemed to have disappeared which means this specific kind of surviving heritage needs to be preserved.

For some new excavations, detailed inventories were made similar to those associated with the A19 project. For extending the industrial estate of Boesinghe (Boezinge), the provincial administration sought archaeological advice to evaluate four possible sites. One site (Cake Trench and Helme Trench) was excavated. Geophysical research was carried out at a different location near an old windmill that was used as a German lookout during the war at Houthulst. According to some sources there used to be an underground system of trenches there. Because the monument may be restored in the near future, and this underground system could cause stability problems, the Institute was asked to do a survey. The system is put to further use in offering archaeological advice for future industrial or residential expansion projects.

There are some situations in which you cannot use aerial photos because there is not enough time to find and/or analyze them or because subsequent events have rendered their information unusable. Older trenches can sometimes be found in the 1915–18 imagery but in the Ypres Salient, many traces disappeared due to fighting and the incessant artillery shelling. Therefore, other resources such as maps and other documents are more useful. These are also necessary to make good inventories of specific kinds of sites (e.g. deep dugouts). Some cases have to be treated quite urgently, and then there is not enough time to geo-reference all the images necessary. In these cases, a quick basic inventory can be made using only trench maps. Meanwhile, three institutions in Flanders deal with the inventory of aerial photographs: the In Flanders Fields Museum (Ypres Salient), the Flemish Heritage Institute (Ypres Salient) and the University of Ghent (Belgian Frontline—based on the collections of the Royal Museum of the Armed Forces and Military History Brussels). When these inventory projects are finished, trench maps will no longer be needed to solve urgent problems. Even then, trench maps will still be useful as an additional source of information. Although most information on these maps was originally based on aerial photography, they are not always accurate. Nevertheless, they are still good guides to study the battlefields and more specifically, the aerial photographs. But the photographs offer a much more reliable image. They show a clear evolution in the appearance of the trenches, while the same trench is sometimes depicted in a totally different manner on different trench maps of the same period.

WORLD WAR I ARCHAEOLOGY IN FRANCE

In France there are archaeologists dealing with World War I heritage. The teams of Alain Jacques (Service Archéologique de la ville d'Arras) and Yves Desfossés (DRAC Nord–Pas-de-Calais) carried out several excavations on World War I sites. One project included the discovery of a British hospital known as Thomson's Cave. This hospital could accommodate 700 soldiers and was built in one of the underground caves near the city. Originally chalk quarries, these "boves" were dug from the tenth century onwards and used for various purposes through the ages. The network of galleries, which covers the size of the town and beyond, also served as a shelter and rallying point for allied troops in 1917 as they awaited their decisive attack, the Battle of Arras. The hospital was equipped with all the necessary services required for the medical staff. Information gathered during the research allowed archaeologists to better understand the materials used and efforts made by British forces to transform the underground premises into real quarters capable of accommodating over 24,000 men. They even found inscriptions from Maori and other New Zealand soldiers. The team also investigated the graves of soldiers who died during the Battle of Arras and at several other sites. In another project, they excavated trenches running directly through a Gallo-Roman site. Safety is one of the major concerns of the team and it is also the official motive invoked by the authorities for not developing this type of research. It is also a reason not to excavate all trenches to the bottom. Bodies might be missed in this manner, but unexploded ordnance is too dangerous to take the risk.

Another group that also worked together on some projects in Flanders with the AWA (Association for World War Archaeology) and the Flemish Heritage Institute was the No Man's Land Team. This team of professional archaeologists, historians, and specialists uses archaeological evidence "to supplement and in some cases challenge the historical record." Some of the major projects were carried out in Auchonvillers (a British trench system and reconstruction), Serre (Excavation of German Heidenkopf trenches), Thiepval, La Signy (an observation post), and the Salisbury Plain and Silloans (Otterburn, Northumberland) in Britain. World War I archaeology in the United Kingdom has focused on British training trenches which are still partially preserved on grounds owned by the Defense Estates. The work was primarily to confirm the use and date of the site (the site at Otterburn was used from 1914–40). Much can be learned by comparing training trenches to the trenches excavated on the real frontline. How well were soldiers prepared to do battle and dig trenches? How did they apply that training in a real war situation? Did they have the time to dig trenches as written in the manuals?

GREAT WAR ARCHAEOLOGY: CONCLUSION

What special role can archaeology play in the study of World War I? Historians have long studied this period intensively and theories about some aspects still change every year. Typologies exist for most objects that are found. Nevertheless, archaeology can uncover a sometimes forgotten material reality. Even some of the best known battles are not completely clear to scholars studying the First World War. The archaeological excavations make the horror of the lives of the soldiers during the First World War more real and immediate than paper relics. Living in trenches, waiting in a shelter for the next attack: the entire picture becomes clearer as archaeology reveals more remains. The archaeological information is much more detailed than any other resource about the war (i.e., aerial photographs, maps, written accounts).

With archaeological research, more can be learned about daily life in the trenches, evolution of trench systems, and some military actions. Sometimes, the reality seems to be very different from the written history. Of course, all this information should be combined to rebuild the whole story. This is a big challenge for the future. World War I archaeology has an important social-anthropological dimension because the main attention goes to the reality in the trenches, and the lives of the soldiers. The confrontation with aerial photography, topography, and the current landscape is also an important issue. The unlocking of all this information is a real challenge.

The inventory and archaeological research play an important role in the protection and management of the sites. The A19 project is a good example. Home and industrial developers and governmental organizations take World War archaeology more into account when working on a new project. An important action is to integrate the information in the urban planning process. The emphasis will have to be on conservation, protection, but also maintenance, information, and sensitization. The international importance of the site was recognized with the decision not to extend the A19 highway.

Is it necessary to excavate everything? In some cases it is not, certainly if time is limited. Then the archaeologist should focus on lesser unknown aspects of the war. On the other hand, in some areas the issue is too sensitive, particularly in areas where there are human remains. In that case, it is almost obligatory to excavate everything that is under threat.

In terms of conservation, the main threats to the archaeological remains are erosion, construction activities, illicit excavations by collectors, and the natural processes of corrosion and decay. Thus, it is necessary to recover and collect for conservation exposed remains as quickly as possible. Another problem is the decay of the sites. A good example is the deep dug-outs. Now you can still go inside, examine, and draw them. However, most are completely constructed of wood and will eventually collapse. Other examples are the corrugated iron, duckboards, textiles, and leather. How long until these remains all disappear? This degradation should be monitored. There is currently no answer to this question. Nowadays, most excavations are done in areas under threat and it is very difficult to get a permit for pure scientific research. But it may be necessary to focus on "unthreatened" World War sites before it is too late.

Archaeology of the Great War is unique for a couple of reasons. An important aspect is the risk you take by excavating a trench system. While digging, you come across ammunition. British scientists like to speak about "the archaeology of lethal behavior." To guarantee the safety of the staff there is good cooperation with the Belgian Bomb Disposal Unit (DOVO). They give instructions on how to handle the ammunition to the fieldworkers and their expertise and knowledge about the different types of ammunition is indispensable. Once every few days, they pick up all (potentially) dangerous artifacts. Sometimes they can even help the archaeologist to interpret them; and help explain certain contexts. Looking at the site from a military point of view can supply very useful information.

Another major issue is the traces you find on a site: trenches, bomb craters, gun emplacements etc. You need specialists on the sites including people who have expertise with certain materials (bullets, shoes, uniforms, ammunition, etc.). For this reason, the Institute collaborated with several international institutions and persons on the work at most sites. They all had specific knowledge, and a different view on the case.

A big difference of treatment is seen in the process of recovering bodies. On a Roman site, the bones are examined and some tests are conducted and after the work the bones are put in an archive or exhibited in a museum. When digging on a World War I site, there are still children, grandchildren, and other family members who remember this man, who lost a father or grandfather. These soldiers are still reported as "missing in action" and their names engraved on several monuments. These remains must be treated with more respect. At the very least, researchers try to find out which regiment they belonged to, and when possible try to identify them. When human remains are found a strict procedure must be followed. The police have to be informed and they assemble the body on the site after it is uncovered, drawn, and photographed. They also take the objects found with the body. Next, the remains are transferred to the country the body belongs to. Luckily, archaeologists can work together very well with the organizations of the several countries dealing with the bodies (the Commonwealth War Graves Commission [CWGC] and Volksbund Deutsche Kriegsgräberfürsorge e.V.).

Several specialists have the chance to carry out research on the bodies. The physical anthropologist reveals information about the age, health, and cause of death. Others examine the remains of the shoes, socks, uniform, leather webbing, cap badges etc. After a while; the bodies are re-buried in one of the many cemeteries along the frontline. German and British soldiers are buried with full ceremony in an individual grave. French soldiers are put in one of the "ossuaries" (mass graves) at one of the French cemeteries.

Also unique is the attention such an excavation gets. Besides the press and documentary makers, excavations get many visitors from Belgium, as well as the Commonwealth and Germany who come to the salient to remember the war. Once, the daughter of a soldier killed during the war somewhere around where an excavation took place, visited the site. Afterwards she took off her shoes, put them in a box, and promised to herself to never wear them again, as a memory to her lost father and the mud in which he disappeared. Sometimes it is strange to see an archaeological site with "remembrance crosses" and poppies, put there by visitors, on the sites where bodies were found. Because it is a very sensitive issue, you have to be extremely careful with the media.

Another challenge is to work on good collaborations between professional and amateur archaeologists. Before professionals were involved, most sites were the exclusive terrain for amateurs. Nowadays this causes some difficulties but because the World War I excavations have proven valuable, efforts must be made to work together.

CHAPTER THIRTEEN

History, Archaeology, and the Battle of Balaclava (Crimea, 1854)

PHILIP FREEMAN

"Much that is dark and inscrutable about the Balaclava question might be cleared up, . . . but the secret history of the 25th of October 1854— a narrative which would prove no less interesting to the civilian than pregnant with instruction to the soldier—may not, perhaps, be told in our day"

A REGIMENTAL OFFICER 1859:256

The "fog of war" is an axiom that explains the confusion that goes with a military engagement, where combat chaos frequently causes confusing, if not contradictory, recollections. Historians attempt to reconcile evidence and make sense of what happened to produce a rational, "acceptable" version of events. Their purpose is often as much to attribute blame as to rationalize why individuals or units behaved the way they did. The traditional resolution of such problems is through critical analysis of historical sources, occasionally complemented by battlefield visits. Military history is replete with attempts to re-examine military events this way. Recently, archaeology has been introduced in the hope that the evidence it can add might complement explanations, if not resolve particular problems.

The systematic study of battlefields as archaeological resources is a relatively recent innovation but one that utilizes a range of methodologies. In conventional "battlefield archaeology" there are, in essence, three basic approaches. The oldest, and most commonly deployed, is to use archaeology to embellish the accepted story of the events that has been derived from written sources that are, in turn, based on eyewitness accounts. Where there are several accounts of the same battle, certain sources are often emphasized over others. Here, archaeology is used to clarify details or add to the historical framework. A second use of archaeology is to illuminate poorly reported engagements while the third approach is a halfway position. In this middle ground, archaeology is used to reconcile the problematic aspects of an engagement, or to correct conventional interpretations. Because there is a temptation to try and demonstrate how traditional versions of an engagement are "wrong," archaeology becomes the arbiter of veracity. Archaeology tends to be regarded as neutral, not laden with values but independent and objective. Such confidence is misplaced. Archaeological data are not neutral, but are the consequence of decisions made about where to work and which strategies and techniques to use. Furthermore, the quantity of evidence recovered is usually small, a problem compounded because few battlefield archaeological studies explore the entire site. Even textbook examples of archaeologically driven battlefield studies (i.e., the Little Big Horn, Kalkriese, and Towton) investigated only fractions of the total scene. Last, but not least, accepting this approach risks throwing the "baby out with the bath water." The arbiter approach makes the fundamental mistake of failing to appreciate why the historical version of a particular battle is constructed the way it is. Bad historical method is replaced by the poor application of archaeological data.

THE CAMPAIGN

The Crimean War and the engagement that became known as the "Battle of Balaclava" can be used to illustrate the interplay of these elements. In the traditional version of the event, on 14 September 1854, British and French forces landed north of Sebastopol, Russia. Six days after disembarkation, they engaged and defeated a Russian army under Prince Alexander Menshikov at the River Alma. On 23 September, the Allies continued southward, marching around Sebastopol to attack its southern side (fig. 13.1). When the Allies ran into Menshikov's baggage train evacuating Sebastopol, the situation was misread as a Russian attack that caused the Allies to

march into the Balaclava Valley (fig. 13.2). By the 26th, British troops occupied the southern end of Balaclava.

The change in Allied strategy meant the loss of any advantage they may have had. The delay caused by preparing their siege meant bombardment of the city did not commence until 17 October. In the meantime, the Russians improved their defenses while Menshikov led his command into interior Crimea. The British position east of the city was precarious. Access to Balaclava, some 10 km southeast of Sebastopol, involved a difficult ascent from the valley to the Sebastopol plain via an unsurfaced track. Menshikov's control of the north end of the Balaclava Valley enabled Sebastopol to be supplied and put the Russian army in position to threaten the only British

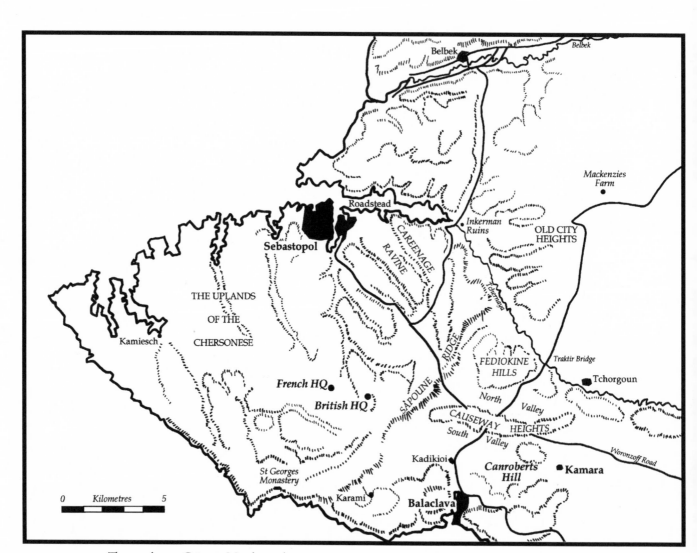

FIGURE 13.1. The southwest Crimea. Map by author.

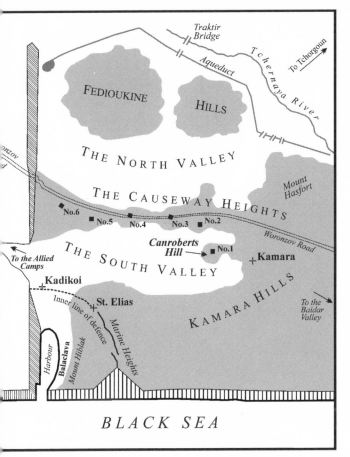

FIGURE 13.2. The Valley of Balaclava. Map by author.

supply route. In early October, British engineers erected six artillery redoubts on Causeway Heights, an east-west running ridge through the valley. By the time of the "battle," only four were complete, each armed with British guns and Turkish garrisons. The easternmost battery and the most important fortification, was Redoubt No.1 on Canrobert's Hill (figs. 13.3, 13.4, 13.5).

The Battle of Balaclava, 25 October 1854, culminated in the "Charge of the Light Brigade," an event that attained iconic status. Its significance was appreciated almost as soon as it occurred. Within hours of the "disaster," accusations and recriminations were flying and with them a concern to attribute blame for what was regarded as a glorious debacle. Within weeks, the same was happening in London, which added to a rising sense of public disquiet about the management of the campaign and the competence of the English commanders. Questions asked in Parliament were followed by commissions that endeavored to explain events and attribute blame to certain individuals while absolving others. The debate fostered often acrimonious claims and counterclaims

FIGURE 13.3. Canrobert's Hill today. Photograph by author.

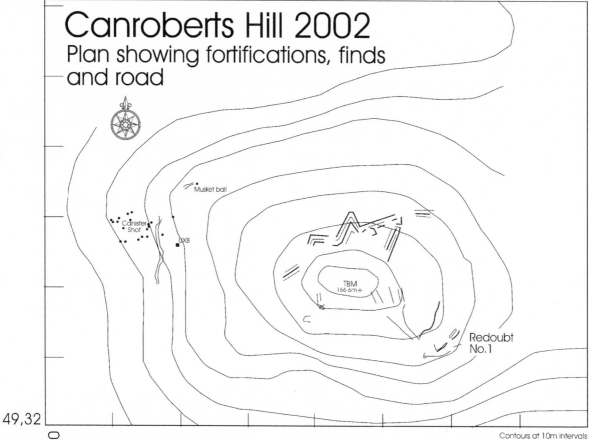

Canroberts Hill 2002
Plan showing fortifications, finds
and road

Musket ball

Canister
Shot

UXB

TBM
166.6m+

Redoubt
No.1

49,32

65,00

Contours at 10m intervals

FIGURE 13.4. Plan view of Canrobert's Hill where Redoubt No. 1 was located during the Battle of Balaclava. Map by author.

protesting innocence or apportioning guilt. The debate continues to this day. In the intervening decades, the Crimean campaign, and the "battle," has been the subject of innumerable studies. As in the days, months, and years afterward, there is still an unhealthy preoccupation in wanting to attribute blame for the charge. With recurring analyses, the situation has reached the point where it now seems virtually impossible to create a "new" perspective on the "battle." Indeed, the debate has become for some a matter of dogma, vilification, and entrenched (academic) posturing.

FIGURE 13.5. Canrobert's Hill viewed from the west. Photograph by author.

The Landscape and Canrobert's Hill

Topographically, Balaclava Valley is divided into two parts: the so-called North and South valleys. Causeway Heights is a stretch of slightly higher ground running west-east for about 4 km north of Balaclava. Along this low ridge dividing the valley ran the so-called Woronzov Road linking Sebastopol with Sapune Heights on the western side of the valley. The Russians held the North Valley; the British controlled the South Valley where the 93rd Highland Regiment and two cavalry brigades were encamped.

For much of the modern era, the valley was off-limits. In the half-century or so after the war, some veterans returned (Wood 1895:125) but in general, the region was closed to non-Soviet, non-military visitors, meaning that most of what has been written is by writers unable to visit, or at best with limited or surreptitious access. With the collapse of the Soviet Union, access to Crimea has been relaxed. Restrictions lifted, tourists arrive in parties, often on "battlefield tours," and are taken around Crimean War sites. The tours, however, seem based on limited, one-dimensional, synthetic accounts and are almost universally underpinned by reference to the "definitive" authorities. In other words, physical inspection of the valley is used to make sense of the literary version. Landscape is little more than a facet of literary history. The interpretations are rarely assisted by any critical familiarity with the topography of the valley. There is an additional dimension to reading the landscape, however. The topography has been altered since the mid-nineteenth century by intensive, mechanized viticulture, along with destruction inflicted in World War II between late 1941 and 1943. This activity rearranged the valley to an extent not widely appreciated, so that what visitors see today may not have been the topographic situation at the time of the battle in the 1850s.

On the northern side of Canrobert's Hill, the ground climbs abruptly. The southern edge is almost cliff-like, with a sheer drop to the valley floor. The eastern and southeast sides are also difficult to scale. To the north-northeast, there is a saddle, one of two lines of ascent. The other easier way up, a relatively gentle incline, is on the southwestern and western sides of the

hill. Today, virtually all the lower slopes of Canrobert's are covered by dense woodland. Extensive remains of trench and bunker systems constructed in World War II are masked by the ground cover. There is an incredible amount of military debris still lying around and recent illicit diggings have exposed human remains.

The "Battle of Balaclava"

The following summary is a composite, constructed from a number of modern sources (Hibbert 1961; Sweetman 1990; Adkin 1996; Kerr 1997; Fletcher and Ischenko 2004). The reason for using these accounts rather than "primary" (or eyewitness) accounts is to make the point that many modern "authorities" rarely acknowledge their sources. When they do, most tend to use a limited group but rarely explain why they prefer, and by implication omit, certain sources (Seaton 1977; Hargreave Mawson 2001; Fletcher and Ischenko 2004; Springman 2005).

The "Battle of Balaclava," as the conventional version of events has it, commenced at daybreak with the Russians taking the village of Kamara, installing a battery there and launching a ferocious bombardment on Canrobert's Hill before assaulting Redoubt No. 1. With the fall of Redoubt No. 1, the Russians turned on No. 2, then No. 3 and finally No. 4. The Turks fled first from No. 1 to No. 2 and then from No. 2, then No. 3 and from No. 4 towards Balaclava. Taking the redoubts allowed movement of a large body of Russian cavalry into the South Valley.

The next phase involved a squadron of Russian cavalry detaching from the main body and advancing toward Kadikoi, outside Balaclava. This squadron unexpectedly engaged the 93rd Highlanders. This regiment, Russell's "thin red streak tipped with steel" (hereafter TRS), supported by some Turks Sir Colin Campbell managed to rally, repulsed the Russians. Shortly after this, the Heavy Brigade's five dragoon regiments (hereafter C-HB) charged the main body of Russian cavalry. This resulted in another British "victory" on and around Causeway Heights. About this time, the Russians decided to call it a day and withdrew, taking the cannon from the English redoubts.

This development was viewed by the Commander-in-Chief of British forces, Lord Raglan, from his vantage point on the western heights. He subsequently sent a message to attack and retrieve the guns to Earl Cardigan's Light Brigade in the South Valley. The message relative to where the recipients received it was ambiguous. It caused what came to be known as the Charge of the Light Brigade (hereafter C-LB), when the flower of the British cavalry were sent to attack the guns; not the small group of cannon from the redoubts, but well-established Russian batteries north of the Woronsov Road. Recriminations, accusations, and name-calling about who was responsible for the debacle commenced almost as soon as the first stragglers made their way back. They ranged from why the Turks performed so badly and why they were left so isolated in such poor fortifications to why, and on whose authority, the Light Brigade was ordered into action. The one component in the "battle" descriptions that tends to be lost in modern accounts is what happened at the beginning of the initial Russian attack on the redoubts, in particular in and around Redoubt No. 1. (Fletcher and Ischenko 2004:163–84). Most authors gloss over the assault, while the better ones only discuss the performance of the Turks.

Archaeological Survey

Against this backdrop, and in an effort to resolve the circumstances of the C-LB once and for all, a television production company sponsored an archaeological survey at Balaclava in 2002. This was probably the first attempt, certainly by western Europeans, to look at the Crimean War archaeologically. The television people were interested in a variety of themes, including the attack on Redoubt No. 1. In this case, the producers were intent on demonstrating how the Turkish performance created conditions where the "battle" did not become a total British defeat. Contradictions existed in contemporary accounts about the redoubt attack. While some eyewitnesses say the Turks fled almost as soon as the Russian bombardment started, others claimed they held out for some time. Since Canrobert's Hill was supposedly captured sometime between 7 A.M. and 8.30 A.M. and the British response was not until about 10:30 A.M., the South Valley was open to the Russians for up to three hours which was time enough for Raglan to organize his response.

Could archaeology shed any light on these events? What might be said about the appearance of the redoubt? While contemporary British descriptions were almost universally contemptuous, Russian accounts were more complimentary. The TV production team had plans to conduct a metal detector sweep (Wason 2003). The program, created by the production team and not those who did the fieldwork, was designed to show the Turks as heroes. In this dramatization they did not flee the redoubts, but put up a resistance sufficient to buy the Allies time to organize. They hoped archaeological evidence might "prove" it to be so. Unsurprisingly, the archaeological research found what the program makers were after, although it was pointed out at the time that there was a much better story that might be told. Work since 2002 has continued to explore these possibilities and some implications are reported here.

Security restrictions meant it was not possible to import handheld GPS for use in documenting the site. Instead, a 1990s IKONOS satellite photograph of the valley was provided by the Institute of Classical Archaeology (ICA), University of Texas. The photograph showed World War II entrenchments, a star-shaped fortification, and less clearly, a bank with three indentations. The satellite image was sufficient for establishing a grid over Canrobert's Hill by way of a conventional theodolite survey. The theodolite data were then superimposed on the satellite image.

The archaeological component of the survey was somewhat disappointing. The ability to recover Crimean War artifacts was compromised by the volume of World War II material scattered across Canrobert's Hill. Despite the skill of the project metal detectorist, his equipment was unable to differentiate between massive quantities of Crimean, World War II, and other metal. The number of ferrous and non-ferrous (usually aluminum alloy) targets made it impossible to dig them all. The hill is crisscrossed with earthworks, a consequence of the Crimean War and two World War II sieges. As a result, it contains masses of materiel scattered across its surface including unexpended ordnance.

Nothing was found by metal detecting the spur of ground at the southwest corner of Canrobert's Hill postulated as the line of retreat taken by the Turks. The top of the hill was also swept with little success.

On the mid-slope on the west side of the hill, a sweep recovered 21 large spherical lead balls, a small pistol ball, and an impacted musket ball. The larger balls were identified as case shot, probably an overshot Russian shell fired from Kamara or, less likely, a British round from Redoubt No. 2, west of Canrobert's. The failure to recover other Crimean War material on the southwest slope, other than the canister shot, suggests the Turkish flight was not over this ground.

The landscape survey revealed that the star-shaped fortification typical of the nineteenth century visible on the IKONOS image is still very clear on the ground. It is reasonably certain that the star-shape, which had been extensively reused in the World War II, was a late Crimean War period fortification, probably thrown up in April 1855, as shown on an unpublished map in private possession. The satellite image led to the identification of another, presumably earlier, fortification on the southeast corner of the hilltop. This earthwork predated World War II as evidenced by foxholes, slit trenches, and a pillbox that had been cut into it. The fortification was a simple embankment set on a natural terrace about 75 m long and up to 1.5 m high. Cut into the parapet were three openings interpreted as artillery embrasures. The terrace upon which the redoubt was positioned was reached by a track that traversed the crest of the hill before descending along its southern edge into the fortification. This redoubt faced the village of Kamara. There was no obvious source of water. There was no evidence of magazines or other structures. If they existed, they were re-used later and altered beyond recognition, adding credence to the notion that the Turks were billeted in the open.

A second survey discovery was a track running along the contours of the southeast side of the hill. This track is visible on the satellite photograph and also indicated on the 1855 map. From what is shown on the original map, the photograph, and found by the survey, it appears to have neither a start nor an end. All that survives is the middle section, part of which was enhanced by a curb. A search of the lower end revealed remnants at the base of the hill. It was a Crimean era road and probably the way by which the Turkish/British (and later World War II troops) on the hill were provisioned.

If the embankment is the Turkish redoubt, then its most striking features are: (1) its relatively small size;

(2) that it was provided with only one parapet and no encircling defenses or outworks; and (3) that its position would seem to face the wrong way; not north, where the Russian assault was assumed to have come, but east toward Kamara. Its location cannot have been random. It used the lay of the ground, presumably for two reasons. The redoubt was sited partially to cover the slope that runs up the east side of the hill while the Redoubt No. 2 battery would have dealt with anything coming from the north.

The engineers who designed the redoubt may have positioned it for another reason. Between the redoubt and Kamara is a defile leading into the South Valley of Balaclava, far removed from the Allied guns on Sapune Heights. It would make sense for the Russians, if they were moving on Balaclava, to use this route, and British engineers positioned Redoubt No. 1 to cover the gap between Canrobert's Hill and Kamara. The location of the redoubt caused its downfall. It was too exposed to Kamara and the Russian bombardment pinned down the garrison and permitted Russian infantry to approach from the northeast before gunners and the Turks in Redoubt No. 1 could respond. If the British had anticipated this possibility, the position of No. 1 was not quite right. In this respect, the comments of a Russian participant about (mis)placing the guns in No.1 is revealing: " . . . the enemy artillery positioned on the very steep heights, especially in fortification No. 1, could not fire upon the foot of the hill it occupied, which our riflemen very skillfully used to their advantage, and in their most critical moments the attacking columns were able to close up and advance in the formation required for an attack with cold steel. Most of the guns worked through embrasures and consequently did not have that full coverage of the terrain necessary for defence. Our guns, on the other hand, were deployed mostly by divisions separated by significant distances and concentrated their fire only on the fortification" (Ushakov in Conrad 2006).

This is precisely what the survey found. Is there anything in the new landscape information that might have implications for the historical version of the engagement? Precisely identifying the position of Redoubt No. 1 led to reviewing contemporary accounts to see if they revealed previously unsuspected "facts" because the minimal archaeological survey reveals discrepancies and anomalies that are not easy to explain.

Documentary Sources

The Crimean War is well-documented, including official documents generated by Boards and Commissions of Enquiry. Because the campaign became a sedentary affair, the troops had much free time, thus there is a plethora of military firsthand accounts describing many of the same events and complementing those of visitors. The war has also been described as the first officially documented war with press correspondents and war photographers. Finally, a number of magisterial histories appeared relatively soon after the campaign. Much diverse material has been integrated by "modern" authorities into a reasonably coherent narrative, but it is clear that source use can be selective and, in some cases uncritical, at least in addressing certain source contradictions.

Although many veterans and their descendants published letters and diaries or wrote accounts, the two best-known contemporary authorities are Russell (1855) and Kinglake (1863–67). To a large degree their accounts form the standard version for some, and their opinions permeate much writing about events culminating in the C-LB. Russell was a special correspondent for *The Times* of London. His dispatches, critical of the management of the campaign, caused a scandal back home. After the war, Russell cashed in on his celebrity, editing and republishing many reports, first as *The War From the Landing at Gallipoli to the Death of Lord Raglan* (Russell 1855) and later, as a conventional history, *The British Expedition to the Crimea* (Russell 1877). In the aftermath of the war, Kinglake wrote a multi-volume history. His credibility is based in part on the methodical way in which he approached his writing. It took him until 1887 to complete his history, during which he consulted leading Allied and Russian participants (Sweetman 2004a). Kinglake's description of the war has been described as "the standard account" (Massie 2003:122). He is the only writer to try to describe what might have happened on Canrobert's. Many British officers in Crimea were critical of the access these writers enjoyed and the detail contained in their reports. They believed the reporters informed the Russians implying that what they wrote contained more than a touch of accuracy.

Many others wrote about events around Redoubt No.1, including the British expeditionary force commander in Crimea. Lord Raglan sent home numerous reports based largely on those provided by his subordinates. Raglan's nephew and Aide-de-Camp was Somerset John Gough Calthorpe, who published his letters, originally anonymously (An Officer of the Staff 1857) " . . . in book form because he realised how much calumny and abuse were unjustly heaped upon Lord Raglan's head" (Calthorpe 1979:7). Unlike many other eyewitnesses, Calthorpe made the simple yet very significant observation that there were parts of the "battlefield" that he could not see (Calthorpe 1979:73). Capt. Henry Berkeley Fitzhardinge Maxse, Coldstream Guards, and later Raglan's Aide-de-Camp, published articles about the war in *The National Review Periodicals* (London). There is also a letter he wrote his mother describing the 25th (Maxse 1854).

Gen. George Charles Bingham, third Earl of Lucan, commanded the British cavalry forces. He felt he had been unfairly scapegoated by Raglan. In an attempt to restore his honor, Lucan petitioned the House of Lords and made a speech to the House in March 1855. His speech provided a summary of the events as he saw them, supplemented with a map of the Balaclava Valley showing the redoubts (Lucan 1855; Sweetman 2004b). John Blunt, Lucan's civilian interpreter, eventually put down his own memories (Austin, in press). Blunt is a significant authority because he describes Lucan's movements over the "battlefield" up to the moment of the C-LB, and claimed to have inspected the redoubts before 25 October.

Lucan's *bette noir* was the brother-in-law he despised, Maj. Gen. James Thomas Brudenell, Earl of Cardigan. As the commander of the Light Brigade, Cardigan wrote a memorandum to Raglan, summarizing what occurred. Back in Britain, Cardigan was as busy as Lucan in broadcasting his part. In a February 1855 speech, he provided a brief resume of the Russian attack on the redoubts (Cardigan 1855). When Calthorpe defended Raglan, he was attacked by Cardigan who brought a slander case against him.

Others in Cardigan's command wrote of the C-LB. Some discussed events in and around Redoubt No. 1. Lord George Augustus Frederick Paget of the 4th Light Dragoons kept a journal that was later published for private circulation. Following publication of Kinglake's history, Paget (1810) revised his account as

The Light Cavalry Brigade in the Crimea. With regard to the Heavy Brigade, there are the letters of Richard Temple Godman of the 5th Dragoon Guards (Warner 1999). Godman's letters were addressed to various family members and so give slightly different slants to particular events. Godman is an important source because he says he was 300 yards behind Redoubt No. 1 when it was attacked. Not only does he describe the circumstances of the C-HB, he provides detailed information about the preliminaries of the Russian attack as far back as 7 October.

On 25 October, the defense of Balaclava was the responsibility of Sir Colin Campbell. In the aftermath of the "battle," he submitted a report to Raglan. Campbell kept a now lost diary, but some letters to his sister survive (Forbes 1895). Like Lucan's report, Campbell's report to Raglan was published in *The Times* (and republished by Forbes in 1895). Anthony Sterling was attached to Campbell's staff. Sterling edited his letters, adding comments on contentious matters and providing corroborative material, including a copy of Campbell's "Despatch of the Battle of Balaklava" (Sterling 1895). Sterling is valuable because not only was he close to the action, but was privy to much incidental information. Not surprisingly, he has some waspish observations about events in and around the "Turkish" redoubts. It is also an advantage that he made, and subsequently published, maps of the Balaclava Valley. Another individual on Campbell's staff was Lawrence Shadwell who wrote a biography about Campbell, which contains much detail about circumstances outside Balaclava (Shadwell 1881; Forbes 1895).

Edward Hamley, Royal Artillery, wrote a series of letters for *Blackwood's Magazine* that were later published as a collection. In its preface, Hamley (1855:v) observed how "Regimental officers must, from their isolated position and want of reliable information, frequently form erroneous ideas of the objects of movements, and of the state and position of the army." Thirty-five years on, Hamley "wrote his masterly one-volume War in the Crimea, essentially repeating the view in his 1855 Blackwood's letters" (Lloyd 2004:944; cf. Hamley 1891).

Strange Jocelyn served in the Scots Fusilier Guards in the 1st Division and sent home a flow of letters. Frances Elizabeth Ogilvy, otherwise Mabell [*sic*], the Countess of Airlie, edited her great-uncle's letters

interspersed with a narrative of the war, largely derived from Hamley's history (Airlie 1933). In the same regiment was Assistant Surgeon Frederick Robinson (Robinson 1856) who admitted he contemplated editing his original impressions but elected to retain the rumors, gossip, and other opinions. An officer of the Coldstream Guards who wrote home about the C-LB was Lord Frederick Paulet (1854). Another prolific writer was Grenadier Guard Henry Percy, whose letters, and those of brother officers, have been published (Percy 2005). From information provided in a diary kept from February until November 1854, the "Regimental Officer" (A Regimental Officer 1859) was probably C. T. Wilmott of a Guards regiment.

One of the earliest personal accounts from the 4th Division was by George Schuldham Peard (1855) of the 20th Regiment. He decided to publish his diary when he returned to England: "I have not heard that any 'combatant' has hitherto published the result of his observations; and it has sometimes been thought by me, that, however imperfectly I may have described scenes and incidents . . . the following . . . may not be wholly uninteresting to the Public, because they contain a true and authentic account of what came under my own observation." (Peard 1855:iii–iv). Peard's detailed description of 25 October was assisted by the fact his regiment was initially positioned above the Balaclava Valley, from where he witnessed the early elements of the "battle" before his division was sent to support Campbell and the two cavalry brigades. His account is invaluable, especially because it contains information that does not appear elsewhere. There are some elements, which based on current evidence are confusing, cannot be located, or are otherwise contradictory. Another less detailed writer was G. F. Dallas of the 46th Regiment, positioned outside Sebastopol (Hargreave Mawson 2001). Henry Roberts, Royal Marine Artillery, was involved in arming South Valley redoubts on the morning of the 25th (Roberts 1854).

There are other 25 October memoirs, most of which are hard to place on the field, e.g. those of the Timothy Gowling of the 95th Regiment and W. Lowe, a ranker in the Royal Regiment of Artillery (Jackson 1982). Gowling witnessed the Turkish flight and their pursuit by Russian cavalry from afar (Fenwick 1954:29). Henry B. Roberts wrote from "Camp Balaklava" while with Battery No. 4, Royal Marine Artillery.

He was probably part of the contingent that assisted the 93rd Regiment in repulsing the Russian cavalry. Roberts has interesting information concerning the construction of the redoubts.

Sir Henry Evelyn Wood was a member of the Naval Brigade assisting in the artillery bombardment of Sebastopol. After revisiting Crimea with at least one veteran, Wood published a series of recollections in *The Fortnightly Review Periodical* (London), later expanded into a monograph in which he compared Crimea "then and now." Wood (1895:vii) claimed his account was accurate because the " . . . habits of precision enforced in the Navy by the keeping of a log or journal, and my daily letters written to my mother, have assisted a naturally retentive memory, and I have had many letters from comrades of both Services in the trenches, expressing general concurrence in my statements." While Wood's description concentrates on the cavalry, he commented on the redoubts. It is unfortunate that he did not describe from where he saw the various actions, but we might assume it was from the camp of his brigade outside Sebastopol. He admitted to not seeing the C-LB. However, he might be regarded a reliable source not only for revisiting Crimea in the years afterwards, but because he quotes from parliamentary papers, "historians," and unnamed Russian sources as well as British comrades and Russian veterans in 1894.

The best known civilian accounts are by the "war correspondents," Russell and Kinglake. A third journalist was Special Correspondent to *The Morning Herald Newspaper* (London), Nicholas Woods, whose contribution to war scholarship is a two-volume history, based partly on his original reports as well notes he made at the time (Woods 1855, 1885). What makes his version valuable is that he says he interviewed a number of, admittedly unnamed, participants as well as offering some trenchant comments on British leadership. Not much can be said about the author of *A Pictorial History of the Russian War* (Dodd 1856) but his account is useful.

James Skene served on the staff of Viscount Stratford de Redcliffe, HMG Ambassador to Constantinople (Skene 1883). Skene's account is more a general description and not arranged in a strictly chronological fashion. It contains a mix of fact, gossip, and anecdote, as he freely admitted. Present in Balaclava soon after its occupation in September 1854, Skene interviewed "battle" participants, although there is no evidence he saw the events of 25 October.

Frances (Fanny) Duberly, accompanied her husband, Henry (8th Royal Irish Hussars), on campaign and sent home letters to her family. Extracts of her correspondence ended up in the *London Times*, which led Fanny to ask her brother-in-law to edit them as her *Journal Kept During the Russian War* (Duberly 1855). Nearly a century later, Tisdall (1963) wrote a narrative of Mrs. Duberly's time in Crimea and the Indian Mutiny but drew more on letters to her sister. Her journal polarized contemporary society. Although some disliked many of her comments, most welcomed her frank description of a campaign going wrong. As such, her narrative, including her account of riding out of Balaclava at the time of the TRS, is regarded as reliable. There is no known Turkish version of what happened.

Accessing Russian accounts is difficult so it is fortunate that Mark Conrad translated many contemporary and near contemporary descriptions (Conrad 2006). Seaton (1977) also cites many (non-official) Russian accounts, but does not normally reference sources in all details. He has a tendency to make unsupported comments about their reliability and highlights disputes between different Russian participants. In addition to eyewitness accounts, Seaton (1977), Fletcher and Ishchenko (2004) also utilize Russian histories.

The commander of Russian forces in Crimea, Menshikov, provided a report for Tsar Nicholas I. Responsibility for the attack on Balaclava lay with Lt. Gen. Pavel Petrovitch Liprandi who reported to Menshikov on the 26th. Parts of Liprandi's version were questioned by Koribut-Kubitovich, a cavalry officer who published an 1859 account, but admitted not seeing events. V. M. Krudener, of the Azov Regiment, the captor of Canrobert's, is also quoted by Seaton. N. Ushakov, a junior officer in the 12th Artillery Brigade, described what he (erroneously) called the Russian attack on the Kadikoi Heights on 25 October—a theme so truncated that it arouses suspicion. Indeed, he has been described as "none too reliable a witness" (Seaton 1977:148; cf. Conrad 2006). Although supposedly an eyewitness ("Having taken part in the battle that I have described in the capacity of an orderly officer for artillery to General Liprandi, I was an eyewitness of all the manoeuvres of our forces as well as the enemy's, and was able to observe the course of events and note all the circumstances"), unless we assume he followed Liprandi around, it is difficult to place Ushakov. Conrad also translated the memoirs of an anonymous Don Regiment artilleryman. Published in B. M. Kalinin's (1907) *Material dlia istorii Donskoi artillerii* (*Material for the History of the Don Artillery*, see translated excerpt in Conrad 2006), this account contains factual errors, but has been overlooked by English-language writers. Another example of the dispute between Russian sources concerns Stefan Kozhukov, 8th Light Battery of the 12th Artillery Brigade, who was positioned somewhere in the north end of the valley as the "battle" developed. He was in a good position to see affairs in the North Valley. His account should be read in conjunction with I. I. Ryzhov's (in Conrad 2006) account of the engagement and subsequent vanquishing of his cavalry squadron by the 93rd Highlanders and the Heavy Brigade. Kozhukov criticized Ryzhov and his apportioning of blame for the Russian failure. An even more critical analysis of some Russian accounts is found in V. I. Genishta and A. T. Borisevich's 1904–1906 history of the Ingermanland Hussars (in Conrad 2006). Their section on 25 October is derived from reminiscences of Ye. F. Arbuzov. In analyzing the performance of the regiment, they criticize other eyewitnesses. They are largely dismissive of most other Russian accounts but do prefer the versions by Arbuzov and Ryzhov. Indeed, whereas British scholarship is fixated with the causes and blame for the C-LB, for their Russian counterparts, the issue is more what happened with the TRS/C-HB and why.

Documentary Analysis

When one looks more closely at the "facts" reported by the various "eyewitnesses," problems emerge. Certain episodes summarized in modern accounts can be found in eyewitness descriptions but many cannot. Because many modern authorities rarely cite sources for their assertions, it is difficult to disentangle material derived from primary accounts from pure conjecture. Elsewhere, there are discrepancies that might be the result of general sloppiness or uncritical reading of primary sources. It is a matter of personal choice which authority/ies is preferred.

There remains a fundamental weakness in virtually all descriptions about the redoubt attacks, especially on No. 1. No Briton who wrote about the events was actually there and only witnessed the assault from afar, a fact appreciated by Kinglake (1863–67). For simplicity's sake, we can divide writers into two general groups: those who saw the events from Sebastopol, and those who saw them from somewhere in the South Valley.

Most British accounts are unanimous in recounting how the Turks fled west from Redoubt No. 1 to No. 2 because their line of retreat to Balaclava (to the southwest) was cut off by Cossack skirmishers. Since Redoubt No. 2 had not yet fallen, the implications are that the Cossacks entered the South Valley below Canrobert's eastern side. After the collapse at No. 2, the Turkish flight continued to No. 3, although some fugitives turned south for Balaclava, where they ran into Sir Colin Campbell and the 93rd Regiment.

Most modern descriptions of what happened on Canrobert's Hill and their assessments of the resistance by the Turks miss the point about the visibility of the events. A close reading of many accounts reveals evidence and contradictions which have been ignored, or have not made it in to the "definitive" accounts. Some differences can be found in table 13.1. The problems are myriad and it is difficult to know where to start.

Distant eyewitnesses tend to dismiss the Turkish performance while those in the valley are more sympathetic. There are similar problems in the Russian versions because they cannot agree on certain issues. As a generalization, they are critical of the quality of the redoubts, but tend to be more generous in assessing the performance of the Turks. If there is confusion about the Russian attack, there is one issue where the primary sources are in accord: the quality of the construction of the redoubts. Shadwell's (1881:327–29) assessment was scathing:

> The outer line of works consisted of a chain of redoubts placed on the crest of the low range of hills separating the valley of Balaklava from that of the Tchernaya, and from about 2000 to 2500 yards in front of the inner line. These redoubts, which had

TABLE 13.1. Differences in how details of the attack on Redoubt No. 1 (Canrobert's Hill), South Valley, Balaclava were reported by various sources.

Attributes of the Attack	Details Reported	Sources
THE TIMING OF EVENTS IN THE SOUTH VALLEY		
Russian forces moved out of camp at or just before dawn	5:00 A.M.	Kinglake (1863–67), Koribut-Kubitovich[1]
	5:30 A.M.	Kozhukhov[1]
	6:30 A.M.	Seaton (1977), Ryzhov[1], Todleben[1]
British cavalry fell in 1 hour before Russian attack/bombardment		A Regimental Officer (1859), Kinglake (1863–67), Jocelyn (1911), Calthorpe (1979), Godman[1]
THE TIMING OF RUSSIAN BOMBARDMENT		
	At an early hour	Dodd (1856), Peard (1885)
	Before daybreak	Wood (1895)
	At breakfast	Robinson (1856)
	6:00 A.M.	Paulet (1854), Seaton (1977), Kozhukhov[1]
	Before 7:00 A.M.	A Regimental Officer (1859)
	7:30 A.M.	Koribut-Kubitovich[1]
	Between ca. 8:00 A.M. and 8:30 A.M.	Duberly (1855), Calthorpe (1979)
THE TIME OF THE RUSSIAN ATTACK		
	6:00 A.M.	Lucan (1855), Arbuzov[1]
	After 6:00 A.M.	Paulet (1854)
	After 6:30 A.M.	Woods (1855/1885)
	7:00 A.M.	Sterling (1895)
	8:00 A.M.	Duberly (1855), Ushakov[1], Koribut-Kubitovich[1]
NUMBERS/TYPE OF RUSSIAN FORCES ATTACKING CANROBERT'S HILL		
	5 battalions of infantry supported by 6 others	Kinglake (1863–67), Hamley (1891), Wood (1895)
	5 battalions of infantry flanked by cavalry and 30 guns	Wood (1895)
	5 battalions	Jocelyn (1911)
	18–20 battalions against redoubts No. 1, No. 2 and No. 3, 30–40 guns and cavalry	Dodd (1856)
	Skirmishers, 8 battalions of infantry and 16 guns	Sterling (1895)
	4000 Russians in 4 columns	Blount (n.d.)
	1200 Russians in 1 column	Calthorpe (1979)
WHO CAPTURED CANROBERT'S HILL?		
Infantry?	Russian skirmishers	Robinson (1856), Sterling (1895), Calthorpe (1979), Godman[1], Koribut-Kubitovich[1], Ryzhov[1], Todleben[1], Ushakov[1] Roberts (1854)
	A dense mass of Russian columns with hand-to-hand fighting	A Regimental Officer (1859)
	By the Azov Regiment under Semiakin and Krudner	Menshikov[1]
	By Liprandi and Semiakin with the Azov and Dneiper regiments	Liprandi[1]
Cavalry?	Turks fled as Russian cavalry skirmishers approached	Shadwell (1881), Woods (1855), Percy (2005)
	By a cavalry charge	Hamley (1891)

[1] Conrad (2006)

been commenced on the 7th October and were still unfinished, were of slight profile and were destined to be armed with 12 lber [pounder] iron guns and to be garrisoned with Turks . . . The chief defect of this position lying in the great distance between the outer and inner line and its purpose, did not escape Sir Colin's . . . observation: but the point which he regarded with much greater anxiety was the extreme right of the inner line, which could be approached from the hills to the eastward by the narrow rib or ledge that connects them with the Balaklava heights. This was the key to the position.

Sir Colin Campbell (in Forbes 1895) said the redoubts as a whole "were very weak." Raglan admitted the four redoubts were small and "hastily constructed," with No. 1 a work of more importance. Sterling reported that by 22 October, "We have made lots of redoubts but Campbell does not like them; and we are making batteries of positions, and improving our defences daily." Sterling implies the construction work commenced before 14 October. On that day, Calthorpe wrote of another 4000 Turks sent to occupy the forts being built. According to Shadwell and Roberts, the work was not really completed by the 25th. A shortage of artillery pieces meant that No. 5 and No. 6 were left unarmed. Hamley variously describes them as ". . . small intrenched [sic] works," provided with "parapets," as ". . . slight field works" (a phrase repeated by Wood) ". . . attacked by an army." The "redoubts and works nearest our heights were so weakly constructed as to be rather a cover for the defenders than an obstacle to the assailants;" and finally, ". . . it was believed to be necessary only to throw up a few shovelfuls of earth and any Turk posted behind them would live and die there" (Hamley 1855:60, 80, 1891:110). Henry Percy had no reason to be familiar with Canrobert's Hill but judging from his description of the fortifications he must have had access to a good source, or had the opportunity to visit them, as he wrote his father: "The action that took place at Balaklava [sic] . . . began by the Turks being attacked in some earthworks about 1 mile in advance of Balaklava which they gave up without apparently a struggle. These earthworks were faultily made, the gorge on the right flank, and would you imagine it, no gate—not even a tree cut down and thrown across . . . our engineers might have seen that

they might have connected the redoubts with a steep ditch—which would have stopped cavalry effectively" (Percy 2005:45–46).

Russell offers surprisingly little about the redoubts although he purports to record circumstances of their construction: the 5 "tumular ridges" were thrown up by a party of 2,000 Turks (Kinglake 1864:86, says 3000), under the direction of Captain Wagman, a Prussian engineer (Adkin 1996:75). Of the Turks defending the fortifications, he continues: "These poor fellows worked most willingly and indefatigably, though they had been exposed to the greatest privations. . . . the Turkish government sent instead of the veterans who fought under Omar Pasha, a body of soldiers of only two years service . . . Still they were patient, hardy and strong" (Russell 1858:140). Shadwell recounts how ". . . the exposed situation of that port . . . , had from an early date engaged Lord Raglan's attention, and measures were already in progress to strengthen the position" (Shadwell 1881:326).

While most authorities acknowledge the inherent weaknesses of the redoubts, there are differences of opinion with respect to whose fault it was. A Regimental Officer (1859:253) blamed the British. "Upon the summits of the mounds . . . the Turks under the directions of an English engineer, had thrown up six ill-designed earthen redoubts . . . the land defences of Balaclava consisted of four earth forts, insufficiently armed, insufficiently garrisoned, imperfectly constructed, altogether without support and distant from the place they were supposed to protect." The "miserable" forts with a "low mud parapet," "the earthworks thrown up to crown that line of defence, were despicable, both as to design and execution; were, moreover, weakly armed, and slightly occupied by crude levies, without support of any kind."

These were sentiments repeated by others as well. For Dodd (1856:253), however, "these redoubts were manned by the Turks . . . the defenders in this case were raw recruits, . . . they had lately arrived from Tunis, and had never seen fire; and, moreover the redoubts were too far in the rear of the Allied camps to receive proper support."

Kinglake's description is reminiscent of what others said. Of No. 1, he reports it was "a slight work," one weakly constructed with ". . . a slight breastwork, with its salient towards the northeast." In No. 1, the Turks had to face a massive attack over "a feeble parapet on the top of an isolated hillock." Following the Russian bombardment, the Turks there "moved . . . from the unsheltered part of the work to the side where more cover was offered." Finally, "They were of very weak profile, and a horseman, as was proved by the Cossacks, could well enough ride through and through them." Of the evacuation of the other redoubts, he noted the Turks took "with them their quilts and the rest of their simple camp treasures." Todleben (in Conrad 2006) also reports the capture of tents, powder caissons and pioneer tools.

Raglan wrote in a dispatch that, following the retreat of the Russians, he decided not to reoccupy the "extreme positions" the Turks had occupied because they proved "wholly inadequate." This sounds similar to Sterling's (1895) opinion that the redoubts were too far advanced to be supported properly, and could not be defended because "the ditch and parapet, although as deep as time allowed them to be made were very poor defences. The 'Cossacks' rode over them." Sterling believed it would have been better to place a cavalry piquet behind Canrobert's which "would have answered every purpose" while the "Turks would have been available to man the strong positions to the east of Balaclava by which the Russians were effectively stopped while flushed with their partial success." Kinglake claimed the engineers "chose it apparently as a makeshift which might more or less baffle a hitherto unenterprising enemy."

To the Russians, the redoubts were isolated, without depth, and entirely unsuitable for coordinated defense. Koribut-Kubitovich (in Conrad 2006) wrote: "One may suppose that special attention was paid to the defence of Balaklava [sic], whose loss would be [a] decisive blow to the allies . . . English engineers . . . were undertaking the construction of a series of redoubts around the camp [at Balaklava] on the heights which formed a belt so to speak, around Balaklava. . . . four redoubts, very compact and not providing mutual flank defences to each other, had been built by the time we advanced on the enemy positions, but they were still not fully provided with guns and were occupied by several hundred Turks who had been provided with English officers and artillerymen."

Todleben (in Conrad 2006) was especially critical of the quality of the redoubts. His Russian authorities were critical of the failure of the Turks to clear the thorn and scrub covering the lower slope later used by the Russians in their approach, facts repeated by Ushakov, the Don artilleryman, and Kozhukhov (in Conrad 2006). Seaton (1977) reports how the Turks "sat there quietly for several weeks and had done little to prepare the positions." Ushakov (in Conrad 2006) has them as much more substantial and problematic objectives. Redoubt No. 1 was situated on a steep hill, where the terrain was naturally favorable to defense, all the more so where it was supplemented with field fortifications and artillery. Ushakov felt Canrobert's capture was due to an exceptionally well coordinated attack combining infantry with artillery, although he adds that the incorrect positioning of the guns in No. 1 helped since the artillery "could not fire at the foot of the hill it occupied," where at "the most critical moments the attacking columns were able to close in and advance in formation for bayonet attack." "Most of the guns worked through embrasures, and consequently did not have that full coverage of terrain." Ushakov's comments are fair, if that was the purpose of the guns and the redoubt, but it seems that the pair, guns and redoubt, was meant to fulfill a slightly different role.

These are the issues concerning events on and around Canrobert's Hill but there is another dimension. One reason the discrepancies have not been subjected to serious scrutiny is that the assault on the redoubts is normally read as the "starter" to the main or best-remembered event of the Battle of Balaclava, the C-LB. As the preamble to the "battle," Canrobert's is relegated to little more than a skirmish.

I have been careful to call what happened on the 25th a "battle." The quotation marks are deliberate. Rather than regarding it as a sequence of four interlinked engagements, or as Sweetman (1990) calls it, four phases, it is perhaps better to characterize it as four semi-articulated events. Each occurred as a consequence of the preceding one, but the repercussions could not have been anticipated. In fact, 40 years after the event, one participant wrote " . . . the battle of Balaklava would be called by the Germans a 'Treffen' or meeting" while Jocelyn (Airlie 1933:78) referred to it as one of two "rather serious Skirmishes." In this sense, what became the "battle" commenced as a Russian assault to get into the South Valley. The affair developed following the capture of at least one Turkish redoubt and a failure of the Russians to exploit the situation. The next stage came when a Russian cavalry squadron attempting to seek out a British battery at Kadikoi, had the misfortune to run into Campbell's command. In an equally disjointed manner, another Russian cavalry squadron was unlucky to encounter the Heavy Brigade. Liprandi (in Conrad 2006), losing confidence, ordered withdrawal of captured British/Turkish artillery, starting a new sequence that led to Raglan's order that resulted in "the Charge."

Emphasis on cavalry and artillery overlooks two substantial issues. The first is where was the Russian infantry after the redoubts were captured? It is clear that a few thousand were in reserve north of Causeway Heights but the bulk, possibly as many as 25,000, are otherwise anonymous. To cut the story short, they were probably held for a crucial two or three hours southeast of Canrobert's Hill in the South Valley. They probably arrived there through that important pass east of Redoubt No. 1. Russian cavalry also moved through that defile and cut off the most obvious Turkish escape route. The most important element is that the Russians appreciated the capture of Redoubt No. 1 as the most important objective. Once taken, the other redoubts would fall in rapid succession.

Emphasizing that Canrobert's Hill was central to Russian plans, Raglan repeated the "enemy commenced their operations by attacking the work on our side of the village of Camar [sic] and after very little resistance carried it." Canrobert's was the primary target because a major part of the Russian advance was meant to open up access to the less well protected eastern flank of the South Valley. Capturing Redoubt No. 1 guaranteed a reasonably secure route into South Valley and opened a clear way into Balaclava. Ushakov appreciated how the guns in No. 1 were not positioned to facilitate its defense per se, but looked to the further distance, a fact appreciated by at least one modern authority (Pemberton 1962). The purpose of the redoubts was not to protect the east-west Woronzov Road but to repel attacks coming from the North Valley.

On the side of the Allies, the only protection for the route running into the South Valley was the battery placed on Canrobert's, even if the "work on Canrobert's Hill was perilously exposed to any

artillery which be might be placed in battery on the neighboring side of Kamara; and no arrangements were made for preventing the enemy from seizing this vantage-ground" (Kinglake 1864: 88). Hamley (1891) noted this when he observed that after entering the South Valley, the Russians kept to the side of the valley nearest Kamara. A Regimental Officer (1859) offers the same explanation; Liprandi (in Conrad 2006) pushed "a heavy column of foot" [to the] right of No. 1 redoubt, which being the nearest of the series to Kamara and crowning Canrobert's Hill, was in fact the key of the rest of the works."

Sterling likewise implies that the Russians occupied positions east of Balaclava and how the capture of Canrobert's was a "partial success." When Fanny Duberly rode out of Balaclava to reach the camp of the 8th Hussars, and before she rode across the front of the 93rd Highlanders, she was advised by an English officer " . . . to keep as far to the *left* [emphasis added] as possible, and, of all things, to lose no time in getting among our own men, as the Russian force was pouring on us" (Tisdall 1963:95). The chances are that the attack on Canrobert's involved something like a partial flanking operation. Woods implied this when he pointed out that by maneuvering around and across the Woronzov Road and sending four infantry battalions across the road heading for Kamara, ". . . Liprandi thus formed a line at right angles with the line of the Turkish redoubts which he was enabled to advance upon 3 sides" (Woods 1885:59). The capture of lightly defended Kamara was the hinge to the British line. The Russians were in the South Valley, behind Canrobert's, before Redoubt No. 1 was captured as implied by Godman's (Warner 1977:73) account of Heavy Brigade pickets to the rear of the Causeway Heights being almost overrun. Finally, the Cossacks were able to cut down the fleeing Turks making for Redoubt No. 2 or Balaclava. Once Canrobert's fell, the remaining redoubts could be taken out, in effect by "rolling up" the line. This is what occurred, according to Ushakov (in Conrad 2006).

If these facts were so, then there is the possibility that there was an assault on the rear of Canrobert's as well as the frontal assault most modern accounts describe. If this speculation is plausible, then it leads to the second question: in such a carefully executed set of maneuvers, what exactly was the purpose of the

Russian attack on the South Valley? British explanations have it as the capture of Balaclava, but a slightly different picture comes from Russian sources.

CONCLUSIONS

To conclude, and returning to a theme highlighted in the opening paragraphs, a particular line of interpretation can overly influence the subsequent scholarship that follows. What an archaeological survey undertaken with minimal reference to documentary sources brought home is the relative poverty of the treatment of the "Battle of Balaclava" by historians. It is clear there is much that conventional descriptions of the "battle" omit. The omissions are made intolerable because there is no attempt to explain why such information should be excluded. With the number of contemporary accounts, it is not surprising there are discrepancies. The quantity of such accounts might now be described as finite, with the prospect of more hitherto unpublished accounts coming to light becoming increasingly remote. Unless something new can be introduced, other than higher standards of source analysis, there is not much hope that the understanding of the "battle: will improve.

One potential source of new data is better recognition of the archaeological detritus of the "battle."

Systematic fieldwork has much to offer in reassessing military actions. This is not to say that the field survey of Redoubt No. 1 resulted in any new or innovative insights, but there is still a need for a more detailed battlefield survey just as there is for a more comprehensive review of the contemporary accounts. Systematic fieldwork, in the sense of recording and mapping, is an increasingly pressing necessity as Crimea undergoes massive redevelopment and metal detecting.

Can re-reading the sources add anything new? What if the sources, contemporary and modern, cannot be made to agree or otherwise be reconciled? Surely, a "safe" explanation is better than none? Yes, the analysis is valid and indeed necessary. At the very least, it should make for a more informed understanding that permits a more nuanced comprehension of the "battle" rather than one that focuses only certain elements. This would redress the balance where there has been the perpetuation of the same arguments and dialogue but where discussion has not really advanced since the 1860s. Analysis of the two sets of evidence, archaeological and literary, might leave us in no better position to determine what happened at the start of 25 October. The picture is as confused as it was on the day. What the archaeology does is to open eyes to the fact that the conventional account of the "battle" is far from clear-cut.

CHAPTER FOURTEEN

Cultural Landscapes and Collateral Damage

Fredericksburg and Northern Spotsylvania County, Virginia,

in the Civil War

CLARENCE R. GEIER AND KIMBERLY TINKHAM

INTRODUCTION

On 12 August 1864, Private Marion Epperly of the 54th Virginia Infantry manning the defenses of Atlanta, Georgia, stated the following: "They [the Union] keep shelling the town study/They have all most runed the plase with shells: they have kild and wounded a great many women and children/I can tell you they see very hard times and are in a grate deel of dainger/ . . . I cannot tell what they doo for provision here/the [Confederate] soldier has taken every thing out of the Gardens that they could Get" (Epperly 1862–65, original spellings preserved).

On 10 August 1863, Private Daniel Snyder, of the 11th Virginia Cavalry was encamped on Confederate lands at Culpeper Court House, Virginia. He stated: "Of all the countries I ever got into this is the hardest and the people the meanest. If it were not wrong I almost wish the Yankees could stay in here with such a class. We were better treated in Pennsylvania than by these stuck up Tuckahoes. The fact is they hate to see a soldier come near their houses" (Snyder 1862–65).

These two insights comment powerfully on the often overlooked, or taken for granted, fact that military engagements rarely take place in cultural isolation. Further, the character of those actions when considered in concert with existing domestic communities can have significant and potentially devastating short- and long-term impacts. With respect to the American Civil War, it can be argued that as with all warfare and military actions, its end as a military experience typically marked the beginning of significant political, social, and economic changes in the lives of individual families, regions, and the nation. It is the purpose of this paper to consider how the analysis of military battles can be used to generate models of pre-existing natural and human landscapes over which they were fought and to assess the "collateral" impacts of those actions on them. To illustrate these points, the impact of the Civil War on the community of Fredericksburg is presented as a case study.

CONCEPT AND THEORY

To understand the impacts of a broad range of military activities on the environment and human communities, it is essential to put military sites into an appropriate conceptual context. Modern texts on archaeological method (Sharer and Ashmore 2003:124–26; Renfrew and Bahn 2004:75–78) draw attention to the importance of the analysis of archaeological data within the context of a region and to an associated branch of archaeology, landscape archaeology. Both of these are directly relevant to the study and interpretation of military sites and ultimately, to an understanding of their historic importance and impact.

A region is "a definable area bounded by topographic features such as mountains and bodies of water" (Sharer and Ashmore 2003:124). An archaeological region is the largest and most flexible of the spatial clusters of archaeological data, the definition of which allows archaeologists to investigate a wider range of activities beyond those attributed to single sites. Such regions may include ecological and cultural factors along with physiographic traits and boundaries. In addition, an archaeological region "may be defined as the sustaining area that contains a series of interrelated (contemporary) human communities sharing a single cultural eco-system" (Sharer and Ashmore 2003:124). Such regions logically vary in scale, complexity, and in the patterns of use reflected in the spatial distribution of sites attributed to the contemporary and interacting human communities. The delineation of such regions is the challenge of the individual archaeologist or historical-archaeologist. Certainly, the archaeological region as a military construct is useful when studying the nature of the interaction between armies as distinct social and political entities occupying or contesting regions housing an already established domestic, civilian community.

Sharer and Ashmore (2003) present landscape archaeology as a branch of the larger field that works to make the regional approach more comprehensive, particularly as it relates to revealing and documenting the manner in which resident human communities exploited, modified and adapted the natural environment for their use. They define landscape archaeology as "an approach within archaeology that emphasizes examination of the complete landscape, focusing on dispersed features and on areas between and surrounding traditional sites as well as on the sites themselves" (Sharer and Ashmore 2003:124, G-9).

Physiographic and ecological features have long been recognized as issues to be addressed or accommodated by armies and military groups as they shape the structure and location of diverse military sites. These factors may include the presence of water, appropriate space and topography, seasonality, aspect, wind direction, available sunlight, viewscapes, and defendability. These factors influence the timing and positioning of countless activities including encampment, offensive and defensive fortification, lines and sources of supply, and the conduct, strategies, and tactics of battle. Evidence for this can be seen in the historical record in the publication and instruction of military guidelines on encampment (United States War Department 1861), fortification (Mahan 1862), and battle (Casey 1862). At the same time, evidence reflected in the archaeological record and in historic commentary reveals a common need in field application to deviate from guidelines so as to adapt to the nuances of natural and cultural circumstances at hand (Geier et al. 2006).

Consistent with the logic of an archeological region is the fact that armies rarely move and wars are rarely, if ever, fought in cultural voids. Previously existing cultural features such as roads, towns, industrial centers, rail lines, agricultural fields, and residences, etc., were often as important in shaping the facts of encampment, fortification, and contest as were physiographic or ecological features. In the United States, the National Register of Historic Places (NRHP), working through the National Park Service (NPS), has taken a lead in defining, documenting, evaluating, preserving, and interpreting diverse and historically significant military landscapes. In addition, state and local governments have been instrumental in furthering preservation and interpretation of these resources.

With reference to guidelines for resource preservation outlined by the NPS, the interaction between the domestic and military communities that occupied geographic regions are conceptualized as cultural landscapes, historic landscapes, and battlefield landscapes. A cultural landscape is defined as "a geographic area, including both cultural and natural resources and the wildlife or domestic animals therein, associated with a historic event, activity, or person exhibiting other cultural or aesthetic values" (NPS 1994:1). In a military setting, such a unit can be as small as a picket post less than an acre in size or as great as a battlefield and its supporting encampments and lines of supply that cover many square miles of land. Such constructs include pre-existing, manmade features produced by the resident group to enhance the utility of a natural setting along with existing ecological and topographic features.

A historic landscape is a cultural landscape that is "composed of a number of character-defining features which, individually or collectively, contribute to the landscape's physical appearance as they have evolved over time" (NPS 1994:1). A unique battlefield, encampment, or fortification can be identified as a single historic site in that it constitutes a landscape that is associated with a particular historic event or activity. At the same time, within National Register logic, such a site can also be one part of a historic vernacular landscape or a historic landscape that "evolved through the use by the people whose activities or occupancy (cumulatively) shaped that landscape" (NPS 1994:2). This latter conceptualization is useful in that it directs the researcher to interpret a military site within the context of the natural and pre-existing cultural features that define the terrain within which the military event(s) under study took place.

In the United States the most clearly recognized military landscape for purposes of legislated commemoration, preservation and interpretation is the battlefield or "the landscape over which the armies contended" (NPS 1995:Section 5). Battles typically follow certain rules of logic based on standardized troop movements, deployments, and tactics. These standardized actions were modified as needed depending on the strength of a military force, range, and capability of available weaponry, and existing obstacles and advantages of terrain. However, each engagement must be treated as a unique event in terms of the way these elements combined on a particular field of battle (NPS 1995:Section 5). Terrain, in this context, includes not only natural topographic features but human alterations such as roads, farms, etc. that served to shape the ground over which the forces engaged. Some fields of action were deliberately shaped or prepared to attract or protect against anticipated military action. This can be seen in the case of the planned but evolving fortification systems at Richmond, Petersburg, or Atlanta. In other cases, military actions were spontaneous and were more clearly influenced by the nuances of the pre-existing natural and cultural terrain. The Civil War battle of Gettysburg fought in July 1863, the Battle of Wilderness fought in May 1864, and the Third Battle of Winchester fought in September 1864 are examples of the latter. While the flow of each of these battles reflects a line of decisions made by the competing field commanders, the actual selection of a battlefield was coincidental. No previous agreement had been made to meet and fight in these places. No previous planning or shaping of the field of battle had taken place. Instead, each involved the tactical exploitation of the existing natural and cultural landscape locally modified by the construction of hasty earthworks.

The preservation and interpretation of military battlefields has typically concentrated on commemoration and the study of military tactics. Popular interests in military reenactment and the scholarly and popular study of military history have begun, however, to move beyond these more traditional topics. Certainly the topic of military encampment and its historic significance has become of increasing interest as more and more historic sites are threatened by agriculture and the development of new industrial, residential, and support complexes in areas of past military activity (Geier et al. 2006). Given statistics that note as many as six out of every seven casualties of the Civil War can be attributed to disease and events occurring when encamped (Robertson 1984:78), the need to recognize the historic nature of camps and to expand commemoration to include sacrifices made by the men who died in service to their countries while in camp are significant issues. For the purposes of this discussion, military encampments along with other types of sites such as defensive fortifications, field hospitals and cemeteries, military supply depots at rail and road heads, etc. indicate that the concept of military landscapes significantly transcends the more historically visible battlefield. Within this broader context then, a military landscape is defined as any geographic area that contains evidence of a particular military site type(s) and the natural and cultural terrain features that contributed to its establishment, plan, and the conduct of military actions consistent with its purpose.

Whatever the military site or landscape under study, the presence of an established civilian community is a key component. In this relationship the resident community can benefit through defense or commerce from the presence of the military community. However, the interaction can also have short- or long-term negative impacts. Negative impact can be measured in terms of the destruction of buildings, the decimation of fields and livestock, and the loss of civilian life or material destruction coincidental to a military action referred to as collateral damage. In a broader application, collateral damage can also take the form of an economic depression and possible conflicts of interest between military troops and civilian residents resulting from the prolonged presence of a significant armed force. An example would include a long-term summer or winter army encampment, whose troops compete with the resident civilian population for a finite quantity of available food, firewood, and other resources.

Collateral damage can vary in scope, complexity, and duration of impact. Each case, as with a battlefield, is a unique event that needs to be individually studied and assessed. The loss of an individual life can have a direct impact on the viability of a family. In the case of the Civil War, the conduct of a battle and the subsequent burial of the dead coupled with the carnage of the event could destroy the viability of an agricultural field and the productivity of a farm. These losses, when associated with the destruction of a farmhouse and support structures, could displace an entire family forcing them into economic and emotional ruin. The freeing of enslaved labor could make the operation and maintenance of a plantation untenable even if there was no direct military action involved. Efforts to neutralize the economic viability of a region to attain a military objective, such as Sheridan's 1864 burning of the Shenandoah Valley, laid the groundwork for decades of regional economic depression (Heatwole 1998). The continual occupation and reoccupation of a town such as Winchester, Virginia (Mahon 2002), by opposing armies, tore the social fabric of the community as well as the economic viability of the town. Each example is a story to itself. However, the study of collateral damage is integral to understanding the true impact of war or of a military presence (not all occur during time of war) in history at a local, regional, and even national level. Within the realm of traditional local and regional history, such impacts are the facts and factors that shape the subsequent trajectory of individuals, towns, and regions as the armies move off and the wars pass into time.

FREDERICKSBURG: A CASE STUDY

The town of Fredericksburg and the lands that surround it provide an excellent case study for documenting the impact of collateral damage on the communities that occupied the area before, during and after the Civil War. Because all or part of two major military battles (Fredericksburg, Chancellorsville) were fought in the vicinity, their zones of spatial overlap serve to define an archaeological region that can be studied from the joined perspectives of historic, natural, cultural, and military landscapes. The Fredericksburg and Spotsylvania National Military Park (FSNMP) protects and interprets 7369 acres including

land over which the Civil War Battles of Fredericksburg and Chancellorsville were fought. Since 2000, archaeological fieldwork conducted on behalf of FSNMP by researchers from James Madison University has documented the large array of domestic and military sites that lie within the two battlefield landscapes that enclose Fredericksburg (Geier and Lotts 2004; Geier and Tinkham 2006). This research has documented the known sites of farmsteads, industrial features, roads, plantations, military and domestic road systems, along with diverse and varied complexes of military features and battlefield landscapes. As project researchers investigated the specific engagements of the battles involving Fredericksburg, a growing understanding of the natural and human terrain features over which they were fought emerged. Data contributing to these models included both primary and secondary source material. These sources include the Official Records (O.R.), military maps (Davis et al. 1891–95), recorded interviews of soldiers, newspaper accounts from field correspondents and artists, battlefield histories and explanations, recent scholarship spurred by a reawakened interest in the events of the war, and volumes of Civil War photographic images.

Military records and firsthand action accounts provided the initial formulation of these models. However, when these nineteenth century landscapes were enhanced by modern topographic, terrain, and environmental data, and considered in the context of a wider range of primary archival data, demographic information, and local historic records, the models became more detailed, accurate, and interpretively valuable. As data were accumulated, a temporally concise picture emerged of the terrain and of the socially and economically complex human community that occupied and exploited it prior to and through four years of civil war. While creating a context for the study of the respective military actions, the landscape models were also made available to broader, more general, and more traditional historical studies.

The Antebellum Cultural Landscape of Fredericksburg.

Between November 1862 and May 1864, four of the most bloody and devastating battles of the American Civil War (Fredericksburg, Chancellorsville,

Wilderness, and Spotsylvania Court House) were fought across a 12 miles east-west by 3 miles north-south section of the central Piedmont and western margin of the Coastal Plain of Virginia. While the Battles of Fredericksburg and Chancellorsville had a direct impact on the town of Fredericksburg, the close proximity of the 1864 actions at Wilderness and Spotsylvania Court House had a less direct but nonetheless real influence on town life. The conduct of these battles is not discussed further in this text as they took place at some distance from Fredericksburg proper.

Period military maps (figs. 14.1, 14.2) and records document the plan of the town and the somewhat sparse human settlement in the countryside to its west. The most visible human feature in this area is a network of economically and politically important roads keying on the joined east-west trace of the Orange Turnpike and Orange Plank Road. At Fredericksburg (fig. 14.2), this road system joined a transit hub that tied the rural Piedmont to roads and rail lines that extend north to Washington D.C., south to Richmond, and to an intercoastal shipping port on the Rappahannock.

Scattered and even isolated small family or limited scope farms were the norm across much of the Piedmont uplands west of Fredericksburg (fig. 14.2). Larger family and smaller slave-holding farms tended to be found on the uplands near town. The town of Fredericksburg (fig. 14.1) is built on a high terrace remnant in the bottomlands of the Rappahannock River. At the time of the Civil War, it was enclosed by prosperous plantations including Chatham and George Washington's boyhood home, Ferry Farm, on the heights east of the river. South of the town, extensive plantations (fig. 14.1) such as Mannsfield and Smithfield were established across the rich bottomlands of the river. On the high uplands to the west prosperous farms and homes, such as those of the Marye family at Brompton and the Howison's at Brae-head, overlooked the town.

In 1860 the population of Fredericksburg was 5200, one-third of whom were slaves. The town served as an industrial and merchant center, the economic focus of which lay along the Rappahannock waterfront. Along the waterfront stood the town's icehouse, a slaughterhouse, a series of large merchant mills and, below the railroad tracks, seven wharves served the Old Dominion Steamboat Company. The retail community included a wide variety of shops from confectioners to pharmacies and clothing stores to book stores and dry goods stores. The cultural focus included churches, the courthouse, banks, the town hall, and a citizen's hall where debates and theatrical performances were held (Hennessy 2005:6–7).

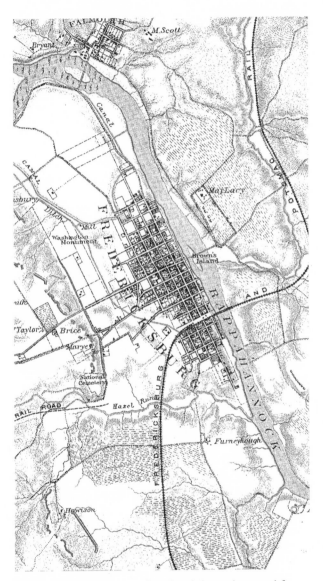

FIGURE 14.1. The vicinity of Fredericksburg abstracted from "Fredericksburg" prepared by Bvt. Brig. Gen. Nathaniel Michler in 1867 (Davis et al. 1891–95: Plate XXX.1). Note the extensive effort to document the cultural landscape over which the Battle of Fredericksburg was fought in December of 1862. Map includes efforts to document terrain, the cleared and prepared plantation and farmlands, as well as roads and natural features.

FIGURE 14.2. Central portion of the project area in the vicinity of the Chancellorsville Inn abstracted from *Sketch of the Battles of Chancellorsville, Salem Church and Fredericksburg* by Confederate cartographer Jed Hotchkiss (Davis et al. 1891–95:Plate XLI.1). Map shows the placement of Catharine's Furnace, the Fairview structure and cemetery, the Chancellorsville Inn, and Bullock House. The map also illustrates the landscape features of the area including woodlines, roads, and clearings, most often related to farming or domestic activity.

The Battles of Fredericksburg and Chancellorsville

Following the Battle of Antietam in Maryland, the Army of Northern Virginia, commanded by Robert E. Lee, dispersed across northern Virginia to recuperate. In turn, the Union Army of the Potomac was placed under a new leader, General Ambrose Burnside. In a daring new plan, Burnside attempted to mass his army of 120,000 and move it quickly to Fredericksburg, cross the Rappahannock and advance on Richmond while the Confederate Army was dispersed. On 21 November 1864, lead elements of the Army of the Potomac appeared on the north bank of the Rappahannock. The bridges across the river had

been destroyed in the spring of 1862 in an effort to hinder an earlier Union occupation of the town. The Union failure to mobilize materials needed to bridge the river and allow a rapid crossing gave General Lee time to mobilize and redeploy his army of 90,000 men. In response to the Union threat, Lee ordered the town abandoned, choosing to create a defense that exploited the natural heights that enclosed the valley of the Rappahannock on the west and south (Marvel 1993; Hennessy 2005; fig. 14.1).

The call for the evacuation of the town resulted in the first and largest flow of refugees that the war had yet seen. By early December, only 1000 of the town's 5200 inhabitants remained, and many of those would leave when faced with the impending battle

(Hennessy 2005:14). Prestigious families such as the Lacy's at Chatham Manor and the Marye's at Brompton were able to move to their country estates as their home and lands were occupied. Others took shelter with friends or generous families in the country as they abandoned their homes and the greater portion of their property and fled into the uncertainties and terror of the harsh winter countryside. Some took residence in abandoned slave quarters, barns and sheds, or wherever shelter could be found. Many families lived in makeshift tents or shelters with little support for the duration of their torment.

Civilian accounts provide insight into the conditions of those forced to leave their homes in Fredericksburg. Jane Beal, a Fredericksburg resident who lived at 307 Lewis Street kept a journal of her experiences at the time. She and her family escaped from Fredericksburg following the Union bombardment of the town. As she passed west of Fredericksburg, she described the scene of a refugee camp near modern day Lafayette Boulevard. "I saw one [woman] walking along with a baby in her arms and another little one not three years old clinging to her dress and crying, 'I want to go home'" (Pfanz 2003:43).

From 11 December 1862 through May 1863, Fredericksburg was in the hands of the Federals, with the 13th of December marking the infamous Union disaster of the Battle of Fredericksburg. During this period of Union presence, soldiers looted homes, started fires and wantonly destroyed private goods (fig. 14.3). The destruction of the town resulted in an outcry from not only the civilians of Fredericksburg, but from the larger South as a whole. Individuals from across the region, including Richmond and Danville, contributed $164,195.45 to aid the civilians of Fredericksburg. Confederate soldiers encamped around Fredericksburg made large contributions to this fund. Montgomery Slaughter, the mayor of Fredericksburg was charged with the task of allocating the funds to the needy citizens (Harrison 1989).

In order to receive reparations, citizens had to present individual claims for their losses to the mayor. Copies of these documents were compiled by historian Noel Harrison. The claims of citizens are particularly telling because many include inventories of the goods that were destroyed. In some cases, Federal soldiers took food items such as flour, corn, rice, and potatoes. They also took knives and even a pistol. It

FIGURE 14.3. Photograph of burned out and destroyed buildings in Fredericksburg following the December, 1862 Battle of Fredericksburg. Photograph by Matthew Brady in May 1864, U.S. Army Military History Institute, Carlisle Barracks, PA.

is quite likely that these items would have been reasonable finds for supplementing their military needs. Other claims indicate that soldiers stole or destroyed items simply for their own personal gain. Mary A. McCoull reported the loss of four dresses, one of which was black silk valued at $50. Books, jewelry and photographs were among the other personal items reported stolen or destroyed (Harrison 1989). Another citizen, Mary A. Layton, lamented the loss of all of her worldly possessions. Her claim, which included a letter, described her situation: ". . . Everything I had in the world was lost distroyed. Not even a bed was left me. I left town the day before the shelling with the intention of getting wagons to get my things out but they commenced shelling the next day so I lost every article of furnature I had so my house [is] not even fit to live in" (quoted in Harrison 1989, original spellings preserved).

In his book, the *Fredericksburg Campaign: Winter War on the Rappahannock,* Frank O'Reilly (2003:125) indicates that some soldiers felt that the Confederacy was a "hotbed of secession," and took their troubles out on the town of Fredericksburg, believing that the state of the country and their personal situations were caused by the rebelling southerners. Based on accounts gathered by O'Reilly, Union soldiers even dressed in women's clothing and paraded down the streets, "scattering smiles and kisses to an applauding crowd" (O'Reilly 2003:124).

During the December 1862 and the later May 1863 (Chancellorsville) battles, the city fell victim to deliberate and inadvertent artillery fire from both sides. Eighty-four buildings (10% of the town) were destroyed and personal wealth is reported to have dropped by 70% (Hennessy 2005:6)

The impact of death from exposure and disease, the emotional stress from the horrors of war, a harsh winter, and a return to destroyed and/or vandalized homes on refugees of all classes and races has yet to be measured. Through the use of historical archaeology, the accounts in the historic record can be enhanced. On Willis Hill, a strong point in the Confederate line immediately west of Fredericksburg, historical records indicate the presence of a residential complex attributed to William Mitchell (fig. 14.4). Based on historic photographs and soldier accounts ". . . there was a little brick house just behind Capt.

Squire's redoubt which was painted white when the battle opened, but it had been so raked with bullets that it was blood red" (Baker 1913:36–52). Shovel test pitting, ground-penetrating radar, and archaeological trenching were used to identify and confirm the location of this structure on Willis Hill, now part of the national park, and place it relative to the artillery line that fronted it. The remains of the structure consisted of a foundation wall, brick rubble, and trash debris that had been used to fill a possible basement where the structure once stood. The fragmented bricks and waste debris indicate that the building was probably never repaired after the war. Instead, it may have been salvaged for reusable building material, and then its cellar filled with remaining debris and trash before the site was covered with fill and turned into a grassy yard. As anticipated from a small number of battle accounts, the structure was found to stand to the rear and right behind the right flank of a line of artillery lunettes manned by the Washington Artillery of New Orleans during the action (Tinkham et al. 2003:49–55).

In May 1863, the Union Army of the Potomac, under a new commander, Gen. Joseph Hooker, initiated a spring offensive. Hooker left an army of 24,000 east of the Rappahannock to attack Lee at Fredericksburg. In an effort to surprise and outflank the Confederates, the remainder of the Union Army moved north of the Rapidan River. From 2–5 May 1863, in the Battle of Chancellorsville, the two armies clashed along the Orange Turnpike corridor west of Fredericksburg. In this action, Fredericksburg was once again devastated as a Union Corps commanded by Gen. John Sedgwick took Marye's Heights (fig. 14.1). Refugee families that had fled the terror of December 1862 and who had thought themselves secure in places such as Salem Church, Catharine's Furnace, and the Chancellorsville Inn (fig. 14.5) west of the town, were again caught in a frenzy of battle. Virtually all the open farmland along the Turnpike from a point two miles west of Chancellorsville east to Fredericksburg was turned into military encampments and/or areas where battles would rage. As the armies moved apart, the Chancellorsville Inn, in particular, was in ruins. The lands enclosing it were littered with dead, both human and livestock that were left where they lay as the armies separated.

FIGURE 14.4. Historic photograph of mill and burned out bridge at Fredericksburg. One of the very few images of structures and military earthworks on Willis Hill is in the distance to the left of the bell tower. A. J. Russell, May 1863; courtesy National Archives.

Like the lands around Chancellorsville Inn, several sites on open terraces over which the December and May actions west and south of Fredericksburg were fought became poorly excavated cemeteries for the large numbers of Union dead who fell before the Confederate defenses of 13 December 1862. A recent description of what the returning refugees found noted: "Looted debris clogged the streets. Amputated limbs lay cast about like litter. Dead animals, including cats and dogs killed by the bombardment, intermingled with human dead. One Confederate

counted 500 dead bodies in town, most of them on a single block . . . Fifty buildings lay smoldering . . ." (Hennessy 2005:20).

As if this was not enough, there were so many Union dead, that many areas on the outskirts of Fredericksburg became temporary burying grounds. Several days after the Battle of Fredericksburg, Union burial parties modified a defensive trench that stretched from Hanover Street just past modern-day Little Page Street into a burial trench including 609 of their fallen fellows (Pfanz 2003:109–10). Hasty

FIGURE 14.5. Chancellorsville Cross Roads during the Battle of Chancellorsville on May 1, 1863 and before its destruction. From pencil sketch by Alfred Waud for Harper's Weekly; Courtesy Library of Congress.

military burials plagued the citizens of the town long after the battle ended. One citizen complained that ". . . parts of them [soldiers], after a short time, showed above the ground, and dogs brought home many a limb. Some corpses were entirely overlooked, and I recollect to have seen two of them untouched as late as the following April" (Edward Heinichen quoted in Pfanz 2003:111). It was not until July 1865 that a national cemetery was created in Fredericksburg in which Union dead would receive a proper burial.

For a brief period after May 1863 the war moved away, but winter of that year found the two armies staring at each other across the Rapidan River well west of Fredericksburg. In 1864 a new Union Commander, Ulysses S. Grant, brought a new style of aggressiveness to the fighting that would drive the Confederacy into the Richmond defenses.

In May, Grant initiated a spring offensive intended to catch Lee off guard and move beyond his line towards Richmond. On 5–6 May, Grant and Lee jockeyed for position along the narrow roadways of northeastern Orange and northwestern Spotsylvania counties in the opening battle, the Wilderness, named

after the dense woodlands across which it was fought. Within days of the Battle of Wilderness, Grant and Lee met again in the Battle of Spotsylvania Courthouse. This extremely bloody battle at the seat of Spotsylvania County lay outside of the project area developed in this text. Nonetheless, the impact on Fredericksburg was direct. On 8 May the town, then occupied by Union forces, was identified by Army of the Potomac Commander, Gen. George Meade, as the interim destination for all Union wounded being evacuated from the battlefields of Wilderness and Spotsylvania Courthouse. Between 8–27 May, 14,000–20,000 wounded flooded the city, each staying several days to a week before being evacuated to more hospitals in Washington, D.C. The response of the citizenry to the wounded enemy ranged from muted to hostile. Virtually every church and public building, as well as dozens of stores and residences, were appropriated as temporary hospitals. Houses not used as hospitals became quarters for more than 500 workers from the U.S. Sanitary Commission or Christian Mission. On 27 May 1864 the last Union hospitals were disbanded and the town never suffered another significant Union intrusion (Hennessy 2005:47–49)

Following the end of the Civil War, the Southern Claims Commission (SCC) was created by an act of Congress to address the material losses of southerners caused by Union troops. In order to receive reparations, citizens had to prove their loyalty to the Union cause throughout the war. Numerous claims were made by civilians residing in and around Fredericksburg. Whether or not the claims were validated by the SCC is interesting, but these claims are invaluable for those researching military landscapes and collateral damage for several reasons.

First, the claims submitted to the SCC were typically very detailed. Individuals associated with the claimant (friends, family, etc.) were interviewed to help determine whether the claimant was indeed loyal to the Union. Through these accounts, researchers can identify various portions of the population resident in the area at the time of the war. The claims often include what type of house or farm was being occupied by the claimant and the location of homes of various interviewees in relation to the claimant. Second, these claims allow researchers to identify the types of collateral damage that individuals or families incurred in terms of losses of private property. Together, this information can provide an idea of make up of the civilian community and the demography of an area as well as an idea of the types and extent of damage caused by military activity in the area.

For example, Absolom McGee, a resident on the battlefield landscape of both Chancellorsville and Wilderness reported a claim for $1,013. According to the claim records, his home was used as a hospital during the Battle of Chancellorsville. During the Wilderness campaign, the advance guard of Grant's army camped on his property. Damages to his land included the loss of his clover crop, which was just ready to bloom, when it was cut to the ground by 500 horses put to pasture in his field. His cattle and hogs were taken for food by Union troops. In addition, his claim included sheets and bedding, 200 pounds of ham, 25 bushels of corn, damage to his home, 30 fowl, 110 cords of wood, shovels, axes, and a saddle and bridle. Mr. McGee was awarded $629.00 of his total claim (Southern Claims Commission Files—Claim number 1013).

John Wycoff, a resident of Spotsylvania County was reportedly operating a 1200 acre plantation associated with the Melville Mine, a gold mining operation along Wilderness Run. He reported the loss of 40 hogs, 10 horses, 500 bushels of wheat, 200 chickens, 2 tons of straw, 10 tons of hay, 300 bushels of corn, and additional valuable livestock among other things (Southern Claims Commission Files—Claim number 22118).

These claims paint a picture of the cultural features that were part of the landscape at the time of the battles, and also provide insights into how the resident community suffered as a result of the war. Documentation of these losses is essential for understanding not only what happened during the war, but also during the process of Reconstruction and recovery that followed.

By 1865, northern Spotsylvania County and the town of Fredericksburg remained devastated. Many large plantation houses such as the Phillips House, that had been the headquarters of General Burnside, and Mansfield south of Fredericksburg had been destroyed. Others such as Chatham and Brompton that suffered varying degrees of damage remained unoccupied. In the absence of slave populations to provide labor, and confronted with fields overgrown from a lack of preparation, some of which still contained unrecovered Union and Confederate dead, the local agricultural and industrial economies were at a stand still. The rural agricultural economy also suffered badly.

Fredericksburg remained in ruins, the resident population being far smaller than at the outset of the war. The wharves had not been rebuilt, rail access was curtailed, and local industry and mercantilism remained badly depressed. In the countryside, iron mining came to an end with the destruction of the blast furnace at Catharine Furnace. In addition, travel centers such as Wilderness Tavern and the Chancellorsville Inn (fig. 14.5) had been destroyed. It would be decades before any significant economic recovery or population growth would take place.

CONCLUSION

Interest in the study and commemoration of military history has increased in modern historians, anthropologists, and the public at large. Thus, the study of battlefield landscapes as natural and pre-existing cultural phenomena can generate "snapshots" of the often complex and diverse human communities that existed when military actions overtook them. Similarly, just as topical areas of interest have changed from a focus on the military events themselves to a growing interest in the lifeways of soldiers in the field and in camp, it is not unreasonable that a continued evolution of topic should proceed to study the area of "collateral" damage and the manner in which that impact shaped the trajectory of local histories. In the case of Fredericksburg, a great deal of the period architecture and material culture has been lost to dramatic growth and expansion of the town, the widening of major roads such as the Orange Turnpike (now Route 3) for modern use, and residential expansion into the countryside. Nonetheless, insights into the mid-nineteenth century cultural landscape remain. Legal records, military action reports, diaries and letters of residents of the community, historical photographs, and observations made by common soldiers are becoming increasingly visible in the published record. As important to the historian and historical-archaeologist, however, are the preserved and protected archaeological remains of sites. These remains provide insights into the lifeways of the people who defined the social and economic make-up of this diverse community at and before the onset of the devastating war.

ACKNOWLEDGMENTS

We wish to acknowledge the very generous willingness of many members of the FSNMP to share their expertise and research on the rich cultural and historical heritage of their park. The enthusiastic support of our fieldwork by individuals such as Robert Krick, retired chief historian, John Hennessy, chief historian, Eric Mink, cultural resource manager, and Francis O'Reilly made our work both successful and enjoyable. We recognize the tremendous historic resource made available to park interpreters by Noel Harrison in his park gazetteer. We also wish to thank John Hennessy in particular for sharing his significant knowledge of the "collateral damage" inflicted on Fredericksburg and its environs by the conduct of the war.

CHAPTER FIFTEEN

Naval Battlefields as Cultural Landscapes
The Siege of Yorktown

JOHN D. BROADWATER

INTRODUCTION

The term cultural landscape, when applied to military sites, typically refers to battlefields or encampments. Even though "landscape" implies a terrestrial setting, the concept is equally valid for describing and analyzing naval battles. In fact, most naval battles were fought near land and were almost always associated with complex multi-national political conflicts. The scope and significance of naval battles rarely ends at the shoreline. Analyzing naval engagements within the broad natural and cultural landscapes across which they took place and with respect to the historic events that define them, imparts additional significance and meaning both to the events and to the natural contexts in which they occurred. In fact, naval battles can only be fully interpreted and given historic meaning by studying them as individual events within the larger context of natural, military, and political events that were taking place. Examples that illustrate the application of the naval landscape concept include:

1. The Spanish Armada: In 1588, Spain launched a long-anticipated invasion of England using a massive fleet of ships of all sizes to transport soldiers across the English Channel. The Armada was defeated by a fortuitous combination of English warships and severe storms that scattered and wrecked many Spanish ships. The naval landscape of the battle included sites of preparation and embarkation in Spain, English shore defenses, and virtually all the waters around the British Isles (Martin and Parker 1999).

2. The Battle of Yorktown: In 1781, a British transport fleet sunk at Yorktown, Virginia, was one component of a battlefield landscape that encompassed American, French, and British land fortifications, a small port town, a group of supply ships, and great opposing fleets at sea, all within the broader theater of the American War for Independence and ongoing conflicts in Europe (Sands 1983, 1988). The Yorktown landscape is explored in more detail later in this chapter.

3. The Battle of Hampton Roads: The famous 1862 battle between the newly-constructed ironclad warships USS *Monitor* and CSS *Virginia* was a pivotal event in the ongoing strategic employment of naval power by the Union to blockade Southern ports thereby strangling the Confederacy early in the American Civil War. The battle landscape included Union and Confederate coastal forts and virtually all the waters of Hampton Roads (Tidewater), Virginia (Davis 1975; Holzer and Mulligan 2006).

4. The Attack on Pearl Harbor: The Japanese carrier-based attack on U.S. military facilities at Pearl Harbor, Hawaii, on 7 December 1941, was a response to deteriorating Japanese-American relationships and a Japanese perception of U.S. weakness in the Pacific. The latter was based on German aggression that threatened to draw the United States into the European war. The Pearl Harbor landscape encompassed a vast Pacific Ocean area beginning west of the Hawaiian Islands, where the Japanese carrier fleet launched their airborne attack, to the coastal waters around O'ahu. This area was all within the larger context of global warfare and the threat of radical shifts in global political and military influence (Prange 1986; Weintraub 1991).

Naval battles such as these provide historical archaeologists with opportunities for interpreting submerged archaeological sites within broader contexts. In fact, data from these "underwater battlefields" can add entirely new perspectives to the written records of a military event at sea. Technology is available for locating and investigating submerged evidence of naval conflict, but special skills and equipment are required to extract valid archaeological data from such sites.

WHAT IS UNDERWATER ARCHAEOLOGY?

The archaeological specialty that deals with submerged sites is generally referred to as underwater, or maritime archaeology (see Conlin and Russell, chap. 5), although the more specific terms nautical and marine archaeology are sometimes used (see glossary). The most important skill for a maritime archaeologist is academic training in historical or prehistoric archaeology, depending on the site types to be investigated. George Bass (1966:13), who paved the way to scientific underwater archaeology, stated: "Archaeology under water, of course, should be called simply archaeology. We do not speak of . . . mountain archaeologists, nor . . . jungle archaeologists. . . . The basic aim in all these cases is the same. It is all archaeology."

Keith Muckelroy (1978:6), a pioneering British maritime archaeologist, provided a definition of maritime archaeology relating to our study of naval landscapes: "[M]aritime archaeology is the scientific study, through the surviving material evidence, of all aspects of seafaring: ships, boats, and their equipment; cargoes, catches, or passengers carried on them, and the economic systems within which they were operating; their officers and crew, especially utensils and other possessions reflecting their specialised [sic] lifestyle.

For this study of naval landscapes, political and military systems should be added to Muckelroy's definition. Some scholars prefer the term anthropology rather than archaeology (Gould 1983), to place more emphasis on behavioral aspects of the events under study. In the United States and elsewhere, underwater archaeology has formed a unique link with the maturing discipline of historical archaeology, which maximizes the diverse methodologies of history and anthropological archaeology with the remarkable technologies currently available for underwater research.

Conlin and Russell (chap. 5, this volume) have presented an excellent discussion of certain modern methods of maritime archaeology using the historic contest between the H L. Hunley and the USS Housatonic as an example. Practicing archaeology under water requires special training and skills in addition to a basic education in history and archaeology or anthropology. These include:

- Maritime archaeologists must be skilled divers as well as trained archaeologists to effectively and safely investigate underwater sites.
- Almost without exception, a well-run underwater "dig" involves specialists such as equipment technicians, dive safety coordinators, geologists, conservators, and others. The principal investigator, who is charged with interpreting the results as well as directing the excavation, must understand the site at a level that identifies what specialists are needed for a given project.
- Planning underwater investigations requires a clear understanding of seasonal weather patterns, average sea conditions, research vessel requirements, nearest port of access, nearest emergency services, and many other logistical and safety considerations. Many an expedition has failed or been compromised due to inadequate planning and preparation.

Several excellent books describe the fascinating variety of underwater archaeology projects around the world (Bass 1972, 1988, 2006; Ruppé and Barstad 2002) while others provide helpful details on methodology and equipment (Graver 2003; Green 2004). The *Encyclopedia of Underwater and Maritime Archaeology* (Delgado 1997) is an excellent reference for all aspects of this archaeological sub-discipline. There are excellent websites, including "Nordic Underwater Archaeology" (Åkesson 2009) and "The Museum of Underwater Archaeology" (Knoerl 2009) that present information ranging from nautical definitions, to projects, methodology, ethical considerations, and necessary equipment. There is also a detailed glossary of terms, with summaries in two-dozen languages.

PREPARING FOR A NAVAL BATTLEFIELD INVESTIGATION

The first step in preparing to conduct an underwater archaeology project is to select a research topic or topics. All too frequently, enthusiastic but inexperienced explorers simply begin searching for underwater sites based on rumors or hunches, only to discover a basic truth: the ocean is a very big place. In fact, the most effective way to begin any project is in the archives.

A thorough document search related to a particular topic or site almost always yields valuable information that will help formulate a survey plan. Each battlefield or shipwreck is unique. So, while most researchers develop a standard research methodology, each project requires a specific archival strategy to provide the information needed to define the relevant naval landscapes and determine the field strategies needed to evaluate them appropriately. Such exhaustive literature searches usually extend well beyond a single archive or record repository.

In spite of the efforts of hundreds of repositories around the world to preserve our past, countless written records have perished, often leaving huge gaps in the historic record as it relates to particular actions or events. Fortunately, formal archives are not the only sources of relevant primary data. Additional sources include fishermen and recreational divers, many of whom have developed extensive shipwreck files, local historians, oral histories, and even descendents of those who participated in the historical events.

Once the initial archival research has been completed, investigators should develop a research design that will guide project search, excavation, analysis, and reporting. In the context of defining naval landscapes, collaboration between terrestrial and underwater archaeologists with shared methodological or topical interests is likely to expand and strengthen the models to be utilized, leading to a more complete and comprehensive landscape interpretation and understanding. Ideally, the same research design that will lead to identifying and locating contributing terrestrial and underwater sites will also provide the natural and historic context needed to interpret site data.

LOCATING SUBMERGED ARCHAEOLOGICAL SITES

Locating submerged evidence from naval battles is often more challenging than locating terrestrial military sites. For one thing, it is often very difficult to pinpoint the exact location where a sea battle took place, even a relatively recent one. Until the advent of military electronic positioning systems during World War II, warships relied on the same navigational method used for more than two centuries: measuring the position of the sun, moon, or stars at a known time. Before the invention of a clock capable of maintaining accuracy at sea, only latitude could be determined. In bad weather, ships and fleets relied on "dead reckoning," that is, estimating their position based on the last accurate "fixed" position. Reported "fixed" positions typically were in error by a mile or more and dead reckoning resulted in much larger spatial inaccuracies. Sea battles also tended to range over wide areas, scattering wreckage and material more broadly than even the largest land battles.

When warships fought, especially in the age of wooden sailing ships, debris often floated away from the immediate battle area before sinking or drifting ashore. Material that sank often disintegrated, or was scattered or buried, leaving little evidence on the seabed. Some materials, particularly wood, were literally consumed. These factors must be considered when developing an underwater survey for the purpose of locating significant, contributing remains.

Although locating submerged archaeological resources can be accomplished by divers, larger areas are more efficiently surveyed using remote-sensing equipment, especially sonar and magnetometers (see Conlin and Russell, chap. 5). These instruments are remarkably effective for locating submerged archaeological material, even small and nearly-buried objects. There also sub-bottom profilers that can produce images of completely buried sites (MIT 2009; Åkesson 2009; Geometrics 2009a, b).

Even with this technology, success depends upon a well-developed research plan and skilled operators. Many underwater sites elude detection because explorers did not attempt to utilize available historical documentation to narrow down search areas. Failure also can result from improper equipment operation or inadequate data analysis.

Modern archaeological research—whether on land or at sea—requires a multidisciplinary approach that often involves specialists from several technological fields including archaeology, history, geology, biology, chemistry, spectrometry, and others. Few, if any, archaeologists ever master all these specializations. However, most principal investigators attempt to learn the basics of any specialties they utilize in their research. It is the responsibility of the project director to anticipate the circumstances and nature of the battlefield remains and create the team of professionals whose skills will be mobilized to enact the established research design, recover and conserve material remains, and interpret the data in a way that gives voice to the historic event under study.

INVESTIGATING SUBMERGED EVIDENCE FROM NAVAL BATTLES

Once a submerged site has been located, remote-sensing equipment should be utilized to the fullest extent to produce accurate, detailed bottom terrain maps showing depth, distribution of ferrous objects, and exposed features (see Conlin and Russell, chap. 5). A large area around the primary site should be mapped to develop a better understanding of the underwater topography and locate scattered objects or features possibly associated with the "battlefield." The data-gathering process follows naturally from a research plan based on the "landscape" concept.

Once all remote-sensing data have been analyzed, the project research design can be updated so that diving (by humans or robotic vehicles) can begin. Once the archaeology team has made a preliminary visual survey, the next step is documenting the site (Green 2004). The first step employed by most archaeologists is installing a reference baseline to facilitate site mapping. It is best to install the baseline parallel to the keel of a sunken ship, either directly over the hull or to one side. If the site is large with multiple scattered features, then the entire study area can be divided into more manageable areas combined on a "master site map." For such large and complex sites, a geographic information system (GIS) is ideal for mapping and

displaying site data (Green 2004; ESRI 2009), and one GIS program has been specifically developed by and for underwater archaeologists (3H Consulting 2009).

CASE STUDY: THE BATTLE OF YORKTOWN, 1781

The above section presented basic definitions, tools, and methodologies of underwater archaeology, along with some very generalized concepts and approaches about naval landscape study. The Battle of Yorktown is a good case study example of an American Revolutionary War landscape study employing these methods.

Events Leading to the Siege of Yorktown

The American War for Independence erupted at an inopportune time for a Britain already embroiled in European conflicts. The American War taxed British military strength and logistics, demanding significant resources on two fronts requiring ships, troops, and supplies to transit the Atlantic Ocean to quell the colonial uprising. By 1778, British forces had failed to subdue the rebellious northern colonies. A new "southern strategy" was adopted that attempted to seize and hold the southern colonies and deny them any opportunity to conduct trade by sea (Sands 1983:25).

Although the British plan met with some initial success, Loyalist support did not prove to be as strong as expected. By the spring of 1781, Sir Henry Clinton, Commander of British Forces in North America, had become frustrated by unsuccessful campaigns in the Carolinas, and was concerned about an allied attack on New York. At the same time, following an inconclusive campaign in North Carolina, the commander of the Southern British Army Major General Charles, Earl of Cornwallis, moved his army to Virginia where he prepared to embark his troops for a voyage to New York (Sands 1983:28–33).

On 8 July, before the ships sailed, Clinton wrote Cornwallis, "By a letter I received this Instant from the Commander in Chief [in England] it is necessary to stop the sailing of the Expedition . . . & remain with the Transports in Hampton Road untill [*sic*] you hear further from me" (quoted in Sands 1983:36). Cornwallis was then ordered to establish a Chesapeake post with a fortified harbor that could serve as an ice-free winter port for the British fleet (Sands 1983:35–36).

Cornwallis eventually selected nearby Yorktown, a small port on the York River. Cornwallis reported to Clinton on 27 July that he would "seize and fortify York and Gloucester [on the opposite shore], being the only harbour in which we can hope to be able to give effectual protection to line of battle ships" (quoted in Stevens 1898:II:107). Thus, Cornwallis's decision to fortify Yorktown was based on the military landscape. Subsequent events would show that the British War Office in London, via its North American Commander-in-Chief in New York, redefined orders to an entire British army and its attending fleet of ships, a move with global consequences.

Cornwallis moved his army, ships, and supplies to Yorktown on 1 August 1781. Cornwallis's ships anchored in the Yorktown harbor while his troops fortified Yorktown and Gloucester by erecting earthworks that protected the army.

Cornwallis's supply fleet was composed of five relatively small warships, about fifty transports and armed merchantmen, at least seven captured prizes and many small sloops, schooners, and rowing craft (Sands 1983:59). With this fleet, Cornwallis possessed the capability to move his army out of Yorktown quickly, should that option become necessary.

When informed that the British had occupied Yorktown, Gen. George Washington recognized a unique opportunity for a major American victory. Quickly, Washington sought assistance from Adm. Francois de Grasse, commander of a large French fleet then in the West Indies. Washington explained that an Allied victory depended upon sea power capable of trapping Cornwallis and that only the French possessed such naval strength (Tilley 1987:252–53).

On 28 August, Washington's efforts were rewarded. The Comte de Grasse arrived at the mouth of the Chesapeake with 26 warships. Cornwallis soon learned of the enemy fleet offshore; however, his small warships were no match for the large French ships-of-the-line, so Cornwallis could only await the arrival of reinforcements from New York.

As Cornwallis's army continued digging in at Yorktown, an important confrontation occured. A British fleet commanded by Rear Adm. Thomas Graves arrived off the Virginia Capes on 5 September. The French fleet sailed out to engage the British in what became known as the Battle of the Virginia Capes. This fleet action was indecisive. However, because of damage suffered by the British fleet and reports of the pending arrival of additional French warships, Graves elected to return to New York to repair and refurbish his ships. This decision left Chesapeake Bay under French control, a situation that proved critical to Yorktown. Thus the Battle of the Virginia Capes, while tactically inconclusive, became a crucial strategic victory for the Allies (Tilley 1987:254–64).

Following withdrawal of the British fleet, the French deployed a squadron at the mouth of the York River, preventing Cornwallis's ships from escaping. Upon learning of Graves' departure, Cornwallis recognized the need to strengthen and hold his post until the British fleet returned. The British considered the situation to be serious, but far from hopeless.

Washington and his French allies were already moving to spring the trap. After feinting an attack on New York and leaving a token force behind, Washington led a rapid overland march to Virginia. His army, reinforced by French troops delivered by de Grasse's ships, brought the total Allied force to 16,645 effectives, a three-to-one advantage over the British who could field only 5953 troops (Sands 1983:49).

Cornwallis was faced with a difficult dilemma: attempt to escape, or hold firm at Yorktown until Graves returned. On 16 September, Cornwallis notified Clinton that he felt that he could hold Yorktown until reinforcements arrived (Stephens 1898:II:157).

Now that his fleet no longer offered a viable means for escape, Cornwallis ordered more than a dozen vessels scuttled along the Yorktown waterfront to obstruct any French landing. On 4 October, Washington received the following report: "Ten or twelve large merchant ships have been sunk before York . . . to prevent our ships from approaching the Town sufficiently to debark Troops" (Washington Papers, quoted in Sands 1983:63). Contemporary reports and maps suggest that the ships were anchored bow-to-stern and sunk in shallow water, forming a continuous barricade along the Yorktown shoreline (fig. 15.1).

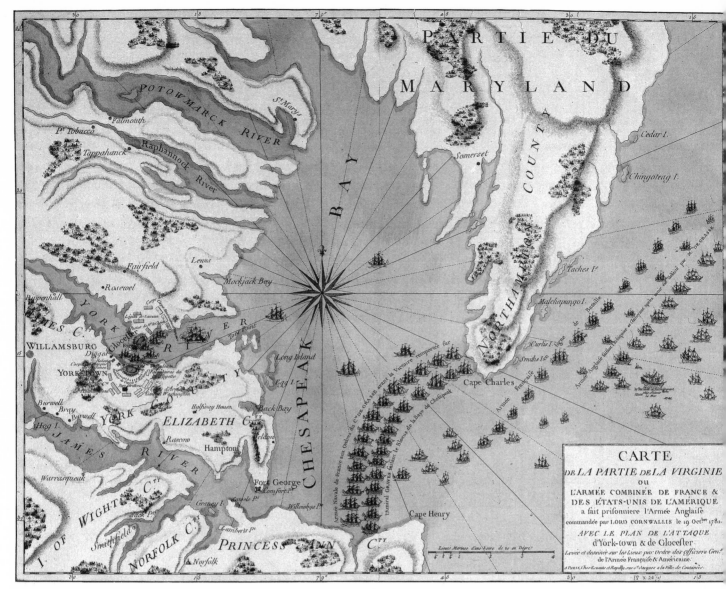

FIGURE 15.1. French map of Tidewater, Virginia, showing major landscape elements and events related to the British surrender at Yorktown, including British and Allied fortifications at York and Gloucester (left, center), the French fleet blocking the entrance to the Chesapeake Bay, and British and French ships battling off the coast. Courtesy The Mariners' Museum.

The siege of Yorktown opened on 9 October, with much early Allied fire directed at the British ships anchored near shore. "The ships were enwrapped in a torrent of fire . . . and presented one of the most sublime and magnificent spectacles which can be imagined" (Thacher 1827:283).

Realizing that reinforcements from New York were not likely to arrive in time, and threatened by the allied siege works that were drawing ever closer, the British began destroying equipment and ships that might fall into enemy hands. Cornwallis recognized

that further resistance was futile and surrendered on 19 October 1781. When the British surrendered, nearly all of Cornwallis's ships lay on the bottom of the York River. At least 26 vessels unaccounted for in the historical record were presumed to remain on the river bottom. Cornwallis's surrender was the final chapter in the unsuccessful British southern campaign during the American War for Independence. The ultimate British defeat is attributable to their failure to retain control of the sea and the logistical support lines that the ocean provided.

Salvage and Archaeology in the Twentieth Century

In 1934–35, the National Park Service, The Mariners' Museum, and the Newport News Shipbuilding and Dry Dock Company conducted recovery operations at several sites on both sides of the York River near Yorktown. Hundreds of objects, ranging from timbers from ships to bottles to cannon, were recovered and documented, and some were preserved. In spite of good intentions, however, no detailed records of artifact provenience or precise site locations were made, thereby greatly limiting the value of the project (Sands 1983:121–31).

As the availability of modern scuba equipment increased in the 1950s, so did diving activity in the York River. There were numerous reports of artifact collecting but, with few exceptions, the impact of this sport diving is impossible to assess (Sands 1983: 133–36).

Official interest in the Yorktown waterfront was renewed in the early 1970s, when the Virginia Historic Landmarks Commission nominated the Yorktown Shipwrecks to the National Register of Historic Places. In 1973, the York River bottom, between Yorktown and Gloucester Point, was designated as the first underwater historic site in Virginia and was one of the first such sites named to the National Register. The National Register designation demonstrates awareness that the Yorktown shipwrecks were essential components of the Battle of Yorktown. In the early 1970s, the efforts of a graduate student and several volunteers followed by a Texas A&M Field School, led eventually to a long-term archaeological project.

Yorktown Shipwreck Archaeological Project

Full-scale research began at Yorktown in 1978, when the Landmarks Commission received a grant from the National Endowment for the Humanities for a comprehensive survey of the Yorktown Shipwrecks area. The 1978 research design, as well the designs for subsequent surveys in 1979–80, specified combining remote-sensing investigations and bottom searches by archaeologists to locate and assess all shipwrecks within the National Register boundaries. The project

discovered a total of nine shipwrecks from the Battle of Yorktown (Sands 1983) (fig. 15.2).

The surveys revealed that the dynamic hydrography of the York River channel has played a major role in site formation processes. Shipwrecks nearest the constriction between Yorktown and Gloucester Point were rapidly eroding, while those further downriver were protected by a deep layer of silt. Three wrecks were found to be exceptionally well preserved, with one, designated 44YO88, appearing to offer the highest research potential (Broadwater 1980, 1981; Sands 1983).

Because of its extremely well-preserved hull and contents, shipwreck 44YO88 was chosen for complete excavation. Its small size indicated that it was a transport or victualler, not a warship. The research design called for the wreck to be examined from several different aspects based on Muckelroy (1978): (1) the ship as artifact; (2) the ship as a former vehicle of commerce; (3) the ship as a small, closed community; (4) the ship as a "time capsule;" and (5) the ship as a troop transport that played a small role in a global conflict.

Whenever possible, established terrestrial archaeological methods and techniques were adapted for the

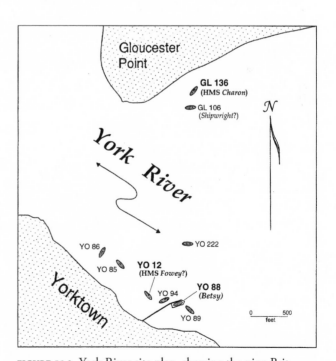

FIGURE 15.2. York River site plan, showing the nine British shipwrecks discovered during the *Yorktown Shipwreck Archaeological Project*. Map by author, courtesy Virginia Department of Historic Resources.

underwater sites at Yorktown. The poor diving conditions prompted some unique approaches, in particular,
the construction of a protective steel cofferdam. The
cofferdam entirely surrounded shipwreck 44YO88, (fig.
15.3) eliminating strong currents, poor visibility, pow-
erboats, and stinging jellyfish that hampered previous
research. The enclosed water was filtered to improve
visibility and facilitate excavation. Mapping hull components, features, and significant artifacts was accomplished via a three-dimensional, direct-measurement
system, consisting of surveyor tapes attached to reference points bolted directly to the rigid cofferdam.

A moveable grid aided mapping, and served as
a scaffold, to prevent divers from damaging fragile
artifacts or disturbing the loose silt and destroying

visibility. Sediment removal was accomplished using
airlifts, which utilize compressed air to create suction
at the intake nozzle. Site overburden traveled up the
airlift pipe and into the river outside the cofferdam. A
"stair-step" pattern of excavation was utilized in order
to minimize the collapse of excavation walls.

Excavation of the Betsy

The Yorktown Shipwreck Archaeological Project produced valuable data from one of the largest groups
of associated sunken vessels in North America. Shipwreck 44YO88 eventually was identified as the British brig Betsy. Its unique construction features and
exceptional preservation offered unparalleled insight

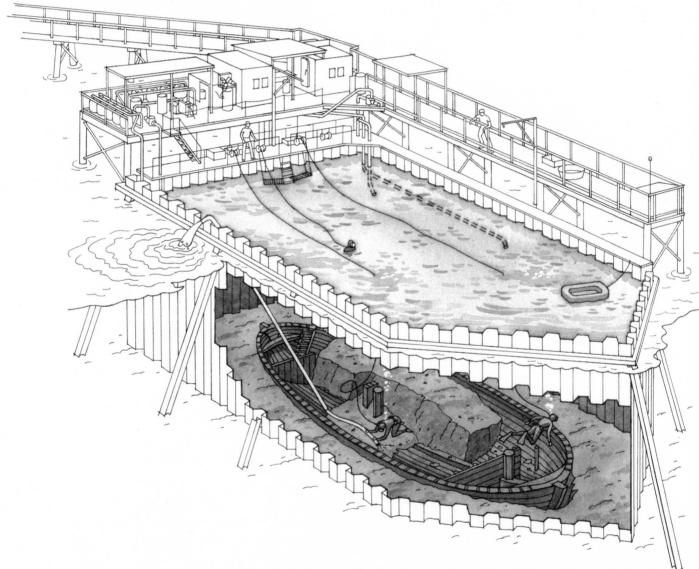

FIGURE 15.3. The Betsy being excavated from the Yorktown cofferdam. Courtesy Pierre Mion / National Geographic Stock.

into eighteenth century ship design and construction as well as shipboard interior appointments and living quarters (fig. 15.4). Subsequent analysis provided insights into the Battle of Yorktown as well.

Excavation revealed that *Betsy* was scuttled by cutting a hole below the waterline. Although the exact date of its sinking is still a mystery, its position in line with five other shipwrecks, parallel to the beach, suggests that it was among the first vessels scuttled on 16 September 1781.

Determining the Function of *Betsy* at Yorktown

The official records of the Royal Navy's Navy Board state that *Betsy* was employed as a victualler, that is, a transport that normally carried food supplies. Documents also revealed that *Betsy* served as a troop transport in July 1781 when it carried 100 men from the 43rd Regiment of Foot from Portsmouth to Yorktown, as verified by five buttons from the 43rd Regiment found on board. Of special interest, there is archaeological evidence that *Betsy* provided an additional and somewhat unique service to the army: assisting with the construction of the land fortifications at Yorktown.

The hold of *Betsy* contained dozens of partially-worked logs and planks that resemble the structures used in wood-and-earth fortifications. It seems likely that British troops felled local trees and sent the timber aboard ships where it was rendered into fortification components. Thus, Cornwallis apparently used this supply vessel as a "floating factory."

The hold also contained additional items that suggested repair activities were being undertaken at Yorktown. Barrels had been patched and rebuilt; shoes had been disassembled as if for repairs and a wooden shoe last was found nearby; an incomplete cannon carriage with one truck (wheel) missing was recovered, and an adze was found among a pile of wood chips. It seems very likely that the crew of the *Betsy* spent the time before sinking their ship fabricating fortification elements and repairing military equipment.

Yorktown as a Battlefield Landscape

The Yorktown Visitor Center (NPS 2007) and the Yorktown Victory Center (Jamestown-Yorktown Foundation 2007) include the sea battle and Cornwallis's fleet in their interpretation. The Yorktown Visitor Center describes the overall land/water elements of the siege and recreates a portion of the gun deck of the HMS *Charon,* while the Victory Center focuses on the role of the British transport *Betsy.*

Thousands of visitors walk the Yorktown Battlefield each year. They stroll through American, French, and British fortifications, complete with earthworks, sharpened stakes, and rows of cannon; then they see "Surrender Field" where the British laid down arms on 19 October 1781. As they follow the self-guided tour routes, they have the opportunity to look over the bluff, down to the York River below and across to Gloucester Point. Hopefully, the extensive museum and battlefield interpretation, along with the impressive river vista, give most visitors an appreciation of the interrelation between the natural environment of Yorktown and crucial events played out on the York River and off the Virginia Capes.

The importance of viewing the Battle of Yorktown from a landscape perspective cannot be overstated. The extended Yorktown battlefield landscape encompassed the territory from Yorktown to the Atlantic Ocean and from the York River to the James River. Significantly, many aspects of the battle, including the selection of Yorktown for Cornwallis's base of operations, were shaped by the physical environment. Yorktown was the only port that met all British criteria: near the entrance to the Chesapeake Bay, deepwater access, easily fortified and defended, and suitable for mooring the British fleet in ice-free conditions through the winter.

Had British ships and troops been able to reinforce the southern British Army in September, as planned, the outcome at Yorktown would have been quite different. The British simply could have sailed out of the bay, leaving Washington and his troops with no enemy to fight, or the strengthened British force, with the support of heavy naval guns, could have turned the tables on Washington's army. The early arrival of DeGrasse's fleet, however, resulted in French naval control of the lower Chesapeake. Without naval support, Cornwallis could not force his way into the bay or ocean, and there was no river outlet above Yorktown. Thus, once again, elements of the landscape influenced the outcome of the battle and, ultimately, the war.

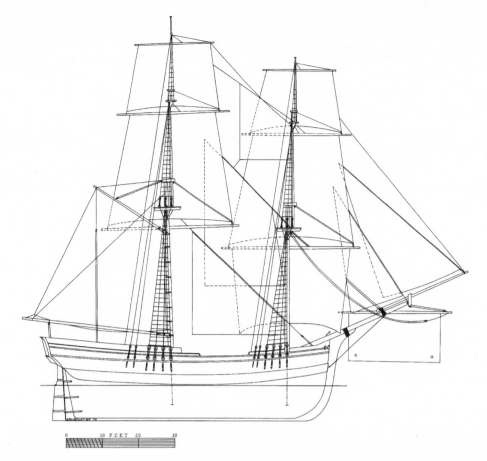

FIGURE 15.4. Reconstructed sail plan of Betsy (top), and scale model based on archaeological analysis (bottom). Drawing by author; photograph by Jennifer Miller.

PLANNING A BATTLEFIELD STUDY

As should now be clear, all aspects of a battle, including both land and water features of the landscape, should be taken into account when planning a battlefield study. Understanding the overall conflict that led to the battle, along with the movements and strengths, supply lines, etc. of the opposing forces, led to the determination—planned or inadvertent—of the battlefield site. The land nearest to naval battles may be miles away, but it may be appropriate to consider that land part of the battle landscape. Conversely, it is not uncommon for terrestrial battlefields to have significant water features, such as a river or creek, or a nearby deepwater river or bay. Such waterways could provide warships with opportunities to bombard opposing land forces, or allow supply ships and boats necessary access to disembark reinforcements, arms, ammunition and food, or evacuate wounded. Therefore, even if the battlefield is on land, water elements should be taken into account, and underwater archaeological investigations may be called for.

Underwater archaeological investigations associated with battlefield landscapes may contribute valuable data for comprehensively interpreting battlefield sites, whether on land on at sea. Archaeological research designs for battlefield investigations should consider the overall battlefield landscape, including all land and water components as discussed in this chapter.

CHAPTER SIXTEEN

The *Maple Leaf*
Wreck Site of a Civil War Transport Ship

FRANK G. CANTELAS AND LAWRENCE E. BABITS

INTRODUCTION

Sunken ships are a unique archaeological resource. In many cases, they can be dated to a fairly close time period, if not a specific event. More importantly, the material culture associated with a ship represents a data assemblage, related in time and space. Others have called wrecks a time capsule (Muckleroy 1978:56). The concept of a shipwreck as a time capsule means that the material culture of a wreck can be used to date other specimens without good provenience, such as artifacts and objects in museum collections where dated items from elite levels of society are often found, but they also have more common artifacts that are not well dated. The British collier *General Carleton* of Whitby, under contract to the Royal Navy when it sank in 1785, provides an example of how shipwrecks can aid museums in studies of material culture. By fortuitous circumstances, over 70 articles of clothing survived. These were used, some exhibited repairs, and chiefly from seamen, rather than officers. When the three dozen stockings were compared with published museum specimens, many interpretive errors were found regarding dating, sizes, and decorative elements. Other items, including a handkerchief (bandana) that belonged to a sailor and a tarpaulin hat, were found to be in use much earlier than previously thought. The clothing assemblage of the *General Carleton* will change interpretations about clothing because the items were dated to a single vessel, on a particular date and represented virtually the entire range of clothing available to sailors at the time (Brenckle 2004).

In those cases where vessel contents have been adequately reported, the huge volume of artifacts often means a long delay in publishing the information. The *Vasa* sank in 1628, was raised in 1961, a museum/preservation center created and numerous small reports on artifacts produced, but the final report series only commenced publication in 2006 (Cederlund 2006). Similarly, the *Mary Rose* sank in 1545 and was raised in 1982. Again a combined museum/preservation center was created and small reports trickled out. The final report series is almost finished with only one volume still due (Gardiner 2005).

In the United States, the *Bertrand* sank in 1865, was excavated during 1969 when its cargo was largely recovered, and two reports have since been issued (Petsche 1974; Switzer 1995). Other in-house reports have been generated but not widely disseminated. Even worse, the USS *Cairo* was sunk by Confederate torpedo 12 December 1862, discovered in 1956, it was virtually destroyed while being raised in 1964, and then nearly disintegrated awaiting proper conservation. The artifacts were scattered and have never been adequately reported (Bearss 1980).

Long delays in producing a final report are due to a variety of constraints, expertise, conservation, and funding; the effect of the latter being magnified in the case of the *Arabia,* a Missouri River steamboat raised by private initiative (Hawley 2005). Without government support, conservation, analysis, and publishing are subject to many distractions, not the least of which is raising funds to continue operations. Such is the case of the *Arabia,* a vessel that sank in 1856, was salvaged and portions raised by 1989, a conservation facility and museum is in operation and some reports have been issued, but the artifact volume has nearly overwhelmed the ability of the investors to complete the project. Still, the *Arabia* project continues, because the group feels obligated to see it through (Corbin 2000; Hawley 2005). Something similar almost happened with the *Maple Leaf,* a Union Army transport sunk in the St. Johns River near Jacksonville, Florida.

THE MAPLE LEAF

The *Maple Leaf* contains a unique legacy from the past, that is an important resource for Civil War history and maritime heritage. Systematic archaeological investigation of the well-preserved cargo revealed aspects of the conflict that do not survive in written form and only in museum collections with poor provenience. The National Park Service designated the site a National Historic Landmark in the fall of 1994.

The mid-nineteenth century saw a great westward movement of people and industry across North America aided by the intricate waterways that are spread across the continent. Among them are the Great Lakes that span the U.S.-Canadian border and empty into the Atlantic Ocean via the St. Lawrence River. This inland marine highway served the growing economies of both countries in a two way trade between extractive interior industries and east coast manufacturing centers. By the 1850s, many types of sail and steam vessels served this trade with an expensive class of wooden sidewheel paddle steamers transporting freight, passengers, and mail.

The *Maple Leaf* was launched at the Marine Railway Yard in Kingston, Ontario, on 18 June 1851. No drawings of her existed until maritime archaeologists recorded the vessel in the 1990s. She was typical of her class, measuring 181 ft long and 26.5 ft in beam (Daily British Whig 1851; fig. 16.1).

The 1850s were a decade of economic decline as reflected in the career of the *Maple Leaf* on the Great Lakes. Her owner, Donald Bethune, held the primary mail contract on Lake Ontario with routes extending along the Canadian shore. The *Maple Leaf* served the mail routes until sold to the Lake Ontario International Steamboat Company in June 1855 (Girvin 1993:79–83). The new company engaged in cross-lake trade, effectively becoming a ferry line serving rail heads for railroad companies on each shore that were actively extending their lines (Union and Advertiser 1857). Ironically, the market downturn for steamboats was largely due to railroad competition, coupled with declining passenger traffic as immigration slowed, and the depression caused by the Panic of 1857 (Mills 1910:153–54; Barry 1973:80; Studenski and Krooss 1963:127).

In 1860, Great Lakes economic conditions for steamboat trade remained bleak. When the American Civil War erupted in the spring of 1861, great economic disparity developed between Great Lakes and East Coast shipping. Depressed market conditions continued on the lakes while government charter fees at the Atlantic ports reached extraordinary heights. As a result, vessels were sold off the lakes for service on the Atlantic (Girvin 1993:103).

In response to the general economic climate, the owners of the *Maple Leaf* negotiated the sale of the steamboat to Boston investors John Lang and Charles Spear on 2 September 1862, for $25,000 (Union and Advertiser 1862; Girvin 1993:106). Government demands for shipping were so great that Lang and Spear signed a charter agreement for the *Maple Leaf* with the U.S. Army the day before they purchased her (Boston Custom House 1962). The army agreed to a one month charter with an option to extend indefinitely at $550 a day (Charter Agreement 1862).

The *Maple Leaf* first operated under the Chief Quartermaster of the 7th Army Corps at Fort Monroe, moving troops and supplies between Baltimore and Jacksonville, Florida (List of Steamers 1862; Thomas 1863). Many of her voyages directly supported military expeditions.

Union Army operations in the southeast included northeast Florida. On 20 February 1864, Union and Confederate forces met at Olustee, 50 miles west of Jacksonville, for the largest Civil War battle in Florida. The Union suffered a defeat and fell back to Jacksonville (Finegan 1864). Federal Gen. Truman Seymour immediately requested reinforcements to strengthen Union positions in east Florida. Three regiments stationed at Folly Island, South Carolina, were sent to Jacksonville, the 13th Indiana, 112th New York, and 169th New York (Itinerary of Military Operations 1864). The troops were given notice to dismantle and pack their camps before boarding transports on 22 February (Hyde 1866:66–67). The men were ordered

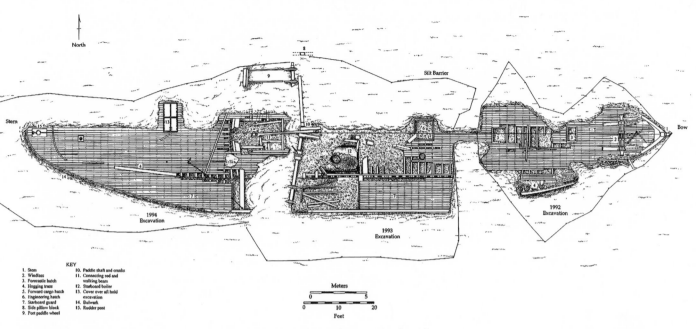

MAPLE LEAF
SITE EXCAVATION
1992 to 1994

KEY
1. Stem
2. Windlass
3. Forecastle hatch
4. Hogging truss
5. Forward cargo hatch
6. Engineering hatch
7. Starboard guard
8. Side pillow block
9. Port paddle wheel
10. Paddle shaft and cranks
11. Connecting rod and
    walking beam
12. Starboard boiler
13. Cover over aft hold
    excavation
14. Bulwark
15. Rudder post

FIGURE 16.1. Plan of *Maple Leaf* site excavation, 1992–94 (Cantelas 1995:89, fig. 13).

to take only essential equipment including weapons, ammunition, five days rations, and shelter tents. Camp and garrison equipment, tents, and baggage were left in charge of the Quartermaster sergeants for later shipment (Hyde 1866:66–67; Foster 1864).

Union warships dominated the waters of Florida and faced little Confederate opposition. In response, a secret Confederate military program concentrated on submerged torpedoes or mines. Several kinds were developed including a barrel type used on the St. Johns River. This consisted of a barrel filled with 70 pounds of powder, anchored to the bottom and floating just below the water surface. It detonated when a vessel struck a contact fuse mounted on the barrel (Dahlgren 1865).

On 26 March, the *Maple Leaf* received orders from the Army Quartermaster to proceed to Pawnee Landing on Folly Island, and take on the camp and garrison equipage of Ames' and Foster's brigades (Dale 1864). This included the baggage of the 13th Indiana, 112th New York, and 169th New York regiments. The cargo also included Foster's brigade headquarters equipment and the property of two sutlers (Hatch 1864a; New York Times 1864).

The *Maple Leaf* arrived in Jacksonville, Florida, on 30 March at 5 P.M., (Dale 1864). Shortly afterward, the captain received orders to transport a detachment of the Independent Battalion of Massachusetts Cavalry to Palatka, about 50 miles south of Jacksonville. Before emptying her holds, the *Maple Leaf* took on board 87 horses, 75 men and some forage, and departed Jacksonville at nine o'clock (Walbridge 1864). River Pilot Romeo Murray guided the vessel through the darkness to avoid sniper fire and arrived at Palatka about 4 A.M. (Murray 1864). The cavalry was debarked and preparations made to return to Jacksonville that evening, departing on 31 March at 11:15 P.M. (Dale 1864).

As a defensive measure against Union forces occupying Palatka, Confederate Maj. Gen. Patton Anderson ordered the St. Johns River to be mined. The "infernal machines" were sent from the torpedo service in Charleston, South Carolina, under supervision of Capt. E. Pliny Bryan. The night of 30 March, almost immediately after the *Maple Leaf* passed the site heading upstream (south), Bryan placed 12 torpedoes across the river channel at Mandarin Point. A little more than 24 hours later, the *Maple Leaf* became the first torpedo casualty on the St. Johns (Bryan 1864; Perry 1965:114–15, 166–67).

Returning downstream to Jacksonville, the *Maple Leaf* rounded Mandarin Point at 4 A.M. and struck a torpedo set the previous night. A tremendous explosion shook the steamboat, causing immediate and catastrophic damage. The torpedo detonated near the bow on the starboard side. Two firemen and two deck hands, asleep in the forecastle, were killed. The pilot house collapsed and the side of the ship "stove in" (Farnham 1864; Jones 1864; Murray 1864).

The vessel settled on the bottom athwart, perpendicular to, the channel, in 24 ft of water (Murray 1864). The saloon deck was partially submerged allowing passengers and crew to easily escape in the lifeboats. They rowed downstream to Jacksonville, arriving about 8 A.M. (Dale 1864). Damage to the *Maple Leaf* was so extensive that re-floating the ship was never seriously considered. The lost cargo of sutler stores and personal effects of the soldiers did not impact the Federal war effort, so no plans were made to salvage the vessel. However, a steamer was sent to the wreck on 9 April to recover ship equipment and anchors (Hatch 1864b).

For years, the sunken *Maple Leaf* threatened river navigation because, as late as 1870, the gallows frame and walking beam still rose above the water (Driggs 1870). Several contracts were awarded by the Army Corps of Engineers to remove obstructions, but the work was not completed until 1890 (Russell 1883; Black 1890). Navigation charts stopped showing the area as a hazard in 1911. Eventually the wreck was forgotten as it slowly settled into the muddy river bottom.

THE MAPLE LEAF ARCHAEOLOGY PROJECT

The obscurity of the *Maple Leaf* ended in 1984 when she was discovered by an expedition led by Dr. Keith Holland of Jacksonville. His group, later organized as St. Johns Archaeological Expeditions, Inc. (SJAEI), would spend the next ten years investigating the site. Only the lower hull, containing the cargo holds and engineering spaces, remains. The main deck, still in place, is buried under 4–8 ft of mud in 21 ft of water. This mud is anaerobic (oxygen-free), creating

remarkable conditions for artifact preservation, especially for organic materials.

Preliminary surveys were made through 1987 as litigation was concluded in a court settlement that recognized government ownership through the U.S. Army while SJAEI was awarded salvage rights. Initial work inside the hull located material associated with the three Union regiments known to have effects on board the *Maple Leaf,* circumstantially confirming the identity of the wreck. In 1992, the Program in Maritime History and Underwater Archaeology at East Carolina University (ECU) was invited to participate and provided archaeological and material culture expertise.

The St. Johns River environment proved daunting. The turbid river is subject to diurnal tidal currents that carry a heavy silt load along the bottom making it impossible to keep an excavation open. The silt layer obscures any visibility a diver might have where artificial lights penetrated only six inches to three feet in the tannic water. To overcome these problems, a barrier was built around portions of the wreck to stabilize the local environment. This silt barrier deflected tidal currents carrying the bottom silt layer, and kept sediment and trash from filling excavated areas. The structure also proved successful in diverting clear river water along the main deck level, thus providing marginal visibility to map and document structural elements. During times of extremely low visibility, divers used water-filled bags sandwiched between the facemask and tape measure with a light shining from the side to take measurements. This technique proved accurate but time-consuming.

Between 1992–94, investigators had two primary goals. ECU documented the starboard side construction of the main deck of the vessel, moving from the bow, past the amidships engineering spaces, and finally the aft deck. The work revealed Great Lakes ship construction techniques and uncovered military artifacts associated with the last mission of the *Maple Leaf.* During the same period, SJAEI conducted excavations in the forward and aft cargo holds. A large collection of material culture was recovered, even though less than five percent of the cargo was retrieved.

Natural processes and salvage attempts have stripped nearly every structural feature above the main deck of the *Maple Leaf* (fig. 16.2). The main deck is intact except for damage near the bow and around the

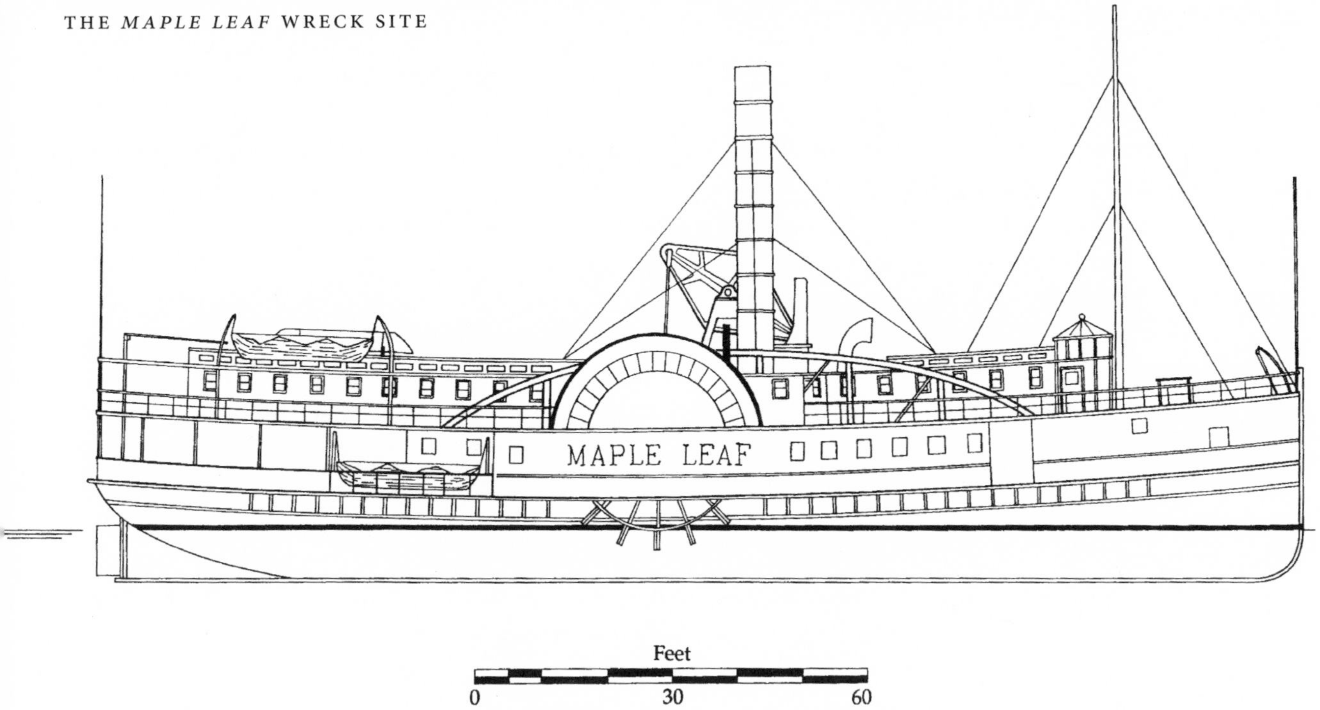

Feet

0   30   60

FIGURE 16.2. Hypothetical profile of the *Maple Leaf* based on 1856 ambrotype and archaeological information (Cantelas 1995:24, fig. 4).

engineering spaces. The lower hull, internal arrangements covered by the main deck, parts of the steam power plant, and propulsion machinery remain.

Physical Remains of The Maple Leaf

The *Maple Leaf* was constructed entirely of wood as a side-wheel paddle steamer. Side-wheelers carried their steam engines in the central hull with paddlewheels extending from the sides amidships. To optimize capacity, paddle wheelers used a sponson hull from which the deck extended beyond the side of the hull to the outer edge of the paddlewheels. The overhanging sponson tapered into the hull at the bow and stern and provided increased deck space. For longitudinal support along the hull length, many side-wheelers carried hogging trusses or bishop arches. These characteristic arches rise above the cabins extending from the bow to stern. The *Maple Leaf* was powered by a single cylinder, walking beam engine, a common power plant for vessels built on the Great Lakes and the East Coast.

The bow contained several significant features (fig. 16.2). The intact hand-powered windlass was used to raise anchors and handle other lifting jobs as needed. The anchors were removed from the vessel shortly after it sank and no trace of them was found. Further aft is the forecastle hatch, leading to the area where four crew members died, and the forward cargo hatch. Between the two hatches, most deck planking was removed in what appears to be an undocumented, and unsuccessful, salvage attempt. Damage from the torpedo explosion exists along the starboard side where the deck was destroyed and slightly further aft, where the hogging truss was broken.

The amidships is filled with the steam power plant. The machinery posed a hazard to navigation for many years after the *Maple Leaf* sank and salvors made several attempts to break it down. Extensive damage to the machinery spaces resulted from this work. Massive timbers forming the A-frame that once supported the walking beam litter this area. While the engine has been removed or destroyed, the paddlewheels and iron paddle shaft remain. The massive iron rod that connected the walking beam and paddlewheel shaft has fallen aft with a section of the walking beam still attached. This piece fell directly through the aft cargo hatch obliterating the structure. The starboard fire tube boiler appears to have suffered an explosion as a result of the initial sinking when cold water came in contact with the hot iron.

The aft deck is relatively intact with very few features providing clues to the cabin structure. Several deck sole plates mark cabin wall locations and a through-deck fitting made of stone probably served to insulate the wooden deck from a heating pipe. Near the stern, the rudder post top rises 7 ft above the deck. A central feature is the hole cut through the deck by SJAEI to gain access to the aft cargo hold.

The intact deck made it difficult to examine interior construction features except in a few locations where damage exposed these elements or in the cargo holds. The most revealing feature is the system of longitudinal supports to keep the long wooden hull rigid. This system consisted of the obvious hogging arches, but also included a substantial shelf and clamp arrangement under the deck. The hogging arches served to brace the vessel and keep the bow and stern portions from sagging. The bracing system was further strengthened by the use of dagger knees, angled wooden braces that supported deck beams and provided additional stiffening. Generally speaking, dagger knees usually angled up and toward the bow in the forward half of the vessel. The reverse was true aft of the midpoint of the vessel.

Excavation of the Hold of the Maple Leaf

Excavation in the forward cargo hold was limited. This area appears to contain the stores of one sutler, but extensive damage makes it a dangerous and difficult area to enter. The aft hold is remarkably intact with a wooden floor installed to keep the cargo above the bilge. Some cargo shifted as a result of buoyancy when the hold filled with water, but a systematic packing arrangement is evident. Heavier boxes and barrels were stacked low and lighter items placed at mid-level. Carpetbags, barrels, boxes, and desks were among these items. Tent poles were laid across the top. The cargo is held solidly in place by sediment that fills the interior of the ship. Many loose artifacts are found in the sediment as a result of packages breaking open as they deteriorated, but the majority of the material culture remains in its original containers.

The containers provided an outstanding means of documenting the packing arrangements. Each container was recorded in relation to those around it. Once in the lab, the contents of each container were treated as a single unit. Accurate measurement of the

containers provided dimensions for the space it once occupied and thus, tied it to the other containers. This recording method was ideal for the low visibility, and supplemented measurements taken underwater.

The *Maple Leaf* served the Union Army well as a transport ship. Her capacity to handle cargo and passengers as a merchant vessel translated to military duty. No specific modifications for Army service are apparent in the existing structure. Accommodations to carry a cavalry detachment on her last trip suggest a large open space was made available on the main deck.

The Artifacts

The *Maple Leaf* contained the personal baggage of an entire Union Army brigade, including three regiments, headquarters, and sutlers. The baggage was separated by regiment, and probably by company. Rather than present a listing of material, this section will focus on the interpreted meaning of some artifacts and their application to better understanding Civil War soldier life. Four categories of artifacts will be addressed, souvenirs, bullets, rubberized cloth, and those representing the last moments of the *Maple Leaf* afloat.

Americans seem to have a penchant for collecting souvenirs. Soldiers in Foster's brigade appear to be no exception to this generalization. Many containers held seashells and regimental memoirs mention shells being collected (Holland et al. 1993:34). Another class of souvenir is material apparently looted from Southern plantations, such as plates and other tableware, and structural embellishments such as door knobs. Virtually all the ceramics were produced by British firms operating in the 1840s and 1850s, some of which ceased operations immediately prior to the Civil War. It is unlikely that infantry on the move would keep heavy, fragile items, so these plates and house furnishings were probably acquired from South Carolina "rebel" plantations to make Folly Island camp life more amenable.

The bullets were a surprise. Testimony during the investigation into the sinking reported that no munitions were aboard (Holland 1993:58–59), but two cartridge crates were recovered that still contained ammunition. From concreted percussion caps found in the crates, it was apparent that these bullets had been packed in lots of ten (with 14 percussion caps) as per regulations (Thomas 1981:10, 15). The two crates were produced at different arsenals and issued to different regiments.

The 13th Indiana received a crate of 1000 bullets from Watervliet Arsenal while at Fort Monroe, Virginia. This crate was marked October 1861 and supplementary markings indicated it was issued to the 13th Indiana (Babits 1995a:121). There were 283 conical bullets in this case, plus an additional ten .69-caliber round balls. These bullets were measured, both across the seam and perpendicular to it. Bullets were also tested by putting them in a modern .58-caliber barrel section and an original 1863 barrel.

Ideally, these bullets should not exceed .574 in because the inside diameter of the barrel was .575 in (Babits 1995a:120). The difference between the outside diameter of a bullet and the inside diameter of the barrel is called "windage," a gap that allowed the conical bullet to be rammed down the barrel. Some bullets issued to the 13th Indiana were too large to be utilized in their rifle muskets. In fact, 281 (99%) bullets exceeded the desired .574 in.

The second crate containing 733 bullets was marked Frankford Arsenal 1863. Associated artifacts indicated this crate was issued to the 112th New York Infantry, a unit armed with the .577-caliber Enfield Rifle, rather than the .58-caliber Springfield (Babits 1995a:122). These bullets were also measured and found to be less defective, but 47 would not fit in the test barrels. That indicates that by 1863, the failure rate had been lowered from ~20% to ~6.5%. A similar figure was obtained by measuring British bullets from an 1862 blockade runner (Babits 1995a:123).

These figures have implications for terrestrial battlefield interpretation. Unfired, or dropped, bullets should be measured to see if they were too large for the soldier's weapon. Failure would be exacerbated during an extended firefight because black powder residue builds up in the barrel, obstructing the bullet. It may now be said that many "dropped" bullets were probably intentionally discarded. A second observation is that early war accounts should mention weapons fouling more than late war accounts. While fouling might have come to be accepted, the *Maple Leaf* bullets show that, after Gettysburg, the Union bullets were, on the average, smaller than they were in 1861 (Babits 1995a:123).

Another artifact class was rubberized cloth, used in the form of "gum" blankets, a poncho, and a rain hat. These articles were fragmentary because the cotton cloth had disintegrated, leaving only impressions on the rubber. The remaining rubber was in fragile condition because the vulcanizing process involved the use of sulphuric acid. The poncho and rubber blankets thus contained the seeds of their own destruction. Since museums rarely have items dated to a particular day, recovering 11 rubber blankets and a poncho from a documented 1 April 1864 sinking, provides a baseline for examining "gum" blankets used during the Civil War.

Although rubber was known to Europeans as early as 1735, experimentation with commercial products did not begin until the early-nineteenth century. The early products proved stiff and brittle in cold conditions and sticky and runny in hot conditions. Charles Goodyear solved the problem with his 1839 vulcanization process (Goodyear 1853). The new vulcanized rubber was strong, elastic, and withstood temperature variations, resisted oils and was not soluble in common fluids such as turpentine. The vulcanized rubber was heated then spread onto cloth, heated in a dry oven, and finally boiled in an alkaline solution to remove sulphurous odors (Goodyear 1853:152–62).

Goodyear held exclusive rights to the vulcanization patent but issued licenses to other firms because the demand was so great. Other companies included Boston Rubber Shoe Company, Phoenix Rubber Company, and the Rubber Clothing Company. Since Goodyear's patent did not expire until 15 June 1865, all rubberized goods were legally required to bear a patent stamp on the fabric side (Woshner 1999:16). At least one company apparently violated the patent rights as one rubber blanket was marked Boott Mills, of Lowell, Massachusetts. Boott Mills was not licensed to produce rubber blankets and does not appear on any listing of Army suppliers (Babits 1995b:61).

The rubber cloth was suitable for a variety of military applications. It was used for knapsacks, haversacks, and headgear and in sheet form, blankets, and ponchos. One rubberized rain hat was recovered along with the gum blankets and poncho. Two comparable rain hats exist; one in the Minnesota Historical Society was made with cotton muslin covered with an oil-based paint (Thomas G. Shaw, personal communication), and the other in the Museum of the Confederacy seems to be rubberized fabric.

The gum blankets and ponchos used by the soldiers were generically referred to as a "gum blanket" (Hinman 1895:50–51). The ones recovered from the *Maple Leaf*, and other museum examples, can be grouped into two general categories based on grommet placing. Type B had two pairs of grommets on one long side, presumably for hooks to fasten the blanket over the shoulders. No *Maple Leaf* rubber blankets exactly match the 1865 Quartermaster dimensions. They range in length from 73.5 in to 62 in. In width they range from 48 in to 32 in. Most have evidence for 16 grommets (type A) or 18 (type B). Gum blankets were utilized for a variety of purposes beyond protection, including game boards, distribution of food, and even for mixing food (Billings 1980:81).

The poncho is basically a gum blanket with a slit in the middle to allow fitting it over the head. The *Maple Leaf* poncho is 48 in x 71 in, about 1 ft narrower than the post-war Quartermaster manual states (Babits 1995b:61, 65). The poncho has no grommets, but it does have a flexible collar that could be closed by a draw string (Babits 1995b:64–65).

A more eclectic, final artifact group reveals undocumented events associated with the last minutes of the *Maple Leaf*. Just above the deck, excavators encountered a shell debris lens. When this occurred, the dredge outflow was connected to mesh bags that caught everything displaced by the dredge. The bags were taken to the surface, emptied and the contents passed through 1/4 in screens. The collection included nearly 100 percussion caps, 48 bullets, 44 buttons, and insignia fragments all in poor condition. Three Enfield rifle muskets, two cartridge box plates, one belt plate, and three bayonets were also recovered.

The insignia included the brass numbers 1, 2, and part of an officer's epaulet ("shoulder board"), and a second lieutenant's bar. New York buttons indicated these items probably belonged to the 112th New York Infantry. This regiment provided the guard detail for the last voyage of the vessel (Babits 1995a:119). The artifacts indicated both a lieutenant and enlisted personnel were aboard. The number of buttons was suggestive of an officer's frock and enlisted four button fatigue blouses because there were more than 16 buttons, including the New York state buttons. Three rifled muskets and cartridge box fragments were also found.

Interpreting these items required a variety of different experiences, knowledge of guard details, accoutrements, insignia, and, to some extent, human behavior. The ship hit the torpedo at 4 A.M. The Army usually posts guards, depending on the situation, about every two hours. It would seem, from the three muskets, bayonets, cartridge boxes, and buttons that one guard relief was asleep in their shirts, along with the officer of the guard, a second lieutenant. The sergeant of the guard was taking the 4 A.M. relief to their posts, and returning with the 2 A.M. guards. These seven men had their fatigue blouses, arms, and accoutrements on. When the ship sank, they kept them. The officer and the off duty guards had only a very short time before the ship sank. They left their weapons, accoutrements, and blouses behind as the ship went down. While particularistic, this interpretive accounting for the artifact mix on deck does explain human behavior during a very short crisis period.

CONCLUSIONS

Taken as a whole, the *Maple Leaf* site provided a wealth of information about Great Lakes ship construction and history. As a vessel contracted to perform military transportation, the cargo of the vessel sheds light on soldier life, battlefield conditions, and the the last moments the *Maple Leaf* was afloat. Since only about 5% of the cargo was recovered, this new information only hints at what could be learned from the well-provenience remainder. The initials clues to military behavior only suggest might be learned if the site were fully excavated.

ACKNOWLEDGMENTS

The authors wish to thank St. Johns Archaeological Expeditions, Inc., the Department of the Army's Center for Military History Museum of the United States Army for allowing us to work on the site and examine these materials. Others who helped are Dean Thomas, Fred Gaede, the late Carlyle Smith, and Mike Woshner. Regrettably, SJAEI's Lee Manley, a key diver and the project's conservator, did not survive to see this chapter completed.

CHAPTER SEVENTEEN

Naval Monuments and Memorials

Symbols in a Contested Landscape

DAVID J. STEWART

INTRODUCTION

Memorials represent a form of material culture that both intentionally and unintentionally reflect the ideologies and values of those who create them. Intentionally because people consciously use memorials to convey ideals: patriotism, honor, and sacrifice, to name but a few. But memorials also encode unconscious messages that their creators may not be aware of and, accordingly, can reveal additional insights into the beliefs of those who created them. These simple premises motivate scholarship on memorials and memorialization, whether related to military or civilian sites. Since the 1960s, archaeologists have studied memorials and the rituals that take place at memorial sites in order to gain a better understanding of the conscious and unconscious beliefs that they convey (see Mytum 2004 for the best recent overview of memorialization studies).

Naval monuments and memorials offer the opportunity to examine two distinct levels of society. Monuments are commissioned by governments to commemorate persons or events deemed significant to the nation as a whole. National monuments date back at least 3000 years, when the Egyptian pharaoh Ramesses III commemorated a victorious naval battle on the wall of his mortuary temple. While the creation of permanent memorials in the distant past was limited to rulers and governments, the last two centuries has witnessed the widespread creation of memorials by all classes of society. These folk-level naval memorials, created by members of the naval profession, often express very different views than their national counterparts. Because of this, memorials

provide an excellent opportunity to examine the interplay between different, and sometimes competing, viewpoints. The struggle over remembrance is not limited to the monuments themselves. In addition to encoding values, both national and folk memorials occupy space in the landscape, and thus have the potential to serve as foci for subsequent activities. Groups that oppose the official version of history told on memorials sometimes use these sites as locations for protest.

This chapter examines how naval memorials function as symbols in the contested landscape of remembrance. The first section discusses themes common to national-level naval memorials. The next section turns to the folk-level, to see how memorials created by naval sailors and officers compare to those of the nation. The final section examines the role that state- and folk-level memorials play in the contested story of remembrance.

Most of the examples of nation-state memorials discussed are drawn from published sources of war memorials. The data for folk memorialization practices, on the other hand, comes from an ongoing study of maritime memorials conducted by the author (Stewart 2004, 2007). The goal of this project is to compare fifteenth through twenty-first century maritime memorials from the United States and the United Kingdom. These memorials represent a cross-section of maritime life from the Age of Sail to the present, including monuments to naval seamen, merchant mariners, fishermen, and whalers, along with shore-based maritime occupations such as shipwrights, merchants, and dockyard workers.

NATIONAL IDEALS

Victory, Glory, Patriotism

Monuments and memorials created by nation-states to commemorate significant persons or events are designed to perpetuate the ideals that the state wishes to associate with itself and the values that it claims to champion. Such monuments thus represent a conscious attempt to interpret history in the way that the nation wants it to be seen. State-sponsored naval memorials are no exception. Common themes on state naval memorials include victory, glory, patriotism, and honoring the dead who gave their lives to the national cause.

Navies are fundamentally tools of war, and therefore it is not surprising that many nation-state naval memorials celebrate victory and the attendant glory that it brings to the nation, its leaders, or naval heroes. In fact, victory and glory form the theme of the earliest known memorial that includes a naval component. The Egyptian pharaoh Ramesses III commissioned a relief for his mortuary temple at Medinet Habu depicting his victory over the Sea Peoples, a group of nomadic raiders who devastated the eastern Mediterranean near the end of the Bronze Age. The battle, which took place ca. 1176 B.C.E, was both a naval and a land engagement. The portion of the relief depicting the naval battle shows Egyptian ships ambushing and defeating those Sea Peoples on the Nile (Wachsmann 1988:166). On the relief, Ramesses is depicted much larger than other figures, in the midst of the battle shooting a bow at the invaders. His size and warlike posture emphasize his personal glory. It seems likely that Ramesses III chose this as one of the events by which he wished to be remembered because the battle represented the glory he earned by defeating a group of invaders and preserving the Egyptian state.

Classical Greek and Roman war monuments were also designed to celebrate victory and glorify the nation and its rulers. One such naval monument commemorates a sea battle that played a decisive role in ancient history. The Roman ruler Octavian rose to power thanks in large part to his victory over the fleet of Antony and Cleopatra at Actium in northwestern Greece in 31 B.C.E. This battle took place between fleets of oared warships armed with rams. When the battle was over, Octavian celebrated his victory by commissioning a monumental wall on a hillside overlooking the battle site. Octavian ordered that the rams from the captured warships be removed and mounted in sockets along the wall (Murray and Petsas 1989:56). The resulting monument provided graphic testament to a defeated and broken enemy. In addition to glorifying Octavian's victory, it served as symbolic placement of Roman power in Greece by marking the spot near Actium as Roman. Indeed, it is not too much of a stretch to say that Actium marks the point where the Roman Republic ended and the Roman Empire began as Octavian went on to become Caesar Augustus. Octavian's campsite memorial at Actium served as both a physical embodiment of the genesis of his power and a reminder for future generations of his lasting glory.

Many state-sponsored naval memorials in modern times follow themes first seen in ancient Egypt and the Classical world (Borg 1991). Classical elements such as columns and triumphal arches remain popular. Nelson's Column in Trafalgar Square, London, arguably the most famous naval monument of the modern era, hearkens back to Roman victory monuments such as Trajan's Column. Victory over a defeated enemy also remains a popular theme. The *Macedonian* Monument, built to honor Stephen Decatur's capture of HMS *Macedonian* during the War of 1812, incorporates cannon taken from the captured British warship. Decatur's victory, along with those of other American naval forces in that war, served as an important catalyst of American national identity, because such victories symbolized that the fledgling nation could emerge victorious against its powerful former rulers. Like Octavian's campsite memorial, the *Macedonian* Monument served as a permanent physical marker for the creation of a new national identity. As noted by Mayo (1988:130–31), the placement of the monument on the grounds of the U.S. Naval Academy in Annapolis, Maryland, training site for naval officers, also serves as an example of the type of conduct that the nation expects from its future naval leaders. This is a common function of military memorials as a whole (Mytum 2004:150).

Warships themselves, the most visible symbols of naval power, can also be preserved to serve as floating monuments. Despite the high costs involved in maintaining wooden or steel warships, numerous examples are preserved by nations throughout the world. Not surprisingly, the vessels chosen are typically those that symbolize an important naval victory. Of these, the most famous in the Western world are probably HMS *Victory*, Nelson's flagship at Trafalgar, and the USS *Constitution* ("Old Ironsides"), celebrated for its victories against the British in the War of 1812. Many other examples from World War I and World War II may also have been preserved in both Great Britain and the United States.

Closely related to victory—and often found on the same monuments—patriotism is also an important ideal that nation-states wish to perpetuate. Patriotism is often symbolized by commemorating a heroic individual who is put forth as an exemplar for those in naval service as well as the nation at large. The British naval hero Adm. Lord Horatio Nelson provides perhaps the best known example of this phenomenon. Nelson died hours after being wounded by a sniper while standing on the quarterdeck of HMS *Victory* at the Battle of Trafalgar on 21 October 1805. The battle, in which a smaller British force captured or destroyed 22 French and Spanish vessels while losing none of their own, was the most famous in a string of victories by Nelson. The fact that he did not return from it only cemented Nelson's legacy as Britain's foremost naval hero. Public jubilation over the victory at Trafalgar was tempered by despair over Nelson's loss, resulting in a great outpouring of memorials that included the construction of arches, columns, and other monument forms.

While many of the early memorials that served as sites of public patriotic commemoration during the Napoleonic Wars were torn down afterwards, two important symbols of Nelson still mark his legacy. The HMS *Victory*, preserved at Portsmouth Historic Dockyard, and Trafalgar Square in London provide places where national pride and patriotism continue to be celebrated. Ceremonies are held annually at both sites on the anniversary of the battle. These widespread celebrations, regularly attended by state officials, demonstrate the importance that Nelson's legacy continues to hold in British national identity.

In addition to individuals, memorials that commemorate important events can be used to focus national feelings of patriotism. A good modern example of this is the USS *Cole* memorial, which honors the 17 sailors killed when that vessel was damaged in a terrorist attack while in port at Aden, Yemen, on 12 October 2000. The Cole memorial was dedicated in the destroyer's home port of Norfolk, Virginia, on the first anniversary of the attack. The dedication ceremony probably would have garnered little national press coverage except for the fact that it took place just one month after the devastating September 11 terrorist attacks. As it was, the ceremony was carried live by many major television networks. In this manner, the Cole memorial while designed to honor only 17 victims, functioned for a time as a proxy memorial for all those who had lost their lives in the recent tragedies. The dedication, which included such patriotic symbols as a military color guard and U.S. flags, also served as a forge for patriotic feeling in the wake of the tragedies of the previous month.

Honoring the Lost

Another important function of nation-state naval memorials is to honor the sacrifice of those who lose their lives while in service, whether in war or peace. While this function existed in war memorials since the nineteenth century, it only became widespread following the First World War. There is no doubt that the horrific scale of death in that conflict accounts in large part for the wave of memorialization that followed in its wake (King 1998; Mytum 2004:99–100, 151). Monuments were erected on many battlefields to honor those who fell there, while numerous communities built public monuments to honor their dead. Whether on battlefields or in villages, these types of commemorations typically included lists of the names of the fallen.

Three famous British naval memorials exemplify the tradition that became widespread following the First World War. The Royal Navy wished to honor its dead, but faced the problem that many sailors lost their lives at sea, where their bodies were either buried or lost and could not be recovered. With no way to create markers at the site, it was decided to erect monuments at Portsmouth, Plymouth, and Chatham, the three principal Royal Navy manning ports (Borg

1991:87–88). The three identical monuments take the form of tall columns rising from pedestal bases. The corners of the bases include buttresses supporting lions, much like those at Nelson's Column in Trafalgar Square, while the top of each column includes a similar treatment, with the sculpted prows of four ships representing the four winds. Each column is topped by a copper globe, which can symbolize both the global reach of the Royal Navy as well as those who died in the seas around the world. Brass plaques mounted on the pedestals record the names of all the men from that port who died during the war. The memorials were completed in the 1920s, and following the Second World War, additional space and plaques were added to record the names of sailors lost in that conflict. The dedicatory inscription included on each monument reads:

> In honour of the Navy and to the abiding memory of those ranks and ratings of this Port who laid down their lives in the defence of the Empire and have no other grave than the sea.

The phrase "to the abiding memory," coupled with the inclusion of the names of all the men—some 66,000 from both World Wars among the three monuments—demonstrate the modern importance of the need to remember those who sacrificed their lives in national naval service as individuals, not just through monuments that celebrate victory or patriotism. Listing the names of the dead has become so much the accepted way of memorialization, in fact, that it would now be unthinkable to create a national memorial, whether naval or not, that did not include such a feature. It is important to note, however, that although the tradition of recording lists of names did not begin with national monuments. It was instead a folk tradition originally practiced by individuals to honor their comrades.

Summary

Ideals such as victory, glory, patriotism, and honoring those who served form the dominant ideology on naval memorials commissioned by nation-states. While the object of the state is to solidify these national values in material form, such monuments rarely contain only one unambiguous meaning. Different groups within society can and do interpret memorials to suit their own beliefs, an idea that is more fully explored in the third section of this chapter.

FOLK MEMORIALS

The sentiments expressed by those in the naval profession themselves—the officers and sailors—along with those of others who, by kinship or occupation, are tied to naval seafaring, in some cases express and reinforce the values of national governments. In other cases, different values are celebrated or emphasized. Such differences in focus will serve as a launching point for discussion of the ways that memorials and memorialization practices exist in a contested landscape, with different societal groups striving to make their voices heard in permanent, material form.

Seafaring has been, and remains, one of the most dangerous occupations practiced by humans. Disease, shipwreck, and accidents have killed untold millions of sailors over the centuries. In addition to these threats, naval seamen also face the possibility of death in battle. To cope with such a dangerous working environment, mariners have developed a number of shared group values that are often communicated on maritime memorials and gravestones. In contrast to state-level naval memorials, memorials created by sailors or other members of the maritime community tend to emphasize values pertaining to the maintenance and protection of the group in the face of the hardships and difficulties that they face. The need to remember the lost and take care of their families is expressed prominently as well.

Bravery and Duty

Sailors expected their shipmates to stand firm in the face of adversity, and not surprisingly, bravery and attention to duty form common themes on naval folk memorials. Such memorials celebrate courage in several situations, from combat to natural disasters. At the church of St. Mylor, near Falmouth, Cornwall, a

FIGURE 17.1. Monument honoring Royal Navy Capt. Colin Andrew Campbell. Highland Road Cemetery, Portsmouth, Hampshire, UK. Photograph by author.

plaque commemorates Edward Bayntum Yescombe, commander of the packet *King George,* who "lost his life in bravely defending his ship against the enemy" in August 1803. American sailors also valued courage. Old Burial Hill in Marblehead, Massachusetts, contains the grave of U.S. Navy Capt. Joseph Lindsay, who died in 1826. Lindsay's family chose to emphasize his service to his country in the War of 1812. His epitaph notes the "coolness, skill, & bravery" that Lindsay exhibited as sailing master of the schooner *Ticonderoga* during the Battle of Plattsburg Bay on Lake Champlain in September 1814.

Terms such as "service" and "attention to duty" figure prominently in folk naval memorials, just as they do in military commemoration in general (Mytum 2004:150). Attention to duty in the face of danger

forms the theme of the memorial to Royal Navy Captain Colin Andrew Campbell. In this case, Campbell's actions during a fire at sea formed one of the significant events of his life, as described in the inscription:

HE SERVED WITH DISTINCTION IN THE CRIMEAN, CHINESE, AND ABYSSINIAN WARS
HE COMMANDED HMS BOMBAY WHEN SHE WAS
BURNT OFF THE COAST OF BRAZIL
14TH DECR 1864,
AND BY HIS PROMPT AND JUDICIOUS MEASURES
WAS THE MEANS OF SAVING THE LIVES OF THE GREATER PART OF THE SHIP'S COMPANY

In addition to the epitaph, Campbell's monument in Highland Road Cemetery, Portsmouth, includes a bronze panel depicting the fire aboard HMS *Bombay* (figs. 17.1, 17.2). The illustration shows the ship engulfed in flames and smoke, while crowded boats lie close alongside rescuing survivors. On the boat in the foreground, one sailor can be seen hauling a shipmate from the water. Fire ranked among the greatest fears of the crews of wooden sailing vessels. Not only were vessels made of wood, but deck seams and rigging elements were coated with highly flammable

FIGURE 17.2. Detail of Captain Campbell's monument, showing the fire aboard HMS *Bombay.* Photograph by author.

tar as protection against the elements. In addition, naval vessels carried large stores of gunpowder, which demanded extreme caution in the use of fire aboard ship. It is easy to see why Captain Campbell's family chose to emphasize his actions during the fire aboard HMS *Bombay.* A captain who could attend to duty and save most of his crew when faced with the horror of fire at sea deserved recognition for his actions.

Service to the Group

High-context groups such as sailors place particular emphasis on loyalty to other group members. One common way that sailors took care of one another was to pay for memorials for the family of a deceased shipmate. At St. Budeaux in Plymouth, Devon, the officers and workmen of Devonport dockyard erected a gravestone for Thomas Atwill, who was accidentally killed there in 1901. The two stanzas of Atwill's epitaph express the sentiments of both colleagues and his wife. The first stanza reads:

> YES WE MISS HIM O HOW SADLY
> NONE BUT ACHING HEARTS CAN TELL
> EARTH HAS LOST HIM, HEAVEN HAS
>   FOUND HIM:
> JESUS DOETH ALL THINGS WELL.

While the first stanza, with its sentiment of "yes we miss him," could indicate a tribute from his colleagues as well as his family, the sentiment expressed in the second stanza of the epitaph is clearly from Atwill's wife:

> SLEEP ON DEAR HUSBAND AND TAKE THY
>   REST
> FOR GOD HAS CALLED WHEN HE
>   THOUGHT BEST.
> THE LOSS IS GREAT THAT WE SUSTAIN
> BUT IN HEAVEN WE HOPE TO MEET AGAIN.

Providing a grave for other mariners applied even in the case of enemies. The British, for example, gave a proper burial and erected a headstone to honor William Henry Allen, commander of the U.S. brig *Argus,* who died of wounds received when his vessel was captured by the British brig *Pelican* in August 1813.

Self-Sacrifice

Taking care of other group members included putting one's own life in danger if necessary in order to save a brother sailor. At the church of St. Mary in Plympton, near Plymouth, Devon, a monument commemorates Edward F. Tucker of HMS *Jackal,* who "died while drowning in attempting to save his shipmate" in 1895. This characteristic of Royal Navy seamen is shown most eloquently by a monument in Kingston Road Cemetery in Portsmouth. This cross-shaped monument is prominently situated next to one of the main paths near the entrance to the cemetery, yet today it is easily overlooked because it is so heavily overgrown with ivy (fig. 17.3). After listing the names of those who were lost, the inscription provides salient details of the tragic event, which occurred aboard HMS *Ariadne:*

> ON THE 8TH MARCH 1872 OFF THE COAST
>   OF PORTUGAL,
> WHEN THE SHIP WAS PROCEEDING TO
>   GIBRALTAR, WERE CAPSIZED
> IN THEIR CUTTER AND DROWNED WHILST
>   BRAVELY ATTEMPTING
> IN A HEAVY SEA TO RESCUE AN UNFOR-
>   TUNATE SHIPMATE WHO HAD FALLEN
>   OVERBOARD

Sacrifices such as this were not uncommon among U.S. naval seamen as well. For example, in Cedar Grove Cemetery, New London, Connecticut, the gravestone of B. F. Skinner describes his loss off Cape Hatteras, North Carolina, in March 1865 while attempting to rescue survivors from the sunken steamer *General Lyon.*

Remembering the Lost

As previously discussed, national memorials such as the Royal Navy monuments at Portsmouth, Plymouth, and Chatham were designed to honor sailors whose bodies were lost at sea and who thus had no proper grave. The practice of honoring the missing became widespread on post-World War I state memorials such as these. Nevertheless, in a maritime

FIGURE 17.3. Monument honoring 11 sailors from the HMS *Ariadne* who died trying to rescue a drowning shipmate in 1872. Kingston Cemetery, Portsmouth, Hampshire, UK. Photograph by author.

context, memorializing the missing had its roots in much earlier folk practices. Erecting memorials to sailors who were lost or died at sea became a common practice in maritime communities throughout Great Britain and the United States around the end of the eighteenth century (Stewart 2004:208–10). Naval seamen participated in this phenomenon as well. A gravestone at the church of Portsea St. Mary's, dedicated to those lost in HMS *Royal George* near Portsmouth in 1782, provides an early example of this. The gravestone originally marked the final resting place of 35 victims of the tragedy who were buried in a mass

grave in St. Mary's churchyard (Brewer and White n.d.:8–9). The stone's epitaph makes it clear that it also commemorates the hundreds of others whose bodies were never recovered:

> A testimony of
> sympathy
> for the unfortunates
> who perished by the sinking
> at Spithead of the
> HMS Royal George
> August 29th 1782
> erected by one who
> was a stranger both to officers
> and the ship's company

Around the middle of the nineteenth century, it became common for the crews of ships to erect monuments to lost comrades upon returning from voyages. While forms varied from mural plaques inside churches (fig. 17.4) to monuments in cemeteries (fig. 17.5), the inscriptions of these crew memorials are remarkably similar. Each records the name of the vessel, the names of those who died, the circumstances of death, and dates of death. Royal Navy crews were also in the habit of including the name of the overseas station to which the vessel was assigned and the dates during which the cruise took place. In addition to these common details, additional information such as the sailor's age at time of death and position aboard ship were often included. Some feature epitaphs as well.

Typically, the dead were listed in rank order, reflecting the shipboard hierarchy that was a fundamental part of naval life. However, such monuments do not discriminate on the basis of socioeconomic class or ethnicity; all who died were included. To naval seamen, membership in the group took precedence over ethnicity.

Families also commemorated naval sons, fathers, and husbands who never returned from the sea. The names of the missing and descriptions of their fate were commonly included on family memorials, while in some cases memorials solely for the lost sailor were erected instead. Such memorials for the missing often highlight the desired qualities of naval seamen. The inscription on a memorial brass in Bristol Cathedral dedicated by one Royal Navy widow exemplifies this type:

FIGURE 17.4. HMS *Severn* crew memorial. Portsea St. Mary's Church, Portsmouth, Hampshire, UK. Photograph by author.

FIGURE 17.5. HMS *Boadicea* crew memorial at the Haslar Royal Navy Cemetery, Gosport, Hampshire, UK. Photograph by author.

TO THE MEMORY OF
MY BELOVED HUSBAND
JOHN SANDERSON,
A CAPTAIN IN THE ROYAL NAVY,
WHO DIED WHILE ON ACTIVE
SERVICE, IN COMMAND OF
HER MAJESTY'S SHIP "ARCHER"
OFF THE CONGO RIVER, SOUTH-
AFRICA, JUNE 27TH 1859, AND
WAS BURIED AT LOANGO.

In cases such as these, it is likely that emphasis on duty was an attempt by family members to reassure themselves that the death of their loved one had a purpose. Naval families seem to have used these cenotaphs to remind society of the great price in lives paid for national glory.

THE CONTESTED LANDSCAPE OF MEMORIALIZATION

The form and inscriptions of national memorials are controlled so that they include only the symbolism and ideology espoused and approved by the state. National memorials, however, serve not only for remembrance and the display of values, but are also meant to be visited. While some are meant only to be viewed, the form of many invite participation from visitors. Since access to many monuments is either open or not tightly controlled, the actions that visitors undertake at memorial sites are sometimes not what the state desires. Therefore, the sites of national memorials are sometimes used by opposition groups to contest the official version of history.

Folk memorials are much less tightly controlled. National governments typically do not have the power or means to enforce the official view of history on memorials created by individuals. This allows folk memorials to be used by those with opposing viewpoints who might not otherwise have a voice. This section explores how naval memorial sites function as contested space, focusing on two themes: the contest over Western imperialism and capitalism, and the debate over the ownership of the past. The contest of space at memorial sites also extends to who "owns" the memory of the event and how history will be represented. The classic example of this in a naval context is the site of Pearl Harbor, which has been covered in depth elsewhere (Linenthal 1991) and will not be examined here.

Examining the ways by which indigenous peoples and minorities protest Western imperialism and capitalism has become a chief concern of historical archaeology (Orser 1996). Naval memorials provide testament to this struggle. Over the past five centuries, navies have been active agents of Western imperialism, and thus naval memorials can be viewed as symbols of domination and oppression. The symbolism of imperialism is not always necessarily intended by the designers of monuments, but nevertheless becomes apparent in the forms chosen. Nelson's Column, for example, can be viewed as a symbol of imperialism because of its form, which hearkens back to the Roman Empire, as well as the victory that it symbolizes. Even the Royal Navy Memorials at Portsmouth, Plymouth, and Chatham, although designed to honor those lost at sea, can also denote empire due to their columnar forms and grand scale. Moreover, the globes that surmount these monuments can be viewed as symbolic of the British attempt to rule the oceans of the world through the instrument of the Royal Navy.

Vessels preserved as floating memorials, such as HMS *Victory* and the USS *Constitution,* can also be viewed as symbolizing the attempt by western nations to enforce their will worldwide through armed force. In some cases, there seems to be an almost conscious attempt to blunt the warlike and imperialistic nature of warship memorials by placing them at locations synonymous with more virtuous national ideals. *Constitution,* for example, forms part of Boston's Freedom Trail, a historical walking tour that includes the site of the Boston Massacre, the Old North Church, and Bunker Hill, among others. Most of the locations on the Freedom Trail are linked with the American Revolution, and thus symbolize freedom and independence. The *Constitution,* on the other hand, is most famous for its actions in the War of 1812. While fought in part due to British incursions against American sovereignty, the War of 1812 also represents the United States' first imperial war, because one of the U.S. war goals was to capture and annex Canada. Similarly the USS *Olympia,* a monument to the Spanish American War, is moored near Independence National Historic Park in Philadelphia. Like *Constitution,* this can be seen as an attempt to mask its role in imperialistic endeavors by situating it at a location symbolic of freedom (Mayo 1988:165).

The symbolism of imperialism is not lost on those who oppose such ideas, however, and for this reason sites such as war memorials are sometimes chosen for protest. Since its construction in the 1850s, Trafalgar Square has a long history of use as a forum for social protest (Mace 1976). Anti-imperialism, along with other concerns such as the rights of workers and women, are just a few of the social movements that have used the square to proclaim their messages. The choice of Trafalgar Square is no doubt partly due to the fact that it provides a large open space in a prominent location within the capital city of England. Nevertheless, this choice has probably also been motivated by the fact that it is a fundamental symbol of British Empire and the status quo.

Action at memorial sites sometimes moves beyond protest. In the post-colonial world, some naval memorials have fallen victim to symbolic acts of resistance. In Havana, Cuba, the Plaza del Maine commemorates those who died when the Battleship *Maine* was destroyed there in 1898. The memorial, built by pro-U.S. Cubans in 1928, included chains and cannon salvaged from the wreck, a plaque containing the names of those who died, and a spread-winged American eagle atop two columns. After the Communist takeover, the eagle was removed because "its pose was interpreted as symbolically maintaining a perch of U.S. power" over the island (Mayo 1988:160). The rest of the monument, however, is still maintained by the Cuban government in honor of the dead.

The spread of Western power and commerce around the globe over the past 500 years has cost thousands of naval seafarers their lives. As discussed earlier, many sailors were lost or died at sea, leaving their families with no body to bury. Creating memorials to these men provided a place for family remembrance, and likely served another function as well. Many of the memorials for the missing are situated in prominent places where they would be viewed by many people. Examples of such locations include mural plaques next to doorways in churches and cenotaphs placed at the intersection of major pathways in cemeteries. The placement of these memorials does not seem to be accidental. Rather, they invite fellow seafarers and the public at large to participate in the process of remembering those who will never return. As such, these memorials functioned to remind the public that ideals such as imperialism, nationalism, and patriotism are not merely abstract ideas but carry real-world consequences and personal cost.

By way of example, the widow of naval lieutenant Charles Webbe dedicated a plaque to her husband, who was lost in the North Atlantic in 1839 (fig. 17.6).

FIGURE 17.6. Mural monument honoring Lt. Charles Webbe, who was lost at sea in 1839. St. Mylor Church, Falmouth, Cornwall, UK. Photograph by author.

In the inscription chosen by Mrs. Webbe, the phrase "is supposed to have perished" emphasizes the lingering doubt regarding the exact fate of her husband, while "deeply mourning" highlights her grief. Like so many others, Webbe simply sailed from port and was never heard from again. While state-level monuments often proclaimed the success of naval enterprises, the unheralded memorials of thousands of naval seamen speak of the horrific toll that these endeavors cost in human lives.

Contests for space at memorial sites also extend to who "owns" the memory of the event and how history will be represented. We have already seen how different social groups can use memorial sites such as Trafalgar Square to protest prevailing social norms. This struggle also includes debate as to what form memorials will take, whose views are to be represented upon them, and who is allowed to participate in ceremonies at the memorial site.

A classic example of this theme in a naval memorialization context is the struggle over the memorial for the battleship USS *Arizona,* which sank in Pearl Harbor during the Japanese attack in December 1941 that launched the United States into World War II.

The *Arizona* Memorial symbolizes victory rising from defeat and preserves the memory of the 1177 men who perished aboard her, many of whom still lie entombed with the sunken hull (Linnenthal 1991; Mayo 1988). Even before its completion in the early 1960s, controversy regarding how the event would be portrayed had begun. A 1961 proposal that called for Japanese participation in the planning of the memorial was quickly dismissed because of continued anger against the "treachery" of the Japanese attack (Linenthal 1991:179). The National Park Service, which operates the *Arizona* Memorial, has received complaints from some who view the presence of Japanese tourists at the site as inappropriate (Linenthal 1991:192). In 1987, an outcry arose over plans to display the personal belongings of a Japanese airman who had participated in the attack. While the National Park Service saw this as a way to humanize the historical event, others viewed it as an insult to the memory of those who died (Linenthal 1991:196). As recently as 1999, Yuko Tojo, granddaughter of the Japanese leader who ordered the Pearl Harbor attack, was criticized for visiting the memorial. While her purpose was to pay homage to those who were lost, not all Americans thought that she had the right to do so. One World War II veteran is quoted as saying, "I don't think it's her place to be here" (DiPietro 1999). Long after the war, the site of the *Arizona* Memorial remains contested ground where remembrance of the event is still debated.

CONCLUSIONS

Memorials are one way by which nations and individuals commemorate events and persons of significance. The ideas expressed on naval monuments vary according to their creators. National monuments tend to emphasize ideals such as victory, patriotism, and glory, while those commissioned by mariners themselves regard values such as bravery, performance of duty, and the care of their comrades as more important. The main value held in common by both state- and folk-level memorials is the need to remember the dead. Even this, however, takes somewhat different forms. State memorials usually include little or no information beyond the simple listing of names of those who die in service. Fellow sailors and family members, on the other hand, provide the personal details that give lost sailors their individuality and indicate the grief felt by those left behind. Competition regarding how events should be remembered sets the stage for memorials as a contested landscape, in which different societal groups vie to record their points of view in permanent material form.

In the future, naval memorialization will no doubt evolve into new forms. Two new areas of naval memorialization are already growing in importance. First, modern technology now allows vessels lost in the depths of the oceans to be located and marked. HMS *Hood,* sunk by the German battleship *Bismarck* in May 1941 with the loss of 1413 lives, was discovered in July 2001. Shortly thereafter, the last remaining *Hood* survivor, Mr. Ted Briggs, laid a wreath on the surface above the site, which lies more than 10,000 ft beneath the North Atlantic. A bronze plaque was also placed on the seabed near the warship's bow (Robinson 2001). True to form, the plaque lists all those who died aboard. British divers who helped raise the ill-fated Russian submarine *Kursk,* which sank in the Barents Sea killing all 118 crew members, placed a memorial plaque at the site in memory of the tragedy (Sunday Mercury 2001).

While submersible technology now allows previously inaccessible wreck sites to be marked, computer technology has resulted in a new form of memorialization in cyberspace. Online commemorations abound, not only for victims of tragedies, but also as a way for family and friends to pay tribute to loved ones. Websites provide virtual forums for many of the ideals and values discussed in this chapter. Because the internet is also widely accessible to a broad section of society, online memorials also provide voices for those who wish to challenge the official version of events. One online tribute to the USS *Cole* (http://www.timjacobs.com/america_uss_cole.htm), a U.S. destroyer damaged by a terrorist attack in Yemen in 2000, provides photos and tributes to the 17 sailors killed in the attack. The backdrop includes red, white, and blue patriotic motifs and quotes reiterating the value of the military. The site also includes the full text of an article claiming that President Clinton was complicit in the terrorist attack that damaged the vessel.

Memorials are necessary because they provide a focal point for the expression of values, beliefs, and emotions. They offer a place at which to remember the past, but also allow multiple reinterpretations of that past. As long as there are publicly-accessible memorial sites, whether on land, under water, or in cyberspace, people will continue to use them to express their views. While specific forms will change, naval memorialization will continue because individuals and nations feel a need to honor the dead, promote national and group ideology, and make sense of history.

CHAPTER EIGHTEEN

"We Must Act Under Our Own Chiefs According to our Own Customs"

Understanding Indigenous Military Archaeology

RON WILLIAMSON

INTRODUCTION

Prior to the arrival of Europeans, war was waged both among northern Iroquoian-speaking groups and between them and some of their Algonquian-speaking neighbors (fig. 18.1). The region occupied by Northern Iroquoians constitutes most of what is now known as southern Ontario, southwestern Quebec, New York, and northern Pennsylvania.

The term "Iroquoian" should not be confused with "Iroquois," an Algonquian word used by Europeans to refer to the Five Nations Confederacy of New York State (Trigger 1969:6) that, from west to east included the Seneca, the Cayuga, the Onondaga, the Oneida, and the Mohawk. These tribes, while joined in confederation, were culturally distinctive due to their long separate developments as reflected in differences in language and material culture as well as clan organization, kinship terms, and mortuary patterns.

The Huron-Wendat, the northernmost of the Iroquoians, historically inhabited the peninsula between Georgian Bay on Lake Huron and Lake Simcoe in south-central Ontario (Trigger 1969, 1976; Tooker 1964). The relatively small Tionnontate or Petun Nation lived immediately southwest of the Huron (Garrad and Heidenreich 1978). They resembled the Huron in most linguistic and cultural respects.

The tribes of the Neutral Confederacy, called Attiwandaron by the Huron, lived farther south between the lower Grand River Valley and the Niagara River (Lennox and Fitzgerald 1990). The French had named them the Neutral Confederacy to signify the peace, albeit tenuous, between the Neutral and the Huron as well as the Neutral's refusal to participate in a long-standing feud between the Huron and the Iroquois. However, the Neutral were certainly engaged in blood feuds with Algonquians to their west.

The Huron and the Neutral were driven from southern Ontario in the mid-seventeenth century by the Iroquois. Following their dispersal, the Seneca and Cayuga established villages along the north shore of Lake Ontario only to be supplanted in the 1690s by Mississauga peoples who migrated from the north shore of Lake Huron. At the conclusion of the American Revolutionary War, the Iroquois were relegated to reserves of land in both New York State and southern Ontario where they have since resided with neighboring Mississauga groups.

Many important strategies and tactics of intertribal warfare such as ambushes and trophy taking are reflected in the ethnographic and archaeological records of northern Iroquoian peoples and many of their neighboring groups. It is the contention of this paper that these practices continued to inform their participation in eighteenth and early- nineteenth century conflicts when they fought alongside European allies. While little archaeological evidence has emerged of the aboriginal presence in those battles, this discussion will explore the ways in which important aboriginal contributions might be documented when opportunities arise for their archaeological exploration.

TRADITIONAL IROQUOIAN WARFARE— THE ARCHIVAL RECORD

There is a rich seventeenth century ethnographic record of the lives of Northern Iroquoians and indirectly of

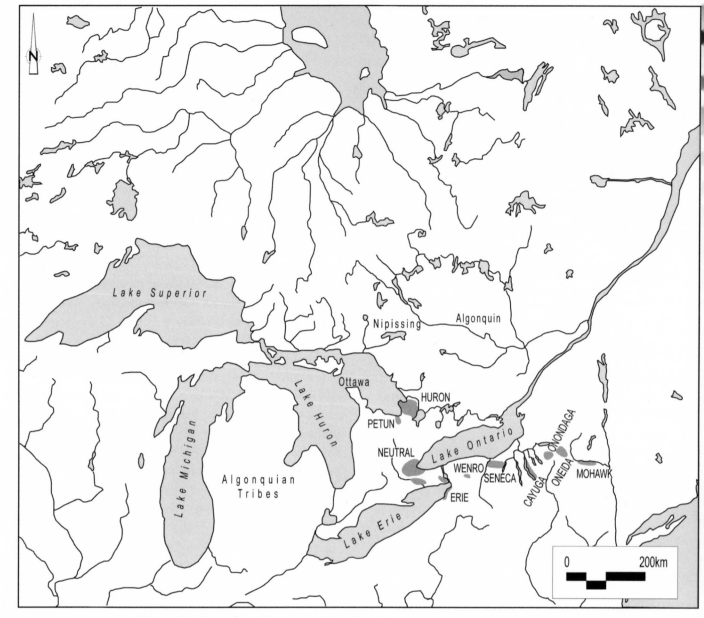

FIGURE 18.1. Map showing location of Northern Iroquoian and neighboring Algonquian Nations Courtesy Archaeological Services, Inc.

their neighbors. From this context, it would seem that the most common reason for traditional warfare among all northern Iroquoian and Algonquian groups was to avenge the death of a kinsman at the hands of an enemy. The entire community, particularly the relatives of the deceased, felt obligated to raise a war party to seek retaliation (Thwaites 1896–1901, 10:225–27; 17:11). This kind of warfare has been described as "Mourning Wars" in which traditional enemies were captured, some of whom were then either symbolically or actually adopted into the group to replace a loved one (Engelbrecht 2003:36). In contexts such as these, warfare was a spiritual act with an emphasis not on killing

in battle but rather on bringing a prisoner back for either sacrifice or adoption.

This view of warfare is consistent with a focus on ambush as the predominant military tactic as well as trophy-taking, where a scalp or even a head, imbued the victor with the spiritual power of the deceased, i.e., a form of soul capture (Engelbrecht 2003:42–43). Gabrielle Sagard, from his life with the Huron, told of 500 or 600 young men going annually to Iroquois territory where they scattered into groups of five or six to lay in wait for the enemy. They laid flat on their bellies in fields, woods, and along the main paths, even stealing into villages at night to capture a prisoner. If they took them alive, they carried them back to their own country and put them to death over a slow fire. If, on the other hand, they had either clubbed or shot them to death with arrows, they carried off their heads or, if too encumbered, took the scalps with the hair on them, later tanning them and putting them away for trophies (Wrong 1939:152–53).

The Jesuits recorded similar practices for members of the Iroquois League (Trigger 1976:650; Thwaites 1896–1901, 29:251; 47:141–53). An indirect reference to Mohawk practice was recorded by Roger Williams, the Puritan cleric who founded Providence, Rhode Island. He described the Mohawks as man-eaters who made a "monstrous dish of the head and brains of their enemies" (Williams 1643:58). Mohawks were also known to have spared the lives of some captives so that they might be naturalized into Iroquois families (Trigger 1976:638).

Among the Huron and Iroquois, the call to arms was made by two or three war chiefs who traveled from village to village to explain their plans and persuade other warriors to join them in their efforts. These chiefs would design the strategies, tactics, and necessary force complements, as well as conduct

needed military training (Biggar 1922–36:159; Wrong 1939:151).

At the time of European contact, the Iroquois were not unfamiliar with linear warfare (fig.18.2), a front line of archers was often used to send volleys of arrows at the enemy. A second line of wood-armored warriors using wooden clubs would then advance for face-to-face combat; these warriors were supported by the archers from the frontline. These tactical groups resembled a kind of light infantry that could redeploy effectively even within wooded terrain. They persisted into the early-nineteenth century and required a considerable amount of training to be successful (Benn 1993:67–72). One means of military training designed to ensure the maintenance of their ranks was described by the explorer, Samuel de Champlain, who spent the winter with the Huron in 1615–16 (Biggar 1925 2:88–89):

The chiefs take sticks a foot long, as many in number as they are, and signalize their chiefs by somewhat larger ones, then go into the woods and clear a space of five or six feet square where this chief, as Sergeant Major, puts all these sticks in order, as it seems good to him, then calls all his companions who all come

FIGURE 18.2. Battle of Lake Champlain, 30 July 1609, from Champlain's Voyages of 1613. Courtesy Public Archives of Canada.

armed, and shows them the rank and order which they will have to observe in fighting their enemies. All the Indians regard attentively, noticing the design the chief has made with these sticks and afterwards withdraw and begin to form ranks according to the plan showed by the said sticks; then they [fall out], move around and return again into order, repeating [this maneuver] two or three times; and they all take their place which they know very well how to keep without getting out of line. That is the rule which they observed in their warfare.

The onset of European contact resulted in almost immediate changes to warfare patterns and intent. Trigger (1976:658–61), for example, discussed the growing need for European goods among the Onondaga, Cayuga, and Seneca in the 1640s that led to the development of a more economically oriented and motivated warfare. He described more intensive conflict that involved pillaging and burning of villages to steal skins and other valuables.

In pre-contact times, weapons used by northern Iroquoians included wooden clubs and bows and arrows with tips made from flint from which they were protected, in part, by a sort of wooden armor and shield (Wrong 1939:154). By the 1640s, easier access to iron weapons resulted in inflicting more serious injuries on their traditional enemies on the part of some groups (e.g., Trigger 1976:624). The later possession and use of guns conferred an obvious military advantage over others not so armed. However, the initial power of the gun might have been mostly psychological since the traditional bow and arrow, in the hands of an experienced archer, was both lighter and more maneuverable than a musket (Trigger 1976:629). Perhaps the most important change to aboriginal warfare resulting from European contact was the increasing importance of prisoner adoption as a means of maintaining population levels in the face of depopulation from intensified warfare and European disease (Richter 1983:530–531).

The Archaeological Record

There is substantial archaeological evidence for intertribal warfare, the prisoner sacrifice complex and trophy-taking on Northern Iroquoian sites (Milner et al. 1991; Milner 1995; Williamson 2007). A number of detailed studies have been conducted to document and interpret modifications to human skeletal elements and the distribution of such remains within sites to examine links between patterns of scattered human bone in the sites of large Iroquoian villages and rituals of prisoner sacrifice and cannibalism (Jamieson 1983; Cooper 1984; Rainey 2002; Fontaine 2004). The correlation of scattered human bone with the remains of sacrificed prisoners is equivocal. Such scatters may also have been the product of the preparation of primary inhumations for secondary, ossuary burial in the Huron "Feast of the Dead," commonly practiced when a village was about to be abandoned and moved. In this re-burial process, extremities and skeletal elements could easily have been left behind.

Trophy-taking is clearly evidenced archaeologically. Large numbers of cranial elements among scattered human bones found on sites, many with parallel, transverse or oblique cut marks on the anterior, lateral, and posterior portions of the cranial vault near the hairline, are characteristic of scalping (Milner et al. 1991:584). Given the ethnographic record of the removal of both arms and legs during episodes of torture, and the taking of arms as trophies (e.g., Biggar 1922–36, 5:231), the recovery of numbers of long bones, more arms than legs, in site debris is also not surprising.

Intact crania are also found in various contexts on Iroquoian sites (e.g., Dupras and Pratte 1998; Robertson et al. 1998:40–41). Given the absence of ethnographic evidence for ancestor worship, they may be interpreted as trophy heads. For example, at the Alhart Site in western New York, which was occupied during the late-fifteenth or early-sixteenth century, 15 male crania were found buried together in a storage pit over the partially charred remains of maize. That most of the skulls were found articulated with their mandibles and upper cervical vertebrae suggested that they had been placed within the pit as in-the-flesh, severed heads (Hammel 1987:51).

Evidence of trophy-taking and body mutilation occurs in some rare cases of burials of single or multiple individuals thought to have suffered personal violence at the hands of their enemies but who were, nevertheless, buried either where they fell or returned to their home villages. For example, at the Draper site, a large, late-fifteenth century ancestral Huron village

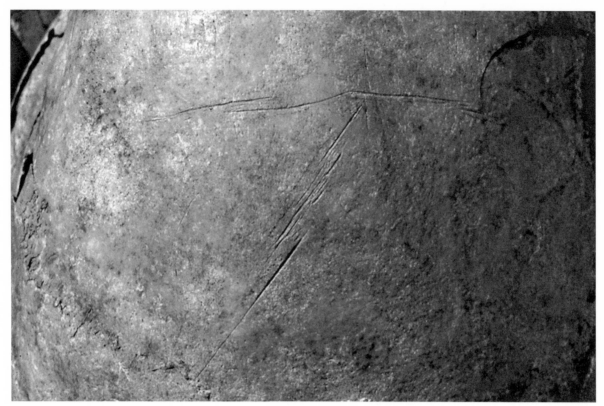

FIGURE 18.3. Scalping marks, fifteenth century ancestral Huron Draper site, Burial 6. Photograph courtesy Museum of Ontario Archaeology.

located northeast of Toronto, Ontario, an elderly male appears to have been shot in the leg from behind with a chert-tipped arrow. He was then speared or stabbed in the chest when prone, scalped (fig. 18.3), and partially dismembered to remove his arms, which, along with his scalp, were likely taken as trophies (Williamson 1978; Forrest 2005:37–42; for similar examples see also Molto et al. 1986; and Wray et al. 1991:211).

Additional evidence of trophy taking is suggested by the presence of certain artifacts made of human bone: human skull rattles or gorgets, beads made from drilled phalanges, and ulna daggers. All have been found on late-fourteenth through sixteenth century northern Iroquoian sites and are likely to have been manufactured from the body parts of captives.

Military Encounters: The Archival Record

Aboriginal warriors involved in eighteenth and nineteenth century conflicts, allied with one European nation or another, fought on their own terms, following their own chiefs. Seneca war chief, Little Billy, told Americans in September 1812, "we must act under our

own chiefs; according to our own customs," and "be at liberty to take our own course in fighting" (Benn 1993:85). More often than not, that course of fighting involved ambush, often at night, as well as trophy-taking, following millennia-old traditions of warfare (e.g., Benn 1993:115–20).

While ambush was a successful tactic, rigid linear field formations were avoided because of the small numbers of aboriginals involved in these hostilities and their need to minimize casualties (Benn 1993:70). Yet, warfare still provided the most important opportunity for individual warriors to display initiative, heroism, and obtain status. What evolved was a form of warfare based on aboriginal tradition but influenced by European practice and association.

According to Maj. John Norton, a Mohawk diplomat and war chief, there were two kinds of warfare undertaken by aboriginals during this period (Klinck and Talman 1970:126–30). The first involved occasional excursions, generally carried out independently by war chiefs, and consisting of small parties of 10–50 warriors. These encounters involved great stealth and preparation. Waiting in ambush required previously prepared provisions since cooking fires would never be lit near an enemy encampment. Norton noted one instance in which two men and one boy successfully delayed a European advance by concealing themselves under bushes and occasionally killing one or two of the enemy (Johnston 1964:33).

The second kind of warfare was a cooperative venture where runners were dispatched by chiefs to neighboring groups to assemble an imposing force. Once the warriors assembled at the appointed rendezvous, with sufficient provisions in hand, a chief was appointed to lead the war party. Typical strategies employed in such encounters included some of the same field tactics featured in early European accounts of inter-tribal conflicts such as the use of cover, firing from a prone position, and a preference for close combat (Klinck and Talman 1970:129–30). Yet, European influences were also apparent:

> When they have reason to expect that the enemy is advancing towards them, or that they draw near to his station, scouts are always sent in front. When they are ready to engage, they either take post in some advantageous position, by which the enemy must pass or march to attack him, which method has been more generally attended with success. In marching to the attack, they advance by files, leaving such intervals between each, as may enable them to outflank him. As soon as they come in contact, they all run up and form; not so exact perhaps as regular troops, but sufficiently so to support each other. If the Action commences with firing, they cover themselves by trees and ravines. In plains where these advantages are not to be had they lie on their faces. Parties advance with their guns loaded, which they discharge on the enemy, these are immediately succeeded by others, until they come in close contact, when they use the spear and tomahawk. Against regular troops, they prefer using fire arms, until they have thinned or broken their ranks, before they charge; but against militia, they prefer coming to close quarters, as soon as the situation in which they meet will admit, because these are good marksmen, but have not discipline to enable them to withstand the impetuosity of an onset.

One tactic that is consistent in descriptions of both early inter-tribal warfare and later periods is the tactical use of landscape features in conflict. Warriors often used knolls, crests, and ridges as natural breastworks for protection and forested areas for natural cover, especially in preparation for ambushes. A particularly noteworthy tactical use of landscape, mentioned in more than one account of the War of 1812, involved the aboriginal use of the thick woods on the top of the Niagara Escarpment which extended parallel to the lakeshore lowlands where the British and American forces operated. From this high point, British-allied warriors could watch American movements on the plain below without being seen and could attack at the most opportune moments (e.g., Allen 1992:139; Klinck and Talman 1970:308, 349).

This did not mean that European nations with which aboriginal forces were allied did not have an influence on how they fought or that there were no differences in the ways in which warriors were engaged. Carl Benn, in his analysis of the Iroquois in the War of 1812, argues that the British profited from their native alliances more than the Americans. The British were more willing to cooperate with their aboriginal allies on their own terms, and used their strengths in more productive ways, alongside their regular troops (Benn 1993:5). During a Niagara skirmish in 1813, for example, the British troops fought beside native allies while on the American side, the regular troops remained several hundred paces behind their native allies (Klinck and Talman 1970:339).

This level of cooperation and understanding had not always been the case among the British. For example, in 1775 during the American Revolutionary War, Governor Guy Carleton thought that warriors should only be used in defense or as scouts. However, Guy Johnson, superintendent of the Indian Department, argued that they would be used more efficiently as raiders carrying out devastating strikes against the rebels in the back settlements of New England, New York, and Pennsylvania (Allen 1992:48). By the War of 1812, however, the British not only used their native allies in physical warfare, but also as a form of psychological terror, playing on the fears of the Americans by building up the "spectre of massacre." As British General Brock informed American General Hull in 1813 in advance of their taking Detroit, "it is far from my intention to join a war of extermination, but you must be aware that the numerous body of

Indians who have attached themselves to my troops will be beyond control the moment the contest commences" (Benn 1993:49–50; Graves 1993:9). Brock was aware that the men in Hull's army were terrified of the natives and Hull eventually surrendered without much of a fight.

The British, in contrast to the Americans, "tended to accept the fact that warriors would only fight under their own leaders, following their own customs," and understood that it was not in their best interest to try to assert authority over them or attempt to change their ways of fighting (Benn 1993:158). Whether this was truly understood, or if they were simply uncertain of how to lead them, leaving the warriors to their own devices was the general course taken by the British, not always to their satisfaction. In 1812, for example, the Wyandot, operating with British regular forces along the River Raisin just south of Detroit, ravaged the area, much to the mortification of British army officers (Allen 1992:138).

There are varying accounts as to the extent to which aboriginal warriors mutilated the dead. While warriors attempted to remove their own dead and wounded from the field so that they would not fall into enemy hands, the remains of enemies were not treated as kindly. Indeed, trophy-taking, in particular scalping, transpired with some frequency. Despite being aware of such aboriginal traditions, most European officers were not comfortable with the practice. In contrast, there are also accounts of aboriginal excursions conducted with "a uniform display of good discipline," and others where warriors retreated without spilling a drop of blood upon the orders of their captain (Allen 1992:130, 138).

Weapons that could be attributed to Iroquoians in warfare during the contact period include traditional bows and arrows with both stone or metal tips, tomahawks, wooden war clubs embedded with iron or steel spikes or blades, hatchets embedded with iron blades, knives (pocket, clasp, and butchers' varieties), swords, lances, spears, half axes, pipe-tomahawks, and British muskets, rifles, and pistols (Allen 1992; Benn 1993; Graves 1994; Richter 2001). Richter (2001:49) has argued that at least initially after European contact, the fundamental change was not the introduction of firearms, but the use of arrows tipped with brass as well as metal hatchets and metal cutting edges embedded

in war-clubs. He argues the latter made for far more deadly hand-to-hand combat while the former were lighter and far more lethal, and certainly capable of piercing traditional wooden armor, although the use of such armor had largely been abandoned shortly after European contact (cf. Benn 1993:71).

Tomahawks were made of brass or iron with steel blades while spears, primarily used as thrusting weapons, were either supplied by the British Indian Department or manufactured by warriors by attaching blades to the end of poles or by carving a point on the end of a shaft and hardening it in a fire (Benn 1993:75).

Wooden war-clubs likely have their origin in pre-contact times (Wrong 1939:98, 154). They were described as ball-headed war clubs (casse-têt) made from a very hard wood, measuring 2–2.5 ft long, squared on the sides, and widened or rounded, to the width of a fist at the end (Fenton and Moore 1977, II:115). These remained in use into the nineteenth century although after European contact they featured iron spikes embedded in their striking ends. Some of these were painted and bore etchings or carvings representing the clan affiliation of the owner, his exploits, or likenesses of his guardian spirits or of those spirits identified with war or the underworld (figs, 18.4 and 18.5). Other traditional clubs resembled inverted gunstocks and also featured metal striking points on their underside although a variation of this club used a short, sharpened deer horn particularly useful for inflicting deep wounds (Benn 1993:76).

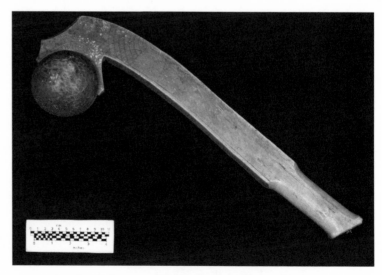

FIGURE 18.4. Iroquoian war club. Photograph courtesy Ruthven National Park Collection, Archaeological Services Inc.

FIGURE 18.5. War club detail of totems or stories. Courtesy Ruthven National Park Collection; Archaeological Services Inc.

In the case of firearms, the British provided their aboriginal allies with muskets, chief's guns, rifles, and pistols, although often smaller caliber and with shorter barrels (lighter construction) than they themselves used. Chief's guns were weapons of better quality and were decorated on the wrist or stock with inlaid silver showing the likeness of a native. Aboriginals allied with American forces were supplied with more rifles than muskets. Sometimes, however, firearms were in such short supply that native warriors were forced into combat with no other arms than traditional clubs, spears, and tomahawks (Benn 1993:72–74; Klinck and Talman 1970:272).

Aboriginals sometimes modified European firearms. Algonkian-speaking groups, for example, damaged or removed dragon side plates from trade muskets because of spiritual beliefs related to hunting and Mishipizheu, the water lynx (Fox 1992). The combs on gunstocks were also sometimes altered to improve sighting of weapons by enabling warriors to line up their eyes along the barrel better (Benn 1993:71). While the British provided their Iroquois allies with buckshot, most of it was likely used for hunting. Alternatively, some Americans suffered

buckshot casualties during the war, possibly from Iroquois weapons (Benn 1993:74). Obviously, any weapon might fall into the hands of a warrior through trade or as battlefield trophies (e.g., bayonets, military muskets).

Warriors also carried strings or belts of wampum, matunip lines (long, plaited vegetable fiber belts that could be used to secure prisoners and dyed black, decorated with tin cones, red-dyed moose hair, and red, black, and white porcupine quills), powder horns, pouches (often decorated with images of guardian spirits such as the thunderbird, underwater panthers, and horned serpent) containing war charms, ammunition or spare flints, scalp lock ornamentation (including feathers, horsehair, and silver ornaments), and circular or crescent-shaped gorgets worn on the chest. The gorgets were originally made of bone or stone. By the early-nineteenth century they were made of silver or gilt with representations of the sun probably because of the traditional association of the sun with war (Trigger 1989:97). Many warriors also wore European-style, crescent-moon shaped gorgets likely because of their association with European military leadership (Benn 1993:76–78).

Eighteenth and Nineteenth Century Military Encounters: Potential Archaeological Record

Unfortunately there are few, if any, systematic archaeological investigations of eighteenth or nineteenth century battles in which northern Iroquoians played a substantial role. Richard Gramly (1978) has reported on some archaeological evidence from investigations at the American Revolutionary War era Fort Laurens, situated in Ohio. He documented a mass grave of 17 men who had been killed in a cleverly concealed aboriginal ambush within sight of the fort as well as the graves of other soldiers who had been killed in other instances of ambush. He also documented evidence of a fire that had occurred at the fort. According to the diary of Rev. David Zeisberger, in July 1780, a major portion of Fort Laurens was set ablaze by a party of aboriginals who were on their way to Fort Pitt. Gramly (1978:9) found charred sections of a palisade and chunks of fire-reddened clay daubing which likely originated from the clay packed among the logs of the structures.

The most thorough analysis of aboriginal participation in a battle, based on both archival and archaeological evidence, is Richard Fox's (1997) examination of Custer's Last Stand in 1876. He used a deductive rather than an inductive approach to trace physical evidence left by native combatants since the inductive approach, which he employed with the American archaeological remains, relied on prescribed tactics that had clear predictive implications (Fox 1997:21). Since the native warriors generally used different firearms with different ammunition than the American troopers, distribution of their spent cartridge cases provided the groundwork for determining individual positions and movements of soldiers and aboriginals (Fox 1997:77–87).

Archaeological investigation helped provide a more accurate description of the battle than one based on archival documents and oral testimony alone. Using the locations of fired bullets and cartridge cases, lost weapons, human remains and burials, he reconstructed the pathways and combat styles of aboriginal participants reaching the conclusion that many aboriginal warriors had acted on their own in the absence of any tactical doctrine to which all adhered (Fox 1997:22). The distribution of cartridge cases also confirmed that warriors used the top of ridges and knolls as natural breastworks (Fox 1997:96–99, 116).

His analysis indicated that warriors reached positions very close to the soldiers, confirming historical accounts of aboriginal tactics such as infiltration and skirmishing. In areas where there were many soldier deaths, but few associated aboriginal bullets and cartridge cases, warriors seemed to have abandoned their guns in favor of hand-to-hand combat, confirming historical accounts that substantial numbers of aboriginals fought armed with clubs, knives, and hatchets (Fox 1997:113). Metal arrowpoints were also found indicating the presence of warriors armed with bows and arrows rather than firearms.

Human remains found during archaeological investigations also revealed evidence of aboriginal activity in the forms of decapitation and dismemberment although Fox (1997) noted that such practices were not necessarily restricted to one side. On the other hand, aboriginal custom dictated mutilation of the enemy for cultural and spiritual reasons in that maimed enemies could not confront one in the hereafter.

CONCLUSIONS

The use of detailed oral testimony and the presence of a rich archaeological record rendered the task of reconstructing the aboriginal involvement in Custer's last battle not only possible but of considerable significance. Indeed, Fox (1997) managed to archaeologically confirm many premises outlined above concerning aboriginal participation in warfare during the contact period and provided researchers with a rationale and model for pursuing similar investigations. Not only do aboriginals appear to have acted on their own terms in accordance with their own customs, but the archaeological evidence has confirmed the tactical use of higher ground, the propensity for hand-to-hand combat with traditional weapons, and the continuing practice of trophy-taking in historic period conflicts. Fox (1997) did so by recording the precise locations on the battlefield of discarded aboriginal weapons, both contemporary and traditional, ammunition casings, and modified human remains and graves.

Some evidence of participation in battles may be found off the battlefield, for example, scalps taken in these encounters. Many scalps were stretched onto wooden frames and painted red, then given either to war chiefs as symbols of their commitment, or to relatives of lost warriors. In Iroquoian tradition, a spirit freed by death could not rest until another had been adopted to replace its loss, having assumed the name of the deceased. This view of adoption as the symbolic reincarnation of the dead is reflected in the painting of the hair and skin of trophy scalps red. The scalps were adopted as "living relatives" symbolically equating them with a prisoner awaiting adoption and the status of the dead person being mourned (Hall 1997:33–35). Weapons used in battle may themselves bear evidence of their use in specific episodes. In the case of war clubs, their carved, incised, and painted decorations may provide tallies or stories of the exploits of a warrior.

In summary, it is clear that accurate reconstructions of aboriginal involvement in battle are possible through detailed examinations of curated weapons and trophies and careful, deductively modeled, archaeological investigations of battlefields conducted in the context of landscape analyses and exhaustive archival research. Such a goal should also be viewed as critical given that these early conflicts involved many autonomous nations, both European and aboriginal, all of which acted according to their own customs and objectives.

ACKNOWLEDGMENTS

I would like to thank Annie Veilleux and Debbie Steiss for their research assistance and Andrea Carnevale and David Robertson for their editorial assistance and help in the preparation of the figures.

CHAPTER NINETEEN

Tragedy of the Nez Perce War of 1877

An Archaeological Expression

DOUGLAS D. SCOTT

INTRODUCTION

The year of 1877 was tragic for the Nez Perce. Broken promises, misunderstood treaties, and conservative factions on both sides caused open warfare between the Nez Perce and the U.S. government. In July, the Nez Perce fled Idaho, at first to find refuge in Montana and then, in a final desperate bid for freedom, they attempted to reach Canada. This trek became an epic event in U.S. history. The flight ended in October at Snake Creek near Bear Paw, Montana, with the surrender of most Nez Perce under the leadership of Chief Joseph. The Nez Perce fought several skirmishes and at least six pitched battles with the army. A number of the battle sites along the Nez Perce flight route are now preserved and interpreted by various state and federal agencies as memorials. One of those sites is the Big Hole National Battlefield in southwestern Montana. The Battle of the Big Hole site is now considered sacred by the Nez Perce for the events that occurred there in August 1877. As a memorial, the site highlights the tragic outcome of hostile relationships between two cultures.

The premise of this contribution is that the modern study of a battlefield requires a combination of historical sources and archeological data. In solving a crime, police rely upon two very different types of evidence. Detectives interview witnesses while forensic scientists gather fingerprints, blood samples, and other physical evidence. These investigators address different types of evidence using unique methods. Evaluated together, this partnership enhances the likelihood of solving the crime. In this analogy, the detectives are historians, the witnesses the documents and oral histories, and the forensic scientists are archaeologists. The records and documents that historical archaeologists use, especially first-hand accounts of historical events, are tantamount to eyewitness testimony that can generate hypotheses to be tested against the archaeological record. They also furnish the basis by which archaeologically observed patterns can be assigned historically meaningful identities. The archaeological or physical evidence record contains clues in the form of artifacts and their contextual relationships. These relationships, which include distributions and spatial associations of various types of artifacts, can reveal a great deal about the activities that were carried out at a site. The historical archaeologist continually compares both sets of data as work progresses in order to explain the events under scrutiny. Sometimes history and archaeology may be at odds, necessitating, on occasion, significant revisions in current perceptions of historical events.

For the past 130 years, the Battle of the Big Hole has been the subject of diverse opinion. Specific issues surrounding the nature of events during the fight fall squarely into the analytical domain of historical archeology and the archeological record. The historical issues and oral traditions surrounding the events of the fight provide direction in the research and aid in understanding battle events. Realizing that there exists a behavioral relationship between historical events and the physical remains of events, behavior on the battlefield can be understood by exposing these relationships and evaluating them in historical context.

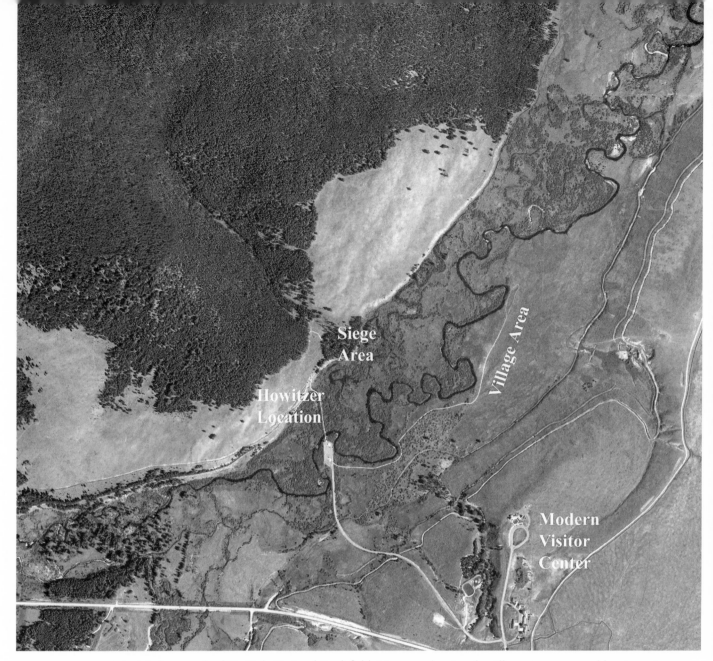

FIGURE 19.1. Aerial photograph of Big Hole National Battlefield, Montana showing the village, siege area, and howitzer site locations. From USGS seamless data distribution Web site http://seamless.usgs.gov/. Courtesy Archaeological Services Inc.

THE BATTLE OF THE BIG HOLE, MONTANA

In a pre-dawn attack on 9 August 1877, the 7th U.S. Infantry led by Col. John Gibbon surprised a Nez Perce camp on the banks of the North Fork of the Big Hole River (fig. 19.1). The infantry suffered a decisive loss, but the Nez Perce, although winning the day, suffered an irreplaceable loss of 80–90 women, children, and men. Discussion of and interest in what happened began virtually as the gun smoke cleared from the field and continues today.

An outline of the events leading to the Big Hole battle, and the sequence of the battle as described in the primary sources (Howard 1881; Shields 1889; Beal 1963; Brown 1982) as well as from the synthetic work of Aubrey Haines (1991) is synopsized here.

The Nez Perce had agreed, in 1877, to a reduced reservation area as a result of increased Euro-American settlement in Idaho and Washington. There was disagreement and hard feelings among and between tribal bands and individuals regarding the loss of ancestral lands. Some bands, particularly Joseph's, were reluctant to give up their lands but they planned to do so. Some Nez Perce bands requested a time extension for moving to the new reservation due to the need to assemble all their members and associated stock. The government denied the extension, which exacerbated an already tense situation.

Even as anxiety built over preparations for leaving their homeland, a taunt by one or more tribal members over not revenging the death of his father, led a young warrior, Wah-Lit-its-to, and two cousins, to search for the white settler responsible. Not finding the settler, they raided a number of ranches and homesteads in the Carson's Prairie and Salmon River, Idaho area, killing several people. This incident, created an unalterable cycle of events that led to the open hostilities between the Nez Perce and the U.S. Army.

After fighting several pitched battles, the Nez Perce made their way into Montana and continued on to find their Crow friends. In the meantime, Col. John Gibbon, commanding the District of Montana, began to assemble his scattered 7th Infantry. The companies reached Missoula on 3 August and left the next day to find the Nez Perce.

Gibbon's column, less his wagons and a guard that were left about 3.5 miles from the battlefield, found the Nez Perce camp late in the afternoon of 8 August. At 11 P.M. that night the command of 17 officers, 132 enlisted men, and 34 volunteers started down the mountain toward the village in the Big Hole Valley.

Gibbon moved his men along an old trail down into the valley. Passing over a wooded point of land, an old alluvial fan (fig. 19.1), Gibbon noted it as a good defense point should a retrograde movement become necessary. In hindsight, this was a wise observation because it would become known as the Siege Area to history. Gibbon continued north of the fan and deployed his men along the trail situated on a steep hillside above the swampy, willow-covered land west of the Big Hole River. The Nez Perce village was arrayed in a slightly V-shaped line along the east side of the river in a camas meadow.

Gibbon planned to charge the village at daylight. However, a lone Nez Perce was seen coming out of the village just before dawn, and he was fired upon by a volunteer. This killing opened the battle. The command fired volleys into the sleeping camp and then charged across the river. The Nez Perce were surprised and initially confused. Many Nez Perce men grabbed their arms and scattered to the north, south, and east finding refuge in the willows, along river meanders, and on the terraces east of the camp. Women and children did the same. Some Nez Perce, reportedly mostly women and children, ran across the meadow to the terraces east of the village. The warriors quickly returned fire from their cover.

Although the attack was initially successful in taking most of the village, the soldiers were still under fire from the Nez Perce. Gibbon committed his reserves. Gibbon left his command position along the western hillside and rode into the village where, in order to deprive the Nez Perce of shelter and other amenities, he ordered the teepees burned. The assumption was that, without horses and shelter, the Nez Perce would be destitute and would return to the reservation a humbled group. Several women and children were hiding in the tepees and a great loss of life occurred when the army fired into them. While the burning was going on, Gibbon's command suffered several casualties, many in fighting near the southern end of the village.

The Nez Perce, rallied by the exhortations of their leaders such as Looking Glass, poured heavy fire into the village. Within an hour, the now slightly wounded Gibbon realized his position in the village was untenable. The command was ordered to fall back across the river, through the willows, to the timber-covered point of land he had noted earlier. As the demoralized command began to retreat, the Nez Perce warriors pressed the battle and the soldiers bunched up causing a halting retreat. There was some hand-to-hand fighting along the retreat and several more soldiers were killed. The retreat became somewhat chaotic.

As the command reached the alluvial fan, several Nez Perce were already there and began to fire. The soldiers charged up the steep toe of the fan and pushed the Nez Perce across a gulch that dissected the fan and up hills on either side of the fan. Upon reaching the fan, Gibbon deployed his men. As some men began dragging in logs to form firing positions, the men of Companies A and I, who had experimental trowel bayonets, began to dig rifle pits (fig. 19.2). Others used knives and makeshift tools to create cover. The Nez Perce in the timber on the south side of the fan, as well as on the hill slopes above the soldiers, continued their fire.

FIGURE 19.2. Detail of the Siege Area showing a riflepit occupied by Gibbon's soldiers and volunteers. Photograph courtesy Midwest Archealogical Center, National Park Service.

A well-known warrior, Five Wounds, was at or near the Siege Area when he learned that his war mate, Rainbow, had been killed. A pledge to die on the same day had to be honored so Five Wounds took a partially loaded magazine rifle and rushed up the mouth of Battle Gulch. He nearly gained the lip of the gulch when he was cut down in a hail of bullets. His body was not recovered by the Nez Perce and was later mutilated by Gen. O. O. Howard's Bannock scouts of the army relief column.

The Nez Perce essentially surrounded the rifle pits. They fired from the timber to the east and west of the entrenchments as well as from the hillsides to the north and west. Some warriors positioned in a group of pines south of the entrenchments opposite the mouth of Battle Gulch were able to direct their fire very effectively. On the hill north of the rifle pits, the warriors used trees as cover to fire at the soldiers and volunteers.

A boom of a howitzer was heard while the men were digging in at the Siege Area. This was a 12-pounder Mountain Howitzer mounted on a Prairie Carriage and drawn by six mules. The howitzer was following the command guided by a civilian volunteer. The gun was crewed by six hastily trained infantrymen, only one or two of whom had any artillery experience.

The howitzer was set up above the trail (fig. 19.1) well south of the village and high on a timbered slope. The Nez Perce, probably alerted to the presence of the gun by its first discharge, assaulted its location. The gun crew fired two shots, apparently at the village, before they were overrun. One crewman was killed and two were wounded. The survivors fled back to the wagon train. The Nez Perce dismounted the gun's wheels and rolled them down the hill. The ammunition from the limber was scattered, the tube was hidden in some brush or buried, the rammer and sponge were carried off, and the carriage wrecked.

While some warriors engaged the entrenched soldiers, others returned to the village and were joined by surviving women and children. The Nez Perce began to mourn and bury their dead. Some were apparently buried in ovens that had been prepared for roasting the locally abundant camas root. Others were buried along the riverbank, and still others were carried away and buried by their surviving families. As the dead were buried, the Nez Perce attempted to salvage what they could from the village.

During the night of 9 August, the Nez Perce warriors continued to fire harassing shots at the soldiers.

The main body in the camp packed what belongings they could find and prepared to depart. With sunrise the camp and most of the people left the valley and departed to the east. A few warriors, perhaps 15, were left behind to keep the soldiers at bay. They did so until about eleven o'clock the night of 10 August, when they fired a departing volley and left.

These warriors joined their grieving families on a trek that would take them on a route south into Idaho and then east through Yellowstone National Park and two months later to the final battle on Snake Creek near Bear Paw, Montana. There the majority of the surviving Nez Perce, now under the general leadership of Chief Joseph, would surrender 5 October and close the Nez Perce War.

The Archaeological Evidence

The basic tenet of anthropology and archeology is that human behavior is patterned. Accordingly, the residue of that behavior should also be patterned and reflect, in varying degrees, details of that behavior. This archeological tenet argues that artifacts, the leavings of behavioral acts, will occur in recognizable and interpretable patterns. Pattern analysis is as old as professional archeology. Patterns are the way in which artifacts are found in/on the ground and the relationships an artifact or a group of artifacts have with other items—context and provenience. Battlefields represent the most violent expressions of human behavior, and the premise is that physical evidence of violent behavioral patterns is likely to be evident (Fox and Scott 1991).

Warfare has special rules by which it is practiced. Within our own culture this may be seen in the preparation and training given members of the military. This training is given, and this was also true in 1877, to ensure that those engaged in battle will perform their duties based on their training and respond to orders without dwelling on the consequences (Dyer 1985). That is patterned behavior. While the warriors of the Nez Perce did not have the same training or respond to orders in the same manner as the soldiers, they nevertheless had a culturally established warfare behavioral pattern.

The fundamental principles used by contemporary forensic firearms examiners to associate fired bullets and fired cartridge cases with the firearm in which they were discharged have not been generally available to battlefield investigators and archeologists. Yet these principles and the methods for associating ballistic evidence to both selected firearms manufacturers and specific firearms are just as applicable to historic items as they are to recently fired bullets and cartridge cases at a modern crime scene. These principles, as synopsized in the following, were applied to the Big Hole firearms artifact collection, which, in concert with other pattern recognition analyses, resulted in some surprising new conclusions regarding the 1877 battle.

Class and Individual Characteristics

The basic principles in firearms identification are divided into two categories: the determination of class characteristics and the subsequent comparison of individual characteristics. Class characteristics can be thought of as those features that the manufacturer intended to be present in the firearm. They include such obvious things as the caliber of recovered bullets and general rifling features imparted on them by the responsible firearm. Certain manufacturing features associated with fired cartridges provide additional information to the modern day firearms examiner regarding the firearm that discharged them.

This is also true for a number of firearms of antiquity. Fired cartridge cases found on a battlefield may offer even better insight into the type or types of firearms involved in the battle. General construction such as internal priming vs. external priming, rimfire vs. centerfire, copper cases vs. tin-plated cases vs. brass cases and, of course, any headstamp information present on recovered cartridges all provide useful, sometimes definitive clues as to the source firearm. Class characteristics serve as a rapid and relatively common-sense means for quickly eliminating certain firearms and narrowing the search to a much-reduced number of candidates (fig. 19.3).

Individual characteristics consist of the unintended features on the various working surfaces of a firearm that often mark bullets and fired cartridges. These arise either through impact (such as the firing pin) or through a dynamic scraping or rubbing action that occurs when a projectile is driven down the bore of a firearm. Even in a new and carefully made firearm there will be microscopic imperfections in the various

FIGURE 19.3. Example of two .50-70-caliber cartridge case heads showing differences in firing pin marks on the primers. The differences denote each cartridge was fired in a separate firearm. Photograph by author.

surfaces that contact the cartridge and the bullet. These arise during the manufacturing process or use/abuse of any firearm and subsequently serve as the means of specifically associating a fired cartridge or fired bullet with the responsible firearm (fig. 19.4).

It is important to note that possession of the actual firearm is not necessary for an examiner to determine that a group of fired cartridges or fired bullets were fired by a single firearm. The identity of the source can be established as long as the class characteristics are in full agreement and that there is sufficient correspondence in individual characteristics is present between the items. Virtually all of this is relevant and applicable to historic firearms and ammunition components.

Digging In and Fighting in the Siege Area

The Siege Area is also the site that has received the most intense post-battle usage by the Forest Service, and then Park Service, which has undoubtedly affected some of the archaeological patterns related to the fighting. Even with all the impacts, the archaeological data attributable to the Battle of the Big Hole has survived surprisingly well (Scott 1994).

The entrenchments or rifle pits dug by Gibbon's men are clearly evident in the Siege Area today (Scott 1994). At least 23 rifle pits of different sizes are arranged in a roughly shaped rectangle. In addition, three isolated pits occur along the sides of Battle Gulch and another is located northeast of the main group. An old prospect pit west of Battle Gulch was also used by some volunteers (Haines 1991).

Numerous battle-derived artifacts occur including buttons, pieces of equipment, cartridge cases, and bullets (Scott 1994). Fifty-nine, .45-70 cartridge cases were recovered representing 26 individual Army Springfield firearms. The .50–70 cartridge cases found tend to concentrate in the western rifle pits, this distribution being consistent with the historically documented location of most volunteers during the latter stages of the battle. Other bullets found in this area include one .44-caliber rim fire cartridge case fired in a Model 1860 Colt Conversion and one .50–70 cartridge case fired in a Remington Rolling Block rifle.

Warrior-fired bullets of various calibers were found in and around the entrenchments as well as in the areas historically identified as Nez Perce positions. The .45–70-caliber bullets were found throughout the Siege Area. A few were found among the entrenchments, but most were outside the entrenchment proper. A large concentration was noted on the northeastern edge of the alluvial fan, with smaller concentrations to the south and upslope about 250 yards to the west.

Those caliber bullets more likely associated with the Nez Perce have a similar distribution. However, more lead scraps (unidentified bullets and bullet fragments) as well as .50–70-caliber and .44-caliber bullets were found among the entrenchments than .45–70 bullets. Many of the other caliber bullets were found embedded in the fan edge or to the northeast.

The Siege Area occupation is exceptionally well-documented in the source materials. Not only did surviving soldiers and volunteers identify which shelter pit they occupied, they also pointed out trees and other places where Nez Perce took shelter. The Nez Perce also vividly recalled the names of the warrior

FIGURE 19.4. Enlarged view of two rimfire .44-caliber firing pin marks using a comparison microscope. The class and individual characteristics match, indicating these cartridges were fired in the same firearm. Courtesy Ruthven National Park Collection, Archaeological Services, Inc.

participants and which individual trees they used for cover (McWhorter 1986, 1991). This makes the Siege Area one of the most thoroughly documented battle sites in the West. While the archaeological evidence is somewhat biased due to the intensity of post-battle occupation and site use, the nature and distribution of archaeological data does agree with the historic documentation. The distribution of .45–70 cartridge cases demonstrates that the army reached the Siege Area under fire and then entrenched. There was little movement of the soldiers and volunteers after that episode.

The incoming Nez Perce-related cartridge case and bullet distributions indicate the soldiers were definitely under fire from most directions during the remainder of the battle. While extensive, the Nez Perce fire appears to have originated from a limited number of firearms; four different .44-caliber rim fire Henry or Model 1866 Winchesters, one or more Sharps, a Spencer, captured .45–70 army weapons, and .50–70 Springfields, as well as at least one Remington Rolling Block rifle.

The army believed they were under fire by numerous Nez Perce during the latter part of 9 August and during 10 August. However, in their chronicling of the battle, the Nez Perce indicated that less than 15 warriors kept the army at bay during 10 August. The cartridge case evidence suggests at least eight firearms used by the Nez Perce were employed against the soldiers. This number represents about half the number of Nez Perce identified by Yellow Wolf (Haines 1991:99) and is certainly in agreement with the Nez Perce accounts. It is also consistent with the percentage of army firearms represented in the archaeological recorded as discussed previously.

The Howitzer Incident

Previously reviewed battlefield history noted that while soldiers were digging in at the Siege Area, a 12-pounder Mountain Howitzer mounted on a Prairie carriage and drawn by six mules went into action. It fired two rounds before it was overrun by the Nez Perce. Archeological evidence of the Howitzer episode consists of a military style D-ring from a saddle girth, a lynch pin from a cannon carriage wheel, and cartridge cases and bullets found high on the slope west of the Siege Area. Fragments of sabot strapping for the explosive shells were recovered and a few additional possible fragments of strapping were found in 1991 in the same area.

The most conclusive evidence of combat action in the area is the firearms data. Twenty .45–70-caliber cartridge cases from five different Springfield rifles were found clustered in the vicinity of the so-called howitzer pit. One gun fired 11 rounds, one fired 4 rounds, two guns fired 2 rounds each, and one gun fired only 1 round. Other firearms-related artifacts consist of unidentified bullet fragments, .45–70 bullets, .50–70 bullets, .40 Sharps bullets, a .44 or .45 Sharps bullet, and .44 Winchester or Henry bullets. A variety of cartridge cases were also found including nine .44 rim fire cases from five individual Henry or Model 1866 Winchester guns and fourteen .50–70 cases from eleven Springfields. Two of those cases, fired from the same gun, are .45–70-caliber that split when fired in the larger caliber gun. In addition, a single percussion cap and the ramrod to a Model 1841 "Mississippi" rifle were recovered in this vicinity.

Since there were only six soldiers with the howitzer, it may be logical to assume that the .45–70 cases represent the soldiers and their position. If the ammunition mule attendant and the civilian guide were near the howitzer then a total of eight men were in the vicinity. The ammunition mule attendant may have been armed with a shotgun. Assuming that the cases that were not .45–70-caliber represented the Nez Perce combatants, at least 18 different Nez Perce fired on the soldiers. Eleven were armed with .50–70 Springfields, five with .44-caliber Henrys or Model 1866 Winchesters and at least one each with a .40-caliber Sharps and a .44- or .45-caliber Sharps firearm. It is also necessary to consider that some Nez Perce were armed with captured .45–70 Springfields and perhaps some cases actually represent additional Nez Perce instead of one of the six soldiers attached to the cannon.

Nez Perce cases and bullets were found all around the zone of the cases attributed to the soldiers. This suggests the soldiers were nearly surrounded by the Nez Perce. There is limited evidence of movement found among the cartridge case distribution. Five .45–70 cases, all fired in the same soldier-associated gun, run in a line north of the main cluster of cases. In his official report of the battle, Gibbon (Haines 1991:76) states that Sergeant Daly and Sergeant Fredrics as well as Corporal Sayles made the best resistance possible

before they were overrun. Perhaps the 11 cases and the evidence of movement of that gun represent one of those soldiers.

Yellow Wolf's (McWhorter 1991:149–50) account of the howitzer incident identifies six, mounted Nez Perce as responding to the cannon movement. Yellow Wolf and the other warriors had been near the Siege Area when the howitzer was spotted. They rode up the hill and fired at the soldiers killing one and driving the remainder away. Wattes Kunnin (McWhorter 1991:149) was also involved in the attack on the howitzer. He described the incident by noting two Nez Perce came down the hill towards the cannon, while he rode up the hill. When he arrived at the cannon, only one soldier, possibly Corporal Sale, was left. He was firing, possibly over his shoulder, at the attackers before he was killed. Yellow Wolf (McWhorter 1991:150–51) thought they had run off about 10–11 soldiers in the howitzer and pack mule fight. He also believed that about 30 Nez Perce were gathered around the captured ammunition crates after the fight. The time interval between the fight and Yellow Wolf's interview with McWhorter may have exaggerated the total numbers of individuals involved in his mind and it is possible that he collapsed two separate but closely spaced incidents into a single episode in the re-telling. Still, Yellow Wolf appears to have remembered the ratio of Nez Perce to soldiers fairly well, if the archeological firearms data portrays the fight accurately.

Gibbon (Haines 1991:76) suggested the private soldiers, who were recent recruits and escaped the howitzer fight, were cowards who fled without a fight. The cartridge case evidence does point to limited firing by three individuals who had .45–70 Springfields. Assuming that all .45–70 cases represent soldiers and not Springfields in Nez Perce hands, the cartridge case distribution patterns indicate the soldiers were outnumbered at least two-to-one by the Nez Perce. The Nez Perce brought at least 18 firearms to bear against the soldiers, including five repeaters. They also surrounded those using the .45–70 Springfields. The cowardice issue aside, the soldiers with the howitzer were surrounded by a force of superiorly armed Nez Perce. Their choice seems simple, fight to the death or retreat in the face of superior forces, which was the choice they made.

The archaeological evidence begs the question of how so many Nez Perce warriors managed to surround the six or so soldiers so quickly, and in a manner that

FIGURE 19.5. Viewshed or weapons fan analysis of the Howitzer site. The shaded area shows the view of the howitzer crew. Note that they could not see to the north, northwest, or west of their location; the direction that the attacking Nez Perce used to overrun the crew and force the abandonment of the gun. Courtesy Ruthven National Park Collection, Archaeological Services Inc.

they were surprised and driven off. The steep hillside where the cannon was positioned provides a commanding view of the countryside. When Geographic Information System (GIS) viewshed or terrain analysis is applied to a landscape model of the area a surprising result emerges. Viewshed, or as the military terms it, Weapons Fan analysis, uses computer power to calculate what can be seen from a specific location at specific heights above the ground. In effect, this analysis can illustrate what a person using a weapon can see from a given position and for specified distances. In the case of the Howitzer Incident, the viewshed shows the soldiers manning the cannon could see great distances to the east and south, but their view to the northwest and west was limited to some 50 m to 100 m because of intervening terrain (fig. 19.5). The Nez Perce oral history accounts note that the warriors, some mounted, attacked from the north and likely the west. The Nez Perce were able to get to within less than 100 m of the soldiers before they were discovered. This is well within rifle range of the weapons wielded by the Nez Perce and they not only outnumbered the soldiers, but they surprised them with superior fire power. That is what caused the loss of the cannon, superior fire power, superior numbers, and the effect of surprise, and not cowardice on the part of the soldiers.

CONCLUSIONS

At the Big Hole Battlefield, archaeological evidence melded nicely with historical documentation and Nez Perce oral tradition. The archaeological evidence presented on the fight is usually supported by the testimony of the soldiers and Nez Perce battle participants. With the eyewitness accounts available it might seem the archaeological data would be redundant or superfluous. The archaeological database is important precisely for this reason. The recovery of archaeological information from the Big Hole Battlefield can be directly correlated with historical accounts. On the one hand, correlation of archaeological data and interpretations with the historical accounts provides a means to assess the accuracy of the interpretations drawn from the archaeological record. In essence, if the interpretations of the archaeological record demonstrate positive correlations with the historical record, then the archaeological interpretations are strengthened. A second point is that where the historical record is incomplete or even silent on individual movements, archaeological data has the opportunity to elucidate those levels of individual movements or participation.

Archaeological studies of historic sites are often used in a confirmation role. Validation studies have been undertaken to determine correlation levels of archaeological and historical data. It is at this point that the value of historical archaeology becomes apparent. Historical archeology can add new details to the story, but its real value is in the fact that it is not history, but anthropology. Historical archeology is a means to study the recent past with an eye toward gaining a greater understanding of social and cultural behavior. In the case of battlefields, the focus of the study becomes cultural approaches to conflict. With the Big Hole, as well as other Indian Wars battle sites, the opportunity is to study the particulars and general trends of disparate cultures in conflict (Fox and Scott 1991).

Archaeological investigations at Little Bighorn Battlefield National Monument, as an example, provided new perspectives on various elements of the 1876 Battle of the Little Bighorn. Those investigations led to developing a Post-Civil War Battlefield Model (Fox and Scott 1991). The Big Hole Battlefield study demonstrates the utility of that model. Combatant positions have been identified, firearms identified and

quantified, and the sequence of events has been eluci-
dated, history enhanced, and in some areas revised.

Fox and Scott's (1991) definition of a Post-Civil War
Battlefield Pattern is predicated upon an axiom basic
to archaeological investigation. Human behavior is
patterned. Behavioral patterns are expressed through
individual behaviors constrained by the norms, values,
sanctions, and statuses governing the group within
which the individual operates. Among standing
armies, military groups are rigidly defined and hier-
archically ordered; they are less well-defined among
guerrilla forces, and individual behavioral roles are
structured accordingly. Thus, the tactical operations
of warfare, both defensive and offensive, precipitate
individual behaviors that are carried out within and
on behalf of the military unit to which the individual
belongs. War tactics, which represent patterned behavior, include establishment of positions and the deployment and movement of combatants. The residues of
tactics in warfare, artifacts, features, and their contextual relationships, should also be patterned and reflect
details of battlefield behavior. That behavior is clearly
reflected at the Big Hole. The distribution of army
cartridge cases and bullets attests to the structured
organization of the military unit at the beginning of
the battle. The archeological data provided evidence
that Gibbon organized his command into wings and
deployed and employed them according to the prescribed tactics of the day. The archaeological evidence
also demonstrates that Gibbon's tactical organization
dissolved after the attack on the village. Some sem-
blance of order was restored during the initial stages
of the retreat through the willows, but that order
disintegrated the deeper into the willows and swampy
ground the command retreated. Gibbon regained
control of his command when they reached the Siege
Area. Order and tactical resolve are evident in the
organization of the entrenchments and the minimal
movement of individuals in those entrenchments.

The archeological data also tell the tale of the Nez
Perce. Their combat strategy was much more individually oriented and the artifact distributions definitely reflect this. The firearms artifacts demonstrate
the Nez Perce were armed with a variety of firearms,
perhaps 16 different types. Most appear to have been
cartridge firearm types, but older muzzle-loading firearms, including at least two Model 1841 "Mississippi"
rifles were present. The Nez Perce dispersed during the

initial attack, taking cover and refuge east, north, and
south of their village as the situation dictated. Rallied
by their leaders, the warriors fought from available
cover, firing into Gibbon's exposed position in the village. Once Gibbon began his retreat, the Nez Perce
pressed the attack individually as well as through sniping activities. The individual fighting style of the Nez
Perce served them well in the combat on the retreat
line. They were able to keep pressure on the command
from numerous sides causing a tactical disintegra-
tion of Gibbon's command structure. Gibbon had no
formally identified enemy to focus his fire upon thus
disrupting the ability of the command to function in
a normal military mode.

Even with Gibbon's more organized defense of the
Siege Area, the Nez Perce were able to keep the command at bay with less than 15 warriors through 10
August. The archeological evidence identifies the position of the command as well as positions of the Nez
Perce. The warriors took advantage of the terrain and
available cover to fire into Gibbon's entrenchments.
The archeological data demonstrate the culturally
prescribed and different fighting behaviors of the two
combatant groups. Thus when individual patterns are
integrated, unit patterns emerge and this patterning is
recognizable on the battlefield.

The integration of individual patterns provided the
basis on which unit patterns were constructed. This
involved tracing positions and movements but at the
unit pattern level. In effect, the deployment of combat
units was identified and traced archeologically.

The Battle of the Big Hole provides a relevant
application of the Post-Civil War Battlefield Pattern
for several reasons. The artifact inventory, including
ammunition components, was readily amenable to the
kind of analyses necessary in establishing the pattern.
The Big Hole battle furnishes a test of the Post-Civil
War Battlefield Pattern as it applies to two types of
military organization virtually at polar opposites, the
rigid military structure and the comparatively unstruc-
tured, individually based tactics of the Nez Perce.

It is also important to reiterate that these data exist
in a recognizable form in space on a field of battle,
where organization is supposedly unlikely to exist. In
this case, those organizations and culturally opposing forces are recognizable. This study then becomes
another step in defining the archaeological aspect of
the anthropology of war.

A-tent or wedge tent. An A-tent consisted of a 16 ft square of material placed over a ridgepole. The resulting inverted 'V' shaped shelter could house up to six soldiers.

Accidental death. Death as the result of an accident without premeditation, malice, or negligence or a reckless act.

Ammunition impact area. Portion of a target range where ammunition hits the ground. See "beaten zone."

Amplitude "time slices." Computer-processing technique that correlates and compares GPR reflection amplitudes in all profiles within a grid.

Antemortem. Before death.

Anthropology, shipwreck. Used in some academic circles to emphasize an anthropological approach to research. Maritime and underwater archaeology are more commonly used terms.

Archaeological region. The sustaining area that contains a series of interrelated (contemporary) human communities sharing a single cultural eco-system (see "region") (Sharer and Ashmore 2003:124).

Archaeology, marine. Archaeology associated with the ocean environment usually, but not always, involving shipwrecks.

Archaeology, maritime. A comprehensive term encompassing archaeology associated with the oceans, inland waters, lakes and rivers; water-related skills and trade; and maritime cultures. The resources are not necessarily underwater.

Archaeology, nautical. Archaeology that normally focuses on ships and their construction and operation.

Archaeology, underwater. A general term for archaeology conducted underwater on any type of site,

regardless of age or affiliation; historic or prehistoric, and fresh or salt water.

Army, organization of or military structure (See www .nps.gov/archive/gett/gettour/armorg for structure of U.S. military at time of American Civil War)

- Squad or mess. Smallest unit of the army, commanded by a sergeant (SGT). Ideally at least two squads composed a platoon.

- Platoon. Commanded by a lieutenant (LT), at least two platoons were in a company. Platoons were organized into squads led by a sergeant or a corporal.

- Company. Ideally led by a captain (CAPT), there were a minimum of four companies in a battalion. At various times this has been an administrative unit and a tactical unit. "A company is to be formed in two ranks, at one pace distance, with the tallest men in the rear, and both ranks sized, with the shortest men of each in the center. A company thus drawn up is to be divided into two sections or platoons; the captain to take post on the right of the first platoon, covered by a serjeant [sic]; the lieutenant on the right of the second platoon, also covered by a serjeant; the ensign four paces behind the centre of the company"(Riling 1966:6–7). Company size varied dramatically from 200 men in the British Guards to as few as 20–25 in militia.

- Battalion. Led by a lieutenant Colonel (LTC), there were a minimum of two battalions in a regiment. During many wars, battalion and regiment were used interchangeably because the regiment was under strength. "A body of foot composed of several companies, armed with firelock, bayonet, and sword. In the late war [Seven Years War] no particular number of companies was ascertained to compose a battalion" (Simes 1768). ". . . each regiment consisting of more than one hundred and sixty files, is to be formed into two battalions . . . When a regiment is reduced to one hundred and sixty files, it is to be formed in one battalion" (Riling 1966:8). "A body of foot composed of four or eight companies" (Hoyt 1811:360).

• Regiment. Led by a Colonel (COL), and ideally composed of a minimum of two battalions and thus of at least eight companies. A regiment, "battalion, or corps, are the same thing, except that some regiments have more battalions than one" (Simes 1768). For the infantryman, the most important unit. At full strength it numbered over 1000 officers and men, although it was often smaller because of attrition through combat or disease. At the time of the Civil War a regiment consisted of ten companies of 100 men each when at full strength (www.nps.gov/archive/gett/gettour/armorg.htm).

• Brigade. Led by a Brigadier General (BG) and composed of at least two regiments. Primary organization used by commanders in a battle. Often advanced or defended positions in cooperation with fellow brigades.

• Division. Composed of at least two brigades and led by a Major General (MGEN) or a brigadier general. During the eighteenth century, a tactical formation composed of two companies was also called a division.

• Corps. Composed of at least two divisions and led by a lieutenant general (LTGEN). Largest single organization of an army. A corps in the U.S. Army at the time of the Civil War included three infantry divisions, and an artillery brigade.

• Army. Composed of either divisions, or corps and led by a Lieutenant General or General (GEN). In the U.S. at the time of the Civil War, each army was a structured organization that included a general headquarters, infantry, artillery, cavalry, signalmen, engineers, quartermaster and commissary departments (nps.gov/archive/gett/gettour/armorg.htm).

Artillery. "In a general sense signifies all sorts of great guns or cannon, mortars, howitzers, petards, and the like together with all the apparatus and stores" (Duane 1810:16). Artillery is divided into field artillery and siege and garrison artillery. Usually organized by regiments, a company is referred to as a battery (nps.gov/archive/gett/gettour/armourg.htm). Artillerymen carried no weapons of their own but were part of a team that operated a single weapon, the cannon. Requiring special training to perform duties, each man perform a task to help move, load, aim, and fire the cannon. Horses typically pulled the cannon from site to site (nps.gov/archive/gett/getteducation/bcast-5.htm).

Artillery, basic ordnance categories.

• Bolt. "An elongated projectile, usually made of solid iron, without a cavity or fuse. Most often a rifled projectile" (Melton and Pawl 1994:10).

• Canister. "A cylinder of tin, iron, or sometimes lead, with a removable thin iron top . . . The cylinder had metal balls, most often made of lead or iron, which were arranged in rows . . . designed to be used in close range against enemy troops" (Melton and Pawl 1994:10).

• Case shot. "Similar to the common shell except that the walls of the projectile are thinner . . . bursting charge usually located in thin metal container usually made of tin or iron . . . internal cavity was filled with lead or iron balls in a sulphur or pitch matrix" (Melton and Pawl 1994:10).

• Shell. "A hollow projectile filled only with a bursting charge of black powder. Sometimes called a common shell" (Melton and Pawl 1994:12).

• Solid shot. "A solid iron projectile without the ability to contain a bursting charge or fuse. Commonly called a bolt in rifled ordnances. Designed to knock down fortifications . . . or to be fired at lines or columns of troops" (Melton and Pawl 1994:12).

Autonomous underwater vehicle (AUV). Self-propelled, untethered craft that can follow a preprogrammed course or set of instructions, then return to the surface or a predetermined location. AUVs can carry a variety of instrumentation, including equipment for detecting and mapping shipwrecks.

Ball. "In the military art, comprehends all sorts of balls and bullets for fire-arms, from the cannon to the pistol" (Duane 1810:30–31).

Battlefield landscape. "The landscape over which the armies contended" (NPS 1995:Section 5).

Bayonet. "A kind of triangular dagger, made with a hollow handle, and a shoulder, to fix on the muzzle of a firelock or musket, so that neither the charging nor firing is prevented by its being fixed on the piece" (Duane 1810:52). A long, pointed blade mounted on the end of a musket. The bayonet allowed men to attack and defend themselves when their musket was unloaded.

Bivouac. A temporary encampment. "A night guard, performed by the whole army, when there is any kind of danger from the enemy" (Simes 1768). "When army does not encamp, but lies under arms all night, it is said to bivouac" (Duane 1810:54; Hoyt 1811:369). Often used to refer to an overnight camp.

Boves. Chalk quarries beneath Arras, France, excavated from the tenth century onwards and used for various purposes. The network of galleries served as a shelter and rallying point for Allied troops in 1917 as they awaited an attack in the Battle of Arras.

"California" stove, oven or furnace. A colloquial term used by Civil War soldiers to describe a tent heating device where a firepit is a hole in the ground and the flue consists of a trench buried beneath the tent floor. Some California stoves may have acted as radiant heating devices.

Caltrop. "A piece of iron having 4 points, all disposed in a triangular form; so that 3 of them always rest upon the ground, and the 4th stands upwards in a perpendicular direction. . . . They are scattered over the ground and passages where the enemy is expected to march, especially the cavalry" (Duane 1810:71).

Camp. "The spot of ground occupied by an army, for a night or more; and where they pitch their tents" (Simes 1768). " . . . there should not be more ground occupied by the camp of a body of men, in front, than the extent of their line when drawn out in order of battle" (Duane 1810:72–73).

Canister. "Are always cylindrical . . . antipersonnel projectiles used at short range. . . . Canister contain no explosive charge. They are usually made with thin sheet metal sides that disintegrate as the canister is fired" (Bell 2003:90). Case shot was the term in the 17th and 18th centuries.

Cannon. "Pieces of ordnance, imply all sorts of great guns or machines for discharging large bullets" (Hoyt 1811:377).

Cantonment. A large camp made up of the encampments of several regiments. A cantonment can be spread across a large area.

Cartridge (cartouche) box (pouch). "A case of wood or turned tin, covered with leather, holding thirty rounds of powder and ball; is wore upon a belt and hangs a little higher than the pocket-hole" (Simes 1768).

Cavalry. Cavalrymen traveled on horseback. A cavalryman carried three different weapons: a saber, a carbine, and a pistol, as well as personal equipment. Often identified as the eyes of the army serving as scouts or screens for an advancing army as well as actually engaging in combat (nps.gov/archive/gett/getteducatio/bcast01/gcast-5.htm).

Chain-of-custody. The paper trail that shows that a piece of evidence can be accounted for at all times between the time it was collected and the time it is used in court.

Class characteristics. Features that the manufacturer intended to be present in the firearm. They include such things as the caliber of bullets and general rifling characteristics imparted on them by the responsible firearm.

Collateral damage. Negative impact on a human community brought about by the actions of a co-resident military force. Such damage is often measured in terms of the destruction of buildings, the decimation of fields and livestock, and the loss of civilian life.

Complex resistivity. Quantity observed when analyzing the response of materials to alternating electric fields. Polarization within the medium results in the voltage and applied current being out of phase, that is, their ratio becomes a complex number with real (resistivity) and imaginary (reactivity) parts; also known as spectral IP.

Crimean oven. Radiant heating device consisting of an aboveground firebox attached to a flue buried beneath the ground. The top of the flue was covered in sheet iron. A tent or several tents were erected over the flue. This heating device was adopted by the medical corps as a method of heating hospital tents.

Crimes against humanity. Widespread attacks against civilian populations, including murder, rape, torture, deportation, imprisonment, and other inhumane acts that intentionally cause great suffering or serious injury (physical or mental).

Cultural landscape. "Geographic area, including both cultural and natural resources and the wildlife or domestic animals therein, associated with a historic event, activity, or person exhibiting other cultural or aesthetic values" (NPS 1994:1).

Daubert v. Merrell Dow Pharmaceuticals, Inc. A 1993 Supreme Court ruling that outlines the criteria on which expert testimony will be allowed.

Deep dugout. World War I underground (wooden) shelter dug behind the front line where soldiers could sleep, arrange meetings, take a rest or be cared for if wounded.

Depositional process. Activity that results in the creation or modification of an archeological site.

Dielectric permitivity. Quantity that describes how an electric field affects and is affected by a medium, and is determined by the ability of a material to polarize in response to the field and thus the ability of the material to transmit (or "permit") an electric field.

Diffraction. Bending of electromagnetic waves as they pass around corners or through holes smaller than the wavelengths of the waves themselves.

Direct measurement system (DMS). A relatively simple system for accurately and efficiently mapping an archaeological site. Measurements from three or more reference points to an object or feature on the site are converted by computer software to x-y-z locations on a three-dimensional site map.

Duckboard. Slatted wooden structure that was placed in the bottom of a World War I trench, on top of an inverted A-frame, or on muddy grounds; in an attempt to keep the feet dry.

Earthworks, glossary of terms and features

• Abatis. "Formed by cutting down many entire trees, the branches of which are turned towards an enemy, and as much as possible entangled one into another" (Duane 1810:1). "A row of obstructions made up of closely spaced, felled trees with branches trimmed to points and interlaced" (Robinson 1977:197). "The trunks of the trees are sometimes buried in the ground" (Hoyt 1811:347).

• Banquette. "A kind of step made on the rampart of a work near the parapet, for the troops to stand upon in order to fire over the parapet; it is generally 3 feet high when double, and 1 ½ when single and about 3 feet broad and 4 ½ feet lower than the parapet [top]" (Duane 1810:173).

• Barracks. "Building to lodge Officers and soldiers in" (Simes 1768).

• Bastion. "Projection in the enceinte, made up of two faces and two flanks, which enabled the garrison

to defend the ground adjacent to the enceinte" (Robinson 1977:197). "A Bastion is a part of the inner inclosure of a fortification, making an angle towards the field, and consists of two faces, two flanks, and an opening towards the center of the place, called the Gorge" (Simes 1768).

• Beaten zone. "The pattern formed by the rounds within the cone of fire striking the ground or the target. The size and shape of the beaten zone changes when the range to the target changes or when the machine gun is fired into different types of terrain. On uniformly sloping or level terrain, the beaten zone is long and narrow. As the range to the target increases, the beaten zone becomes shorter and wider. When fire is delivered into terrain sloping down and away from the gun, the beaten zone becomes longer. When fire is delivered into rising terrain, the beaten zone becomes shorter" (U.S. Army 1984:7–2).

• Berm. "In fortification, is a little space or path, of about 3, 4, 6, or 8 feet broad, according to the height and breadth of the works, between the ditch and the parapet, when made of turf, to prevent the earth from rolling into the ditch" (Duane 1810:34). In modern (and incorrect) usage, berm now refers to a mound.

• Blockhouse. "This name is sometimes given to a brick or stone building on a bridge, or the brink of a river, serving not only for its defence, but for the command of the river . . ." (Duane 1810:55). "A small fortified building used as a place of retreat or as a flanking device in forts. It was generally constructed from logs, although other materials, such as earth and stone, were commonly used in conjunction with wood" (Robinson 1977:197). "A kind of wooden fort built with square timber bullet proof" (Hoyt 1811:369).

• Bombproof. "A structure designed to provide security against artillery fire" (Robinson 1977:197). A bomb was a shell, and in "gunnery, are hollow iron balls to throw out of mortars or howitzers with a fuze hole of about an inch diameter, to load them with powder, and to receive the fuze" (Duane 1810:633). "Powder-Magazine . . . ought to be . . . bombproof" (Smith 1779:155).

• Breastwork. See parapet (Duane 1810:60; Hoyt 1811:370).

• Bulwark. "The ancient name for bastion or rampart" (Duane 1810:69).

- Caponier. "Passage made from one work to another, of 10 or 12 feet wide, and about five feet deep, covered on each side by a parapet, terminating in a glacis. Caponiers are sometimes covered" (Duane 1810:80).

- Casemate, or casement. "A work made under the rampart, like a cellar or cave, with loopholes to place guns in it, and is bombproof" (Simes 1768). "A vault, or arch of mason-work, in that part of the flank of a bastion which is next the curtain, made to defend the ditch, and the face of the opposite bastion" (Duane 1810:86).

- Cavalier. "A work raised generally within the body of the place, ten or twelve feet higher than the rest of the works; their most common situation is within the bastion, and made much in the same form" (Simes 1768).

- Chevaux-de-Frise. "Large joints or beams, stuck full of wooden pins, armed with iron, to stop breaches, or to secure a passage of a camp against the enemy's cavalry" (Simes 1768). "The body or beam of a chevaux-de-frize is generally made 9 feet long, and 6 inches square, and weights 41 pounds. The spears are 33 in number, weighing 2 lb. each, and 5 feet long, and 1 ¼ inches square. They are placed 9 ½ inches asunder" (Duane 1810:94).

- Counterguard. "Small ramparts, with parapets and ditches, to cover some part of the body of the place" (Duane 1810:106).

- Countermine. "Used when the besiegers have, notwithstanding the opposition of the besieged, passed the foss [sic], and put the miner to the foot of the rampart. They are of two sorts, being either made when the bastion is raised, or afterwards, when it is attacked . . . pits sunk deep in the ground, where the miner is supposed to be, from whence they run out branches, in search of the enemies mine, to frustrate the effect of it" (Simes 1768).

- Counterscarp. "The outside of a ditch, opposite to the parapet of the work, behind the ditch" (Simes 1768). "The exterior side of the ditch-the side away from the body of the place" (Robinson 1977:198). ". . . exterior talus, or slope of the ditch, on the farther side from the place, and facing it. Sometimes the covert way and glacis are meant by this expression" (Duane 1810:107).

- Covered, covert, way. "A space of ground, level with the country, about three or four fathoms wide, covered by a parapet, which goes quite round the place" (Simes 1768).

- Cresset. "Any great light upon a beach, lighthouse, or watch-tower" (Duane 1810:110).

- Curtain. "Part of the rampart of a place . . . between the flanks of two bastions, and is the best defended of any part of the rampart" (Simes 1768). ". . . section of a bastioned fortification that lies between two bastions" (Robinson 1977:198).

- Dead space. "Places where the soldier's waist [while walking out from the gun] falls below the gunner's line of aim, dead space exists" (U.S. Army 1984:8–6). In effect, dead space is a zone not covered by direct fire.

- Demibastion. "Half bastion, is a work with only one face and one flank" (Duane 1810:116).

- Demilune. "Half-Moon . . . an outwork that has two faces which form a salient angle, the gorge of which resembles a crescent" (Hoyt 1811:405). See ravelin (Duane 1810:176; Hoyt 1811:404).

- Detached work. "Totally unconnected with any of the works of the place, by any covert way" (Duane 1810:196).

- Ditch. In fortification, "a large deep trench made round each work" (Duane 1810:176), or "A wide, deep trench around a defensive work, the material from the excavation of which was used to form the ramparts" (Robinson 1977:198). Fosse and moat are other terms for ditch.

- Dugout. "Deep holes in the trenches . . . supposed to be shell proof" (Empey 1917:289).

- Embrasure. "Openings made in the flanks of a fortification, or in the breastwork of a battery, about two feet and a half within, eight or nine without, and three feet from the bottom, for part of each gun to enter and fire through" (Simes 1768).

- En barbette. "Arrangement for cannons in which they were mounted on high platforms or carriages so that they fired over a parapet instead of through embrasures" (Robinson 1977:198).

- Enciente. "The wall or rampart, which surrounds a place; it is, properly, composed of bastions and curtains" (Simes 1768). ". . . works of fortification-walls, ramparts, and Parapets—that enclose a castle, fort, or fortress" (Robinson 1977:198).

- Enfilade. "A work is said to be enfiladed, when a gun can be fired into it, so that the shot may go all along the inside of the parapet" (Simes 1768). ". . . places, which may be scoured by the enemy's shot, along their whole length" (Duane 1810:136).

- Face, of the bastion. "Section of any bastion between the flanked angle and the shoulder angle" (Robinson 1977:198).

- Fascine. "A kind of faggot, made of branches, tied in two or more places, of about six or eight inches diameter. They serve to keep up the earth in trenches . . . instead of stone or brick walls" (Simes 1768).

- Field fortification. "fortifications de campagne," French. Consists in the art of fortifying, constructing, attacking, and defending all sorts of temporary field works during a campaign" (Duane 1810:192).

- Firing port. See loophole.

- Firing step. A low wooden bench was placed on the banquette to enable soldiers to fire over the parapet then reload in greater safety. See banquette.

- Flank of the bastion. "A part between the face and curtain. The flank of one bastion serves to defend the ditch before the curtain and face of the opposite bastion" (Simes 1768).

- Flank (-er, -ing). "That part of a work which defends another work, along the outside of its parapet" (Simes 1768). " . . . any parts of a work, which defend another work along the outsides of its parapet" (Duane 1810:177).

- Fleche. "Work of two faces, often constructed before the glacis of a fortified place, when threatened with a siege in order to keep the enemy as long at a distance as possible" (Duane 1810:177).

- Fort. "A small fortification, made in a pass near a river, or at some distance from a fortified town, to guard the pass, or to prevent the approach of ships, or an enemy by land: they are made of different figures, some made small, and some greater" (Simes 1768). "A small fortified place, environed on all sides with a ditch, rampart, and parapet" (Duane 1810:170).

- Fortification. "A general name for any work made to oppose an enemy" (Simes 1768).

- Fortress. "A general name for all places that are fortified by nature or art" (Simes 1768).

- Fosse. "A work established for the defense of a land or maritime frontier, of an approach to a town, or of a pass or river" (Robinson 1977:203). Also ditch or moat.

- Fougass. "In mining, a small mine, from 6 to 8 feet under ground: It is generally placed under the glacis or dry ditches" (Duane 1810:198). In more recent times, a buried barrel of fuel detonated by explosive to spread a fire cone onto attackers.

- Foxhole. A one- or two-man fighting position.

- Fraise. "Stakes of palisades, placed horizontally on the outward slope of a rampart of turf, to present the work being taken by surprise [sic]" (Simes 1768). "A row of palisades planted horizontally or obliquely in the ground at the edge of a ditch or other earthwork" (Robinson 1977:203).

- Full bastion. When the level ground within is even with the rampart; that is, when the inside is quite level, the parapet being only more elevated than the rest" (Simes 1768).

- Gate. "A main entrance in the enceinte of a castle, fort, or fortress" (Robinson 1977:203).

- Glacis. "That part of a fortification, beyond the covert-way, to which it serves as a parapet, and terminates towards the field in an easy slope" (Simes 1768). ". . . the part beyond the covert way, to which it serves as a parapet and terminates towards the field in an easy slope" (Duane 1810:177). The glacis was designed to cover the lower fortification elements and bring attackers onto a plane swept by defensive grazing fire. The slope caused shot to bounce over the defenses. The term is still applied to the sloping front of an armored vehicle (Alger 1985:153).

- Gorge. "That part next the body of the place, where there is no rampart or parapet" (Simes 1768). ". . . of a bastion, is the interval between the extremity of one flank and that of the other" (Duane 1810:177). The entrance to a bastion or a fort.

- Gunslit. See firing port, loophole.

- Headlog. A log placed on the parapet, but raised above it, creating an opening to fire through without exposing the head.

- Hornwork. "Is composed of a front, and two branches. The front is made into two half bastions and a curtain" (Simes 1768).

- Intrenchments [sic]. "Are all sorts of works, made to fortify a post against an enemy. A post is intrenched, when it is covered with a foss and parapets" (Simes 1768). "A fieldwork comprised of a ditch and an earth parapet" (Robinson 1977:203).

- Liles. "Pits three feet deep were dug, narrowing gradually towards the bottom; embedded into them were smoothed logs as thick as a man's thigh, with their tops ends sharpened and charred, so that only four inches projected above ground. To keep these logs firmly and securely in position earth was thrown into the pits and stamped down hard, to a depth of one foot, the rest of the pit being filled with twigs and brushwood to hide the trap. These were planted in sequences of eight rows three feet apart. The soldiers called them "lilies" from their resemblance to the flower" (Julius Caesar cited in Keppie 1989:183). The only archaeological examples are found at Rough Castle, on the Antonine Wall, Scotland, where the pits were arranged in such a way as to direct foot traffic away from the gates. The modern equivalent is a pit with punji stakes.

• Line of defense. "The distance between the salient angle of the bastion, and the opposite flank; that is, it is the face produced to the flank . . . may extend (though not exceed) 150 fathoms" (Duane 1810:172).

Loophole. "Square or oblong holes made in the wall to fire through with muskets" (Simes 1768). Loopholes "are either square, or oblong holes, made in the wall, to fire though with musquets [sic]. They are generally 8 or 9 inches long, 6 or 7 inches wide within and 2 or 3 feet without; so that every man may fire from them direct in front, or oblique to right or left" (Duane 1810:178).

• Lunette. "A small work raised sometimes in the middle of the foss before the curtain, forming an angle, its terre-plein rising but a little about the surface of the water, about twelve feet broad, with a parapet of eighteen feet. There is another sort of lunette which is larger, and raised to cover the faces of the half moon; and is likewise composed of two faces; a longer and a shorter" (Simes 1768).

• Magazine. "A place in which stores are kept, or arms, ammunition, provisions" (Duane 1810:357). ". . . place for the storage of gunpowder, arms, provisions, or goods" (Robinson 1977:203).

• Moat. "Ditch, or foss, is a depth or trench round the rampart of a place to defend it and prevent surprises. The brink of the moat next the rampart is called the scarp; and that opposite, on the other side, is called the counterscarp, which forms a re-entering angle before the center of the curtain. A dry moat round a place that is large and has a strong garrison, is preferable to one full of water, because the passage

may be disputed inch by inch" (Simes 1768). See fosse or ditch.

• Outwork. "A work inside the glacis but outside the body of the place" (Robinson 1977:204).

• Palisade. A kind of stakes made of strong split wood, of about nine feet long, three feet deep in the round, in rows about six inches asunder. They are placed in the covert-way, at three feet from, and parallel to the parapet or side of the glacis, to secure it from being surprised" (Simes 1768). "Palisadoes, in fortification, [are] stakes made of strong split wood, about nine feet long, six or seven inches square, three feet deep in the ground, in rows about 2 ½ or three inches asunder, placed in the covert-way, at three feet from and parallel to the parapet or side of the glacis" (Duane 1810:503). "A high fence, for defensive enclosure, made of poles or palings planted in the ground from six to nine inches apart" (Robinson 1977:204).

• Parados. "The rear wall of a trench" (Empey 1917:303).

• Parallel. "At a siege, signify the trenches or lines made parallel to the defence . . . deep trenches, fifteen or eighteen feet wide, joining the several attacks together. They serve to place the guard of the trenches in, to be at hand to support the workmen when attacked" (Simes 1768).

• Parapet. "An elevation of earth, designed for covering the soldiers from the enemy's cannon, or small shot; wherefore, its thickness is from eighteen to twenty foot, its height is six on the inside, and four or five on the side next the country. It is raised on the rampart, and has a slope, called the superior talus, to the glacis of the parapet. . . . The height of the parapet being six foot on the inside, it has a banquet or two for the soldier who defend it, to mount upon, that they discover the country better; as likewise the foss and counterscarp, to fire as they find occasion" (Simes 1768). "A parapet, to resist cannon should never be less than 18 feet thick in earth and 8 or 9 in masonry. A wall need only be two feet thick in masonry to resist musketry. The parapet should always be 4 ½ feet above the banquette, and 7 ½ or 8 feet above the rampart, or terreplein" (Duane 1810:195). "In fortification, a work of earth or masonry forming a protective wall over which defenders fired their weapons" (Robinson 1977:204).

- Rampart. "An elevation of earth raised along the faces of any work of ten or fifteen feet high, to cover the inner part of that work against the fire of any enemy" (Simes 1768). "A mass of earth formed with material excavated from the ditch to protect the enclosed area from artillery fire and to elevate defenders to a commanding position overlooking the approaches to a form or fortress" (Robinson 1977:204).
- Ravelin. "Works raised on the counterscarp before the curtain of a place and serve to cover the gate, and bridges of a town. They consist of two faces, forming a salliant angle, and are defended by the faces of the neighbouring bastions" (Simes 1768). "A work placed before the curtain to cover it, and prevent the flanks from being discovered sideways, it consists of 2 faces meeting in an outward angle" (Duane 1810:179).
- Redan. "Indented works, are lines or faces forming salliant [sic] and re-entering angles flanking one another, and are generally used on the side of a river which runs through a garrisoned town" (Simes 1768). ". . . are a kind of indented works, lines, or faces, forming sallying and re-entering angles, flanking one another" (Duane 1810:578).
- Redoubt. "A place more particularly intrenched, and separated from the rest by a fosse" (Simes 1768). "a square work without any bastions, placed at some distance from a fortification, to guard a pass" (Duane 1810:179).
- Reentering or reentrant angle. "An angle pointing toward the interior of a fortification" (Robinson 1977:204). ". . . angle whose point turns inwards, or towards the place" (Duane 1810:173).
- Reverse slope. The back side of a hill. ". . . on the back or behind . . . a reverse commanding ground" (Duane 1810:600).
- Revetment. "A strong wall, built on the outside of the rampart and parapet, to support the earth, and prevent its rolling into the ditch" (Simes 1768).
- Salient angle. "Is that which points outwards or whose legs open toward the place" (Duane 1810:173). "An angle pointing outward" (Robinson 1977:204).
- Sally ports. "Postern-gates, as they are sometimes called, are those . . . which lead from the inner to the outward works . . . When they are constructed for the passage of men only, they are made with steps at the entrance and outlet. They are about six feet wide" (Duane 1810:613).

- Sap. "A trench, or an approach made under cover, of ten or twelve feet broad, when the besiegers come near the place, and their fire grows so dangerous, as not to be approached uncovered" (Simes 1768).
- Sap roller. A gabion placed on its side and rolled ahead of a sap to provide cover for the men digging the sap.
- Scarp. "That whose points turn from the centre of the place" (Simes 1768). "The interior side of the ditch" (Robinson 1977:204). Term used to "express the outside of the rampart of any work next to the ditch" (Duane 1810:179).
- Sods. "Pieces of turf with which works are faced" (Duane 1810:645). These were often held in place by pegs.
- Star Fort. "So called because they resemble that figure . . . commonly made of 4 angles, sometimes of 5, and very rarely of 6; but we find them now made of 7 and 8 angles" (Duane 1810:182). "An enclosed work with a trace made up of a series of salient and reentering angles" (Robinson 1977:204).
- Stockade. "A defensive work-usually eight or more feet high-composed of timbers planted tightly together in the ground. Stockades were generally provided with loopholes, and since these openings were often in the upper part of the fence, banquettes or elevated walks were often necessary parts of the wall" (Robinson 1977:204–05).
- Superior slope. "The top surface of an earth parapet which slants downward toward the country" (Robinson 1977:205).
- Talus. "Or epaulement, is the slope given to the rampart, or wall . . . which is more or less sloped according as the earth is looser or more binding" (Simes 1768). ". . . signifies a slope made either on the outside or inside of any work, to prevent the earth's rolling down" (Duane 1810:179).
- Terreplein. "Of a rampart, is the horizontal superficies of it between the interior talus and banquette, which is used as a common passage by the defendants" (Simes 1768).
- Toise. "A measure of six feet used by French engineers in all their fortifications" (Simes 1768).
- Trace. "Outlines of the horizontal configurations of a fortification" (Robinson 1977:205). See enceinte.
- Traverse. "A parapet, made cross the covert-way, opposite to the salient angles of the works . . . to

prevent enfilades" (Simes 1768). ". . . a parapet . . . to prevent being enfiladed"(Duane 1810:695).

• Trench. "Lines of approach, and attack, is a way hollowed in the earth, in form of a foss [*sic*], having a parapet towards the place besieged, when the earth can be removed; or else it is an elevation of fascines, gabions, woolpacks, and such other things for covering the men as cannot fly into pieces or splinters" (Simes 1768).

Eddy currents. Circular electric currents induced in an electrical conductor by an alternating magnetic field.

Electrical conductivity. Measure of a material's ability to conduct an electric current; it is the reciprocal (inverse) of electrical resistivity.

Evidence. Anything a judge allows in court as relevant to a case.

Fatigue duty. Military work details that may include construction and policing.

Field artillery. "Divided into Battalion Guns, Artillery of the Park, and Horse Artillery. Battalion guns include all the light pieces attached to regiments of the line, which they accompany in all manoeuvres [*sic*] . . . Artillery of the Park is composed of all kinds of field ordinance. It is destined to form batteries of position . . . to occupy advantageous situations" (Duane 1810:17).

Firearm identification. Methods and procedures used to determine weapon type or even the specific gun that fired a projectile or cartridge case. Archaeological applications are derived from modern forensic and criminal investigation methods and theories.

Flintlock. A firearm ignited by a mechanism using a flint striking against a steel to produce sparks. The eighteenth century term was firelock. "Firelock, so called from their producing fire of themselves, by the action of the flint and steel; the arms carried by a foot-soldier" (Duane 1810:158).

Flux-gate magnetometer. Incorporates a sensor constructed from an identical pair of cores made from high-magnetic-permeability material to measure a vector component (such as the vertical component) of the magnetic field.

Forensic science. Application of science to the law.

Forensic archaeology. Application of archaeological techniques to the law.

Frye v United States. A 1923 Supreme Court decision that outlines criteria for expert testimony based on what was generally accepted by the relevant scientific community. This has been replaced in many jurisdictions by the (see) *Daubert v. Merrell Dow* ruling.

Fusil. "A light musket" often lighter and shorter than muskets carried by line infantry (Duane 1810:207).

Gabion. "A cylinder basket, open at both ends, of about three feet wide, and as much in height. They serve in sieges to carry on the approaches under cover" (Simes 1768). "A kind of basket, made of ozier twigs, of a cylindrical form . . . Some gabions are 5 or 6 feet high, and 3 feet in diameter . . . Those used in field-works are 3 or 4 feet high, and 2 ½ or 3 feet in diameter" (Duane 1810:208). See sap roller.

Genocide. Intent to destroy, in whole or in part, a national, ethnic, racial or religious group.

Geographic information system (GIS). A mapping system consisting of computer hardware, software, and geographic data for capturing, managing, analyzing, and displaying all forms of spatially-referenced information. Archaeological data can be displayed along with site data such as seabed contour, sediment type, biological information and many other types of data.

Grapeshot. "A certain number of small shots, of iron or lead, quilted together with canvas and ropes about a pin of iron or wood, fixed upon a bottom in the same manner, so as the whole together weigh as much as the shot of that caliber" (Simes 1768).

Grazing fire. "When the center of the cone of fire does not rise more than 1 meter above the ground" (U.S. Army 1984:7–3).

Gun. "Fire-arm, or weapon of offence, which forcibly discharges a bullet through a cylindrical barrel by means of gunpowder. The term is chiefly applied to cannon" (Duane 1810:244).

(Heavy) Field artillery. Mobile artillery used to support troops at the front. Heavy field artillery is of the largest caliber.

Historic landscape. A cultural landscape that is "composed of a number of character-defining features which, individually or collectively contribute to the landscape's physical appearance as they have evolved over time" (NPS 1994:1).

Historic site. "Historic landscape that is associated with a particular historic event or activity" (NPS 1994:2).

Historic vernacular landscape. Historic landscape that "evolved through the use by the people whose activities or occupancy (cumulatively) shaped that landscape" (NPS 1994:2).

Howitzer. "A sort of mortar, mounted upon a field carriage like a gun. The difference between a mortar and a howitzer [sic] is, that the trunnions are at the end of the first [mortar], but in the middle of the last [howitzer]" (Simes 1768).

Hut. During the winter soldiers constructed above-ground or semi-subterranean domiciles often referred to by the soldiers as huts or shanties. It could be a log or frame building, a log walled, tent roofed structure or a variety of other domiciles. Other terms were shebang and shanty.

Impression evidence. Evidence such as fingerprints, footprints, tool marks, where one object is pressed or stamped against another, allowing the second object to retain characteristics of the first.

Individual characteristics. Markings utilized by firearm examiner in his or her efforts to associate a specific firearm with ballistic evidence. These characteristics consist of the unintended features on the various working surfaces of a firearm that often mark bullets and fired cartridges either through impact (such as the firing pin) or through a dynamic scraping or rubbing action such as occurs when a projectile is driven down the bore of a firearm.

Induced magnetization. Magnetic quantity that exists only in the presence of an external magnetic field.

Induced polarization. Method that compares resistivities as a function of variable frequency input currents (frequency-domain type) or that measures the rate of decay in potential difference after current flow is terminated (time-domain type).

Infantry. Foot soldiers. Traveled from place to place by marching in all types of weather. At the time of the American Civil War each infantryman would carry his own weapon—a rifled musket and bayonet—along with personal belongings and equipment and food for several days (www.nps.gov/archive/gett/getteducation/bcast01/gcast-5.htm).

In-phase. Description of a waveform signal that is shifted 0 (zero) degrees with respect to a reference waveform and thus synchronized with the reference signal.

Inverted A-frame. Wooden structure in an inverted A-shape form put on the bottom of a World War I trench. Duckboards were put on top of the structure. The water and mud could then run underneath the duckboards, through the inverted-A.

Justifiable homicide. Term generally used in self-defense cases where the defendant themselves would have been seriously injured or killed unless they killed the deceased.

Landscape archaeology. "An approach with archaeology that emphasizes examination of the complete landscape, focusing on dispersed features and on areas between and surrounding traditional sites as well as on the sites themselves" (Sharer and Ashmore 2003:124, G-9).

Lee-Enfield Rifle. Standard rifle for the British army from 1895 until 1956. It was also used by Britain's Commonwealth allies and colonies.

Livens-projector. An early type of mortar used to launch chlorine-gas grenades in World War I. They were pipes placed at an angle of 45° in batteries consisting of 20–25 pieces. The bank of projectors was fired by means of an electrical charge.

Magnetic permeability. Quantity, directly related to magnetic susceptibility, which expresses the degree of magnetization of a material that responds linearly to an applied magnetic field.

Magnetic susceptibility. Ratio of induced magnetization to the external magnetic field of the earth.

Magnetometer. Device that precisely measures the magnetic field of the earth along with any anomalies (variations) caused by ferrous materials (iron or steel). Charting the anomalies can indicate the location and nature of ferrous cultural material on the seabed, even if it is completely buried.

Maintained landscape. Landscape, such as a military camp, is an area of land on which a sense of order has been established through the modification, maintenance, and arrangement of activities and features by the group that occupies it.

Manslaughter. Intentional killing without either premeditation or malice.

Meter gauge railway. Narrow-gauge railway system serving the front line trenches in World War I.

Military landscape. Geographic area that houses evidence of a particular military site and the natural and cultural terrain features that contributed to its presence, plan, and the conduct of military actions consistent with its purpose.

Military Ranks (officers and men)

- Captain. "Commands a troop or company; he ought to be very diligent, and preserve good order among the men . . ." (Simes 1768). A captain commands a company (Riling 1966:138–41).

- Captain-Lieutenant. "Commands the Colonel's troop or company" (Simes 1768). The company commander of a company assigned to a field officer, (Colonel's, Lieutenant Colonel's or Major's) company. The field officer was the "official" commander but the Captain-Lieutenant actually commanded.

- Colonel. "Commandant of a corps, commands it in chief" (Simes 1768). Colonel was the usual rank of a regimental commander (Riling 1966:128–31).

- Ensign. "Officer who carries the colours . . . and is the youngest Officer of a company, subordinate to his Captain and Lieutenant" (Simes 1768). An ensign traditionally carried the regimental colors (Riling 1966:143–44).

- Engineer. "Officer of the military branch, who, by the help of geometry, delimiates upon paper, or marks upon the ground, all sorts of forts, and other works proper for offence or defence; who understands the art of fortification" (Simes 1768).

- Lieutenant. "Second Officer in a troop or company; in the absence of the Captain, commands it" (Simes 1768). A junior officer at the company level (Riling 1966:141–42).

- Lieutenant Colonel. "Should be a man of great experience, know how to attack or defend a post, and lead the regiment to battle" (Simes 1768). In the absence of the colonel, the Lieutenant Colonel commanded a regiment.

- Major. "Is to be active, vigilant, and well acquainted with the strength of the battalion and details of a corps, and well instructed in the exercise and every kind of manoeuvre" (Simes 1768). Major was the lowest field grade officer. In a battalion, the major was second in command (Riling 1966:132–34).

Militia. "A force whose services, in general, do not exceed the boundaries of the nation, but which may volunteer beyond them. The American militia has no coherent system, every state has power to regulate its own" (Duane 1810:438). Initially, militia was the colonial self-defense force. During the Revolution, militia was placed in classes called up (drafted) for service as needed. They usually served for short periods, such as 6 weeks or 3 months. In emergencies, they might be called out for only a few days. Generally, militiamen were not well-trained and did not turn out in great numbers or in a timely fashion.

Mine. "A kind of lodgement made under ground to place powder in, which is set on fire in order to blow up the works above it" (Simes 1768).

Mine crater. Pit created by the detonation of explosives in a tunnel beneath enemy trenches.

Mortar. "Made of brass or iron, are used both in the land and sea service for throwing shells and carcasses; those for land are shortest and lightest" (Simes 1768).

Murder. Killing with premediation and/or malice.

Musket. "The most commodious and useful firearms used in the army: they carry a ball at the rate of twenty-nine to two pound of lead" (Simes 1768). The musket was the most common shoulder arm of eighteenth century armies. It was a smoothbore weapon that also used a bayonet. The musket was easier and faster to load than a rifle but its accurate range was under 50 yards. It had a smooth bore (interior barrel) and ranged in caliber from .62 to .75 inch.

Optically pumped magnetometer. Incorporates a photon emitter from a lamp, an absorption chamber containing vapor, such as rubidium, cesium, or helium, a buffer gas through which the emitted photons pass, and a photon detector that measures total magnetic field intensity by observation of the precession frequency of the vapor atoms.

Osteobiographies. Life story of a person as documented through their skeletal remains.

Osteological. Having to do with bones.

Overhauser-effect magnetometer. Incorporates a liquid containing free electrons combined with a liquid containing hydrogen atoms which is exposed to secondary polarization ("lining up") from a radio-frequency magnetic field; the free electrons transfer their energy to the hydrogen nuclei (protons), polarizing the liquid—just like a proton-precession magnetometer—but more pervasively and with less expended power.

Parade. "It is now used in a military sense to signify any place where troops assemble" (Duane 1810:505). It "is the place where troops assemble to go upon guard, or any other duty" (Simes 1768).

Perimortem. Around the time of death.

Permanent camps. Living quarters which do not move, such as domiciles by a fort.

Phase. Position of a particular point in time on a waveform cycle, with a complete cycle defined as 360° of phase.

Picket (more properly picket guard). "An out-guard posted before an army, to give notice of an enemy approaching" (Duane 1810:523).

Picket duty. Detachment of one or more troops held in readiness or advanced to warn of an enemy's approach. A sentry on horseback is called a vedette, not picket.

Pointblank. "The position of a gun when laid level; and pointblank range is that distance which the shot goes upon a level plain" (Simes 1768). "In gunnery, denotes the shot of a piece leveled horizontally, without either mounting or sinking the muzzle. In shooting thus, the bullet is supposed to go in a direct line, and not to move in a curve, as bombs and highly elevated random shots do" (Duane 1810:536).

Policing. Activity related to camp maintenance. As part of daily activity soldiers were detailed to clean up camp and living areas. Policing, as a depositional process, is important in the examination of encampments.

Proton-precession magnetometer. Incorporates a coil to create a strong magnetic field through a hydrogen-rich fluid which causes protons to align their spins. The strong field is then shut off, causing the protons to precess (like a top) with a frequency proportional to the weak field of the earth measured.

Positioning system. The modern positioning system is an electronic unit that receives precise locational data from several satellites and converts those data to an accurate geodetic position on the Earth at the receiver's location. The U.S. and Russia both maintain a constellation of satellites comprising the Global Positioning System (GPS).

Pre-disturbance survey. Examination of an archeological site or sites in advance of excavation or disturbance by archaeologists, often involving remote sensing equipment. Pre-disturbance surveys are important to gather baseline environmental data and to help refine excavation and sampling strategies.

Provincial. American who served in an American military unit on the British side on a full time basis. This term was also used to identify the British Army's American units.

Quartermaster Corps. Provided the quarters and transportation of the army, storage and transport for all army supplies, clothing, camp and garrison equipage, cavalry and artillery horses, mules, fuel, forage, straw and stationary. Paid the incidental expenses of the army including per diem to extra duty men, postage on public service, the expenses of courts-martial, the pursuit and apprehension of deserters, the burial of officers and soldiers, hired escorts, expresses, interpreters, spies and guides, veterinary surgeons and medicine for horses, the supply of water for posts and the authorized expenses for movements and operations of the army not assigned to other departments (www.15thnewyorkcavalry.org/the_quartermaster.htm).

Range. "The distance from the battery to the point where the shot, or shell, touches the ground" (Simes 1768; Duane 1810:566; Hoyt 1811:454).

Reflection. Process of electromagnetic energy emitted at a point, "bouncing off" of an object and returning to the point; the elliptical region of strongest reflection is known as the "First Fresnel Zone."

Region. "A definable area bounded by topographic features such as mountains and bodies of water" (Sharer and Ashmore 2004:124).

Regular. Term referring to the eighteenth century British soldiers who were enlisted for long service and were generally well-trained and disciplined. "When applied to the army, signifies those troops that are inlisted [sic] for a regular period, do duty as soldiers and nothing else; contradistinguished from those who are citizens occasionally exercising the duties of soldiers; thus the militia are not ranked among the regulars" (Duane 1810:583).

Remote-sensing equipment. Electronic equipment designed to record the location and characteristics of material lying on the seabed using electronic sensors towed behind survey vessels or mounted on autonomous underwater vehicles (AUVs). Remote-sensing equipment can cover large areas of seabed in a relatively short time and is often capable of providing researchers with remarkably detailed information on submerged objects without the need for divers.

Remotely-operated vehicle (ROV). Powered underwater craft capable of conducting many tasks that would normally be done by a human diver, such as transmitting video imagery from underwater sites, determining precise locations of submerged objects, and performing skilled operations including simple excavation and recovery tasks. ROVs are particularly useful on deepwater sites, where human divers cannot work.

Rifle. "Gun, a fire arm of a peculiar construction, now much used in regular armies. It has lines or exignous canals within its barrel, that run spirally, forming a female screw, and its ball when projected revolves on an axis, coincident with the axis of the piece prolonged" (Hoyt 1811:111–18, 457). The lands and grooves cut into the barrel are called rifling. They make the bullet spin, thus gyroscopically stabilizing the bullet and increasing accuracy.

Rifle musket. "A weapon that had spiral grooves inserted during manufacture" (Hess 2008:8).

Rifled musket. "A smoothbore weapon with spiral grooves added sometime after its manufacture" (Hess 2008:8).

Rifle pits. Hasty individual entrenchments dug in the field to protect the individual solider. Hasty in this case means to be quickly prepared according to training doctrine and procedure to provide minimum protection and fields of fire for a solider or group of soldiers.

Scuba diving. SCUBA, an acronym for Self-Contained Underwater Breathing Apparatus, consists of a portable air cylinder and demand regulator that supplies air when the diver inhales. Developed in the 1940s, Scuba is used for most recreational diving and some scientific diving.

Shanty. During the winter soldiers constructed aboveground or semi-subterranean dwellings often referred to by the soldiers as huts or shanties.

Shell. "Hollow iron balls to throw out of mortars or howitzers [sic], with a hole about an inch diameter, to load them with powder and to receive the fuze [sic]" (Simes 1768). ". . . are hollow balls to throw out of mortars or howitzers with a fuze hole" (Duane 1810:633).

Shelter tent. Tent intended to be carried by troops. The shelter tent consists of two-halves of a tent. The intent was for soldiers to button them together, and drape the tent over a rope suspended between two poles stuck in the ground. Also called a pup tent or dog tent.

Ship. Generic term for a large seagoing vessel; also a specific vessel type having three masts with square sails set on all three.

Shrapnel. "A shell which bursts in the air and scatters small pieces of metal over a large area" (Empey 1917:308). Exploding shell for field guns (as opposed to mortars) was invented in the late-eighteenth century by the British Army's Henry Shrapnel.

Shot. "All sorts of ball, either for cannon, musquets [sic], carabiens [sic], or pistols" (Simes 1768). Term "given to all kinds of balls used for artillery and fire-arms; those for cannon being of iron, and those for guns and pistols, etc., of lead" (Duane 1810:735).

Sibley (Bell) tent. A tent that could accommodate upwards of 20 men, stood 12 ft high, and had a 16–18 ft diameter footprint. These were often fitted out with a distinctive cone-shaped Sibley stove.

Side-scan sonar. An active marine remote sensing device that uses sound waves to paint a picture of materials on and protruding from the bottom of a lake, river, or portion of the ocean.

Skirmishers. "Detached parties of light troops sent out in front of a battalion" (Duane 1810:643). "Small detached parties of light troops sent in front or on the flanks to attack an enemy" (Hoyt 1811:462). "A battle force sent out from the main line when within range of the enemy during an engagement . . . usually more numerous than a line of pickets and geared for immediate action in support of the battle line" (Hess 2008:122).

Sonar. Electronic system that sends sound pulses through the water and displays the returning echo to produce an acoustic image of the seabed and any objects exposed there. The most commonly used types are multi-beam, side-scanning, and bottom-penetrating sonar.

Sub-bottom profiler. An active marine remote sensing device that uses sound waves to penetrate into sediments on the bottom of a lake, river or portion of the ocean. As sound waves are returned to the instrument they paint a picture of the different geological strata below the bottom.

Stockading. A process where soldiers constructed earthen or wood bases upon which they would erect tents. In some cases the logs were vertical. Stockading effectively increased the height of the tents and created an additional layer of shelter. Stockading can also refer to fortification by erecting a stockade.

Strategy. "The art and science of developing and using political, economic, psychological, and military forces as necessary during peace and war, to afford the maximum support to policies, in order to increase the probabilities and favorable consequences of victory and to lessen the chances of defeat" (Lykke 1983:A-9). "The planning for, coordination of, and concerted use of the multiple means and resources available to an alliance, a nation, a political group, or a commander, for the purpose of gaining an advantage over a rival" (Alger 1985:5). "The art or science of military command" (Hoyt 1811:463).

Sutler. "Follows the army to sell all sorts of provisions . . . They pitch their tents in the rear of each regiment" (Simes 1768).

Tactics. "The employment of units in combat. The ordered arrangement and maneuver of units in relation to each other and/or to the enemy in order to utilize their full potentialities" (Lykke 1983:A-9). "The planning, training, and control of the ordered arrangements (formations) used by military organizations when engagement between opposing forces is imminent or underway" (Alger 1985:5). "The method of arranging or disposing troops to the best advantage in order of battle" (Hoyt 1811:464).

Technical diving. Specialized diving below 40 m that utilizes compressed gasses other than air, along with computer-generated decompression schedules designed for given depth-time parameters.

Trench map. Diagrams made by the several warring parties on which they drew enemy trenches and infrastructure and their own trenches (in most cases less detailed). These were based on aerial photography and ground observations and used to plan and evaluate military actions.

Trench system. Civil War and World War I fortifications, including front line, second and third lines, communication trench, jumping off trench and sap. The real front line was the front line trench; from here a soldier was facing the enemy. These were connected with support (2nd line) and reserve (3rd line) trenches by communication trenches. These were used to transport men, food, ammunition, and equipment. Short trenches called saps were dug from the front line trench into no man's land. In some cases, a jumping off trench was dug, starting from a sap, parallel with the front line trench. These were used to start an attack on the enemy troops.

Vidette. "A sentry on horseback" (Hoyt 1811:467).

Viewshed or terrain analysis. The concept of using computer power of a Geographic Information System (GIS) to calculate what can be seen from a specific location at specific heights above the ground. This viewshed or weapons fan analysis results in a field of view or what a person could see from a given position for specified distances.

War crimes. Serious violations of international humanitarian law (use of gas, treatment of civilian population and prisoners of war in violation of the law, weapons outlawed by treaties, etc.)

Wedge tent. See A-tent

Western Front. Term used in both World Wars to point out the front line between the zones controlled by Germany and the Allied forces in Western Europe. In World War I, the front stretched from Newport (Belgium) to the Swiss Border. There was also an Eastern Front during both wars.

Winter camps. In winter months, when the road network of a region became impassable, Revolutionary and Civil War armies established semi-permanent camps. These camps contain huts built by the soldiers. Winter quarters was another term, and also meant ". . . the time comprehended between the end of one campaign and the beginning of another" (Simes 1768).

Williams cleaner ammunition. Three distinct types of bullet. The intent was to remove powder residue from rifle bores before the gun became fouled. Williams bullets were designed with three parts: body, zinc washer, and disk/plug and were as accurate as the standard issue .577/.58 projectile. Upon firing, the disk/plug would expand the zinc washer, scouring out the barrel.

Wire entanglement. Barbed wire placed in several rows in front of the front line trench as an extra protection.

A Regimental Officer. 1859. *Our Veterans of 1854: In Camp and Before the Enemy.* London: C. J. Skeet.

Abbott, W. W. 1983. *The Papers of George Washington, Colonial Series, Volume 2: August 1755–April 1756.* Charlottesville, Va.: University Press of Virginia.

———. 1984. *The Papers of George Washington, Colonial Series, Volume 3: April 1757–November 1756.* Charlottesville, Va.: University Press of Virginia.

Adkin, M. 1996. *The Charge: The Real Reason Why the Light Brigade Was Lost.* London: Leo Cooper.

Adye, R. W. 1804. *The Bombardier and Pocket Gunner.* Boston: Printed for E. Larkin by William Greenough, Charleston.

Airlie, Countess of (Ogilvy, Mabell). 1933. *With the Guards We Shall Go. A Guardsman's Letters in the Crimea, 1854–1855.* London: Hodder and Stoughton.

Aitchison, K. R. 1994. Culloden Dykes—Documentary Search. Edinburgh, UK: Unpublished report on file at National Trust for Scotland Headquarters.

Aitken, M. J. 1974. *Physics and Archaeology.* Oxford, UK: Clarendon Press.

Åkesson, P. 2009. Side Scan Sonar. Nordic Underwater Archaeology, http://www.abc.se/~pa/mar/sidescan.htm (accessed August 24, 2009).

Albert, A. H. 1976. *Record of American Uniform and Historical Buttons, Bicentennial Edition.* Boyertown, Penn.: Boyertown Publishing Company.

Alger, J. I. 1985. *Definitions and Doctrine of the Military Art.* Wayne, N.J.: Avery Publishing Group, Inc.

Allen, R. S. 1992. *His Majesty's Indian Allies-British Indian Policy in the Defence of Canada, 1774–1815.* Toronto: Dundurn Press.

Allen, W. C. 1995. "In the Greatest Solemn Dignity"—the Capitol's four cornerstones. U.S. Senate Document 103–28. Washington, D.C.: U.S. Government Printing Office.

An Officer on the Staff. 1857. *Letters from Headquarters or the Realities of the War in the Crimea.* London: John Murray.

Anderson, P. 1920. *Culloden Moor and the Story of the Battle,* 2nd ed. Repr., Inverness, Scotland: William Mackay & Son, 1867.

Ansel, D. M. 1984. *Frontier Forts Along the Potomac and its Tributaries.* Parsons, W. Va: McClain Printing.

Aries, P. 1982. *The Hour of Our Death.* New York: Vintage Books.

Arnold, J. B., III, T. J. Oertling, and A. W. Hall. 1999. The Denbigh Project: initial observations on a Civil War blockade-runner and its wreck site. *International Journal of Nautical Archaeology* 28:126–44.

———, ———, and ———. 2001a. The Denbigh Project: excavation of a Civil War blockade-runner. *International Journal of Nautical Archaeology* 30:231–249.

———, ———, and ———. 2001b. The Denbigh Project: test excavations at the wreck of an American Civil War blockade-runner. *World Archaeology* 32:400–412.

Arnold, J. B. III, C. P. Weldon, G. M. Fleshman, C. E. Peterson, W. K. Stewart and G. P. Watts, Jr. 1992. USS *Monitor:* results from the 1987 season. *Historical Archaeology* 26(4):47–57.

Arnold, J. B. III, G. M. Fleshman, D. B. Hill, C. E. Peterson, W. K. Stewart, S. R. Gegg, G. P. Watts, Jr. and C. Weldon. 1991. *The 1987 Expedition to the*

Monitor National Marine Sanctuary: Data Analysis and Final Report. Washington, D.C.: U.S. Department of Commerce, National Oceanic and Atmospheric Administration.

Atkinson, R. J. C. 1953. *Field Archaeology.* London: Methuen.

Austin, D. In Press. *Sir John Blount's Diary of the Crimean War.*

Babits, L., and T. Pecoraro. 2006. Fort Dobbs, 1756–1763 Iredell County, North Carolina, an archaeological study. Statesville, N.C.: Manuscript on file at Fort Dobbs State Historic Site.

Babits, L. E. 1990. A Confederate bombproof's interior. *Military Collector and Historian* 42(4):135–37.

———. 1995a. Bullets from the *Maple Leaf. Military Collector and Historian* 47(3):119–26.

———. 1995b. Rubber poncho and blankets from the Union transport *Maple Leaf. Military Collector and Historian* 47(4):60–67.

Babits, L. E., J. Barnes, T. Foard, R. Leech, S. Simmons, A. S. Walsh. 1987. Archaeological investigations at Causton's Bluff, Chatham County, Georgia. Savannah, Ga.: Manuscript on file at Georgia Historical Society.

Bak, R.W. 1999. *The CSS* Hunley. Dallas: Cooper Square Press.

Baker, H. H. 1913. *A Reminiscent Story of the Great Civil War.* New Orleans: The Ruskin Press.

Baker, H. R., R. N. Bolster, P. B. Leach and C. R. Singleterry. 1969. *Examination of the Corrosion and Salt Contamination of Structural Metal from the USS* Tecumseh. NRL Memorandum Report 1987. Washington, D.C.: Naval Research Center.

Balicki, J. 1995. Archeological resources. In *Historical and Archeological Survey for Fort C.F. Smith, 241 24th Street North, Arlington, Virginia,* vol. 2, ed. C. D. Cheek and P. Benton. Report to Arlington County, Virginia Department of Community Planning, Housing and Development, Community Improvement Division, Arlington, Va. West Chester, Penn.: John Milner Associates Inc.

———. 2000. Defending the capital: the Civil War garrison at Fort C.F. Smith. In *Archeological Perspectives on the American Civil War,* ed. C. R. Geier and S. Potter, 125–47. Gainesville, Fla.: The University Press of Florida.

———. 2006a. "Masterly inactivity" the Confederate cantonment supporting the 1861–1862 Potomac River blockade, Evansport, Virginia. In *Huts and History,* ed. C. Geier, D. Orr, and M. Reeves, 97–136. Gainesville, Fla.: The University Press of Florida.

———. 2006b. Supplemental metal detection investigations associated with structural landscape enhancements, Blenheim Estate. Report prepared for The City of Fairfax, Fairfax, Virginia. Alexandria, Va.: John Milner Associates, Inc.

———. 2007. The Confederate cantonment at Evansport, Virginia. In *Fields of Conflict: Battlefield Archaeology from the Roman Empire to the Korean War,* vol. 2, ed. D. Scott, L. Babits, and C. Haecker, 255–77. Westport, Conn.: Praeger Security International, Greenwood Publishing Group, Inc.

Balicki, J., B. Corle, and S. Goode. 2004. Multiple cultural resources investigations at eight locations and along five tank trails, Marine Corps Base Quantico, Prince William, Stafford, and Fauquier counties, Virginia. Report prepared for EDAW, Inc. Alexandria, Virginia. Alexandria, Va: John Milner Associates, Inc.

Balicki, J., B. Corle, C. Goode, and L. Jones. 2005. Archeological investigations for Quaker Ridge Housing (44AX195) Alexandria, Virginia. Report prepared for Carr Homes, Annandale, Virginia. Alexandria, Va: John Milner Associates, Inc.

Balicki, J., K. Culhane, W. H. Owen II, and D. J. Seifert. 2002a. Fairfax County Civil War Sites Inventory, technical report version. Report prepared for Fairfax County Park Authority, Fairfax, Virginia. Alexandria, Va.: John Milner Associates, Inc.

Balicki, J., K. L. Farnham, B. Corle, and S. J. Fiedel. 2002b. Multiple cultural resources investigations, Marine Corps Base Quantico, Prince William and Stafford Counties, Virginia. Report prepared for EDAW, Inc. Alexandria, Virginia. Alexandria, Va.: John Milner Associates, Inc.

Balicki J. F., K. Holland, and B. Corle. 2007. Documentary study and archaeological investigation 1226 North Pegram Street and Polk Avenue (44AX198), Alexandria, Virginia. Report prepared for Prospect Development Company, Inc., Woodbridge, Virginia. Alexandria, Va.: John Milner Associates, Inc.

Barker, D. B., and J. A. Doolittle. 1992. Ground-penetrating radar—an archeological tool. *Cultural Resources Management* 15(5):25–28.

Barnes, J. 1865. Medical and surgical history of the rebellion containing reports of medical directors and other doctors. Manassas, Va.: Manuscript on file, Manassas National Battlefield Archives.

Barry, J. P. 1973. *Ships of the Great Lakes, 300 Years of Navigation.* Berkeley, Calif.: Howell-North Books.

Bartholow, R. 1863. *A Manual of Instructions for Enlisting and Discharging Soldiers.* Philadelphia: J. B. Lippincott.

Bass, G. F. 1966. *A History of Seafaring Based on Underwater Archaeology.* London: Thames and Hudson.

———. 1972. *A History of Seafaring Based on Underwater Archaeology.* London: Thames and Hudson.

———. 1988. *Ships and Shipwrecks of the Americas.* London: Thames and Hudson.

———. (ed.). 2006. *Beneath the Seven Seas: Adventures with the Institute of Nautical Archaeology.* London: Thames and Hudson.

Beal, M. D. 1963. *"I Will Fight No More Forever."* Seattle: University of Washington Press.

Beasley, J. (ed.). 2005. *Archaeological Overview and Assessment and Identification and Evaluation Study of the Best Farm, Monocacy National Battlefield, Frederick, Maryland.* Occasional Report No. 18, Regional Archaeology Program, National Capital Region. Washington, D.C.: U.S. Department of the Interior, National Park Service.

Bearss, E. C. 1980. *Hardluck Ironclad.* Baton Rouge, La.: Louisiana State University Press.

———. 1981. *History of the First Battle of Manassas.* Lynchburg, Va.: H. E. Howard, Inc.

———. 2006. *Fields of Honor: Pivotal Battles of the Civil War.* Washington, D.C.: National Geographic.

Bell, J. 2003. *Civil War Heavy Explosive Ordnance.* Denton, Tex.: University of North Texas Press.

Bell, M. and R. M. Martore. 1998. *Letter from Melvin Bell and Report from Robert M. Martore and Melvin Bell.* In H.L. Hunley *Site Assessment,* ed. L. E. Murphy, 147–51. Submerged Resources Center Professional Report No. 15. Santa Fe, N. Mex.: U.S. Department of Interior, National Park Service.

Benn, C. 1993. *The Iroquois in the War of 1812.* Toronto: University of Toronto Press.

Bevan, B. W. 1996. Geophysical exploration for archaeology, volume A: archaeological questions and answers. Geosight Inc. Technical Report No. 4. Ontario, Canada: Geosight Inc. Available at http://www.cast.uark.edu/nadag/projects_database/geop_typ_pages/dbase-con.htm

———. 1991. The search for graves. *Geophysics* 56:1310–19.

———. 1998. *Geophysical Exploration for Archaeology—an Introduction to Geophysical Exploration.* Midwest Archeological Center Special Report No. 1. Lincoln, Neb.: U.S. Department of the Interior, National Park Service.

Bevan, B. W., and J. L. Kenyon. 1975. Ground-penetrating radar for historical archaeology. *MASCA Newsletter* 11(2):2–7.

Biggar, H. P. 1922–1936. *The Works of Samuel de Champlain,* 6 vols. Toronto: The Champlain Society.

Billings, J. D. 1980. *Hardtack and Coffee or the Unwritten Story of Army Life.* Williamson, Mass.: Corner House Publishers,

Birch, S., and D. M. McElvogue. 1999. *La Lavia, La Juliana* and the *Santa Maria de Vison:* three Spanish Armada transports lost off Streedagh Strand, Co Sligo: an interim report. *International Journal of Nautical Archaeology* 28:265–76.

Black, G. A., and R. B. Johnston. 1962. A test of magnetometry as an aid to archaeology. *American Antiquity* 28:199–205.

Black, W. M. 1890. Report of operations for the month of January, 1890. Record Group 77, Corps of Engineers, Jacksonville District. East Point, Ga.: U.S. National Archives, Southeast Region.

Blades, B. S. 1981. Excavations at the Confederate picket line, Crater area, Petersburg National Battlefield, Virginia. Petersburg, Va.: Report prepared for the National Park Service, Mid-Atlantic Region.

———. 2001. An archaeological overview and assessment of the main unit, Petersburg National Battlefield, Virginia. Valley Forge, Penn.: Report prepared for the National Park Service, Valley Forge Center for Cultural Resources.

Blondel, F. 1689. *Nouvelle Maniere de Fortifier les Places,* 2nd ed., Amsterdam: Henry Desbordes.

Bond, D. 1974. Frontier forts of Monongalia County.

In *The Monongalia Story: A Bicentennial History,* ed. E. L. Core, 366–412. Parsons, W. Va.: McClain Printing.

Bonner, T. M. 1995. *Becoming a Physician: Medical Education in Britain, France, Germany, and the United States, 1750–1945.* Baltimore: John Hopkins University Press.

Borg, A. 1991. *War Memorials: From Antiquity to the Present.* London: Leo Cooper.

Boston Custom House. 1862. Bill of sale. Record Group 92, Vessel File. Washington, D.C.: U.S. National Archives.

Braley, C. O. 1987. *The Battle of Gilgal Church: An Archaeological and Historical Study of Mid-Nineteenth Century Warfare in Georgia.* Athens, Ga.: Southeastern Archaeological Services, Inc.

Bratten, J. R. 1996. The Continental Gondola *Philadelphia:* a new look at America's oldest surviving warship. In *Underwater Archaeology: Proceedings from the Conference on Underwater and Historical Archaeology,* ed. S. R. James Jr. and C. Stanley, 112–16. Cincinnati, Ohio: Society for Historical Archaeology.

———. 2002. *The Gondola* Philadelphia *and the Battle of Lake Champlain.* College Station: Texas A&M University Press.

Breiner, S. 1973. *Applications Manual for Portable Magnetometers.* Sunnyvale, Calif.: GeoMetrics.

Brenckle, M. P. 2004. Blue jackets and white trousers: British and American sailor clothing, 1750–1851. MA thesis, East Carolina University, Greenville, N.C.

Brewer, R., and T. White. n.d. Tales of St. Mary's: the sinking of the H.M.S. *Royal George.* Portsmouth, UK: Manuscript on file at Portsea St. Mary's Church.

Broadwater, J. D. 1980. The Yorktown Shipwreck Archaeological Project: results from the 1978 survey. *International Journal of Nautical Archaeology* 9(3):227–35.

———. 1981. From collier to troop transport: the *Betsy,* Yorktown, Virginia. In *Beneath the Seven Seas,* ed. G. F. Bass, 200–206. London: Thames and Hudson.

———. 1992. Shipwreck in a swimming pool: an assessment of the methodology and technology utilized on the Yorktown Shipwreck Archaeological Project. *Historical Archaeology* 26(4):36–46.

Broadwater, J. D., R. M. Adams, and M. Renner. 1985. Yorktown Shipwreck archaeological project: an interim report on the excavation of shipwreck 44Y088. *International Journal of Nautical Archaeology and Underwater Exploration* 14:301–14.

Brown, G. W. 2000. Life in the trenches: the archeological investigation of the federal picket line near the Crater, Petersburg National Battlefield. College Park, Md.: Report prepared for the National Park Service, Petersburg National Battlefield and Valley Forge by the Center for Cultural Resources, University of Maryland.

Brown, M. H. 1982. *The Flight of the Nez Perce.* Lincoln, Neb.: Bison Books.

Brown, M. 2004. A mirror of the apocalypse: Great War training trenches. *Sanctuary* 33: 54–58.

———. 2005 Journey back to hell: excavations at Serre on the Somme. *Current World Archaeology* 10:25–33.

Brown, R. H., W. H. Chapman, W. F. Hanna, C. E. Mongan, and J. W. Hursh. 1987. *Inertial Instrument System for Aerial Surveying.* U.S. Geological Survey Professional Paper 1390. Denver, Colo.: U.S. Geological Survey.

Burger, H. R., A. F. Sheehan, and C. H. Jones. 2006. *Introduction to Applied Geophysics.* New York: W. W. Norton.

Bryan, E. P. 1864. Report to Major General P. Anderson, 4 April 1864. In *The War of the Rebellion: A Compilation of the Official Records of the Union and Confederate Armies,* ed. R. N. Scott, Series I, Volume 35, Part 1:381 (1891). Washington, D.C.: U.S. Government Printing Office.

Buttafuso, R. A. 2000. *Civil War Relic Hunting A to Z.* Ann Arbor, Mich.: Sheridan Books.

Calthorpe, S. J. C. 1979. *Cadogan's Crimea: Reprint of Calthorpe's Letters from Headquarters by a Staff Officer, Published 1856, 1857 & 1858.* London: Hamish Hamilton.

Calver, W. P., and R. P. Bolton. 1966. *History Written with Pick and Shovel.* New York: New York Historical Society.

Campana, S. and S. Piro (eds.). 2009. *Seeing the Unseen: Geophysics and Landscape Archaeology.* London: Taylor and Francis.

Campbell, J. D. and M. J. O'Donnell. 2004. *American Military Headgear Insignia.* Alexandria, Va.: O'Donnell Publications.

Cantelas, F. J. 1995. An archaeological investigation of the steamboat *Maple Leaf*. MA thesis, East Carolina University, Greenville, N.C.

Cardigan, Earl of (James Brudenell). 1855. Report of a speech at the Mansion House. *The Times* (London), Feb. 7:10.

Casey, S. 1862. *Infantry Tactics for the Instruction, Exercise, and Manoeuvres of the Soldier, A Company, Line of Skirmishers, Battalion and Brigade or Corps D'Armee*. Reprinted 1985. Dayton, Ohio: Morningside House, Inc.

Catts, W. P., J. Balicki, and P. Siegel. 2006. "A System of Easy Maneuvers . . .": Archeological Evidence of a Musketry Range at Valley Forge National Historical Park, Pennsylvania, USA. Paper presented at: The 4th International Fields of Conflict Conference; 2006, September 29–October 3; Royal Armouries, Leeds, Yorkshire, UK.

Cavanaugh, M. A., and W. Marvel. 1989. *The Petersburg Campaign: the Battle of the Crater: "The Horrid Pit," June 25–August 6, 1864*. The Virginia Civil War Battles and Leaders Series. Lynchburg, Va.: H. E. Howard,

Cederlund, C. O. 2006. Vasa I, *The Archaeology of a Swedish Warship of 1628*. Stockholm: Statens Sjohistoriska Museer (National Maritime Museum of Sweden).

Chalkley, L. 1912. *Chronicles of Scotch-Irish Settlement in Virginia Extracted from the Original Records of Augusta County, 1745–1800*. Washington, D.C.: Daughters of the American Revolution.

Charter Agreement. 1862. Charter between Charles Spear and Captain William McKim, U.S. Army, 1 September 1862. Record Group 92, Water Transport, S.1407, Box 54. Washington, D.C.: U.S. National Archives.

Chelsea Telegraph and Pioneer. 1862. The Mass. First. March 15: 2, Col. 2.

Churchill, W. S. 1995. *Churchill's History of the English Speaking Peoples*. New York: Dodd Mead Co.

Clairic, de la Mamie. 1776. *L'Ingenieur de Campagne; or Field Engineer*. Trans. Lewis Nicola. Philadelphia: R. Aitkin.

Clark, A. J., 2000. *Seeing Beneath the Soil*. New York: Routledge.

Coates, E. J., and D. S. Thomas. 1990. *An Introduction to Civil War Small Arms*. Gettysburg, Penn.: Thomas Publications.

Conlin, D. L. (ed.). 2005. *USS* Housatonic *Site Assessment*. Submerged Resource Center Professional Report 18. Santa Fe, N. Mex.: U.S. Department of Interior, National Park Service.

Conlin, D. L. 2005. Analysis. In *USS* Housatonic *Site Assessment*, ed. D. L. Conlin, chapter 9. Submerged Resource Center Professional Report 18. Santa Fe, N. Mex.: U.S. Department of Interior, National Park Service.

Conlin, D. L., and M. A. Russell. 2006. Archaeology of a naval battlefield: *H.L. Hunley* and USS *Housatonic*. *International Journal of Nautical Archaeology* 35(1):20–40.

Conner, M. A. 2007. *Forensic Methods: Excavation for the Investigator and the Archaeologist*. Lanham, Md.: AltaMira Press.

Conner, M., and D. D. Scott. 1998. Metal detector use in archaeology: an introduction. *Historical Archaeology* 32(4):76–85.

Conrad, M. 2006. Mark Conrad's Homepage—Russian Military History, http://marksrussianmilitary-history.info/ (accessed December 2006). (see for B. M. Kalinen 1907; I. I. Ruzhova; Genishta and A. T. Borlsevich 1904–1906; Todleben; Ushakov; Kazhukov; Liprandi; Godman)

Conyers, L. B., 2004. *Ground-Penetrating Radar for Archaeology*. Walnut Creek, Calif.: AltaMira Press.

Conyers, L. B. and D. Goodman. 1997. Ground *Penetrating Radar—An Introduction for Archaeologists*. Walnut Creek, Calif: AltaMira Press.

Cook, R. B. 1940. Virginia's frontier defenses, 1719–1795. *West Virginia History* 1:119–130.

Cooper, M. 1984. An analysis of scattered human bone from Ontario Iroquoian sites. Toronto: Manuscript on file at the Ontario Heritage Foundation and at Archaeological Services Inc.

Corbin, A. 2000. *The Material Culture of Steamboat Passengers*. New York: Kluwer Academic.

Corle, B., and J. Balicki. 2006. Finding Civil War sites: what relic hunters know; what archeologists should and need to know. In *Huts and History*, ed. C. R. Geier, D. Orr, and M. Reeves, 55–73. Gainesville, Fla.: The University Press of Florida.

Corps of Engineers. 1868. *Professional Papers of the Corps of Engineers*. Washington, D.C.: United States Army.

Creveling, M. C., B. J. Little, W. F. Hanna, C. E.

Petrone, S. R. Potter, and R. C. Sonderman. 1995. Seeking the unknown soldier—geophysical prospecting at Manassas and Antietam battlefields. Society for Historical Archaeology 28th Annual Meeting; 1995, January 4–8; Washington, D.C.; abstract 68.

Crouch, D. 1841. Interview by the Rev. Dabney Shane. Draper Manuscripts, 12CC225–229. Madison: State Historical Society of Wisconsin.

Crouch, H. R. 1995 *Civil War Artifacts: A Guide for the Historian.* Fairfax, Va.: SCS Publications.

Dabas, M., and J. R. Skinner. 1993. Time-domain magnetization of soils (VRM), experimental relationship to quadrature susceptibility. *Geophysics* 58:326–33.

Dahlgren, J. A. 1865. Report to Secretary of the Navy Gideon Welles, 1 June 1865. In *Official Records of the Union and Confederate Navies in the War of the Rebellion,* ed. C. W. Stewart, Series I, 16:385 (1903). Washington, D.C.: U.S. Government Printing Office.

Daily British Whig (Kingston, Ontario). 1851. March 26.

Dalan, R. A., and S. K. Banerjee. 1998. Solving archaeological problems using techniques of soil magnetism. *Geoarchaeology* 13:3–36.

Dale, H. W. 1864. Proceedings of a Board of Survey upon the Steamer *Maple Leaf,* April 2, 1864. Record Group 92, Vessel File. Washington, D.C.: U.S. National Archives.

Dames & Moore, Inc. 1979. Selected inventory, analysis, and mapping of resource variables, phase II—Manassas National Battlefield Park. Manassas, Va: Report on file, Manassas National Battlefield Park Archives.

Daniels, D. J. (ed.). 2004. *Ground Penetrating Radar.* London: Institution of Electrical Engineers.

Davis, W. C. 1975. *Duel Between the First Ironclads.* Mechanicsburg, Penn.: Stackpole Books.

———. (ed.). 1981–84. *The Image of War 1861–1865,* 6 vol. New York: Doubleday.

Davis, G. B., L. J. Perry, and J. Kirkley (eds.). 1891–95. *Atlas to Accompany the Official Records of the Union and Confederate Armies.* Washington, D.C.: U.S. Government Printing Office.

Delgado, J. P. 1992. Recovering the past of USS *Arizona:* symbolism, myth, and reality. *Historical Archaeology* 26(4):69–80.

———. 1996. *Ghost Fleet: The Sunken Ships of Bikini Atoll.* Honolulu: University of Hawaii Press.

———. 1997. *British Museum Encyclopaedia of Underwater and Maritime Archaeology.* London: British Museum Press.

Delgado, J. P., D. J. Lenihan and L. E. Murphy. 1991. *The Archaeology of the Atomic Bomb: A Submerged Cultural Resources Assessment of the Sunken Fleet of Operation Crossroads at Bikini and Kwajalein Atoll Lagoons.* Southwest Cultural Resources Center Professional Papers No. 37. Sante Fe, N. Mex.: U.S. Department of Interior, National Park Service.

de Meyer, M. 2006. A bird's eye view of the Ypres Salient. *In Flanders Fields Magazine* 16 (July): 3–4.

de Meyer, M., and P. Pype. 2004. *The A19 Project: Archaeological Research at Cross Roads.* Zarren, Belgium: Association for World War Archaeology.

——— and ———. 2006. Scars of the Great War (Western Flanders, Belgium). In *Fields of Conflict: Battlefield Archaeology from the Roman Empire to the Korean War,* vol. 2, ed. D. Scott, L. Babits, and C. Haecker, 359–382. Westport, Conn.: Praeger Security International, Greenwood Publishing Group, Inc.

Desfosses, Y., A. Jacques, and G. Prilaux. 2000. Premieres recherches sur la grande guerre dan le Nord-Pas-deCalais. *Archeologia* 367:32–38.

———, ———, and ———. 2005. *L'archeologie de la Grande Guerre.* Archeologie en Nord-Pas de Calais 10. Pas de Calais, France: D.R.A.C. Nord, Service Regional de l'Archeologie.

Dickey, T. S., and P. C. George. 1993. *Field Artillery Projectiles of the American Civil War.* Mechanicsville, Va.: Arsenal Publications II.

Diderot, D. (ed.). 1763. *Encyclopedie, ou Dictionnaire Raisonne des Sciences, des Arts et des Metiers,* 17 vols. Paris: André Le Breton, Michael-Antoine David, Laurent Durand, and Antoine-Claude Briasson.

Dinwiddie, R. 1884. *The Official Records of Robert Dinwiddie, Lieutenant-Governor of the Colony of Virginia, 1751–1758.* With notes by R. A. Brock. Richmond, Va.: The Virginia Historical Society.

DiPietro, B. 1999. Tojo's Granddaughter Visits Pearl Harbor. *Associated Press* March 30, 1999.

Dodd, G. 1856. *Pictorial History of the Russian War 1854–1856.* Edinburg, UK: Chambers.

Doddridge, J. 1824. *Notes on the Settlement and Indian*

Wars. Pittsburgh, Penn.: John S. Ritenour and William T. Lindsey.

Doyle, P. 1998. *Geology of the Western Front, 1914–1918.* London: The Geologists' Association.

Driggs, J. 1870. Report to Secretary of the Treasury George Boutwell, 29 August 1870. Record Group 56, General Records of the Department of the Treasury, Correspondence of the Office of the Secretary of the Treasury. Washington, D.C.: U.S. National Archives.

Drummond, J. (ed.). 1842. *The Memoirs of Sir Ewen Cameron of Locheill.* Edinburgh, Scotland: The Abbotsford Club.

Duane,W. 1809. *The American Military Library; or, Compendium of the Modern Tactics.* Philadelphia: Printed by B. Graves, for the author.

———. 1810. A Military Dictionary. Philadelphia: Printed and published by the author.

Duberly, Mrs. Henry. 1855. *Journal Kept During the Russian War from the Departure of the Army From England I April 1854, to the Fall of Sebastopol.* London: Longman, Brown, Green, and Longmans.

Duffy, C. 2003. *The Forty Five: Bonnie Prince Charlie and the Untold Story of the Jacobite Rising.* London: Cassell.

Dupras, T., and D. Pratte. 1998. Crainiometric study of the Parsons crania from midden 4/feature 245. In *The Archaeology of the Parsons Site: A Fifty Year Perspective,* ed. R. F. Williamson and D. Robertson, *Ontario Archaeology* 65/66:140–45.

Dupras, T. L., J. J. Schultz, S. M. Wheeler, and L. J. Williams. 2006. *Forensic Recovery of Human Remains: Archaeological Approaches.* New York: Taylor and Francis.

Dyer, G. 1985. *War.* New York: Crown Publishers.

Ellwood, B. B. 1978. Measurement of anisotropy of magnetic susceptibility—a comparison of the precision of torque and spinner magnetometer systems for basaltic specimens. *Journal of Physics E: Scientific Instruments* 11:71–75.

Empey, A. G. 1917. *Over The Top.* New York: G. P. Putnam's Sons.

Engelbrecht, W. 2003. *Iroquoia: The Development of a Native World.* Syracuse, N.Y.: Syracuse University Press.

Equipo Argentino de Antropolgia Forense (EAAF). 2005. Annual report 2005: covering the period January to December 2004. Buenos Aires, Argentina and New York: Argentine Forensic Anthropology Team/Equipo Argentino de Antropolgia Forense.

Epperly, D. 1862–65. Compiled letters of Daniel Epperly and his wife during the Civil War. Harrisonburg, Va.: On file, James Madison University Archaeological Research Library.

Espenshade, C. T., R. L. Jolley, and J. B. Legg. 2002. The value and treatment of Civil War military sites. *North American Archeologist* 23(1):39–67.

ESRI. 2009. What is GIS? http://www.gis.com/whatisgis/index.html (accessed August 31, 2009).

Evans, M. E., and F. Heller. 2003. *Environmental Magnetism—Principles and Applications of Enviromagnetics.* New York: Academic Press.

Ewing, C. B. 1894. The selection and physical examination of the recruit. In Transactions of the Third Annual Meeting of the Association of Military Surgeons of the National Guard of the United States; August 9–10, 1893; Chicago, Illinois. St. Louis, Mo.: Buxton and Skinner Stationary Co. p. 166–192.

Farnham, C. H. 1864. Proceedings of a Board of Survey upon the steamer *Maple Leaf,* April 2, 1864. Record Group 92, Vessel File. Washington, D.C.: U.S. National Archives.

Fassbinder, J. W. E., H. Stanjek, and H. Vali. 1990. Occurrence of magnetic bacteria in soil. *Nature* 343:161–163.

Feinman, G. M. 1997. Thoughts on new approaches to combining the archaeological and historical records. *Journal of Archaeological Method and Theory* 4(3/4):367–377.

Fenton, W., and E. Moore (eds.). 1974. *Customs of the American Indians Compared with the Customs of Primitive Times by Father Joseph Francois Lafitau.* Toronto: The Champlain Society.

Fenwick, K. (ed.). 1954. *Voice from the Ranks. A Personal Narrataive of the Crimean Campaign by a Sergeant of the Royal Fusiliers.* London: Folio Society.

Ferguson, L. G. 1973. *Exploratory Archaeology at the Scott's Lake Site (38CR1) Santee Indian Mound—Ft. Watson summer 1972.* Research Manuscript Series 36. Columbia, S.C.: University of South Carolina, Institute of Archaeology and Anthropology.

Finegan, J. 1864. Report to Brigadier General Thomas

Jordon, 26 February 1864. In *The War of the Rebellion: A Compilation of the Official Records of the Union and Confederate Armies,* ed. R. N. Scott, Series I, Volume 35, Part 1:330–333 (1891). Washington, D.C.: U.S. Government Printing Office.

Finnegan, T. J. 2006. *Shooting the Front: Allied Aerial Reconnaissance and Photographic Interpretation on the Western Front—World War I.* Washington, D.C.: National Defense Intelligence College.

Fiorato, V., A. Boylston, and C. Knisel (eds.). 2000. *Blood Red Roses: The Archaeology of a Mass Grave from the Battle of Towton, AD 1461.* Oxford, UK: Oxbow Book.

Fletcher, I., and N. Ishchenko. 2004. *The Crimean War: A Clash of Empires.* London: Spellmount Publishers.

Foard, G., and T. Perdita. 2005. *Scotland's Historic Fields of Conflict: An Assessment for Historic Scotland.* Norwich, Scotland: The Battlefields Trust.

Fontaine, A. 2004. Scattered bones: human fragmentary remains from the Lawson Site. MA thesis, University of Western Ontario, London, Ontario, Canada.

Foote, S. 1974. *The Civil War: A Narrative.* New York: Random House.

Forbes, A. 1895. *Colin Campbell Lord Clyde.* London: Macmillan.

Forbes, R. 1896. *The Lyon in Mourning.* Edinburgh, UK: Edinburgh University Press for the Scottish History Society.

Forrest, C. 2005. The in-house burials at the Late Ontario Iroquoian Draper Site (AlGt-2). MA thesis, University of Toronto, Toronto, Ontario, Canada

Foster, R. S. 1864. Special Order 48. Transcribed copy in Company Order Book, Company E, 13th Indiana Regiment. MacClenny, Fla.: Richard Ferry Collection.

Fox, R. A. Jr, 1993. *Archaeology, History, and Custer's Last Battle: The Little Big Horn Reexamined.* Norman, Okla.: University of Oklahoma Press.

Fox, R. A. Jr. and D. D. Scott. 1991. The Post-Civil War battlefield pattern. *Historical Archaeology* 25(2):92–103.

Fox, W. 1992. Dragon sideplates from York Factory: a new twist on an old tail. *Manitoba Archaeological Journal* 2(2):21–35.

Frassanito, W. A. 1983. *Grant and Lee; The Virginia Campaigns 1864–1865.* New York: Charles Scribner's Sons.

Gaede, F. C. 2001. *The Federal Civil War Shelter Tent.* Alexandria, Va.: O'Donnell Publications.

Gaffney, C. F., and J. A. Gater. 2003. *Revealing the Buried Past—Geophysics for Archaeologists.* Stroud, Gloucestershire, UK: Tempus Publishing.

Gardiner, J. (ed.). 2005. *Before the Mast: Life and Death Aboard the Mary Rose.* Portsmouth, UK: Mary Rose Trust.

Gardner, W. M. 1990. *In Search of the Stockade: Archeological Testing at Fort Edwards Hampshire County, West Virginia.* Woodstock, Va.: Thunderbird Research Associates.

Gardner, W. M., K. A. Snyder, and G. J. Hurst. 1999. A Phase I archeological investigation of the 12 acre Blenheim Property, City of Fairfax, Virginia. Woodstock, Va.: Report prepared for the City of Fairfax, Virginia by Thunderbird Archeological Associates, Inc.

Garrad C., and C. Heidenreich. 1978. Petun. In *Handbook of North American Indians Volume 15, Northeast,* ed. B.G. Trigger, 394–397. Washington, D.C.: Smithsonian Institution Press.

Garrison, E. G. 2003. *Geophysical Techniques for Archaeology.* New York: Springer-Verlag.

Geier, C. R., and S. Lotts. 2004. The battlefields of Fredericksburg and Chancellorsville and the associated properties of Chatham and Jackson's Shrine: report of findings and archaeological site descriptions to 2004, vol. 2: an overview and assessment of archaeological resources and landscapes within lands managed by Fredericksburg and Spotsylvania National Military Park. Harrisonburg, Va.: Report submitted to Fredericksburg & Spotsylvania National Military Park.

Geier, C. R., and K. Tinkham. 2006. Park histories, previous research, cultural resources and significant military and domestic themes, threat to resource with recommendations for resource management and interpretation, vol. 1: an overview and assessment of archaeological resources and landscapes within lands managed by Fredericksburg and Spotsylvania National Military Park. Harrisonburg, Va.: Report submitted to Fredericksburg & Spotsylvania National Military Park.

Geier, C. R., and S. E Winter (eds.). 1994. *Look To The Earth: Historical Archeology and the American Civil War.* Knoxville, Tenn.: University of Tennessee Press.

Geier, C. R., D. Orr, and M. Reeves. 2006. *Huts and History: the Historical Archaeology of Military Encampment During the American Civil War.* Gainesville, Fla.: The University Press of Florida.

Geometrics. 2009a. Marine Magnetometers. http://www.geometrics-products/geometrics-magnetometers (accessed August 21, 2009).

Geometrics. 2009 b. Magnetic Search in the Marine Environment. ftp://geom.geometrics.com/pub/mag/Literature/MarineSearch.pdf (accessed August 21, 2009).

Gibbon, J. 1860. *Artillerist's Manual.* Repr., Westport, Conn.: Greenwood Press, 1970.

Gibbs, M. 2006. Cultural site formation processes in maritime archaeology: disaster response, salvage and Muckelroy 30 years on. *International Journal of Nautical Archaeology* 35(1):4–19.

Gillett, M. C. 1987. *The Army Medical Department, 1775–1818.* Washington, D.C.: Center of Military History, United States Army.

———. 1991. *The Army Medical Department, 1818–1865.* Washington, D.C.: Center of Military History, United States Army.

———. 1995. *The Army Medical Department, 1865–1917.* Washington, D.C.: Center of Military History, United States Army.

Gilmore, Q. A. 1865. *Engineer and Artillery Operations Against the Defences of Charleston Harbor in 1863.* New York: D. Van Nostrand.

Girvin, G. T. 1993. *Maple Leaf's* story prior to the Civil War. In *The Maple Leaf: An Extraordinary American Civil War Shipwreck,* ed. K. V. Holland, L. B. Manley and J. W. Towart, 63–111. Jacksonville, Fla.: St. Johns Archaeological Expeditions, Inc.

Gonzalez, N. G., P. De Vivies, M. J. Drews and P. Mardikian. 2004. Hunting free and bound chloride in the wrought iron rivets from the American Civil War submarine *H. L. Hunley. Journal of the American Institute for Conservation* 43(2):161–74.

Goodyear, C. 1853. *Gum-elastic and its Varieties, with a Detailed Account of its Applications and Uses and of the Discovery of Vulcanization.* New Haven, Conn.: Published by the author.

Gould, R. A. 1983. The archaeology of war: wrecks of the Spanish Armada of 1588 and the Battle of Britain, 1940. In *Shipwreck Anthropology,* ed. R. A. Gould, 105–42. Albuquerque: University of New Mexico Press.

———. 1990. *Recovering the Past.* Albuquerque: University of New Mexico Press.

———. 2000. *Archaeology and the Social History of Ships.* Cambridge, UK: Cambridge University Press.

Gould, R. A. (ed.). 2007. *Disaster Archaeology.* Salt Lake City: University of Utah Press.

Gourevitch, P. 1998. *We Wish To Inform You That Tomorrow We Will Be Killed With Our Families: Stories from Rwanda.* New York: Picador.

Gramly, R. M. 1978. *Fort Laurens 1778–9: The Archaeological Record.* Richmond, Va.: William Byrd Press.

Graver, D. K. 2003. *Scuba Diving,* 3rd ed. Champaign, Ill.: Human Kinetics Publishers.

Graves, D. E. 1993. *The Battle of Lundy's Lane on the Niagara in 1814.* Baltimore, Md.: The Nautical & Aviation Publishing Company of America.

Green, J. N. 2004. *Maritime Archaeology: A Technical Handbook,* 2nd ed. San Diego, Calif.: Elsevier Academic Press.

Griffith, P. 1986. *Battle in the Civil War: Generalship and Tactics in America 1861–65.* Fieldhead, UK: Field Books.

Groome, D. 2001. *The Handbook of Human Rights Investigation: A Comprehensive Guide to the Investigation and Documentation of Violent Human Rights Abuses.* Northborough, Mass.: Human Rights Press.

Haecker, C. M. and J. G. Mauck. 1997. *On the Prairie of Palo Alto: Historical Archaeology of the U.S.-Mexican War Battlefield.* College Station: Texas A&M University Press.

Hagerty, Gilbert. 1971. *Massacre at Fort Bull.* Providence, R.I.: Mowbray Company.

Haglund, William, Melissa Connor, and Douglas D. Scott. 2001. The archaeology of mass graves. *Historical Archaeology* 35(1): 57–69.

Haines, Aubrey. 1991. *An Elusive Victory: The Battle of the Big Hole.* West Glacier, Mont.: Glacier Natural History Association.

Hale, John P. 1896. Trans-Allegheny Pioneers. Repr., Raleigh, N.C.: Derretth Printing Company, 1971.

Hall, R. 1997. *An Archaeology of the Soul: North*

American Indian Belief and Ritual. Chicago, Ill.: University of Illinois Press.

Hall, W., and R. Wilbanks. 1995. *Search for the Confederate Submarine* H. L. Hunley *Off Charleston Harbour, South Carolina: Final Report.* Charleston, S.C.: National Underwater and Marine Agency.

Halleck, Henry W. 1862. *Elements of Military Art and Science.* New York: D. Appleton.

Hamley, E. B. 1855. *The Story of the Campaign of Sebastopol.* London: William Blackwood and Sons.

———. 1891. *The War in the Crimea.* London: Seely and Co. Ltd.

Hammel, G. 1987. The Alhart Site: the cultural reconstruction. Draft manuscript in the possession of the author.

Hanna, William F. 1977. Weak-Field Magnetic Susceptibility Anisotropy and Its Dynamic Measurement. U.S. Geological Survey Bulletin 1418. Washington, D.C.: U.S. Government Printing Office.

Hanson, Mark D. 2005. Target architecture of a suspected firing range at Fort Steele, Wyoming. *Historical Archaeology* 39(4):45–58.

Hargreave Mawson, M. (ed.). 2001. *Eyewitness in the Crimea. The Crimean War Letters of Lieutenant Colonel George Frederick Dallas.* London: Greenhill Books.

Harper's Weekly. 1862. Building huts for the Army of the Potomac. January 18, 6(264):38.

Hatch, J. R. 1864a. Report to Brigadier General J. W. Turner, 1 April 1864. In *The War of the Rebellion: A Compilation of the Official Records of the Union and Confederate Armies,* ed. R. N. Scott, Series I, 35(1):380 (1891). Washington, D.C.: U.S. Government Printing Office.

———. 1864b. Letter to Brigadier General John W. Turner, 9 April 1864. In *The War of the Rebellion: A Compilation of the Official Records of the Union and Confederate Armies,* ed. R. N. Scott, Series I, 35 (2):47 (1891). Washington, D.C.: U.S. Government Printing Office.

Harrington, J. C. 1957. *New Light on Washington's Fort Necessity A Report on the Archaeological Explorations at Fort Necessity National Battlefield Site.* Richmond, Va.: Eastern National Park and Monument Association.

Harrison, N. G. 1989. Appendices for gazetteer of historic sites related to Fredericksburg and Spotsylvania National Military Park. Fredericksburg, Va.: On file at Department of Interior, National Park Service, Fredericksburg and Spotsylvania National Military Park.

Hawley, G. 2005. *Treasure in a Cornfield.* Kansas City, Mo.: Paddlewheel Publishing,

Heatwole, J. L. 1998. *The Burning; Sheridan in the Shenandoah Valley.* Charlottesville, Va.: Rockbridge Publishing.

Henderson, W. D. 1998. *Petersburg in the Civil War: War at the Door.* Lynchburg, Va.: H.E. Howard, Inc.

Hennessy, J. J. 1989. *The First Battle of Manassas: An End to Innocence, July 18–21, 1861.* Lynchburg, Va.: H. E. Howard, Inc.

———. 2005. For all anguish, for some freedom: Fredericksburg in the war. *Blue and Gray Magazine* 22(1):6–53.

Hess, E. J. 2005. *Field Armies and Fortifications in the Civil War.* Chapel Hill: The University of North Carolina Press.

———. 2008. *The Rifle Musket in Civil War Combat.* Lawrence: University Press of Kansas.

———. 2009a. *Old Armies and Fortifications in the Civil War.* Chapel Hill: University of North Carolina Press.

———. 2009b. *In the Trenches at Petersburg; Field Fortifications and Confederate Defeat.* Chapel Hill: University of North Carolina Press.

Hewett, J. B. (ed.). 1994. *Supplement to the Official Records of the Union and Confederate Armies.* Wilmington, N.C.: Broadfoot Publishing Company.

Hibbert, C. 1961. *The Destruction of Lord Raglan: A Tragedy of the Crimean War 1854–55.* London: Longmans.

Higgins, T. 1985. Efficient action in the construction of field fortifications: a study of the Civil War Defenses of Raleigh, North Carolina. MA thesis, College of William and Mary. Williamsburg, Va.

Hinman, C. 1895. *Corporal Si Klegg and his "Pard."* Cleveland, Ohio: N. G. Hamilton.

Holland, K. V., L. B. Manley, and J. W. Towart. 1993. *The* Maple Leaf *an Extraordinary American Civil War Shipwreck.* Jacksonville, Fla.: St. Johns Archaeological Expeditions, Inc.

Holland, T. D., B. E. Anderson, and R. W. Mann. 1993. Human variables in the postmortem alteration of human bone: examples from U.S. war casualties. In *Forensic Taphonomy: The Postmortem Fate of Human Remains,* ed. W. D. Haglund and M. H. Sorg, 263–274. New York: CRC Press.

Holschlag, S. L., and M. J. Rodeffer. 1976a. Ninety Six: siegeworks opposite Star Redoubt. Washington, D.C.: Manuscript on file, National Park Service, Office of Archaeology and Historic Preservation.

———— and ————. 1976b. Ninety Six: the stockade fort on the right. Washington, D.C.: Manuscript on file, National Park Service, Office of Archaeology and Historic Preservation.

———— and ————. 1976c. Ninety Six: exploratory excavations in the village. Washington, D.C.: Manuscript on file, National Park Service, Office of Archaeology and Historic Preservation.

Holschlag, S. L., M. J. Rodeffer, and M. L. Cann. 1978. *Ninety Six: The Jail.* Ninety Six, S.C. Star Fort Historical Commission.

Holyoak, V. and J. Schofield. 2002. *Military Aircraft Crash Sites, Archaeological Guidance on Their Significance and Future Management.* Swindon, UK: English Heritage

Holzer, H., and T. Mulligan (eds.). 2006. *The Battle of Hampton Roads: New Perspectives on the USS* Monitor *and CSS* Virginia. New York: Fordham University Press.

Howard, O. O. 1881. *Nez Perce Joseph.* Repr., New York: DaCapo Press, 1972.

Hoyt, E. 1811. *Practical Instructions for Military Officers.* Repr., Westport, Conn.: Greenwood Press, 1971.

Hunter, J. W. III. 2004. The Phinney Site: the remains of an American armed vessel scuttled during the Penobscot Expedition of 1779. *International Journal of Nautical Archaeology* 33(1):67–78

Hunter, J., and M. Cox. 2005. *Forensic Archaeology: Advances in Theory and Practice.* London: Routlege.

Hyde, W. L. 1866. *History of the One Hundred and Twelfth Regiment N.Y. Volunteers.* Fredonia, N.Y.: W. McKinstry and Co.

ICTR (International Criminal Tribunal for Rwanda). 1995. *Case No.: ICTR-95–1–1 The Prosecutor of Tribunal against Clement Kayishema, Ignace Bagilishema, Charles Sikubwabo, Aloys Ndimbate, Vincent Rutaganira, Mika Muhimana, Ryandikay,*

Obed Ruzindana. First Amended Indictment. Arusha: International Criminal Tribunal for Rwanda.

————. 1999. *The Prosecutor versus Clement Kayishema and Obed Ruzindana. Case No ICTR-95-I-T.* Arusha: International Criminal Tribunal for Rwanda.

Irvine, W. T. 1891. Old 35th Georgia: a brief history of the 35th Regiment of Georgia Volunteers from its organization to its surrender at Appomattox Court House, April 9, 1865. *The Sunny South,* May 2.

Itinerary of Military Operations. 1864. Itinerary of military operations, January 1 to November 13, 1864. In *The War of the Rebellion: A Compilation of the Official Records of the Union and Confederate Armies,* ed. R. N. Scott, Series I, 35(1):23, (1890). Washington, D.C.: U.S. Government Printing Office.

Jackson, C. O. (ed.). 1977. *Passing the Vision of Death in America.* Westport, Conn.: Greenwood Press.

Jackson, S. W. 1982. Crimean experiences by William Lowe. Journal of the Society for Army Historical Research 60: 103–111.

Jamestown-Yorktown Foundation. 2007. Homepage. http://www.historyisfun.org/yorktown/yorktown.cfm (accessed January 3, 2007).

Jamieson, J. B. 1983. An examination of prisoner-sacrifice and cannibalism at the St. Lawrence Iroquoian Roebuck Site. *Canadian Journal of Archaeology* 7(2):159–76.

Jarrell, E. W. 2004. *The Randolph Hornets in the Civil War: a History and Roster of Company M, 22nd North Carolina Regiment.* Jefferson, N.C.: McFarland & Company, Publishers.

Jeffery, B. 2004. World War II underwater cultural heritage sites in Truk Lagoon: considering a case for World Heritage listing. *International Journal of Nautical Archaeology* 33(1):106–21.

Jensen, T. L. 2000a. "Gimmie Shelter": Union shelters of the Civil War, a preliminary archeological typology. MA thesis, The College of William and Mary, Williamsburg, Va.

————. 2000b. Civil War archeology at Fort Pocahontas: life between the trenches. *Quarterly Bulletin, Archeological Society of Virginia* 55 (3):126–34.

Jirikowic, C., G. J. Hurst, and T. Bryant. 2004. Phase I archeological investigation at 206 North Quaker Lane, Alexandria, Virginia. Woodstock, Va.: Draft report to Meushaw Development Company, Alexandria, from Thunderbird Archeological Associates, Inc.,

Jocelyn, J. R. J. 1911. *The History of the Royal Artillery (Crimean Period)*. London: John Murray.

Johnson, J. K. (ed.). 2006. *Remote Sensing in Archaeology—An Explicitly North American Perspective*. Tuscaloosa: University of Alabama Press.

Johnston, C. J. (ed.). 1964. *The Valley of the Six Nations: A Collection of Documents on the Indian Lands of the Grand River*. Toronto: University of Toronto Press.

Johnston, R. B. 1990. *West Virginians in the Revolution*. Bowie, Md: Heritage Books.

Johnston, R. M. 1996. *Bull Run: Its Strategy and Tactics*. Carlisle, Penn.: John Kallmann, Publishers.

Jolley, R. L. In Review. An archaeological survey of the Confederate Left Flank, 3rd Battle of Winchester, Virginia, September 19, 1864. *Quarterly Bulletin, Archaeological Society of Virginia.*

Jones, J. B. 1999. "Our Brigade has never been in Winter Quarters, but Always in Tents & Moving About . . .": lessons learned from the archeological evaluation of Camp Mason, an early Confederate winter encampment near Winchester, Virginia. *Quarterly Bulletin, Archeological Society of Virginia* 54 (1):20–35.

Jones, S. D. 1864. Proceedings of a Board of Survey Upon the Steamer *Maple Leaf,* April 2, 1864. Washington, D.C.: U.S. National Archives, Record Group 92, Vessel File.

Joseph, M. 1996. Cultural landscape inventory: northeast quadrant. Manassas, Va.: Manuscript on file, Manassas Battlefield Park.

Joyce, C., and E. Stover. 1991. *Witnesses from the Grave: The Stories Bones Tell*. Boston, Mass.: Little, Brown and Company.

Kellogg, L. P. 1916. *Frontier Advance on the Upper Ohio, 1778–1779*. Madison: The State Historical Society of Wisconsin.

———. 1917. *Frontier Retreat on the Upper Ohio, 1779–1781*. Madison: The State Historical Society of Wisconsin.

Kelso, W. M. 2006. *Jamestown: The Buried Truth*. Charlottesville, Va.: University of Virginia Press.

Kennedy, F. H. 1998. *The Civil War Battlefield Guide*. Boston, Mass.: Houghton Mifflin.

Kepecs, S. 1997. Introduction to new approaches to combining the archaeological and historical records. *Journal of Archaeological Method and Theory* 4(3/4):193–98.

Keppie, L. 1989. The Roman Army of the Later Republic. In *Warfare in the Ancient World,* ed. J. Hackett, 169–91. New York: Facts on File.

Kerchevel, S. 1833. *A History of the Valley of Virginia*. Repr., Bowie, Md.: Heritage Books, 2001.

Kerr, P. 1997. *The Crimean War*. London: Boxtree.

King, A. 1998. *Memorials of the Great War in Britain: The Symbolism and Politics of Remembrance*. Oxford, UK: Berg.

King, W. K. 1980. *Tombstones for Bluecoats: New Insights into the Custer Mythology*. Marion Station, Calif.: Published by the author.

Kinglake, A. W. 1863–1867. *The Invasion of the Crimea: Its Origin and an Account of Its Progress Down to the Death of Lord Raglan*. London: Blackwood.

Klinck, C. F., and J. Talman (eds.). 1970. *The Journal of Major John Norton 1816*. Toronto: The Champlain Society.

Kloeppel, J. E. 1987. *Danger Beneath the Waves: A History of the Confederate Submarine* H.L. Hunley. Orangeburg, S.C.: Sandlapper Publishing.

Knoerl, T. K. 2009. The Museum of Underwater Archaeology. http://www.uri.edu/artsci/his/mua/MUA.htm.

Koontz, L. K. 1925. The Virginia Frontier, 1754–1763. Repr., Bowie, Md.: Heritage Books, 1992.

Kurland, M. 1997. *How to Try a Murder: The Handbook for Armchair Lawyers*. New York: MacMillan.

Kvamme, K. L. 2001. Current practices in archaeogeophysics: magnetics, resistivity, conductivity, and ground-penetrating radar. In *Earth Sciences and Archaeology,* ed. P. Goldberg, V. T. Holliday and C. R. Ferring, 353–84. New York: Plenum Publishers.

———. 2005. Terrestrial remote sensing in archaeology. In *Handbook of Archaeological Methods,* vol. 2, ed. H. D. G. Maschner and C. Chippindale, 423–77. Walnut Creek, Calif: AltaMira Press.

Lawson, C. C. P. 1961. *A History of the Uniforms of the British Army,* vol. III. London: Kaye and Ward.

Le Blond, M. 1764. *Elements de fortification, Contenant Les Principes & la description raisonnee des differens ouvrage qu'on on emploie a la Fortification des Places; les Systemes ses principaux Ingenieurs, la Fortification irreguliere, &c.* Paris: Charles-Antoine Jombert.

Le Borgne, E.1955. Susceptibilité magnetique anormale du sol superficiel. *Annales de Geophysique* 11:399–419.

Legg, J. B., and S. D. Smith. 1989. *"The Best Ever Occupied . . .": Archeological Investigations of Civil War Encampment on Folly Island, South Carolina.* Research Manuscript Series 209. Columbia, S.C.: The South Carolina Institute of Archaeology and Anthropology, University of South Carolina.

———— and ————. 2007. Camden: salvaging data from a heavily collected battlefield. In *Fields of Conflict: Battlefield Archaeology from the Roman Empire to the Korean War,* vol.1., ed. D. Scott, L. Babits, and C. Haecker, 208–33. Westport, Conn.: Praeger Security International, Greenwood Publishing Group, Inc.

Lenihan, D. J. (ed.). 1989. *Submerged Cultural Resources Study: USS* Arizona *Memorial and Pearl Harbor National Historic Landmark.* Professional Papers No. 23. Santa Fe, N. Mex.: U.S. Department of Interior, National Park Service, Submerged Cultural Resources Unit.

Lenihan, D. J., and L. E. Murphy. 1998. Research design. In H. L. Hunley *Site Assessment,* ed. L. Murphy, 15–20. Submerged Resources Center Professional Report No. 15. Santa Fe, N. Mex.: U.S. Department of Interior, National Park Service.

Lennox, P., and W. Fitzgerald. 1990. The culture history and archaeology of the Neutral Iroquoians. In *The Archaeology of Southern Ontario to* A.D. *1650,* ed. C. Ellis and N. Ferris, Occasional Publications of the London Chapter of the Ontario Archaeological Society No. 5. London, Ontario, Canada: Ontario Archaeological Society.

Leslie, F. 1896. *Frank Leslie's Illustrated History of the Civil War,* ed. L. S. Moat. New York: Published by Mrs. Frank Leslie.

Lewis, E. R. 1979. *Seacoast Fortifications of the United States.* Annapolis, Md.: Leeward Publications.

Lewis, V. A. 1906. Pioneer forts, stockades and blockhouses in West Virginia during the Border Wars. In *First Biennial Report of the Department of Archives and History of the State of West Virginia,* Appendix VIII:191–250. Charleston, W. Va.: The Tribune Printing Co.

Lightfoot, K. G. 2005. *Indians, Missionaries, and Merchants: The Legacy of Colonial Encounters on the California Frontiers.* Berkeley, Calif.: University of California Press,

Linenthal, E. T. 1991. *Sacred Ground: Americans and Their Battlefields.* Urbana, Ill.: University of Illinois Press.

Linford, N. T. 2006. The application of geophysical methods to archaeological prospection. *Reports on Progress in Physics* 69:2205–257.

List of Steamers. 1862. List of steamers in the employ of the War Department. In *Official Records of the Union and Confederate Navies in the War of the Rebellion,* ed. E. K. Rawson and C. W. Stewart, Series I, Volume 8:54 (1903). Washington, D.C.: U.S. Government Printing Office.

Liston, M. A., and B. J. Baker. 1995. Reconstructing the massacre at Fort William Henry, New York. *International Journal of Osteoarchaeology* 6:28–41.

Lloyd, E. M. 2004. Hamley, Edward Bruce. In *The Oxford Dictionary of National Biography,* vol. 24, ed. H.G.C. Matthews and B. Harrison, rev. R.T. Stearn, 942–45. Oxford, UK: Oxford University Press.

Lord, Francis A. 1965. *Civil War Collector's Encyclopedia: Arms, Uniforms, and Equipment of the Union and Confederacy.* New York: Castle Books

Lowry, Thomas P. 1994. *The Story the Soldiers Wouldn't Tell: Sex in The Civil War.* Mechanicsburg, Penn.: Stackpole Books.

Lucan, Earl of (Brudnell, James). 1855. Recall of the Earl of Lucan—Report of the Battle of Balaclava— Statement of the Earl of Lucan. *Hansard Parliamentary Debates* 137 (2 March 1855–2 May 1855): 730–74.

Lykke, Arthur F., Jr. (ed.). 1983. *Military Strategy: Theory and Application.* Carlisle Barracks, Penn.: U.S. Army War College,

Macbane, D. 2001. The expert sword-man's companion (1728). In *Highland Swordsmanship: Techniques of the Scottish Swordmasters,* ed. M. Rector, 24–87. Union City, Calif: Chivalry Bookshelf.

Mace, Rodney. 1976. *Trafalgar Square: Emblem of Empire.* London: Lawrence and Wishart.

Mackay, H. 1833. *Memoirs of the War carried on in Scotland and Ireland, 1689 to 1691.* Edinburgh, UK: Bannatyne Club.

Mahan, D. H. 1862. *A Complete Treatise on Field*

Fortification. Repr., Dayton, Ohio: Morningside Books, 1968.

Maher, B. A., and R. Thompson (eds.). 1999. *Quaternary Climates, Environments and Magnetism.* Cambridge, UK: Cambridge University Press.

Mahon, M. G. (ed.). 2002. *Winchester Divided: the Civil War Diaries of Julia Chase and Laura Lee.* Mechanicsburg, Penn.: Stackpole Books.

Mardikian, P. 2004. Conservation and management strategies applied to post-recovery analysis of the American Civil War Submarine *H. L. Hunley* (1864). *International Journal of Nautical Archaeology* 33(1):137–48.

Martin, C., and G. Parker. 1999. *The Spanish Armada.* New York: W. W. Norton.

Marvel, W. 1993. *The Battle of Fredericksburg.* National Park Civil War Series. Conshohocken, Penn.: Eastern National Park and Monument Association.

MIT (Massachusetts Institute of Technology). 2009. AUV lab at MIT SeaGrant. http://auvlab.mit.edu (accessed August 25, 2009).

Massie, A. (ed.). 2003. *A Most Desperate Undertaking: The British Army in the Crimea 1865–56.* London: National Army Museum.

Maxse, A. 1854. Letter from Fitz Maxse to his mother. http://www.crimeantexts.org.uk.sources (accessed December 2006).

Mayo, J. M. 1988. *War Memorials as Political Landscape.* New York: Praeger.

McAllister, J. T. 1913. *Virginia Militia in the Revolutionary War.* Repr., Bowie, Md.: Heritage Books, 1989.

McBride, W. S. 1994. Civil War material culture and camp life in central Kentucky. In *Look to the Earth: Historical Archaeology and the American Civil War,* ed. C. R. Geier, Jr. and S. E. Winter, 130–57. Knoxville.,Tenn.: The University of Tennessee Press.

———. 2001. *"For the Protection of Your Lives and Fortunes . . ." Archaeological Excavations at Fort Edwards, Hampshire County, West Virginia.* Lexington, Ky.: Wilbur Smith Associates.

———. 2005. *Report of the 2004 Archaeological Investigations at Fort Edwards, Hampshire County, West Virginia.* Lexington, Ky.: McBride Preservation Services.

McBride, W. S. and T. Gruber. 1999. *Historical and Archaeological Investigations of the Fort Edwards Properties.* Lexington, Ky.: Wilbur Smith Associates.

McBride, W. S., and K. A. McBride. 1991. *An Archaeological Survey of Frontier Forts in the Greenbrier and Middle New River Valleys of West Virginia.* Program for Cultural Resource Assessment Archaeological Report No. 252. Lexington, Ky.: University of Kentucky Program of Archaeological Research.

——— and ———. 1993. *Forting Up on the Greenbrier: Archaeological Investigations of Arbuckle's Fort, 46Gb13.* Program for Cultural Resource Assessment, Archaeological Report No. 312. Lexington, Ky.: University of Kentucky Program of Archaeological Research.

——— and ———. 1998. Archaeological investigations of Fort Arbuckle. *Journal of the Greenbrier Historical Society* 6(6):15–45.

——— and ———. 2003. *Archaeological Survey of Frontier Forts in Monroe, Pocahontas, and Randolph Counties, West Virginia.* Kentucky Archaeological Survey Report 79. Lexington, Ky.: Kentucky Archaeological Survey.

——— and ———. 2006. Archaeological investigations of Fort Donnally. *Journal of the Greenbrier Historical Society* 8(2):21–36.

McBride, W. S., and W. E. Sharp. 1991. *Archaeological Investigations at Camp Nelson: A Union Quartermaster Depot and Hospital in Jessamine County, Kentucky.* Program for Cultural Resource Assessment, Archaeological Report 241. Lexington, Ky.: University of Kentucky Program of Archaeological Research.

McBride, W. S., K. A. McBride, and G. Adamson. 2003. *Frontier Forts in West Virginia: Historical and Archaeological Investigations.* Charleston, W. Va.: West Virginia Division of Culture and History.

McBride, W. S., K. A. McBride, and J. D. McBride. 1996. *Frontier Defense for the Greenbrier and Middle New River Country.* Program for Cultural Resource Assessment, Archaeological Report No. 375. Lexington, Ky.: University of Kentucky Program of Archaeological Research.

McBride, W. S., S. C. Andrews, J. H. Beverly, and T. A. Sandefur. 2003. From supply depot to emancipation center, the archaeology of Camp Nelson, Kentucky. Lexington, Ky: Report prepared for the Kentucky Transportation Cabinet, Division of

Environmental Analysis, Frankfort, Kentucky by Wildur Smith Associates.

McCarthy, M. 2000. *Iron and Steamship Archaeology: Success and Failure on the SS* Xantho. New York: Kluwer Academic/Plenum Publishers.

McGuinn, W. F., and B. S. Bazelon. 1988. *American Military Button Makers and Dealers: Their Backmarks and Dates.* Chelea, Minn.: Bookcrafters, Inc.,

McKee, W. R., and M. E. Mason, Jr. 1980. *Civil War Projectiles II: Small Arms & Field Artillery with Supplement.* Orange, Va.: Publisher's Press, Inc.

McNeill, J. D. 1985. The galvanic current component in electromagnetic surveys. Geonics Limited Technical Note TN-17, Mississauga, Ontario, Canada

McWhorter, L. V. 1986. *Hear Me My Chiefs! Nez Perce History and Legend,* ed. Ruth Bordin. Caldwell, Idaho: Caxton Printers.

———. 1991. *Yellow Wolf: His Own Story.* Caldwell, Idaho: Caxton Printers.

Melton, J. W. Jr., and L. E. Pawl. 1994. *Introduction to Field Artillery Ordnance, 1861–1865.* Kennesaw, Ga.: Kennesaw Mountain Press.

Mercur, J. 1889. *Elements of the Art of War.* London: MacMillan.

Mills, J. C. 1910. *Our Inland Seas.* Repr., Cleveland, Ohio: Freshwater Press, 1976.

Milner, G. 1995. Osteological evidence for prehistoric warfare. In *Regional Approaches to Mortuary Analysis,* ed. L. A. Beck, 221–44. New York: Plenum Press.

Milner, G., E. Anderson, and V. G. Smith. 1991. Warfare in late Prehistoric and early Historic eastern North America. *American Antiquity* 56:581–603.

Miscellaneous Wrecks, 1871–1888, Record Group 77, File #1125, Atlanta Ga.: U.S. National Archives, Southeast Region.

Molto, J. E., M. W. Spence and W. A. Fox. 1986. The Van Oordt Site: a case study in salvage osteology. *Canadian Review of Physical Anthropology* 5(2):49–61.

Moore, A. 1983. *He Died Furious.* Baton Rouge, La.: Ortlieb Press.

Moore, J. W. 1981. *The Lowcountry Engineers: Military Missions and Economic Development in the Charleston District, U.S. Army Corps of Engineers.* Washington, D.C.: U.S. Government Printing Office.

Moore, W. S. 1998. Age determination of sediments at the *Hunley* site using ^{210}PB. In H. L. Hunley *Site Assessment,* ed. L. E. Murphy, 158–62. Submerged Resources Center Professional Report No. 15. Santa Fe, N. Mex.: U.S. Department of Interior, National Park Service.

Morrison, C. 1975. Frontier forts in the South Branch Valley. *West Virginia History* 36:131–39.

Morse, D., J. Duncan, and J. Stoutamire. 1983. *Handbook of Forensic Archaeology and Anthropology.* Tallahassee, Fla.: Rose Printing.

Morton, O. F. 1916. *A History of Monroe County, West Virginia.* Staunton, Va.: McClure Company.

Mosse, G. L. 1990. *Fallen Soldiers: Reshaping the Memory of the World Wars.* New York: Oxford University Press.

Muckelroy, K. 1978. *Maritime Archaeology.* Cambridge, UK: Cambridge University Press.

Muller, J. 1747. *The Attack and Defense of Fortify'd Places.* London: Printed for J. Millan.

———. 1756. A Treatise Containing the Elementary Part of Fortification. London: Printed for J. Nourse.

———. 1783. *The Field Engineer of M. le Chevalier de Clairac.* London: Printed for J. Millan.

Murphy, L. E. 1997. Remote sensing. In *Encyclopaedia of Underwater and Maritime Archaeology,* ed. J. P. Delgado, 340–44. London: British Museum Press.

———. (ed.). 1998. H. L. Hunley *Site Assessment.* Submerged Resources Center Professional Report No. 15. Santa Fe, N. Mex.: U.S. Department of Interior, National Park Service.

Murphy, L. E., and T. G. Smith. 1995. Submerged in the past: mapping the beguiling waters of Florida's Biscayne and Dry Tortugas national parks. *GeoInfo Systems* 5(10):26–33.

Murphy, L. E., M. A. Russell, and C. F. Amer. 1998a. Site description. In H.L. Hunley *Site Assessment,* ed. L. E. Murphy, 73–85. Submerged Resources Center Professional Report No. 15. Santa Fe, N. Mex.: U.S. Department of Interior, National Park Service.

Murphy, L. E., M. A. Russell and C. F. Amer. 1998b. Site analyses. In H. L. Hunley *Site Assessment,* ed. L. E. Murphy, 87–117. Submerged Resources Center Professional Report No. 15. Santa Fe, N. Mex.: U.S. Department of Interior, National Park Service.

Murphy, L. E., M. A. Russell, T. G. Smith, and S. M. Shope. 1998. Predisturbance remote sensing survey. In H.L. Hunley *Site Assessment,* ed. L. E. Murphy, 45–62. Submerged Resources Center Professional Report No. 15. Santa Fe, N. Mex.: U.S. Department of Interior, National Park Service.

Murray, R. 1864. Proceedings of a board of survey upon the steamer *Maple Leaf,* April 2, 1864. Washington, D.C.: U.S. National Archives, Record Group 92, Vessel File.

Murray, W. M., and P. M. Petsas. 1989. Octavian's Campsite Memorial for the Actian War. *Transactions of the American Philosophical Society* 79 (4):1–172.

Museum of Underwater Archaeology. 2009. Home-page. http://www.uri.edu/mua (accessed August 24, 2009).

Mytum, H. 2004. *Mortuary Monuments and Burial Grounds of the Historic Period.* New York: Kluwer Academic/Plenum Publishers.

Nabighian, M. N., V. Tien, J. S. Grauch, R. O. Hansen, T. R. LaFehr, Y. Li, J. W. Peirce, J. D. Phillips, and M. E. Ruder. 2005. The historical development of the magnetic method in exploration. *Geophysics* 70(6):33–61.

NPS (National Park Service). 1994. *Protecting Cultural Landscapes; Planning Treatment and Management of Historic Landscapes.* Bulletin 36, Preservation Briefs. Washington, D.C.: U.S. Department of the Interior.

———. 1995. *Shenandoah Civil War Sites Study: Battlefield Resources.* Washington, D.C.: U.S. Department of the Interior. Available at http://www.cr.nps.gov/hps/abpp/shenandoah/svs1–5.html.

———. 2007. Yorktown Battlefield. http://www.nps.gov/york/ (accessed August 24, 2007).

Nelson, D. 2006. "Right Nice Little House[s]": winter camp architecture of the American Civil War. In *Huts and History,* ed. C. Geier, D. Orr, and M. Reeves. Gainesville, Fla.: University Press of Florida.

Nesmith, J. H. 1824. *The Soldier's Manual.* Facsimile edition, Philadelphia: Riling, 1963.

Neyland, R. S., and C. F. Amer. 1998. Administrative history. In H. L. Hunley *Site Assessment,* ed. L. E. Murphy, 5–13. Submerged Resources Center Professional Report No. 15. Santa Fe, N. Mex.: U.S. Department of Interior, National Park Service.

North, N. A. 1976. Formation of coral concretions on marine iron. *International Journal of Nautical Archaeology* 5(3):253–258.

O'Connor, J. M. 1817. A Treatise on the Science of War and Fortification, 2 vols. Trans. of S. F. G de Vernon *Traite elementaire d'art militaire et de fortification* (1805). New York: J. Seymour.

O'Donnell, M., and J. D. Campbell. 1996. *American Military Belt Plates.* Alexandria, Va.: O'Donnell Publications.

O.R. (Official Records of the Union and Confederate Armies). 1997. *The War of the Rebellion: A Compilation of the Official Records of the Union and Confederate Armies.* CD-ROM version, originally published 1880–1901. Carmel, Ind.: Guild Press of Indiana.

O.R.N. (Official Records of the Union and Confederate Navies). 1999. *Official Records of the Union and Confederate Navies in the War of the Rebellion.* CD-ROM version, originally published 1894. Oakman, Ala.: H-Bar Enterprises.

Olson, C. 1995. Investigations of the CSS *Curlew:* a victim of the Battle of Roanoke Island, North Carolina. In *Underwater Archaeology: Proceedings from the Conference on Underwater and Historical Archaeology,* ed. P. F. Johnston, 28–33. Washington D.C.: Society for Historical Archaeology

Ordnance Department. 1861–1865. Summary statements of ordnance and ordnance stores in the hands of regular army and volunteer artillery regiments. Record Group 156, entry 109. Washington, D.C.: National Archives.

Ordnance Survey Map. 1867, 1st ed. Viewable at: http://www.oldmaps.co.uk/indexmappage2.aspx.

O'Reilly, F. A. 2003. *The Fredericksburg Campaign: Winter War on the Rappahannock.* Baton Rouge, La.: Louisiana State University Press.

Orser, C. E. 1996. *A Historical Archaeology of the Modern World: Contributions to Global Historical Archaeology.* New York: Plenum Press.

Osterburg, J. W., and R. H. Ward. 2004. *Criminal Investigation: A Method of Reconstructing the Past,* 4th ed. Cincinnati, Ohio: Anderson Publishing Company.

O'Shea, J. M. 2002. The archaeology of scattered wreck-sites: formation processes and shallow water archaeology in western Lake Huron. *International Journal of Nautical Archaeology* 31(2):211–27.

Owsley, D. W., W. F. Hanna, M. L. Richardson, and L. E. Burgess. 2001. *Bioarcheological and Geophysical Investigation, The Soldiers Plot, Emmanuel Lutheran Church Cemetery, New Market, Virginia (Site No. 44SH364)*. Archeological Society of Virginia Special Publication 41. Richmond, Va.: Archeological Society of Virginia.

Owsley, D. W., M. L. Richardson, and W. Hanna. 2003. Bioarcheological investigation and exhumation of the grave of remains of William D. Farley, Confederate Scout. *Quarterly Bulletin of the Archeological Society of Virginia* 58(2):94–113.

Paget, G. A. F. 1810. *The Light Cavalry Brigade in the Crimea: Extracts from the Letters and Journal of the Late General Lord Paget During the Crimean War*, ed. C. S. Paget. Glasgow, Scotland: John Murray.

Parasnis, D. S. 1996. *Principles of Applied Geophysics*. London: Chapman & Hall.

Parrington, M. 1979. Revolutionary war archaeology at Valley Forge, Pennsylvania. *North American Archaeologist* 1(2):161–76.

Papatheodorou, G., M. Geraga and G. Ferentinos. 2005. The Navarino Naval Battle Site, Greece—an integrated remote-sensing survey and a rational management approach. *International Journal of Nautical Archaeology* 34(1):95–109.

Paulet, F. 1854. Unpublished letter, (NAM 7305. 75). London: National Army Museum.

Peard, G. S. 1885. *Narrative of a Campaign in the Crimea*. London: Richard Bentley.

Peebles, M. D. 1995. CSS *Raleigh*: the history and archaeology of a Confederate ironclad in the Cape Fear River. In *Underwater Archaeology: Proceedings from the Conference on Underwater and Historical Archaeology* ed. P. F. Johnston, 20–27. Washington D.C.: Society for Historical Archaeology.

Pemberton, W. B. 1962. *Battles of the Crimean War*. London: Batsford.

Percy, A. 2005. *A Bearskin's Crimea. Colonel Henry Percy VC and His Brother Officers*. Barnsley, UK: Leo Cooper.

Perry, M. F. 1965. *Infernal Machines*. Baton Rouge, La.: Louisiana State University Press.

Petsche, J. E. 1974. *The Steamboat* Bertrand: *History Excavation and Architecture*. National Parks Service Publications in Archaeology No. 11. Washington, D.C.: U.S. Government Printing Office.

Pfanz, D. C. 2003. *War So Terrible: A Popular History of the Battle of Fredericksburg*. Richmond, Va.: Page One History Publications.

Pfeiffer, S., and R. F. Williamson. 1991. *Snake Hill, An Investigation of a Military Cemetery from the War of 1812*. Toronto: Dundurn Press.

Phillip, J. (of Almerieclose). 1888. *The Grameid: An Heroic Poem Descriptive of the Campaign of Viscount Dundee in 1689 and Other Pieces*. Edinburgh, UK: Edinburgh University Press for the Scottish History Society.

Pollard, T. 2006 Archaeological Survey of Culloden Battlefield. GUARD report 1981, University of Glasgow. Glasgow, UK.

———. 2009a. Mapping mayhem: Scottish battle maps and their role in archaeological research. *Scottish Geographical Journal* 125 (1):25–43.

———. (ed). 2009b. *Culloden: the History and Archaeology of the Last Clan Battle*. Barnsley, UK: Pen and Sword.

Pollard, T. and Oliver, N. 2002. *Two Men in a Trench: Battlefield Archaeology, the Key to Unlocking the Past*. London: Michael Joseph/Penguin UK.

——— and ———. 2003. *Two Men in a Trench II: Uncovering the Secret's of British Battlefields*. London: Michael Joseph/Penguin UK

Potter, S. R., R. C. Sonderman, and M. C. Creveling. 2000. No maneuvering and very little tactics—archaeology and the Battle of Brawner Farm. In *Archaeological Perspectives on the American Civil War*, ed. C. R. Geier and S. R. Potter, 3–28. Gainesville, Fla.: University Press of Florida.

Prange, G. W. 1986. *Pearl Harbor: The Verdict of History*. New York: McGraw-Hill.

Quinn, R. 2006. The role of scour in shipwreck site formation processes and the preservation of wreck-associated scour signatures in the sedimentary record—evidence from seabed and sub-surface data. *Journal of Archaeological Science* 33:1419–432.

Rainey, D. L. 2002. Challenging assumptions: an analysis of the scattered human remains at the Keffer Site (AkGv-14). MA thesis, University of Western Ontario. Ontario, Canada.

Ratner, S. R., and J. S. Abrams. 2001. *Accountability for Human Rights Atrocities in International Law: Beyond the Nuremberg Legacy*, 2nd ed. Oxford, UK: Oxford University Press.

Records, S. 1842. Letter. Draper Manuscripts, 22CC95–97. Madison: Wisconsin State Historical Society.

Reeves, M. B. 2001. *Dropped and Fired: Archeological Patterns of Militaria from two Civil War Battlefields, Manassas National Battlefield Park.* Occasional Report No. 15, Regional Archaeology Program. Washington, D.C.: U.S. Department of the Interior, National Park Service, National Capital Region.

———. 2006. Under the forest floor: excavations at a Confederate winter encampment, Orange, Virginia. In *Huts and History,* ed. C. Geier, D. Orr, and M. Reeves, 194–216. Gainesville, Fla.: University Press of Florida.

Reid, S. 1998. *Like Hungry Wolves: Culloden Moor, 16 April 1746.* Marlborough, UK: The Crowood Press.

———. 2003. *Battles of the Scottish Lowland, Battlefield Britain.* Barnsley, UK: Pen and Sword.

Renfrew, C., and P. Bahn. 2004. *Archaeology; Theories, Methods and Practice,* 4th ed. New York: Thames and Hudson.

Reynolds, J. M. 1997. *An Introduction to Applied and Environmental Geophysics.* New York: John Wiley & Sons.

Reynolds, R. L., J. G. Rosenbaum, M. R. Hudson, and N. S. Fishman. 1990. Rock magnetism, the distribution of magnetic minerals in the earth's crust, and aeromagnetic anomalies. In *Geologic Applications of Modern Aeromagnetic Surveys,* ed. W. F. Hanna, 24–45. U.S. Geological Survey Bulletin 1924. Denver, Colo.: U.S. Government Printing Office.

Rhodes, R. H. (ed). 1985. *All for the Union: A History of the 2nd Rhode Island Volunteer Infantry in the War of the Great Rebellion As Told by the Diary and Letters of Elisha Hunt Rhodes.* Lincoln, R.I.: Andrew Mowbray Inc.

Rich, E. E. 1976. The fur traders: their diet and drugs. *The Beaver, Magazine of the North,* Summer:42–53.

Richardson, M. L. 2002. The probe—a remote sensing system. *Quarterly Bulletin of the Archeological Society of Virginia* 57(2):72–76.

Richter, D. K. 1983. War and culture: the Iroquois experience. *The William and Mary Quarterly* 40(4):528–59.

Riess, W., and G. Daniel. 1997. Evaluation of preservation efforts for the Revolutionary War privateer *Defence. International Journal of Nautical Archaeology* 26(4):330–38.

Riling, R. (ed.). 1966. *Baron Von Steuben and his Regulations.* Philadelphia: Ray Riling Arms Books.

Roberts, H. B. 1854. Letter of Lt. Henry B. Roberts, Royal Marine Artillery, 27 October 1854, Camp Balaklava, No. 4 Battery. Unpublished letter, NAM 6702. 36 1 and 2. London: National Army Museum.

Robertson, G. 1999. *Crimes against Humanity: The Struggle for Global Justice.* New York: The New Press.

Robertson, J. I. Jr. 1984. *Tenting Tonight: The Soldiers Life.* The Civil War Series. Alexandria, Va.: Time-Life Books.

Robertson, M. G. 2001. Los murales de la tumba del Templo XX sub. de Palenque. In *La Pintura Mural Prehispanica en Mexico, II, Area Maya,* Tomo IV, ed. Beatriz de la Fuente, 381–88. México, D.F.: IIE, Universidad Nacional Autónoma de México.

Robertson, D., R. F. Williamson, and B. Welsh. 1998. Settlement patterns at the Parsons Site. *Ontario Archaeology* 65/66:21–52.

Robinson, A. 2001. Lost crew of Hood is honored. *Plymouth Evening Herald* (London), July 27.

Robinson, F. 1856. *Diary of the Crimean War.* London: Richard Bentley.

Robinson, W. B. 1977. *American Forts—Architectural Form and Function.* Urbana, Ill.: University of Illinois Press.

Rodgers, B. A., W. M. Coble and H. K. Van Tilburg. 1998. The lost flying boat of Kaneohe Bay: archaeology of the first U.S. casualties of Pearl Harbor. *Historical Archaeology* 32(4):8–18.

Ruppé, C. V., and J. F. Barstad. 2002. *International Handbook of Underwater Archaeology.* New York: Kluwer Academic/Plenum Publishers.

Russell, W. H. 1855. *The War from the Landing at Gallipoli to the Death of Lord Raglan.* London: George Routledge & Co.

———. 1877. *The British Expedition to the Crimea.* London: George Routledge and Sons.

Russell, S., and M. A. Fleming. 1991. A bulwark in the Pacific: An example of World War II archaeology on Saipan. In *Archaeological Studies of World War II,* ed. W. Raymond Wood, 13–28. Museum of

Anthropology Monograph Number 10, Columbia, Mo.: University of Missouri Museum.

Russell, M. A., and L. E. Murphy. 1998. Field operations. In H. L. Hunley *Site Assessment,* ed. L. E. Murphy, 63–71. Submerged Resources Center Professional Report No. 15. Santa Fe, N. Mex.: U.S. Department of Interior, National Park Service.

Russell, M. A., L. E. Murphy, D. L. Johnson, T. J. Foecke, P. J. Morris, and R. Mitchell. 2004. Science for stewardship: multidisciplinary research on USS *Arizona. Marine Technology Society Journal* 38(3):54–63.

Russell, W. 1883. Letter from First Lieutenant William Russell to Captain J. C. Post, 13 March 1883. In Record Group 77, Transcript from Entry 1154, Box 2, Jacksonville District, Corps of Engineers, 241–43. East Point, Ga.: U.S. National Archives, Southeast Region.

Sahlins, M. 1992. *Anahulu: The Anthropology of History in the Kingdom of Hawaii.* Historical Ethnography, vol. 1. Chicago, Ill.: University of Chicago Press.

Sandby, T. 1746. *The Plan of the Battle of Culloden, April 16th, 1746.* Windsor, UK: Royal Library.

Sanderson, J. M. 1862. *Camp Fires and Camp Cooking; or Culinary Hints for the Soldier including Receipt for Making Bread in the "Portable Field Oven" Furnished by the Subsistence Department.* Repr., Laramie, Wyo.: Sue's Frou Frou Publications, 1986.

Sands, J. O. 1983. *Yorktown's Captive Fleet.* Charlottesville, Va.: University Press of Virginia.

———. 1988. Gunboats and warships of the American Revolution. In *Ships and Shipwrecks of the Americas: A History Based on Underwater Archaeology,* ed. G. F. Bass, 143–68. London: Thames and Hudson.

Saxe, H. M. (Field Marshal). 1757. *Reveries or Memoirs Upon the Art of War.* London: J. Nourse.

Schabas, W. A. 2000. *Genocide in International Law.* Cambridge, UK: Cambridge University Press.

Scollar, I., A. Tabbagh, A. Hesse, and I. Herzog. 1990. *Archaeological Prospecting and Remote Sensing.* Cambridge, UK: Cambridge University Press.

Scott, D. D. 1989. An officer's latrine at Fort Larned and inferences on status. *Plains Anthropologist* 34:23–34.

———. 1991. Earthworks in the Trans-Mississippi West. In *Society for Historical Archaeology Annual Meeting Abstracts,* Richmond, Va.

———. 1994. *A Sharp Little Affair: The Archeology of the Big Hole Battlefield.* Lincoln, Nebr.: J & L Reprint.

Scott, D. D., and R. A. Fox, Jr. 1987. *Archaeological Insights into the Custer Battle—an Assessment of the 1984 Field Season.* Norman: University of Oklahoma Press.

Scott, D. D., and W. J. Hunt, Jr. 1997. The Civil War Battle at Monroe's Crossroads, Fort Bragg, North Carolina: A Historical Archaeological Perspective. Tallahassee, Fla.: U.S. Department of Interior, National Park Service, Southeast Archeological Center.

Scott, D. D., L. Babits, and C. Haecker (eds.). 2006. *Fields of Conflict: Battlefield Archaeology from the Roman Empire to the Korean War.* Greenwood Publishing Group, Inc.

Scott, D. D., P. Willey, and M. Connor. 1998. *They Died With Custer: The Soldiers' Skeletons From The Battle of the Little Bighorn.* Norman: University of Oklahoma Press.

Scott, D. D., R. A. Fox Jr., M. A. Connor, and D. Harmon. 1989. *Archaeological Perspectives on the Battle of the Little Bighorn.* Norman: University of Oklahoma Press.

Seaton, A. 1977. *The Crimean War: A Russian Chronicle.* London: Batsford.

Seigel, P. E., W. P. Catts, W. J. Chadwick, J. Balicki, M. A. Tobias, and J. Gerhardt. 2006. Phase I and II archeological investigations for the proposed gateway entrance to Valley Forge National Historical Park, S.R. 0422, Section SRC, Upper Marion Township, Montgomery County, Pennsylvania. West Chester, Penn.: Report to Boles, Smyth Associates, Inc., Philadelphia, Penn., from John Milner Associates, Inc.

Sever, T. L. 2000. Remote sensing methods. In *Science and Technology in Historic Preservation,* vol. 4. ed. R. A. Williamson and P. R. Nickens, 21–51. Dordrecht, Netherlands: Kluwer Academic Publishers.

Shadwell, L. 1881. *The Life of Colin Campbell, Lord Clyde.* Edinburgh, UK: W. Blackwood and Sons,

Sharer, R. J., and W. Ashmore. 2003. *Archaeology, Discovering our Past,* 3rd ed. New York: McGraw-Hill Higher Education.

Sharma, P. V. 1997. *Environmental and Engineering Geophysics.* Cambridge, UK: Cambridge University Press.

Sheire, J. W. 1968. Fort Larned National Historic Site, historic structures report part I. Washington, D.C.: U.S. Department of Interior, National Park Service, Office of Archeology and Historic Preservation.

Shields, George O. 1889. *Battle of the Big Hole.* Chicago, Ill.: Rand McNally Co.

Shiman, Phillip. 1990. *Fort Branch and the Defense of the Roanoke Valley 1862–1865.* Hamilton, N.C.: Fort Branch Battlefield Commission.

Shope, S. M., L. E. Murphy and T. G. Smith. 1995. Found at sea: charting Florida's sunken treasures. *GPS World* 6(5):22–34.

Sigler-Eisenberg, B. 1985. Forensic research: explaining the concept of applied archaeology. *American Antiquity* 50:650–655.

Silberman N. A. 2004. In Flanders Fields: uncovering the carnage of World War I. *Archaeology* 57(3):24–29.

Silverstein, J., J. Byrd, and L. Otineru. 2006. Hill 209: The last stand of Operation Manchu, Korea. In *Fields of Conflict: Battlefield Archaeology from the Roman Empire to the Korean War,* vol. 2, ed. D. D. Scott, L. Babits, and C. Haecker, 417–28. Westport, Conn.: Praeger Security International, Greenwood Publishing Group, Inc.

Silvia, S. W., and M. J. O'Donnell. 1996. *The Illustrated History of American Civil War Relics.* Orange, Va.: Publisher's Press, Inc.

Silvia, S. W., T. Law, J. Melton, B. Buttafuso, C. Harris, and M. O'Donnell. 2006. Relic hunting in the 21st century. *North South Trader's Civil War* 32 (2):40–60.

Simes, T. 1768. *An Universal Military Dictionary.* Repr., Ottawa, Ontario: Museum Restoration Services, 1969.

Skene, J. H. 1883. *With Lord Stratford in the Crimean War.* London: Richard Bentley.

Slotkin, R. 2009. *No Quarter: the Battle of the Crater, 1864.* New York: Random House.

Smith, G. 1779. *An Universal Military Dictionary.* London: John Millan.

Smurthwaite, D. 1993. The Complete Guide to the Battlefields of Britain. London: Mermaid.

Smythe, Donald. 1981. Honoring the Nation's dead. *American History Illustrated* 16(2):26–33.

Snow, C. C. 1995. A murder most foul. *The Sciences* May/June:16–20.

Snow, C. C., L. Levine, L. Lukash, L. G. Tedeschi, C. Orrego, and E. Stover. 1984. The investigation of the human remains of the "disappeared" in Argentina. *The American Journal of Forensic Medicine and Pathology* 5(4):297–299.

———, ———, ———, ———, ———, and ———. 1985. Scientists aid search for Argentina's "desparecidos." *Science* 230:56–57.

Snow, D. R. 1981. Battlefield archeology. *Early Man* 3(1):18–21.

Snyder, D. 1862–65. Compiled letters of Daniel Snyder for the period of the Civil War. Harrisonburg, Va.: On file, Clarke County Virginia Historical Society, James Madison University Archaeological Research Library,

Sosin, J. M. 1967. *The Revolutionary Frontier, 1763–1783.* New York: Holt, Rinehart and Winston.

Soubier, L. C. and W. L. Brown III. 1989. Historic furnishings report, Post Hospital, HS-2, New Commissary, HS-4, Old Commissary Storehouse, HS-5, Quartermaster Storehouse, HS-6, Officers' Quarters, HS-7, Fort Larned National Historic Site, Kansas. Harpers Ferry, W.Va.: U.S. Department of Interior, National Park Service, Harpers Ferry Center.

South, S. 1973. *Palmetto Parapets.* Anthropological Studies 1. Columbia, S.C.: University of South Carolina, Institute of Archaeology and Anthropology.

Southern Claims Commission Files. Files related to Fredericksburg Area. Bound Volumes 296–301. Fredericksburg, Va.: On file at Fredericksburg and Spotsylvania National Park.

Souza, D. J. 1998. *The Persistence of Sail in the Age of Steam: Underwater Archaeological Evidence from the Dry Tortugas.* New York: Plenum Press.

Springman, M. 2005. *Sharpshooter in the Crimea: The Letters of Captain Gerald Goodlake VC.* Barnsley, UK: Pen and Sword.

Starbuck, D. R. 1999. *The Great Warpath: British Military Sites from Albany to Crowne Point.* Hanover, N.H.: University of New England Press.

State Historical Society of Wisconsin. 1915. The

Preston and Virginia Papers of the Draper Collection of Manuscripts. Repr., Utica: Ky.: McDowell Publications, 1985.

———, ———, ———. 1991. Calendar of the Frontier Wars Papers of the Draper Collection of Manuscripts. Utica: Ky.: McDowell Publications.

State Historical Society of Wisconsin and M. C. Weaks. 1925. Calendar of the Kentucky Papers of the Draper Collection of Manuscripts. Repr., Utica: Ky.: McDowell Publications, 1991.

Steadman, D. W., and W. D. Haglund. 2005. The scope of anthropological contributions to human rights investigations. *Journal of Forensic Science* 50(1):23–30.

Steere, E. 1948. Genesis of American graves registration, 1861–1870. *Military Affairs* 12(3):149–61.

Sterling, A. 1895. *The Highland Brigade in the Crimea Founded on Letters Written During the Years 1854, 1855 and 1856.* Repr., Minneapolis, Minn.: Absinthe Press, 1995.

Sterling, B. B., and B. W. Slaughter. 2000. Surveying the Civil War. In *Archeological Perspectives on the American Civil War,* ed. C. R. Geier and S. Potter, 305–22. Gainesville, Fla.: University of Florida Press.

Stevens, B. F. 1898. *Facsimiles of Manuscripts in European Archives Relating to America: 1773–1783.* London: Chadwick Press.

Stevens, W. D., and J. M. Leader. 2006. Skeletal remains from the Confederate Naval Sailor and Marines' Cemetery, Charleston, SC. *Historical Archaeology* 40(3):74–88.

Stewart, D. J. 1999. Formation processes affecting submerged archaeological sites: an overview. *Geoarchaeology* 14:565–87.

———. 2004. "Rocks and storms I'll fear no more": Anglo-American maritime memorialization, 1700–1940. Ph.D. diss., Texas A&M University, College Station, Tex.

———. 2007. Gravestones and monuments in the maritime cultural landscape: research potential and preliminary interpretations. *International Journal of Nautical Archaeology* 36:112–24.

Stillé, C. J. 1866. *History of the United States Sanitary Commission: Being The General Report of Its Work During the War of the Rebellion.* Philadelphia: J.B. Lippincott.

Stinson, D. E. 1966. Historic structures report, Fort Larned, Kansas. Washington, D.C.: Manuscript on file, U.S. Department of Interior, National Park Service, Office of Archeology and Historic Preservation.

Stone, R. 1977. *A Brittle Sword: The Kentucky Militia, 1776–1912.* Lexington: University Press of Kentucky.

Stover, E., and M. Ryan. 2001. Breaking bread with the dead. *Historical Archaeology* 35 (1):7–25.

Strutt, M. A. 1991. Rediscovering the dead—practical applications of remote sensing in historic cemeteries. MA thesis, College of William and Mary, Williamsburg, Va.

Strutt, M. A., and W. F. Hanna. 1998. Magnetic story of a brick kiln at Thomas Jefferson's Poplar Forest. Society for Historical Archaeology 31st Annual Meeting; 1998, January 6–10, Atlanta, Ga.; abstract 40.

Stuart, J. 1820. Memoirs of Indian Wars. Repr., Bowie, Md.: Heritage Books, 1994.

Studenski, P., and H. Krooss. 1963. *Financial History of the United States,* 2nd ed. New York: McGraw Hill.

Summers, L. P. 1929. *Annals of Southwest Virginia, 1769–1800.* Abington, Va.: Published by the author.

Sunday Mercury Newspaper (London). 2001. Brit divers pay tribute. October 14.

Sweetman, J. 1990. *Balaclava 1854. The Charge of the Light Brigade.* Oxford, UK: Osprey Publishing.

———. 2004a. Kinglake, Alexander W. In *The Oxford Dictionary of National Biography,* vol. 31, ed. H. C. G. Matthews and B. Harrison, 695–96. Oxford, UK: Oxford University Press.

———. 2004b. Bingham, George Charles, the Third Earl of Cardigan. In *The Oxford Dictionary of National Biography,* vol 5, ed. H.C.G. Matthews and B. Harrison, 753–56. Oxford, UK: Oxford University Press.

Switzer, R. R. 1995. *The Bertrand bottles: A Study of 19ᵗʰ Century Glass and Ceramic Containers.* Repr., Washington, D.C.: U.S. Department of Interior, National Park Service, 1974.

Tanner, J. M. 1981. *The History of the Study of Human Growth.* Cambridge, UK: Cambridge University Press.

Taylor, J. E. 1989. *With Sheridan up the Shenandoah Valley in 1864: Leaves From a Special Artists Sketch Book and Diary.* Cleveland, Ohio: Western Reserve Historical Society.

Telford, W. M., L. P. Geldart, and R. E. Sheriff. 2003. *Applied Geophysics.* Cambridge, UK: Cambridge University Press.

Tennis, C. L. 1995. Exhumation of a hero, Colonel Ben Milam, Milam Park Renovation Phase I. San Antonio, Tex.: The University of Texas at San Antonio, Center for Archaeological Research, Archaeological Survey Report No. 223.

Terry, C. S. 1905. *John Graham of Claverhouse, Viscount of Dundee 1648–1689.* London: Archibald Constable and Company.

Thacher, James. 1827. *A Military Journal During the American Revolutionary War, from 1775–1783,* 2nd ed. Boston: Cottons & Barnard.

Thomas, C. W. 1863. Letter to Captain William McKim, 10 June 1863. Record Group 123. Washington, D.C.: U.S. National Archives.

Thomas, D. S. 1981. *Ready . . . Aim . . . Fire!: Small Arms Ammunition in the Battle of Gettysburg.* Gettysburg, Penn.: Thomas Publications.

———. 1997. *Round Ball to Rim Fire: A History of Civil War Small Arms Ammunition, Part One.* Gettysburg, Penn.: Thomas Publications.

———. 2002. *Round Ball to Rimfire: A History of Civil War Small Arms Ammunition, Part Two: Federal Breechloading Carbines and Rifles.* Gettysburg, Penn.: Thomas Publications.

———. 2003. *Round Ball to Rimfire: A History of Civil War Small Arms Ammunition, Part Three: Federal Pistols, Revolvers, and Miscellaneous Essays.* Gettysburg, Penn.: Thomas Publications.

Thomas, J. E., and Dean S. Thomas. 1996. *A Handbook of Civil War Bullets and Cartridges.* Gettysburg, Penn.: Thomas Publications.

Thompson, R., and F. Oldfield. 1986. *Environmental Magnetism.* London: Allen & Unwin.

3H Consulting, Ltd. 2009. Site Recorder 4. http://www.3hconsulting.com.

Thwaites, R.G. 1896–1901. *The Jesuit Relations and Allied Documents,* 73 vols. Cleveland, Ohio: Burrows Brothers.

Thwaites, R. G., and L. P. Kellogg. 1905. *Documentary History of Dunmore's War, 1774.* Draper Series Vol. 1. Madison: The State Historical Society of Wisconsin.

——— and ———. 1908. *The Revolution on the Upper Ohio, 1775–1777.* Draper Series Vol. 2.

Madison: The State Historical Society of Wisconsin.

——— and ———. 1912. *Frontier Defense on the Upper Ohio, 1777–1781.* Draper Series Vol. 3. Madison: The State Historical Society of Wisconsin.

Tice, W. K. 1997. *Uniform Buttons of the United States 1776–1865.* Gettysburg, Penn.: Thomas Publications.

Tinkham, K., S. Evans, and C. Geier. 2003. "The little brick house alongside of Squire's guns which was white at the beginning of the battle, was perfectly red with bullet-marks at its close": an archaeological assessment of mid-19th century domestic structures on Willis Hill. Harrisonburg, Va.: Report Submitted to Fredericksburg and Spotsylvania National Military Park, Department of Sociology and Anthropology, James Madison University.

Tilley, J. A. 1987. *The British Navy and the American Revolution.* Columbia: The University of South Carolina Press.

Tisdall, E. E. P. 1963. *Mrs Duberly's Campaign. An Englishwomen's Experience in the Crimean War and the Indian Mutiny.* London: Jarrold.

Todd, F. P. 1978. *American Military Equipage 1851–1872.* New York: Charles Scribner's Sons.

———. 1983. *American Military Equipage 1851–1872, Volume II: State Forces.* New York: Chatham Square Press, Inc.

Tooker, E. 1964. *An Ethnography of the Huron Indians 1615–1649.* Bulletin 190. Washington, D.C.: Smithsonian Institution, Bureau of American Ethnology.

Toomey, D. C. 2004. *The Civil War in Maryland.* Baltimore, Md.: Toomey Press.

Trigger, B. G. 1969. *The Huron: Farmers of the North.* New York: Holt, Rinehart and Winston.

———. 1976. *The Children of Aataentsic: a History of the Huron People to 1660.* Montreal: McGill-Queens University Press.

———. 1989. *A History of Archaeological Thought.* Cambridge, UK: Cambridge University Press.

Troiani, D., E. J. Coats, and M. J. H. McAfee. 2002. *Don Troiani's Regiments and Uniforms of the Civil War.* Mechanicsville, Penn.: Stackpole Books.

Trudeau, N. A. 1993. *The Last Citadel: Petersburg, Virginia, June 1864–April 1865.* Baton Rouge, La.: Louisiana State University Press.

Union and Advertiser (Rochester, New York). 1857. March 21.

————. 1862. August 14.

Unrau, W. E. 1957. The story of Fort Larned, Kansas. *Kansas Historical Quarterly* Autumn:257–80.

U.S. Army. 1984. *Machinegun 7.62mm, M60.* Field Manual 23–67. Washington, D.C.: U.S. Government Printing Office.

United States War Department. 1861. *Revised Regulations for the Army of the United States, 1861.* Repr., Harrisburg, Penn.: The National Historical Society, 1980.

————. 1863. *Rules for the Management and Cleaning of the Rifle Musket, Model 1863, for the use of Soldiers with Descriptive Plates.* Washington, D.C.: U.S. Government Printing Office.

————. 1917. *Manual for Noncommissioned Officers and Privates of Infantry.* Washington, D.C.: U.S. Government Printing Office.

Vauban, Marshal de. 1737. *De l'Attaque et de la Defense des Places.* La Haye (The Hague): P de Hondt.

————. 1968. *A Manual of Siegecraft and Fortification,* ed. G. A. Rothrock. Ann Arbor, Mich.: University of Michigan Press. Originally published as *Memoire por servir d'instruction dans la conduite des sieges et dans le defense des places,* Leiden 1740.

Veyrat, E. and M. L'Hour. The wrecks of the Battle of La Hougue (1692): evidence of French shipbuilding in the Royal Dockyards. In *Underwater Archaeology: Proceedings from the Conference on Underwater and Historical Archaeology,* ed. R. P. Woodward and C. D. Moore. Vancouver, British Columbia: Society for Historical Archaeology.

Viet, R. 1996. "A ray of sunshine in the sickroom": archaeological insights into late 19th- and early 20th-century medicine and anesthesia. *Northeast Historical Archaeology* 25:33–50.

Von Schliha, V. E. K. R. 1868. *A Treatise on Coast-Defence: Based on the Experience Gained by Officers of the Corps of Engineers of the Army of the Confederate States.* London: E & F. N. Spon.

Wachsmann, S. 1998. *Seagoing Ships and Seamanship in the Bronze Age Levant.* College Station: Texas A&M University Press.

Walbridge, C. 1864. Orders to Captain Henry Dale, 30 March 1864. Record Group 123, Court of Claims, Case 3705. Washington, D.C.: U.S. National Archives.

Ward, E. 2002. *Army Life in Virginia: The Civil War Letters of George G. Benedict.* Mechanicsburg, Penn.: Stackpole Books.

Ward, I. A. K., P. Larcombe and P. Veth. 1999. A new process-based model for wreck site formation. *Journal of Archaeological Science* 26:561–70.

Warner, P. (ed). 1999. *Letters Home from the Crimea.* London: John Murray.

Wason. 2003. *Battlefield Detectives.* London: Granada Media.

Watts, G. P. Jr., M. Wilde-Ramsing, R. W. Lawrence, and D. B. Hill. 1981 *Excavation of a Fort Fisher Bombproof.* Kure Beach, N.C.: North Carolina Division of Archives and History, Underwater Archeology Branch.

Weems, R. E., and E. J. Lemon, cartographers. 1993. Geology of the Cainhoy, Charleston, Fort Moultrie, and North Charleston Quadrangles, Charleston and Berkeley Counties, South Carolina. Charleston, S.C.: U.S. Geological Survey.

Weintraub, S. 1991. *Long Day's Journey into War: December 7, 1941.* New York: Dutton.

Weymouth, J. W., and R. J. Huggins. 1985. Geophysical surveying of archaeological sites. In *Archaeological Geology,* ed. G. R. Rapp Jr. and J. A. Gifford, 191–235. Newhaven, Conn.: Yale University Press.

Whitehorne, Joseph W. A. 1992. *While Washington Burned: The Battle for Ft. Erie 1814.* Baltimore, Md.: Nautical and Aviation Publishing Co. of America.

————.2006. Blueprint for nineteenth-century camps: castratamentation. In *Huts and History,* ed. C. Geier, D. Orr, and M. Reeves, 28–51. Gainesville, Fla.: University Press of Florida.

Wilbanks, R. L., and W. Hall. 1996. The discovery of the Confederate submarine *H. L. Hunley.* In *Underwater Archaeology: Proceedings from the Conference on Underwater and Historical Archaeology,* ed. S. R. James and C. Standley, 82–87. Cincinnati, Ohio: Society for Historical Archaeology.

Wilhelm, T. 1881. *A Military Dictionary and Gazetteer.* Philadelphia, Penn.: L. R. Hamersly.

Williams, J. C. 1864. *Life in Camp.* Claremont, N.H.: The Claremont Manufacturing Company.

Williams, R. 1643. *A Key into the Language of America.* Repr., Providence, R.I.: Rhode Island Historical Society, 1827.

Williamson, R. A., and P. R. Nickens (eds.). 2000. *Science and Technology in Historic Preservation.* Dordrecht, Netherlands: Kluwer Academic Publishers.

Williamson, R. F. 1978. Preliminary report on human interment patterns of the Draper Site. *Canadian Journal of Archaeology* 2:117–121.

———. 2007. "Otinontsiskiaj Ondaon"—the house of cut-off heads: the history and archaeology of northern Iroquoian trophy-taking. In *The Taking and Displaying of Human Body Parts as Trophies by Amerindians,* ed. R. J. Chacon and D. H. Dye. New York: Springer Press.

Wilson, C. N. 2002. *Carolina Cavalier: The Life and Mind of James Johnston Pettigrew.* Rockford, Ill.: Chronicles Press.

Wilson, D. R. 2000. *Air Photo Interpretation for Archaeologists.* Stroud, UK: Tempus Publishing.

Withers, A. S. 1831. *Chronicles of Border Warfare.* Repr., Parsons, W. Va.: McClain Printing, 1989.

Witten, A. J. 2006. *Handbook of Geophysics and Archaeology.* London: Equinox Publishing.

Wood, E. 1895. *The Crimea in 1854 and 1894.* London: Chapman Hall.

Wood, W. R. ,and L. A. Stanley. 1989. Recovery and identification of World War II dead: American grave registration activities in Europe. *Journal of Forensic Sciences* 34:1365–373.

Woodbury, A. 1862. *A Narrative of the Campaign of the First Rhode Island Regiment in the Spring and Summer of 1861.* Providence, R.I.: Sydney S. Ryder.

Woods, N.A. 1855/1885. *The Past Campaign. A Sketch of the War in the East From the Departure of Lord Raglan to the Capture of Sevastopol,* 2 vols. London: Longman, Brown, Green, and Longmans.

Woshner, M. 1999. *India-Rubber and Gutta-Percha in the Civil War Era.* Alexandria, Va.: O'Donnell Publications.

Wray, C. F., Sempowski, M. L. and L. P. Saunders. 1991. *Tram and Cameron: Two Early Contact Era Seneca Sites.* Rochester Museum and Science Center Research Records No. 21. Rochester, N.Y.: Rochester Museum and Science Center.

Wrong, G. M. (ed.). 1939. *The Long Journey to the Country of the Hurons.* Toronto: The Champlain Society.

Wylie, A. 1999. Why should historical archaeologists study capitalism? The logic of question and answer and the challenge of systemic analysis. In *Historical Archaeologies of Capitalism,* ed. M. P. Leone and P. B. J. Potter, 23–25. New York: Kluwer Academic/Plenum Press.

Yule, Henry. 1851. *Fortification for Officers of the Army and Students of Military History.* London: William Blackwood and Sons.